THE SOUNDS OF THE SILENTS IN BRITAIN

A MONDAY MORNING DIVERSION.
THE AUGMENTED ORCHESTRA.

"A Monday Morning Diversion. The Augmented Orchestra". *Musicians' Journal* 15 (January 1925), 15. Musicians' Union Archive, University of Stirling.

The Sounds of the Silents in Britain

Edited by Julie Brown and Annette Davison

OXFORD
UNIVERSITY PRESS

OXFORD
UNIVERSITY PRESS

Oxford University Press is a department of the University of Oxford.
It furthers the University's objective of excellence in research, scholarship,
and education by publishing worldwide.

Oxford   New York
Auckland   Cape Town   Dar es Salaam   Hong Kong   Karachi
Kuala Lumpur   Madrid   Melbourne   Mexico City   Nairobi
New Delhi   Shanghai   Taipei   Toronto

With offices in
Argentina   Austria   Brazil   Chile   Czech Republic   France   Greece
Guatemala   Hungary   Italy   Japan   Poland   Portugal   Singapore
South Korea   Switzerland   Thailand   Turkey   Ukraine   Vietnam

Oxford is a registered trademark of Oxford University Press
in the UK and certain other countries.

Published in the United States of America by
Oxford University Press
198 Madison Avenue, New York, NY 10016

© Oxford University Press 2013

Library of Congress Cataloging-in-Publication Data
The sounds of the silents in Britain / edited by Julie Brown and Annette Davison.
    p. cm.
Includes bibliographical references and index.
ISBN 978-0-19-979761-5 (hardback) — ISBN 978-0-19-979754-7 (pbk.)   1. Silent film music—Great
Britain—History and criticism.   2. Silent films—Great Britain—History and criticism.   3. Silent films—Great
Britain—Musical accompaniment.   I. Brown, Julie (Julie A.)   II. Davison, Annette, 1971–
ML2075.S687 2013
781.5'42094109041—dc23   2012026330

ISBN: 978-0-19-979761-5 (hardback)
ISBN: 978-0-19-979754-7 (pbk.)

9 8 7 6 5 4 3 2 1
Printed in the United States of America
on acid-free paper

For Arthur Cuthbert (1927–2011) and Tom Cuthbert (2009–)

Contents

Acknowledgements

THIS BOOK GREW out of a research network, *The Sounds of Early Cinema in Britain,* funded by the Arts and Humanities Research Council (AHRC) under the strategic theme *Beyond Text,* whose concerns with ephemeral cultural practices and non-text-based forms of knowledge perfectly matched our own interests in the history of live performance in cinemas. We learned an enormous amount from the productive exchange the network enabled, and we would like to thank everyone who participated in the network's various workshops, conferences, and screenings, and who thus contributed to this volume, whether directly or indirectly. In particular, we would like to thank Bryony Dixon, Laraine Porter, and Neil Brand for embracing the network and for enabling our involvement with the British Silent Film Festival in 2009 and 2011. Robert Rider's imaginative approach to silent film exhibition at the Barbican Cinema, London, led to a very productive partnership there, which also benefitted from the expertise of Erica Rodriguez. Thanks also to Katharine Ellis, Valerie James, and the team at the Institute of Musical Research (School of Advanced Studies, University of London), and the network's advisory committee—comprising Bryony Dixon, Professor Ian Christie, Dr Sarah Hibberd, and Donald Mackenzie—which ensured that the ship was well steered.

We would both also like to thank the staff and students of our respective university departments (Music at Royal Holloway, University of London, and Music at the University of Edinburgh) for their enthusiastic support of our events and for allowing us to develop new courses in this area (and for making them so enjoyable!).

Julie would specially like to thank Chris Morris, Julia Weatherly, Ben Wolf, Laurie O'Brien, Sofie Vilcins, and Reuben Philips for various types of help in gathering materials from the British Library and British Film Institute. She is grateful for the warm assistance always afforded her by the librarians at the British Film Institute. Above all she thanks Štěpán Kaňa for developing an interest in silent film with her, agreeing to come out on Sunday afternoons to screenings with live music, and for all manner of support over the course of this project and book production. Annette would like to thank Trevor Griffiths for generously sharing his knowledge of relevant archives and materials right at the start of the project, and for looking interested when she (over-)enthused about her research. Special thanks go to Colin, Georgia, and Tom (the production baby): Colin for his patience and support, the wee ones for ensuring that there are always distractions from academic work. Sincere thanks also to Norm Hirschy at Oxford University Press for his guidance and support throughout the publication process.

Notes on Contributors

Stephen Bottomore spent two decades directing documentaries in many countries worldwide while pursuing a parallel career as a film historian. He is an associate editor of the journal *Film History* and the author of *"I want to see this Annie Mattygraph": A Cartoon History of the Coming of the Movies* (1995) and *The Titanic and Silent Cinema* (2000) as well as many articles on silent and pre-cinema. He was awarded a PhD by Utrecht University in 2007 for his thesis on early cinema and warfare. He lives in Thailand and in Britain.

Julie Brown is Reader in Music at Royal Holloway, University of London. She has published on television music, horror films, music as on screen metaphor, and silent film scores. Outside screen music studies she publishes on early twentieth-century music, and is author of *Bartók and the Grotesque* (2007) and contributing editor of *Western Music and Race* (2007), which was awarded the American Musicological Society's Ruth Solie Award for a collection of essays of exceptional merit. She is currently working on a book on the sound cultures of film exhibition in 1920s Britain.

Judith Buchanan is Professor of Film and Literature and Director of the Humanities Research Centre at the University of York. She works on silent cinema in encounter with the other arts and on film and literature in engagement with each other. She is author of *Shakespeare on Silent Film: An Excellent Dumb Discourse*

(2009) and of *Shakespeare on Film* (2005) and editor of *The Writer on Film: Screening Literary Authorship* (2013).

James Buhler is Associate Professor at the University of Texas at Austin. Along with David Neumeyer and Caryl Flinn, Professor Buhler edited *Music and Cinema* (2000). He is also author with David Neumeyer and Rob Deemer of *Hearing the Movies*, a textbook on music and sound in film (2009). He is currently working on a book concerning the auditory culture of early American cinema.

Jon Burrows is an Associate Professor in the Department of Film and Television Studies, University of Warwick. He is the author of *Legitimate Cinema: Theatre Stars in Silent British Films, 1908–1913* (2003) and of numerous essays and articles on various aspects of British film culture in the silent era. He is currently working on a research project examining how cinema was transformed into a mass medium in Britain during the Edwardian era.

Ian Christie is a film historian, curator, broadcaster, and consultant. He has written and edited books on Powell and Pressburger, Russian cinema, Scorsese, and Gilliam, and has contributed to exhibitions ranging from *Film as Film* (1979) to *Modernism: Designing a New World* (2006). A Fellow of the British Academy, he is Professor of Film and Media History at Birkbeck College, director of the London Screen Study Collection and vice-president of Europa-Cinemas, of which he was a co-founder. Recent publications include: *Stories We Tell Ourselves: The Cultural Impact of British Film, 1946–2006* (co-author, 2009) and *The Art of Film: John Box and Production Design* (2009), and articles on Méliès and Patrick Keiller. www.ianchristie.org.

Malcolm Cook is a doctoral candidate at Birkbeck College, University of London. He is researching early British animated cartoons prior to the advent of sound cinema, with a particular focus on the relationship between the moving image and the graphic arts and other pre-cinematic entertainments, as well as the neurological processes involved in the perception of these forms. He holds a BA in Film and Literature from the University of Warwick and an MA in History of Art, Film and Visual Media from Birkbeck College.

Annette Davison is Senior Lecturer in Music at the University of Edinburgh. She has published research on music and sound for the screen and the stage in several books and journals. Her most recent monograph was *Alex North's* A Streetcar

Named Desire: *A Film Score Guide* (2009). Current research projects include main title sequences for television serials, a cultural history of live music performance in cinemas in Britain, and music and film narrative.

Fiona Ford has recently completed her doctoral thesis on the film music of Edmund Meisel at the University of Nottingham in 2011. She has published on *The Wizard of Oz* in *Melodramatic Voices: Understanding Music Drama* (2011), is co-editing the *Cambridge Companion to Film Music* with Mervyn Cooke, and preparing a film score guide on Max Steiner's *King Kong*.

Trevor Griffiths is Senior Lecturer in Economic and Social History at the University of Edinburgh. Having initially worked on the nature of working-class society in Britain in the early twentieth century, more recently he has turned to examine aspects of popular culture, especially in Scotland. He has co-edited and part-authored the third volume in the *History of Everyday Life in Scotland* series (2010), covering the nineteenth century, contributing a chapter on work and leisure patterns, and recently published *The Cinema and Cinema-going in Scotland, 1896–c. 1950* (2012).

Andrew Higson is Greg Dyke Professor of Film and Television and Head of the Department of Theatre, Film and Television at the University of York. He has written widely on British cinema, from the silent period to the present day, and on questions of national cinema. His books include *Waving the Flag: Constructing a National Cinema in Britain* (1995), *English Heritage, English Cinema: The Costume Drama Since 1980* (2003), and *Film England: Culturally English Filmmaking since the 1990s* (2011). He is also editor of *Young and Innocent? The Cinema in Britain, 1896–1930* (2002), *British Cinema, Past and Present* (with Justine Ashby, 2000) and *"Film Europe" and "Film America": Cinema, Commerce and Cultural Exchange, 1920–1939* (with Richard Maltby, 1999).

Joe Kember is Senior Lecturer in Film in the Department of English, University of Exeter. He has published widely concerning early cinema and nineteenth-century shows, and his most recent book, *Marketing Modernity: Victorian Popular Shows and Early Cinema* (2009) focusses upon the social and institutional continuities that underpinned the market for popular entertainments across this period. He is co-investigator for the major AHRC project "Moving and Projected Image Entertainments in the South West, 1840–1914," and is currently co-authoring a substantial book on this topic with the project team.

John Riley is a writer, lecturer, curator, and broadcaster. As well as *Dmitri Shostakovich: A Life in Film* (2005) and *Discover Film Music* (2008), he has contributed book chapters to publications by Cambridge and Oxford University Presses, Routledge, BFI, Praeger, and others. The South Bank Centre commissioned him to write and direct *Shostakovich—My Life at the Movies*, which, using film clips accompanied by live orchestra, follows the composer's cinema career. Premiered by Simon Russell Beale and the CBSO, it was then produced at the Komische Oper, Berlin. He has also curated various film seasons and produced a BBC Prom.

Derek B. Scott is Professor of Critical Musicology and Head of the School of Music at the University of Leeds. He is the author of *The Singing Bourgeois: Songs of the Victorian Drawing Room and Parlour* (1989, revised 2001), *From the Erotic to the Demonic: On Critical Musicology* (2003), *Sounds of the Metropolis: The 19th-Century Popular Music Revolution in London, New York, Paris, and Vienna* (2008), and *Musical Style and Social Meaning* (2010). His edited volumes include *Music, Culture, and Society: A Reader* (2000) and the *Ashgate Research Companion to Popular Musicology* (2009).

THE SOUNDS OF THE SILENTS IN BRITAIN

Overture

Julie Brown and Annette Davison

TODAY, AS A result of trail-blazing research by Rick Altman, Richard Abel, Gillian Anderson, Stephen Bottomore, Martin Miller Marks, and others,[1] there now exists a rich picture of the enormous variety of sonic practices used before, during, and around the exhibition of moving pictures during the first thirty-five years of cinema. The wider landscape is still little understood, however. Much of the detailed work to date has focused on the North American context, yet it seems likely that the sonic dimension of exhibition cultures that developed in other countries and cultures, in the context of other musical and theatrical customs, and using different talent experiencing the pressures of other historical and cultural forces, will have been shaped somewhat differently. This book springs from and explores that assumption in the context of Britain.

To stimulate research into the live performance aspect of early film exhibition in Britain we initially formed a research network involving scholars and performers with complementary skills and disciplinary backgrounds. Members of this network included silent film music scholars, archivists and curators of silent film, performers of music for silent films, historians variously of early cinema, theatre and economics, as well as collectors and enthusiasts. Funded by the United Kingdom's Arts and Humanities Research Council (AHRC), the network produced four events over two years, including conferences and performance workshops. Each event featured associated screenings involving live music, sound effects, or voice, ranging from re-imaginings to historically informed reconstructions. Many of the chapters in this volume were developed from papers presented at these events and the dialogue they encouraged, and brought together here they represent the first body of research about the sounds of early cinema in Britain. But while this volume represents a significant step forward in examining the British context, it also points to the need for further research: the practices discussed here are primarily those of England and Scotland, for example. Wales, particularly Cardiff, is often mentioned in the film trade papers, and while Northern Ireland was formed fairly late in the period in question (1921), the sonic and musical practices experienced in its cinemas potentially offer fertile ground for the exploration of the establishment and contestation of nationhood.[2]

FEATURE: BUILDING A PICTURE OF THE SONIC ENVIRONMENT OF THE BRITISH CINEMA

With some notable exceptions, studies of British film exhibition practices of this period rarely make reference to the sonic practices at work.[3] Given the fundamentally ephemeral character of the object of study and related source materials, this is not altogether surprising. Those attempting to address the matter necessarily circulate between the demands of medium-, place-, and performer-specificity and the cultural ubiquity of sound practices. They also grapple with the paradox that their source materials can be simultaneously overwhelming in volume (as with film trade papers, and the body of music that may have been drawn on) and frustratingly patchy and ill-documented in type (as with reception, and detailed accounts of regional practices).

Recent research projects that have focused on film exhibition and other related forms of entertainment at particular times in particular cities and regions have contributed significantly to the generation of a more detailed picture of the situation across Britain. A number of the essays in this book build explicitly upon this work. Joe Kember's chapter draws upon an AHRC-funded project with a regional focus: "Moving and Projected Image Entertainment in the South West, 1820–1914"; Ian Christie's chapter benefits from, and contributes to, the AHRC-funded "London Project", discussed further below.[4] Trevor Griffiths reveals how the practices in one city (Aberdeen in Scotland) could differ markedly from those found elsewhere in Britain, and Jon Burrows's chapter builds upon his extensive archival work on local licensing in London and its boroughs.[5]

An account of exhibition practices in this period must recognize the importance of the First World War (1914–18), though not primarily for its direct impact on or disruption of European markets, but, as Gerben Bakker argues, "because the war prevented European film from taking part in the escalation of quality" in the United States.[6] In large part this was due to an inability to secure the venture capital necessary to participate in the significant escalation in film production costs that began around 1909. With this escalation, access to a large market became increasingly important. Prior to the war the European film market had been surprisingly integrated, but as Bakker shows, once the war began, "consumers became more hostile to products from enemy countries, especially to cultural products such as films": the market disintegrated.[7] The war was also detrimental to the attempts of a small number of European film companies to adopt strategies that would enable them to participate in the escalation necessary to compete with the US film industry.[8] The introduction of entertainment taxes across Europe did not help matters. In Britain an entertainments tax was imposed on cinema tickets from 1916, and had a particularly negative impact on the smallest of venues, since a considerably higher proportion of tax was payable on the cheapest cinema tickets and raising ticket prices meant moving into a higher tax bracket. In her chapter Julie Brown advances this as one explanation for the initial reluctance of small venues to increase overheads by adding elaborate live prologues to their programmes.

The war also had a significant impact on the international exchangeability of films, both between European countries and with North America. In terms of personnel, many German nationals then resident in Britain were interned during the war, as Stephen Bottomore highlights in his chapter about Selsior's dance films. Where those individuals were connected with the film industry there were direct repercussions on production and exhibition in Britain. There was also an impact on the music in cinemas: with cinema musicians first volunteering for and then being conscripted into the armed services, employment opportunities emerged for a variety of players who might not otherwise have entered the sector, as Annette Davison explores. But if this led to a perceived lowering of quality in musical performance in cinemas, the return of musicians at the end of the war was one of several factors that seems to have improved the quality of performance from the late 1910s and on into the 1920s.

Cultural and technological exchange continued in some forms though. Selsior's dance films used a system invented by a Hungarian, for example (see Stephen Bottomore's chapter 9). From 1925 London's Film Society fostered cultural exchange by programming films produced in a variety of other countries, including avant-garde or experimental fare. In many cases, attempts were made to procure original music from abroad, such as scores by the Austrian composer Edmund Meisel for a number of Soviet and German films, as noted in chapters by Fiona Ford and John Riley.

Developing an expanded picture of sonic practices in Britain through the first decades of cinema also means that certain international comparisons can now be drawn—with the nickelodeon period in the United States, for instance. With the rise of the nickelodeon (*c.*1905–1915), sound began to be institutionalized there as a specifically cinematic practice: it came to be determined by the institutions of cinema exhibition and its emerging commerce, rather than guided solely by the type and/or location of venue. Specific spaces for music and musicians were created, and the piano established itself as the all-important instrument for accompaniment, in combination with one or more other instruments in larger venues. In the 1910s, debates about the type and quality of musical accompaniment began to appear in the trade papers, and film producers and companies began to offer suggestions for the accompaniment of their films. There are clear points of similarity between the United States and Britain at this time, particularly in terms of trade paper discourse, as can be seen in Jon Burrows's and Andrew Higson's chapters. Elsewhere, however, Roberta Pearson argues that "Britain had no real equivalent to the American nickelodeon period,"[9] a view supported by Nicholas Hiley, who argues that a regular venue that primarily exhibited motion pictures did not appear in Britain until the cinema building boom that began around 1909, driven by speculative investment in the entertainment industry.[10] In this volume and elsewhere, Burrows challenges these accounts. On the basis of municipal records from London, Burrows argues that there was indeed a robust presence of low-cost moving picture houses between 1906 and 1911, though admittedly the scale of development was significantly smaller than that found in the United States. Due to stringent licensing regulations imposed on entertainment venues by the London County Council (LCC), and particularly the lack of a medium-tier licensing system, many penny theatres were unlicensed, which had particular consequences for music and its relationship to moving pictures.[11] The introduction of the 1909 Cinematograph Act on 1 January 1910, or more specifically, the resolution concerning the performance of music that was introduced soon afterwards following confusion in the exhibition industry, signalled a change in the provision of music. As the first piece of legislation to regulate film exhibition on a national basis, the Cinematograph Act may be understood as the most important factor in the move towards an institutionalization of sonic practices in British cinemas. We would do well to be wary of assumptions that this led to national conformity, however, given that the local authorities that oversaw the Act's enforcement were able to impose additional requirements on venues. As Brown's account of live stage prologues indicates, idiosyncratic local licensing decisions continued to exert a considerable influence on the type and scale of the musical and staged performances that were possible, even through the 1920s. Indeed unravelling the mysteries as to which musical forces were legally permissible in particular areas at particular times is one of the most daunting tasks facing those hoping to understand early film exhibition in Britain, mindful though we must remain of the fact that not all practices used will have been licensed or legal.[12]

THE MIXED PROGRAMME

Familiar concerns and exhibition phenomena lie behind much of the work presented here and ultimately helped us to shape the volume. Its organization into four sections reflects known sonic film phenomena of early film exhibition (speaking to pictures, accompanying pictures, performance in cinemas generally), as well as concerns typical of film studies more widely (institutions). Given the little research that has been undertaken in relation to these sonic practices in Britain, it is perhaps not surprising that such an organization emerged, though the questions the contributors ask and their ways of tackling those questions are often new and inspiring. The essays here offer some startling new perspectives on the role of sound in early film exhibition, while also demonstrating that world events and cultural specificities can impact upon a national cinema-music culture.

The chapters grouped in the first section, "Speaking to Pictures", approach a live sound practice associated with early film exhibition that has been acknowledged in the historical literature for about thirty years. Adding to models of the film lecturing scene in the United States as a series of practices associated with magic lantern traditions, and in France according to improvisatory *bonimenteur* and scholarly *conférencier* practices, these contributions deepen our understanding of the diverse lecturing practices that operated in Britain and around English literature.

The first two chapters both explore the effects of film lecturing. Kember considers the ability of film lecturers in Britain to attract, sustain, and focus the attention of audiences. He notes that adding a lantern-style educative lecturer to moving pictures was one way of addressing concerns emerging in the 1900s that moving pictures themselves did not fix attention. By delving into the detail of exhibition practices at St James's Hall, Plymouth, Kember argues that town hall shows here and elsewhere structured the manipulation of audience attention within new institutional configurations, and did so as early as 1901, not only after 1908 as previously understood. Shows at St James's Hall serve to demonstrate that lecturers could contribute to the creation of new patterns of audience attention, mediating and modulating the various effects involved in moving picture exhibition, and adapting a wide range of oral practices in doing so. Judith Buchanan, by contrast, is interested in the gap between the ideal film lecture advocated in the trade press, and instances of less-than-perfect actual lecturing. Like the lanternist before him, the film lecturer could draw on his live showmanship effectively to "author" a film by an analogous speech act, making and remaking the show as required by the particular live situation. Campaigns in the trade press which promoted the erudition and eloquence of the lecturer, and the publication of set lectures to accompany particular films, contributed to a standardized notion of the cinematic lecture. However, as Buchanan's examination of a detailed transcription of one that accompanied the screening of a film of *Othello* in Berlin in 1912 shows, the reality could be very far from ideal.

The next two chapters focus on the lecturing practices of an individual on the one hand, and a particular city on the other. Bottomore considers star British film lecturer, the actor turned elocutionist Eric Williams, who from about 1911 until at least the end of the First World War was a popular lecturer in England and Scotland. Williams adopted a number of approaches to film lecturing, but notably recited poems and other texts to films that were sometimes referred to as "bioscope ballads". He made and starred in the films, and also often perfectly synchronized his live speaking with the lip movement on screen. Bottomore traces Williams's career from its beginnings to his success touring in the north of England and Scotland, and reflects upon his appeal. As Griffiths shows in the next chapter, the use of elocutionists who spoke to the images from behind the screen persisted in Scotland, or more particularly, in Aberdeen, far longer than has been documented elsewhere in Britain. Making use of the financial and administrative records of individual cinemas, Griffiths shows that as late as 1915 an effective elocutionist could command a salary fifty per cent higher than a cinema pianist, and suggests that the popularity of live dialogue with pictures in Aberdeen had a specific socio-economic base, having been partly associated with halls in poorer districts and with younger audiences.

The essays in the next section, "Accompanying Pictures", focus on musical accompaniment of moving pictures. Although other essays in this volume also refer to these practices, Christie, Higson, Burrows, and James Buhler directly address local evidence of, debates about, and issues arising from musical accompaniment in cinemas. The picture that emerges here sometimes conflicts with, and substantially develops, received wisdom about this period of exhibition in Britain.

Christie explores exhibition in the 1890s and 1900s in light of evidence for the musical accompaniment of forms of screen media exhibited in London from the seventeenth to the nineteenth centuries. He also considers early films in terms of remediation, as with the emergence of films inspired by popular song titles at the turn of the century, and the fact that popular songs formed the principal content for the various synchronized sound systems developed in the 1900s. Christie thus suggests that it may be appropriate to ask: why would music *not* have been used to accompany screen media?

One answer to this question can be found in Burrows's contribution, at least in terms of film exhibition in London from the late 1900s into the early 1910s: compliance with regulations imposed by the LCC concerning the licensing of venues for music. Soon after the Cinematograph Act came into force, miniature orchestras became more common in London cinemas than the lone pianist that some previous histories have identified. Rather than responding moment-to-moment to the images on screen in the manner that an improvising pianist might (or well might not), these orchestras played through a number of "good" musical pieces in their entirety, which might or might not have had a direct correspondence to some aspect of the film or its theme. Thus, despite exhortations in the trade press for such a correspondence between music and film, this doesn't seem to have happened in practice regularly until at least the mid-1910s, a thesis supported by Higson, whose chapter forms a companion piece to Burrows's. Here letters to, and columns in, the trade papers from the early 1910s are brought together, alongside views from manuals and—more unusually—contemporary fiction. As several authors here suggest, some contemporary trade paper reporting might also more usefully be viewed as idealization than as a direct representation of what was heard in cinemas.

The final chapter in this section draws particular attention to the propagandistic nature of certain trade reports, where exaggeration may have been used to serve other purposes. Buhler presents a series of points of comparison and contrast between North America's development of upscale exhibition standards and those in Britain, specifically London, as represented by reports in the North American trade paper *Moving Picture World* from the late 1900s into the 1910s. While British film production was denigrated as inferior to the North American product in such reports, London's exhibition practices were promoted as superior. From the end of 1909, the other purpose this comparison served was to promote to North America the feasibility of more expensive cinemas that excluded vaudeville, but where music played a significant role. Burrows's evidence that orchestras were quickly established as the predominant means of accompaniment in London cinemas after 1910 seems to support the trade view presented by Buhler.

The next three chapters, grouped together under the heading "Performance in Cinemas", explore aspects of the heterogeneity of early film programmes. As Nicholas Hiley reminds us, for over the first twenty-five years of projected moving pictures "the basic unit of exhibition was not the individual film but the programme, and the commodity that most patrons wished to buy from the exhibitor was not access to an individual film, but time in the auditorium."[13] From their very earliest days, programmes within which moving pictures appeared often included not only filmed musical and dance "acts" (initially with live, but later with synchronized, musical accompaniment), but fully live stage performances of a variety of types, sometimes forging explicit dramatic connections with the screened entertainments, and also audience singalongs involving varying degrees of participation.

Bottomore here explores the activities of London-based film company Selsior, which from 1912 to 1917 developed short dance films. Recognizing the importance of close musical synchronization to presenting these films convincingly as species of performance, Selsior developed a sync system which was designed to address the combined

effects of highly variable film projection speeds and the inherent difficulty of conducting live to what may have been a hand-cranked, and hence variable-speed, unscrolling
film. Selsior's early solution to synchronizing music exactly to movement—initially
borrowed from others—was to include in the corner of the screen a filmed image of a
conductor whom a live cinema orchestra was intended to follow. Derek Scott's chapter
also concerns synchronization technology, though here the focus is on the transfor-
mations that the technologies prompted in filmed performances. Focussing on song
performance in British Pathé's early sound shorts, Scott first situates Pathé's sound
films in the longer history of the company's production of performance shorts and
then analyses a number of these screened performances in order to shed light on the
ways early performers and filmmakers grappled with the changes demanded of the new
medium.

Brown's chapter explores the inverse relationship between performance and
screen. Live stage prologues were dramatic and/or musical performances presented
immediately before a feature film. Directly related to the feature and intended to
bridge the gap between "the world of actuality" and the world of the feature, they
sometimes consisted of live enactments of plot summaries or involved a short scene
from the film performed on stage by members of the film cast itself, though they
might equally have involved a thematically related operatic scena or simply a song
performance. In this chapter, Brown focuses on film trade paper reporting of the
prologue phenomenon in Britain, over which she casts a sceptical eye as to its representations of the prologue's genealogy and embrace by British cinemas.

In the final chapter in this section, the locus of performance shifts from the stage
and screen to the auditorium. Here Malcolm Cook explores the place of singing by
cinema audiences in the mixed programmes of the 1920s, in particular the vocal participation encouraged by the release of multiple film song series in Britain through
1926 and 1927. Cook highlights a range of precedents for such participation, but
focuses on a less familiar context: the rise and decline of the community singing
movement in Britain over the same period. While there were similarities between
these two forms of community singing, there were also differences: the repertoire
of the film song series was more heterogeneous than that of the community singing movement, and the series demonstrated a different approach to the possibilities
that technology could bring to the cinema at the crucial moment of transition to
synchronized sound.

In the fourth and final section, "Musicians, Companies, and Institutions", the focus
is on the response of key film institutions and companies to music and sound in this
period. Davison's chapter focuses on the trade union and the collection agency. She
explores the role of the Musicians' Union (and its forerunners) in relation to cinema musicians and its negotiations with the principal employers' organization over

this period. She then turns to the Performing Right Society (PRS), the institution established by publishers and composers in 1914 to collect revenue for the public performance of their music. Here she highlights the vital role that cinemas played in the establishment and survival of the PRS during its infancy, and the periodically difficult relationship between the Musicians' Union and the PRS, in part the result of the society's classification system for the licensing of music in cinemas.

Riley's chapter explores attitudes towards sound at the Film Society, an organization which not only influenced the development of further community based societies elsewhere in Britain but was one of the very first film societies internationally. Riley provides a survey of the variety of musical accompaniment practices used for the society's seasons of monthly screenings in London which ran between 1925 and 1939. He highlights the seriousness with which the society approached musical and other forms of accompaniment for their programmes which not only featured a variety of films, but also often a variety of accompaniment practices.

The Film Society also features in the book's final chapter. The primary focus of Ford's essay, however, is composer Edmund Meisel's commission to create a music and sound effects track for a post-synchronized part-talkie version of *The Crimson Circle* (1929)—now sadly lost—produced by British Talking Pictures. Drawing upon trade promotion concerning Meisel's score and soundtrack, published interviews with the composer, and reviews of the trade show, Ford offers intriguing insights into the company's transition to synchronized sound and the composer's apparent ongoing development of what some critics have called his approach to "visual sound".

RESOURCES

As noted above, the sonic dimension of early film exhibition creates special problems for the researcher, due in part to the ephemerality of the practices involved. One of our aims with this volume was to draw upon the expertise of those approaching the topic from different disciplinary perspectives, and using different types of sources. The particular stories embedded in the various sources give rise in turn to different histories and critical perspectives. Information about many of the individual types of records and documents discussed here can be found in the notes to individual chapters, but extremely useful bibliographies and resource summaries by Burrows and Bottomore are also available in Higson's collection *Young and Innocent? The Cinema in Britain, 1896–1930*. We intend the bibliography to the current volume and this section of the introduction to be taken as a supplement to those earlier lists, one with an emphasis on sonic practices.

From the earliest days of the moving pictures, film trade papers referred to exhibition practices, including sound practices, and are therefore central source material for anyone studying silent film sound. They include advertisements for music publications, for music- and sound-related equipment, as well as various types of commentary about the film music trade in general, which from the early 1910s often included a dedicated music column. Most chapters here make use of such materials, though some draw particular attention to their partiality and potential unreliability (Buhler, Burrows, Brown): film—and potentially musical—trade papers tended to report best practice (as exemplars to be aspired to), worst practice (as negative image), and promote the industry's interests and agenda in general. Many such papers were produced every week for many of the thirty-five years in question, and the need to fill column inches in turn led to considerable redundancy in the music columns, sometimes financial deals with particular music publishers and musical instrument producers, and also a tendency to publish photographs and accounts of exhibition practice supplied to them by individual cinemas, who received free advertising in return. They are vital sources, but should be handled with care.

Alternative perspectives to those of the industry may be found in newspapers (local/regional and London-based nationals), as well as in individual archival collections, where available (see, for instance, Kember, Griffiths). Records of licensing committees provide for the perspective of local authorities and police records present formal accounts of individual compliance with such licenses (Burrows, Griffiths). Detailed records held by patent office archives document particular technological developments used in the creation and dissemination of film sound (Bottomore), and manufacturers' catalogues for lantern slide series present information concerning the scale and period of popularity of song slides in Britain (Cook). Individual special collections in film archives also have the potential to be treasure troves, incomplete though they may be. The Film Society and Ivor Montagu collections at the British Film Institute (BFI) contain correspondence and accounts that provide insights into sonic practices at the Film Society screenings (Riley, Ford), and film holdings at the BFI and Pathé provide access to films, both silent and early synchronized sound (Ford, Scott). Memoirs, such as those of Cecil Hepworth (Buchanan, Christie, Higson) and Ivor Montagu (Riley), fictionalized accounts of sonic practices by novelists (Higson), as well as such quirky sources as a detailed transcription of a film lecture by an academic linguist, complete with all its asides, circumlocutions and dialectic peculiarities (Buchanan), all help to enrich our understanding of sonic practices and individuals' experience of them.

Since *Young and Innocent?* was published, many nineteenth-century British newspapers and journals have been digitized and made freely accessible via the British Library's website, thereby facilitating remote research into the very early years of moving picture exhibition. Other newspapers have now also been digitized for most of the "silent film" era, and are available via various subscription services.[14]

Digitization projects such as these will only increase in number. A number of British music journals also included articles about moving picture music, especially during the 1920s, though offerings tended to be highly intermittent. This is the case with the *Musical Times*, for example. By contrast, the *Musical News and Herald* and *Melody Maker* both ran dedicated columns or (in the case of *Melody Maker*) a "Cinema and Music Supplement" for more substantial periods of time, in the early and late twenties respectively. Stephen Herbert's *A History of Early Film* (three volumes), a collection of primary source materials, includes a relatively small but significant selection of columns and trade manuals referring to music, several of which are cited in Higson's chapter. The BFI recently digitized the first issue of the *Kinematograph Yearbook Programme Diary and Directory* (1914), and the British Cinema History Research Project based at the University of East Anglia includes an online index to two (regrettably brief) periods of *Kinematograph Weekly* that are relevant to further research in this area.[15] The most frequently updated reference guide to relevant digitization projects can be found in the library section of the website *The Bioscope* (http://bioscopic.wordpress.com/), an excellent resource written and administered by Dr Luke McKernan.

Music relevant to the study of early film exhibition in Britain is available in numerous archival collections. Thanks to legal deposit, much published photoplay music (including, in some cases, instrumental parts) is available in the British Library; unlike in the Library of Congress, however, it has not been identified as a discrete collection, nor is it likely to include all music published in Britain. Further problems are created by the intersecting histories of the naming and renaming of our very object of study (moving pictures, motion pictures, film, kinema, photoplay music, kinema music, etc.) and the cataloguing of such vast library collections; ultimately one must be prepared to undertake creative catalogue searching in order to locate individual items, including the small number of full scores held there. Other libraries with useful collections of music include the BFI and Cambridge University Library (both of which have a small number of full "special scores" among their Special Collections), Birmingham City Library and the National Media Museum in Bradford (both of which have large collections of photoplay music, including instrumental parts), and the privately owned and managed library of the British Light Music Society, where music is available to members for hire.[16]

Other resources include the remarkable database that is emerging from the London Project, a major study of the emergence of the film business in London, which is already an essential resource for searching for information about cinemas and film businesses in London before the First World War.[17] More conventional archives of specific significance to the study of early film sound include the recently catalogued Musicians' Union Archive (Special Collections, University of Stirling), and the archive of the PRS. Other useful archival collections relating to silent film music are held by Trinity College of Music, Greenwich. Certain small museums hold individual pieces of early film sound and music technology; for instance, the Black Country Living Museum, Dudley, holds a complete cinema percussionist's kit, while the Musical Museum, Brentford, houses a Photoplayer and various cinema organs. The BFI's National Archive includes many silent films, especially shorts, of specific musical interest.[18] Some of the above collections have become accessible to researchers only over the last two years, and it is hoped more will become available in the future. One remarkable original score was only recently located in a private collection, for instance, and brought to public performance in April 2011 at the Barbican Cinema, London.[19] Performances and reconstructions are worthy of note because they provide a different kind of knowledge, with musical expertise enabling us to put the results of archival and musicological research into practice. The annual British Silent Film Festival provides opportunities to see British silent films with live accompaniment of various types, most often undertaken in a historically conscious idiom broadly defined, sometimes involving full historical recreations. The reconstruction of the musical suggestions for *The Battle of the Somme* (1916), which the film's distributors commissioned from J. M. Hutcheson and were printed in *The Bioscope* that year, represents a significant milestone, and can be heard as one of two score options on the Imperial War Museum's recent DVD release of the film, making it a useful resource for teaching.[20] Mock-up synchronizations of five British produced "special scores" are also available to hear and view.[21]

There is still much to learn about the sonic dimension of early film exhibition in Britain: archives, special collections and personal legacies long buried and forgotten are still coming to light. In some senses we have only begun to scratch the surface. Nevertheless, these traces prove highly enabling when viewed together, sketching out as they do important coordinates for researchers, and pointing the way towards fruitful future research areas, helped in part by the general map constructed from research undertaken elsewhere. Together these essays advance our understanding of how cinema developed in Britain as a sounding and often highly theatrical cultural form, a dimension of film history that can easily get lost amidst debates about film's advance as a form of visual culture.

NOTES

1. See the volume's bibliography for representative examples of work by these authors.

2. For starting points, see Denis Condon, *Early Irish Cinema, 1895–1921* (Dublin: Irish Academic Press, 2008) and Peter Miskell, *A Social History of the Cinema in Wales, 1918–1951: Pulpits, Coalpits, and Fleapits* (Cardiff: University of Wales Press, 2006).

3. Exceptions include Stephen Bottomore, "The Story of Percy Peashaker: Debates about Sound Effects in the Early Cinema", in *The Sounds of Early Cinema*, ed. Richard Abel and Rick Altman (Bloomington: Indiana University Press, 2001), 129–42; Tony Fletcher, "Sound before *Blackmail* (1929)", in *The Showman, the Spectacle and the Two-Minute Silence: Performing British Cinema before 1930*, ed. Alan Burton and Laraine Porter (Trowbridge: Flicks Books, 2001), 6–11; Neil Brand, "Distant Trumpets: The Score to *The Flag Lieutenant* and Music of the British Silent Cinema", in *Young and Innocent? The Cinema in Britain, 1896–1930*, ed. Andrew Higson (Exeter: University of Exeter Press, 2002), 208–24; Toby Haggith, "Reconstructing the Musical Arrangement for *The Battle of the Somme* (1916)", *Film History* 14/1 (2002): 11–24; Michael Allen, "In the Mix: How Mechanical and Electrical Reproducers Mediated the Transition to Sound in Britain", in *Film Music: Critical Approaches*, ed. K. J. Donnelly (Edinburgh: Edinburgh University Press, 2001), 62–87.

4. This project was headed by Dr John Plunkett and Dr Joe Kember of the University of Exeter. See the project website for more information: http://www.sall.ex.ac.uk/projects/screenhistorysw/ [accessed 3 August 2012].

5. See also Jon Burrows's "Penny Pleasures: Film Exhibition in London during the Nickelodeon Era, 1906–1914", *Film History* 16/1 (2004): 60–91; "Penny Pleasures II: Indecency, Anarchy and Junk Film in London's 'Nickelodeons', 1906–1914", *Film History* 16/2 (2004): 172–97.

6. Gerben Bakker, "The Decline and Fall of the European Film Industry: Sunk Costs, Market Size, and Market Structure, 1890–1927", *Economic History Review* 58/2 (May 2005): 316. From around 1910 the European share of released negatives in the US market declined suddenly from around fifty per cent to just twenty per cent, falling only a further five per cent during the war years. By this point US market share had grown massively, however, and "production costs had escalated several times" (ibid., 340). For a more detailed exploration of the combination of factors that contributed to the decline, see Bakker's article.

7. Ibid., 337. The disintegration was later compounded by the introduction of protectionist policies, such as quota systems, by individual nation states.

8. Ibid., 338.

9. Roberta Pearson, "Transitional Cinema", in *The Oxford History of World Cinema*, ed. Geoffrey Nowell-Smith (Oxford: Oxford University Press, 1996), 38.

10. Nicholas Hiley, "'Nothing More Than a "Craze"': Cinema Building in Britain from 1909 to 1914", in *Young and Innocent?*, ed. Andrew Higson, 111–27.

11. Burrows, "Penny Pleasures [I]".

12. As Burrows notes, some penny theatres managed to continue under the radar of the licensing authorities despite advertising and promoting the musical contribution of their programmes in trade papers.

13. Nicholas Hiley, "'At the Picture Palace': The British Cinema Audience, 1895–1920", in *Celebrating 1895: The Centenary of Cinema*, ed. John Fullerton (London: John Libbey, 1998), 97.

14. At the time of writing these include: *The Times, Manchester Guardian, Observer, Illustrated London News, Daily Express, Daily Mirror, Church Times, Scotsman, Stage, Financial Times, Irish Times, Weekly Irish Times*.

15. The two relevant periods are the late 1890s, then under the title the *Optical Magic Lantern Journal and Photographic Enlarger*, and early 1915, as *Kinematograph and Lantern Weekly*. The British Cinema History Research Project online: http://www.uea.ac.uk/ftv/bchrp/kineweekly [accessed 3 August 2012].

16. Details of some of these holdings are available in Miguel Mera and Ben Winters's useful first attempt to document all film music holdings in the United Kingdom: "Film and Television Music Sources in the UK and Ireland", *Brio* 46/2 (Autumn/Winter 2009): 37–65.

17. The London Project online: http://londonfilm.bbk.ac.uk [accessed 3 August 2012].

18. Tony Fletcher has brought some of this material to "performance" or "resynchronization" (in the case of sound-on-disc films) at the British Silent Film Festival over the last few years.

19. Julie Brown, "Finding the Modern in a British Silent Film Score: 'Unusual film-fare' and Frederick Laurence's *Morozko* (1925)" (in preparation). This score is also discussed in Brown, "Audio-Visual Palimpsests: Resynchronizing Silent Films with 'Special' Music" in *The Oxford Handbook of Music in Film and Visual Media*, ed. David Neumeyer (New York: Oxford University Press, forthcoming).

20. *The Battle of the Somme*, DVD. The War Office. 1916; London: Imperial War Museum, 2008. SN6540.

21. The British Academy-funded research project "'Film-fitting' in Britain, 1913–1926", directed by Julie Brown, facilitated the production of these resources, which are available for viewing at Royal Holloway, University of London. Or, contact Julie Brown directly.

PART ONE

Speaking to Pictures

1

Professional Lecturing in Early British Film Shows

Joe Kember

IT HAS NOW been over ten years since Tom Gunning wrote that the film lecturer, far from being an unknown figure for film historians, had in fact been rediscovered regularly over the preceding twenty years.[1] That means it is now more than thirty years since the pioneering work by Norman King and Charles Musser in the United States and Martin Sopocy in Britain reintroduced us to the figure of the lecturer.[2] But even in the wake of substantial investigations of exhibition practices since then, the film lecturer has remained a slippery figure, hard to reconstruct from surviving information. We are left with some fundamental questions inspired, in part, by an apparent paucity of evidence: how extensive was the film lecture within the early industry, and, if present at all, what did film lecturing consist of? In response to the latter question, I have argued extensively elsewhere that the term "lecturer" had accrued a wide variety of meanings in the British marketplace for late nineteenth-century entertainments and that many of these persisted within film shows, where the presence of a lecturer contributed to the sense of "liveness" of film exhibition.[3] At some points, it described a master of ceremonies role; at others, a describer of scenes, commentator, educator, or instructor; frequently, it carried a savour of showmanship, or drew upon a wide range of other performative attitudes, perhaps engaging in limited forms of dialogue, vocal or otherwise, with audiences. In film shows, the term "lecturer" therefore continued to refer to a wide range of speaking practices, embracing most forms of vocal performance taking place between or during the screening of films, and varying from full-blown scholarly lectures, to the delivery of narrative or dialogue, to the practice of reading the titles of films to audiences. Adopting this broad definition—the industry's own—it can be seen that film lecturing was, in fact, a very common practice before 1910, though one must always be careful to specify exactly what it consisted of at any one site, or during any one show.

Not merely associated with the nineteenth-century British professional lecture circuit, which, of course, included a varied set of conventions in itself, film lecturers capitalized fluidly upon much more diverse vocal traditions and aural practices. Their role therefore contrasts with the models for film lecturing described by Rick Altman in the United States in the same period: though many British film lecturers persisted in the conventions associated with lantern shows, or used lectures especially in relation to educative or instructive films, this describes only one part of a much richer vocal heritage.[4] This performative range also extended well beyond the useful French terms applied to lecturers: the lecturer could be both the improvisatory *bonimenteur* and scholarly *conférencier* as required, but he could also be actor, singer, impersonator, chairman, guide, and much more besides.[5] At points, it is important to note, he was also a silent observer of the screen, perhaps becoming, at such moments, the audience's representative on the stage. The inclusive professional dimensions of the role were therefore defined by remarkably varied genres of speech and gesture, justifying Richard Crangle's contention that film lecturing in Britain is best defined as a bricolage of practices adapted from earlier conventions.[6]

This chapter will extend this argument by considering in more detail a function that was common to all forms of film lecturing in this period: the ability to attract, sustain, and focus the attention of audiences. Drawing upon trade and local presses, and especially upon a survey of pre-First World War film and magic lantern exhibition practices in South West England,[7] it argues that film exhibitors demonstrated a sophisticated understanding of varied qualities of attentiveness in their audiences, and employed equally varied genres of public speaking in order to take advantage of these. The task of speaking to such audiences under these conditions was by no means a simple or neutral one, and lecturers participated fully in the continual process of institutional definition that took place within the early industry. Undoubtedly, at such shows, film lecturers had an important role as interlocutors or mediators for the images on screen, for modern media, and even for "modernity" itself (however one might wish to define that term), but the role was not defined by relatively inert qualities of "between-ness" or mediation.[8] Film lecturing was a profession with a distinct, if dispersed, profile and heritage of its own, and lecturers took a constructive role in modifying institutional practices from venue to venue, show to show.

LECTURING AND THE "BATTLE FOR ATTENTION"

The emphasis on film lecturing as a profession also reminds us that, though film lecturing contributed to the vibrant visual culture typified by the cinematograph, we should not lose sight of the equally vibrant, and remarkably varied, pervasive and resilient, oral/aural practices which it drew upon and redeveloped. From recitals of literary works to the ballyhoo of barkers outside shop shows and on fairgrounds, a wide range of existing discursive professions and practitioners had consistently articulated the acquisition and maintenance of audience attention as a substantial challenge. In each case, a fundamental part of the role of a public speaker was to secure the attentiveness of listeners, thus converting a crowd into an audience. The motives behind this ambition varied greatly, including the pedagogue's ambition to instruct, the entertainer's desire to amuse, and the ubiquitous financial imperative to "reel 'em in". Equally, the methods of securing attention were extremely varied, and certainly included the visual attraction, whether on posters, signs, and windows in city streets, or on screens and other illustrations within the shows. However, the ability to sustain attention within and between shows, generating good press, word of mouth, or repeat custom from loyal audiences, was just as significant to most shows, and it is important to recognize the role of the aural as well as the visual in this enterprise.

The problem of attention was not new, and it was certainly not restricted to reports concerning the cinema. As Jonathan Crary has demonstrated in his book *Suspensions of Perception: Attention, Spectacle, and Modern Culture*, the second half of the nineteenth century witnessed both an unprecedented upsurge in philosophical and scientific debate concerning the qualities of human attention, and the creation of technologies, works of art, and other popular forms that reflected, critiqued, or negotiated these ideas.[9] According to Crary, seeking explicitly to qualify the work of Georg Simmel, Walter Benjamin, and others on the distractive experience of modernity, "Attention and distraction were not two essentially different states but existed on a single continuum, and thus attention was, as most increasingly agreed, a dynamic process, intensifying and diminishing, rising and falling, ebbing and flowing according to an indeterminate set of variables."[10] The period thus witnessed the emergence of new forms of "institutionally competent attentiveness", such as that most often displayed by audiences of the cinematograph.[11]

In this light, it is tempting to read the verbal counterparts to visual spectacles, such as those provided by film lecturers, as an institutional mechanism dedicated to sustaining attention and securing long-term business from their audiences. Indeed, this is an important part of the argument I wish to make. The business of lecturing thrived in situations where it was important to acquire, focus, channel, or redirect the attention of audiences, and this explains its significance for religious, educational, and political institutions as well as on the professional lecture circuit and within popular entertainments. As one magic lantern commentator warned his fellow lecturers in the pages of the industry's dedicated trade paper, the chief problem with a poorly delivered lecture was that "you will not carry your audience with you and will not be able to retain their attention however good the illustrations may be".[12] However, in making a claim for lecturers as embodiments of this institutional imperative to secure attention, it is important not to equate the visual in any simple way with distraction, or the aural and verbal with contemplation. Projected images had the capacity to induce prolonged periods of staring-at attention from audiences, as the elaborate staging of many lantern slides or the existence of multishot film series from 1897 onwards implies; equally, the noisy, improvisatory performances of barkers outside of street shows and the battery of vocal talents employed by skilled lecturers demonstrate that accomplished speakers had a practised capacity to function as attractions in their own right.

Moreover, the problem of attention was identified, too, within spoken performances which did not depend upon visual images at all. Handbooks on elocution and public speaking proliferated between the 1870s and 1910s in Britain and the United States, each one setting out a training programme dedicated to securing the interest of audiences for protracted periods.[13] In his 1915 volume, *Public Speaking: Principles and Practice*, James Albert Winans made the connection between oratory and the psychology of attention more explicit. Drawing upon the work of eminent psychologists such as William James and Edward Bradford Titchener in the 1890s, Winans argued that the "the primary aim of a speaker is to hold the attention of his audience", but doing so was no simple matter.[14] In order to succeed in what Winans called the "Battle for Attention", the speaker needed to exploit both "primary" and "secondary" forms of attention.[15] Primary attention was evoked by powerful stimuli such as loud sounds and bright lights, and could be created in lectures by rhetorical "sensational methods" of "novelty", "curiosity", and "suspense". Secondary attention was more active, purposive, and long term, requiring an effort of dedicated concentration on the part of listeners. However, for Winans, looking to stabilize the ebb and flow of an audience's attention span, "it is easily seen that the less the effort involved in attending to a given idea the better, for the power of attention will be less quickly exhausted".[16] What was necessary, then, was the achievement of a state of "derived primary attention", in which high levels of concentration could be achieved without ongoing conscious effort: the listener was, in Titchener's words, "buried or sunk in his task".[17]

Properly regulated and varied speech was to be regarded as both a kind of spectacle in itself and as the means of channelling all kinds of productive concentration and imagination from listeners. For Winans's target readership of educators and instructors, primary attention was most often a means to an end, a first step towards the highly prized, lengthy periods of dedicated concentration that were best practice for listeners in lecture theatres. However, Winans's categories of attention were not mutually exclusive: he advocated the use of rhetorical strategies intended to attract all three types of attention as and when helpful to the speaker. In most film shows, we might note already, a far more mixed economy of speech—and of attentiveness—seems to have been appropriate than was typical of educative lecturing, with each show necessitating regular shifts in register from the educative to the informal to the spectacular. We might further note that Winans's listener/spectator, shifting in this way between primary, secondary, and derived primary types of attention, presents a compellingly inclusive model for attentive as well as distractive modes of film spectatorship, one that is broadly in sympathy with several recent accounts of the ambivalent attractiveness of early cinema.[18]

SPEAKING TO MOVING PICTURES

The early film exhibition business was characterized by both a multiplicity of early venues and a marked propensity for institutional change. As such, it had uses for public speakers of many kinds. Among these, perhaps the best known are those film lectures associated with educational and travel subjects, of the kind popularized by Burton Holmes's "Travelogues" in the United States (and, to a limited extent, in Britain and Ireland, where Holmes toured during 1904–5 to critical acclaim[19]). Most often taking place within respectable lecture theatres and other civic venues, and with ticket prices typically set high at a shilling and upwards, lectures of this kind perpetuated the key features of high-status platform lectures, which, in varied forms, had been popular throughout the nineteenth century.[20] During the aughts, travel and exploration lectures featuring films seem to have been an occasional attraction in most British towns: though irregular, large cities such as Plymouth hosted a film lecturer perhaps every five to six months on average and in smaller towns, such as nearby Torquay, the frequency was more like once during a year.[21] Many were organized by local entertainment agencies, such as Paish & Co. or Moon & Sons in the South West, though others took place under the auspices of nationwide organizations, such as the Royal Geographic Society, which had sponsored lantern shows throughout Britain for some decades. Film lecturing was also adopted by national charitable and missionary organizations such as the Royal National Mission to Deep Sea Fishermen and the Church Missionary Society, which had added subject-relevant moving pictures to the substantial lantern slide collections they held, looking upon them as a new means to garner support and funding for their varied enterprises.

Frequently, the appeal of such exhibitions lay in the claim that the lecturer had journeyed to an exotic location himself, had acquired substantial expertise concerning it, and perhaps had undergone adventures there. Generations of celebrated lantern and panorama lecturers had made similar claims, making the accumulation of views part of a personal narrative that could be retold to good effect. But with the widespread arrival of mass-reproduced photographic lantern slides in the 1880s and moving pictures in the 1890s, this claim also helped to distinguish such performers from competitors using commercially available images. Thus, relatively well-known career-lecturers such as Arthur Malden (the son of famous lantern lecturer Benjamin Malden) and Henry Hibbert used both slides and films in support of lectures that promised virtual tours around popular scenic destinations, most often in Europe.[22] Other lecturers brought more adventurous narratives to their audiences.[23] For example, during 1906, Harry de Windt toured his "Through Savage Europe" show, with films taken by his companion on the journey, Mr MacKenzie, and a lecture which detailed "his travels in some of the coldest and most inhospitable regions of Europe and Siberia".[24] Sandon Perkins toured his "Midst Arctic Snows" lecture during 1908 and 1909, using slides and films he had taken himself, and continuing a longstanding tradition of illustrated lecturing by Arctic explorers (which would soon include Herbert Ponting's celebrated films of Captain Scott's expedition).[25] The authenticity of speaker and footage were equally significant for missionary organizations, which often employed returned missionaries as lecturers, enabling films of natives to be presented as personal narratives of conversion rather than simply as exotic scenes.

The appeal of adventurer/lecturers of this kind was reinforced by their performance styles. According to one reviewer, Harry de Windt was "slim and youthful; he has a good clear voice; and in his remarks he passes quickly from grave to gay, from lively to severe."[26] Such variation of tone and the lively momentum of the lecture were remarked upon by a second review: "Mr. de Windt is a brilliant lecturer who punctuates his narrative with many humorous remarks, and does not allow a dull moment."[27] Lecturing styles varied, but reviews routinely paid more attention to describing the lecturer than the content or quality of the films. In such cases, the personality on the platform, coupled with an engaging speaking style, was the key to generating the absorbed attention of audiences and to distinguishing the show from travel films screened at other locations, helping to justify its high ticket prices.

Though relatively infrequent, lectures of this kind, sometimes given by career lecturers like Malden and sometimes by adventurer lecturers like Sandon Perkins, remained viable during the 1910s and well beyond, both in picture theatres and civic venues. Malden, in fact, remained active as a travelogue lecturer as late as 1927, his publicity still suggesting that films of the Rhine, France, Italy, and Egypt were "specially taken", and could not be seen elsewhere.[28] But attempts to extend and standardize film lecturing practices of this kind remained speculative and largely unsuccessful. Companies such as Pathé and, notably in Britain, the Charles Urban

Trading Company and the British and Colonial Kinematograph Company, released relatively large volumes of educational and travel subjects and often published detailed catalogue descriptions intended to inform lectures during the screening. In a few cases, it was even possible to acquire copies of lecture scripts from such manufacturers, and, from 1903, Urban's flagship entertainment at London's Alhambra variety theatre sometimes included lectures given by the travellers, mountaineers, and scientists who had made the films.[29] But this form of didactic lecture remained too closely tied to the body and spoken performance of the lecturer to lend itself easily to industrial distribution. Moreover, moving pictures had not been widely embraced by the lantern industry, though dominant figures such as Burton Holmes and Malden proved exceptions to this rule. During the late 1890s and 1900s, lantern lectures far outnumbered this type of travel film lecture, with a (conservative) average of three or four still taking place in large towns such as Plymouth each week during the season until about 1905. Partly, this was because the costs of maintaining moving picture equipment and acquiring new films were impossible for such small-scale showmen, but lecturers also complained that it had proved too difficult to combine moving pictures with the educational imperatives of much lecturing. Committed lanternists argued that the "kinematograph appeals to the eye chiefly, if not entirely",[30] and that "lecturing and teaching are more difficult and less effective with moving pictures".[31]

By 1912, even W. T. Stead, a devoted and vocal proponent of the moving pictures as an evangelical tool, diagnosed a similar problem at work in the new cinema theatres:

> The cinema public is like a child whose only literature is picture books; it is apt to be satisfied with looking at the pictures and never learns to read. The approach to the mind is solely through Eye-gate; the approach by Ear-gate is entirely neglected. The cinema challenges, but does not fix attention.[32]

For such commentators, moving pictures were to be resisted or reformed chiefly because they created a cinema that did not "fix attention" and a public that had become childlike, unable to listen or concentrate effectively. The antidote to this problem most often advocated was the addition of a lantern-style, educative lecturer to the exhibition, one who might generate prolonged periods of attention in the manner proposed by Winans. But lectures in the travelogue tradition seem to have remained only an occasional practice in most picture theatres. Although travelogues and other educational lectures were sometimes suggested as a useful alternative to standard programmes by the late aughts and early teens, this strategy seems to have been uncommon or unknown in the locations surveyed across the South West, and even where it did occur the lecturer employed was expected to speak to commercially distributed pictures, most likely without a published script. One cinema manager, hoping to make use of the few commercially available travel lecture scripts, complained in correspondence with *The Bioscope* in 1908 that "there are many exhibitors similarly placed to myself, who have risen from the ranks of the industry and who are not quite geniuses enough to stand up in a hall and deliver a long lecture on a picture which they have probably only seen run through the machine about two or three times."[33]

The alternative, for such managers, was to employ a speaker who did possess such improvisatory talents, and who might, therefore, be able to speak to a wide range of film genres. There was, in fact, a long precedent for doing exactly this, though it was a tradition of public speaking quite different from the script-driven, personalized narratives of celebrity lecturers such as Burton Holmes. Most often working within shows managed and owned by others, film lecturers of this kind seem to have been more common than those directly associated with the platform tradition, but their roles are more difficult to define, partly because their vocal performances were rarely reported, and partly because their profession was largely improvisational. From as early as 1897, the classified pages of theatrical and showman journal *The Era* contained advertisements for moving picture lecturers, indicating that such roles were at least in occasional demand among showmen.[34] John A. Prestwich, better known as an engineer of early cinematographic apparatus, proposed in a 1901 article written to showmen that film entertainments might be improved by merely announcing the titles or "by introducing a jest or short anecdote" now and then.[35] Similar techniques also seem to have been used in certain higher-status exhibitions. For example, in the relatively plush surroundings of Maskelyne and Cooke's famous conjuring show at London's Egyptian Hall, which since 1896 had regularly screened films, it was Nevil Maskelyne himself who introduced each film, or occasionally pointed out important details to audiences.[36] In shows such as this, the lecturer was required to focus audience attention upon the significance of what they were seeing, a feature that could be especially salient in relation to footage of current events or local scenes that might appear meaningless without appropriate signposting.

Within other shows, the role of the lecturer was more elaborate. On the fairground, where films were also exhibited on a relatively grand scale, well-known bioscope showmen, such as Colonel William Clark and William Haggar, regularly hired qualified lecturers to provide more detailed descriptions of films.[37] Though the term "describer" was frequently used in place of "lecturer" at this site, this title did not necessarily indicate that the role was simply a matter of reiterating the events taking place on the screen. One 1901 article in *The Showman*, titled "Animated Pictures and Elocution", suggested that, though "there is nothing calculated to delight the public more than the cinematograph", the public quickly tended to lose interest in moving pictures, chiefly because they were "not so much interested in the history of the subject, for there is no story attached and no ability displayed":

> A good reading by an able elocutionist, illustrated by good pictures, not only pleases the audience as far as the pictures are concerned, but it tells a good story and displays ability. It not only pleases the sight of the individual, but it pleases the brain as it makes him think of what he has seen and heard; the impression and interest gained is based on more lasting feeling.[38]

The combination of speaker and film, for this commentator, created an opportunity for enterprising showmen to make a deeper connection with audiences, one founded upon a prolonged, absorptive form of attention, similar in quality, if not content, to that looked for by generations of platform lecturers.

During the ten years that followed the article, the conspicuous display of oratorical ability, coupled with a good story, was most certainly expected of successful bioscope describers, and the practice was common in Britain. Some became relatively well known, at least within the business itself. According to a 1910 article in *The World's Fair*, James Styles (Figure 1.1) had been regarded for several years as "the best

FIGURE 1.1 Front-page image of James Styles in *The World's Fair*, 19 November 1910. (Courtesy: National Fairground Archive, University of Sheffield Library)

describer on the road", with "a natural gift to weave romances and interesting stories to pictures which he could describe after seeing them once":

> On one occasion when I happened to be among the audience, I heard the remark: "it's just like a play"; another said "they've got a good company, there must be five or six good 'uns in that scene"; yet it was all the work of one man, and that man James Styles, who, with his mimetic description and dramatic power, quite carried away his audience until it was as good as a play. Perhaps the greatest compliment he has been paid is the fact that his words have been copied and used by other describers throughout the country. Some, at least, had the courtesy to ask permission—which was readily granted. Others, however, filched his descriptions in a bare-faced manner, apparently not thinking that it is quite as dishonest to steal a man's brains as his purse, if not in the eyes of the law, at least in principle. A good story is good coin in many places, and talking pictures are now in request. I could give several instances where actors of repute—of unquestionable ability as actors, have tried to re-enact pictures, and failed, which only proves that more credit is due to the man whose success was unquestionable, namely—James Styles.[39]

Like the figure of the showman more generally, Styles was celebrated for his swift and easy ability to improvise a scene and for his capacity to entertain audiences with "fresh talk". The lectures themselves are described as "romances" and "interesting stories", emphasizing Styles's role as professional elocutionist, and suggesting that his ability to "weave" these narratives into the films was both highly skilled and difficult to reproduce. The idea that others had copied Styles's descriptions word for word is impossible to verify, but the existence of a kind of black market for a good lecture is an intriguing possibility, given that lecturers traded principally on the uniqueness of their presence.

The words spoken, of course, depended on Styles himself, and the possibility remained that, in the context of the travelling bioscope show, they might change according to location, audience, or time of day. Perhaps most suggestive, though, is the brief description of Styles's style and the reactions of his audience. The emphasis on "mimetic description and dramatic power" and the idea that these features "quite carried away his audience" closely resemble laudatory accounts of celebrated platform lecturers and their talent for painting word pictures or rendering dramatic realisations for attentive listeners. In Styles's film show, however, the suggestion was that the describer might also fill in the dialogue of the photoplay, in a style that resembled vocal performance traditions such as ventriloquism or the monopolylogue (a kind of character sketch involving multiple impersonations).

As in the US tradition of "talker pictures",[40] similar techniques, in fact, were at work in some picture theatres by 1909, with one correspondent to *The Bioscope* even suggesting that "the manufacturers should issue with their dramatic pictures a copy of the drama or a sketch giving the principle speeches made", so that "by simple phrases, short and to the point, you can convey to your hearers what the man, woman, or child would be saying".[41] The forms of attention generated by such techniques neatly combined the dramatic power exercised by the seasoned public speaker with the narrative absorption associated with the longer, fictional moving pictures that were now becoming more popular, and which, by 1912, would largely supplant the narrative functions sometimes played by lecturers.

Vocal dexterity and improvisatory ability of this kind also characterized the work of lecturers in other early film shows. Large-scale touring panorama shows such as Poole's "Myriorama" and Hamilton's "Excursions" quickly adopted the moving pictures, and imported them into environments that had employed varied public speakers for a number of decades.[42] Since the 1870s, the "Myriorama" had included lecturers, sometimes known as "guides" in order to reflect the world travel theme that governed the show, and by the 1890s the lecture included a "cross-talk" act that introduced a parodic edge to the lecture. In such shows, films might be accompanied by a number of such speakers, and sometimes by others, including comedians, ventriloquists, and popular and choral singers.[43] Relatively new shows, such as Leon Vint's idiosyncratic "Globe Choir and Scenorama", adopted similar strategies, although in this case the chief attraction was a twenty-strong female choir, which performed choruses, duets, trios, and selections on various instruments, before the exhibition of panoramic and moving travel pictures, described by Vint himself and accompanied by pianoforte.[44] Like celebrity lectures, panorama shows often appeared in large public town halls, mechanics' institutes, and other civic venues, but unlike lectures of this kind, they also promised to provide a kind of high-class variety, with a rapid turnover of different visual, verbal, and musical attractions. In this context, lecturers often imparted continuity to the show, becoming a focused point of attention within lengthy multimedia presentations.

These high-status touring panorama shows can usefully be seen as precursors for the touring town hall film shows that became important in larger British cities from approximately the beginning of 1901. Both forms of entertainment were staged on a similar scale, promised high-quality variety, including music and lectures, and were often in competition for the same large, desirable auditoria in city centres, including town halls and legitimate theatres. Perhaps best known among these is Alfred West's touring "Our Navy" entertainment, an early example which by 1899 was over two hours long, contained lantern images and numerous films accompanied by appropriate sound effects, a number of songs, and a patriotic, educative lecture often delivered by West himself.[45] But as recent work by Jon Burrows on T. J. West's shows in Bournemouth and by Vanessa Toulmin on Edwardian exhibition practices has suggested, the range, duration, and significance of town hall shows was much greater than idiosyncratic examples such as West's show suggest.[46] One further example of an eminent town hall film show, at St James's Hall in Plymouth, furnishes us with an unusually clear description of the multiple roles that could be played by lecturers at such high-status venues. It also demonstrates that such lecturers helped create what André Gaudreault and Jean Châteauvert have called a "structured sound space", in which music, lecturing, and other sound characteristics were used primarily to coordinate or discipline audiences in newly institutionalized configurations of spectatorship.[47] However, whereas Gaudreault and Châteauvert identify this aspect of film exhibition primarily with cinema post-1908, town hall shows in Britain provide examples of widespread similar sound practices as early as 1901, suggesting that the structured manipulation of audience attention within new institutional configurations had been more important earlier than has usually been suggested.

LECTURERS AT ST JAMES'S HALL, PLYMOUTH, 1901–2.

Since its opening in 1866, St James's Hall had been Plymouth's leading venue for touring exhibitions of all kinds. Situated in Union Street, an area renowned for its array of ephemeral penny shows, the hall quickly became a permanent fixture for the crowds that flowed from the naval port to the city and back, as well as for the growing population of Plymouth and surrounding areas. With a two-tier auditorium and 3000 seats, the hall delivered high-status amusements compared with other venues along the street, regularly hosting panoramas, musical performances, and a range of popular performers, from protean artists to freak exhibitions. In November 1896, during a period in which the hall was operating as a variety theatre, St James's was also the first venue on Union Street to exhibit film, with a sensational fortnight-long turn of "Paul's Theatrograph". But a more substantial programme of film exhibition began in May 1901, shortly after the hall had begun again to operate as an exhibition venue for hire, with the arrival of the "Royal Animated Picture Company and Gibbons' Phono Bio-Tableaux". The new show began with a speculative run of two weeks, but its popularity was such, with hundreds turned away each night, that the decision was quickly taken to continue. The longest runs for travelling panorama shows at St James's Hall had stretched for ten weeks, with a more typical range of only four. But under the auspices of three different film exhibition companies and four managers of the venue, the film show at St James's persisted as a permanent nightly attraction for the next year and a half, and the hall become known locally by November 1901 as "The Home of Animated Photography". It would retain this title for the next thirteen years, during which period films remained a regular attraction under varied managers, and with numerous lecturers, and by 1914, now an established picture theatre, it would eventually relaunch as "The Home of Movies" (Figure 1.2).[48]

The St James's film show rapidly became a local institution and was a substantial competitor to the elaborate New Palace variety theatre a few doors away, which had dominated popular entertainments in the town since it had opened in 1898. The business practices of the two venues were, in fact, similar in many respects. Both drew broadly similar audiences and were able to charge comparable prices, starting from sixpence for the galleries (the same, or slightly more than was charged by legitimate theatres in the town at this time, and considerably more than picture theatres would come to charge by the early 1910s). Both programmes opened nightly at 7.30 p.m., but the film show also included matinee performances from 3 p.m. on Wednesdays and Saturdays, and these were intended in part for families, with seats available for children at half price. The two shows were well respected by the local press and civic authorities, partly because of the harmless nature of the varieties on offer, and partly

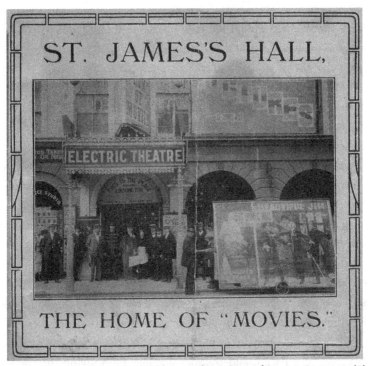

FIGURE 1.2 Front-page image from *St James's Pictorial Magazine and Souvenir Programme* (Plymouth: Valletort Press, 1914). (Courtesy: Plymouth Library Services).

because of the benefit performances they held for local charities. Importantly, the film show was also equally lengthy, typically running for a period of between two and two and a half hours each night, with the general expectation that audiences would arrive at the beginning and sit through a carefully scheduled, varied, and constantly evolving programme. As in all well-respected theatrical venues in the town, the local press especially emphasized the quality of the venue's management, noting that the programme was renewed at least once a week, more regularly than had been possible for the panorama showmen, but closely mirroring hiring practices for artistes at the New Palace.

The 1901–2 St James's show was notable, too, for the variety and quality of its musical and vocal performances. Among these, Gibbons's "Phono Bio-Tableaux", fresh from the London Hippodrome, proved an especially significant attraction in the first months of the show, but most enduring were the pianists, bands, orchestras, choirs, singers, ventriloquists, professional lecturers, and other speakers who performed at the hall during these years. Indeed, though reviews praised the regular changes of programme, the quality of the films, and the provision of scenes of current events or of local views, the most frequently remarked attraction of the hall in the local press was the superiority of its auditory environment. The pianist, William Neale, who subsequently went on to conduct the "Fonobia Orchestra of Soloists" at the hall, was particularly successful, and further positive notices were given to small choral groups that were hired to sing during the pictures in certain weeks. Importantly, as the feature most directly and obviously associated with the management of the hall rather than the moving picture companies that took residence within it, sound practices, and especially vocal performances, seem to have provided evidence for the hall's consistent claim to provide quality entertainment for discerning and higher-spending audiences. It also tended to distinguish this venue from competitor high-status film exhibitions in Plymouth, which in 1901 included the lengthy annual appearance of Hancock's "Winter Gardens" along with its "Bioscope" show, regular screenings in the course of the varieties at the Palace, and the fortnight-long visit of West's "Our Navy" during December.

Sound practices at St James's were carefully balanced across each performance, and, like the films themselves, were also modified, rotated, and withdrawn across the life of the show, becoming a significant aspect of its self-renewing novelty. Its lecturers were an especially significant feature of this careful management of sound. As visible and audible representatives of the hall, placed on the stage and alongside the screen, they tended to provide cues for the projectionist, for other performers, and for audiences, and bore the primary responsibility for moving the show along in a structured, well-paced, and friendly manner. Embodying the show's coherence, it was equally important that they did so in an entertaining and inclusive manner, the performance of personality becoming a key structuring component of the show's stylistics. They were also expected to contribute materially to the show's novelty, with different lecturers hired in order to bolster the hall's provision of choral or popular song, its screening of educational or travel subjects, or its inclusion of variety turns to break up different sections of the film show. Edwin Wallace, who also worked briefly as an assistant manager at the hall, was promoted chiefly as a world traveller and spent one portion of the show vividly relating his experiences in travelogue fashion (Figure 1.3). Mr E. Osmonde, who managed the hall during the same period, also appeared as a lecturer for a number of weeks, with reviews

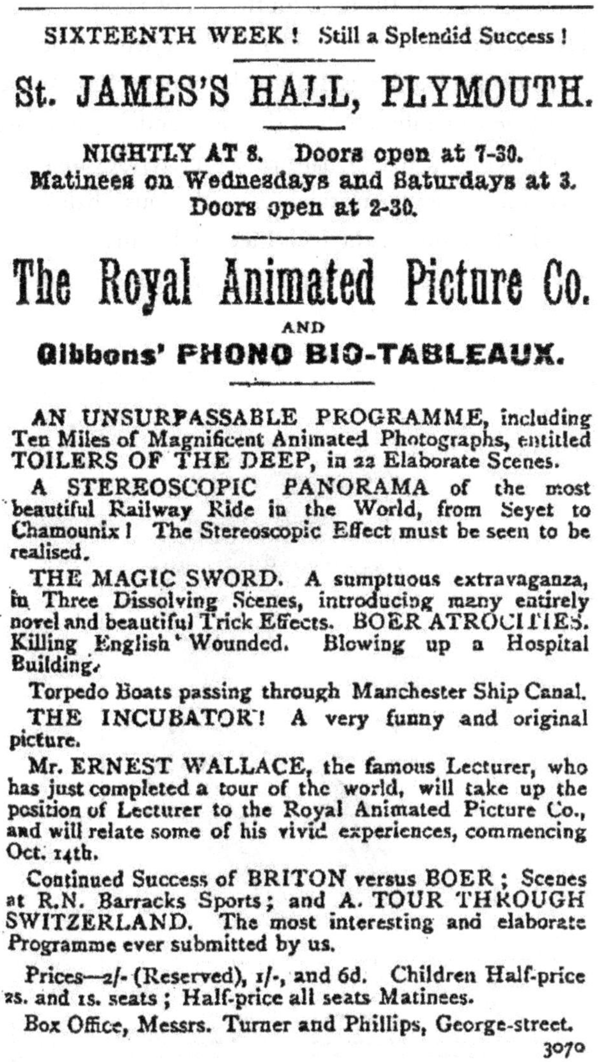

SIXTEENTH WEEK !   Still a Splendid Success !

St. JAMES'S HALL, PLYMOUTH.

NIGHTLY AT 8.   Doors open at 7-30.
Matinees on Wednesdays and Saturdays at 3.
Doors open at 2-30.

The Royal Animated Picture Co.

AND

Gibbons' PHONO BIO-TABLEAUX.

AN UNSURPASSABLE PROGRAMME, including Ten Miles of Magnificent Animated Photographs, entitled TOILERS OF THE DEEP, in 22 Elaborate Scenes.

A STEREOSCOPIC PANORAMA of the most beautiful Railway Ride in the World, from Seyet to Chamounix ! The Stereoscopic Effect must be seen to be realised.

THE MAGIC SWORD. A sumptuous extravaganza, in Three Dissolving Scenes, introducing many entirely novel and beautiful Trick Effects. BOER ATROCITIES. Killing English Wounded. Blowing up a Hospital Building.

Torpedo Boats passing through Manchester Ship Canal.

THE INCUBATOR! A very funny and original picture.

Mr. ERNEST WALLACE, the famous Lecturer, who has just completed a tour of the world, will take up the position of Lecturer to the Royal Animated Picture Co., and will relate some of his vivid experiences, commencing Oct. 14th.

Continued Success of BRITON versus BOER ; Scenes at R.N. Barracks Sports; and A. TOUR THROUGH SWITZERLAND. The most interesting and elaborate Programme ever submitted by us.

Prices—2/- (Reserved), 1/-, and 6d. Children Half-price 2s. and 1s. seats ; Half-price all seats Matinees.

Box Office, Messrs. Turner and Phillips, George-street.

3070

FIGURE 1.3 Newspaper advertisement including notice for the appearance of a new lecturer at St James's Hall. *The Western Figaro*, 18 October 1901: 9.

suggesting that he was well liked for his "genial" attitude to audiences.[49] But by far
the most successful of the hall's lecturers in this period was Edwin Wensley-Russell,
who managed to fulfil all of the functions expected of lecturers at the hall: he introduced titles, commentated or sang to the pictures, provided popular songs in interludes, and, more bizarrely, as the "Human Cello", gave regular vocal impersonations
of Auguste van Biene's well-known solos (Figure 1.4).

Wensley-Russell had been an actor during the 1890s, and in 1899 had advertised
himself in the pages of *The Era* as a "singing light comedian", a career which does
much to explain the versatility of his platform presence during film shows, but
there is no evidence to suggest any history as a lecturer before the St James's show.[50]
However, performing alongside the films for the full two hours of the show, his face
and voice quickly became well known to Plymouth audiences, and his presence was
often advertised in newspapers alongside the titles of new films. As such, it is tempting to read him as a new manifestation of the older and, by 1901, largely displaced
British tradition of the music hall "Chairman", a master of ceremonies whose performance connected the variety performances on the music hall stage and who was
expected to embody the ethos of the hall. Like a Chairman, Wensley-Russell was
charged with moving the programme crisply along from one section to the next, with

St. James's Hall.

Mr. Wellsley Russell,
Lecturer and Human 'Cello.

FIGURE 1.4 Portrait of Edwin Wensley-Russell (misspelled) in local Plymouth press. *The Western Figaro*, 27 September 1901: 8.

reviews suggesting that "he does not let the programme flag for one moment".[51] Also like a Chairman, he was expected to make a personal and enduring connection with audiences, acting "the part of guide and friend" to them as another review noted, adding that "his witty appropriate remarks help muchly towards the enjoyment of the scenes depicted".[52] Thus, although the multiple vocal roles Wensley-Russell played might appear to stretch beyond credibility his professional designation as "lecturer" to the hall, his performance was unified by his central role as master of ceremonies.

As in the case of James Styles, the regular changes of film each week necessitated a good deal of flexibility in Wensley-Russell's performance style and an ability to improvise, having perhaps seen the films in question only a few times before. The films screened were numerous and varied across the two-hour programme, with the most popular subjects in 1901–2 being local films, scenes of current events including some late Boer War films, comedies and trick films, and a number of multiscene "event films", such as the twelve-scene Méliès spectacle *Jeanne D'Arc* (1900). Under such circumstances, Wensley-Russell was called upon variously to provide relevant information and humorous anecdotes concerning local scenes, personalities, or current events, to enhance the gags delivered by the comedies, and to deliver relevant story information for longer fictional films. In addition to the regular flow of commentary he provided, he occasionally took centre stage himself. As well as his renditions as the Human Cello, which remained popular for several months, his versions of popular tunes, such as the "butcher's song" "I'll Throw Sheep's Eyes at You, Love", and short comic sketches concerning other popular singers added further variety. During December 1901, he also sang "Star of Bethlehem" in a performance that took centre stage, while a series of films were screened as yuletide illustrations for the verse.

Providing a degree of continuity between such highly varied films, Wensley-Russell therefore brought the attention of audiences to bear on radically different subjects, but remained a constant, aural reminder that each of these subjects was but one part of the greater show. He was a key part of the scheduling strategy at St James's Hall, enabling a wide variation in film subject matter without producing a jarring or discontinuous experience for audiences. Alongside the hall's orchestra and its well-structured programme, he therefore allowed its managers to capitalize fluidly upon alternative qualities of attentiveness in its audiences, varying from curiosity or fascination with the numerous attractions the moving pictures could offer, to periods of prolonged concentration on educational subjects or complex narratives, to a simple appreciation for the musical qualities of his voice. This expert management of audience attention was not easily accomplished, requiring a virtuosic performative range, a talent for improvisation and fresh talk, a clear understanding of the pragmatics of addressing large audiences across such long periods, and also the occupation of a distinct, authoritative, but personable subject position from which to speak. Unsurprisingly, men such as Wensley-Russell and James Styles who combined these qualities seem to have been much in demand, with Wensley-Russell returning regularly to St James's Hall to bolster the range of attractions on offer. Such men could become invaluable to exhibitors, coming to characterize the shows and even the institutions in which they took place. Indeed, in the decade that followed, St James's Hall employed a series of well-regarded lecturer/vocalists, with Horace Davis, whose funeral was noted in the pages of *The Bioscope* in 1910, becoming perhaps the best known of all these local figures.[53]

Clearly we cannot, without consideration of further examples, take performances at this one venue to typify the profession of film lecturing across Britain at the turn of the century. Indeed, the styles of lecturers, where present, were likely to be as varied as the institutions in which they performed. However, we can conclude, at least, that the dispersed set of traditions called upon by individuals such as Wensley–Russell and Styles exemplifies the variability in the roles played by lecturers in Britain prior to the arrival of picture theatres. Working within and between numerous institutional contexts, lecturers were not merely mediators for the continual processes of institutional redefinition at work within varied exhibition industries, but could be instrumental in creating new patterns of audience attention, actively modulating the provision of spectacle, narrative, and other cognitive effects in tandem with the dynamics of a well-balanced programme. In doing so they adapted a wide range of earlier public-speaking and singing practices, from platform lecturing to popular song to ventriloquism, and at certain points their voices, far from being supplementary to the spectacle, could become the primary point of attention for audiences. Furthermore, lecturers frequently bore an important responsibility for structuring and coordinating the shows in which they participated, calling upon varied modes of audience attentiveness in order to do so. Lecturers thus tended to enact in word and gesture both the adaptation of older institutional formations and the development of innovative or unfamiliar institutional strategies for securing and manipulating attention—a Janus-faced function which would again become especially significant in Britain and North America with the substantial arrival of picture theatres in 1909.[54]

NOTES

1. Tom Gunning, "The Scene of Speaking: Two Decades of Discovering the Film Lecturer", *Iris* 27 (Spring 1999): 67–79.

2. See, for example, Martin Sopocy, "A Narrated Cinema: The Pioneer Story Films of James A. Williamson", *Cinema Journal* 18/1 (1978): 1–28; Norman King, "The Sound of Silents", *Screen*

25/3 (1984): 2–25; Charles Musser, "The Eden Musee in 1898: Exhibitor as Co-Creator", *Film and History* 11/4 (1981): 73–83.

3. Joe Kember, *Marketing Modernity: Victorian Popular Shows and Early Cinema* (Exeter: University of Exeter Press, 2009), 44–128.

4. Rick Altman, *Silent Film Sound* (New York: Columbia University Press, 2004), 134–40.

5. According to Germain Lacasse's concise definition, the *bonimenteur* can be defined as "the person commentating on the screening, improvising film commentary", and the *conférencier* as "the person giving a well-prepared lecture with scholarly explanations". Germain Lacasse, "The Lecturer and the Attraction", in *The Cinema of Attractions Reloaded*, ed. Wanda Strauven (Amsterdam: Amsterdam University Press, 2006), 190. For a detailed description of these and other terms from the French, see André Gaudreault with Jean-Pierre Sirois-Trahan, "Le retour du [bonimenteur] refoulé… (où serait-ce le bonisseur-conférencier, le commentateur, le conférencier, le présentateur ou le 'speacher'?)", *Iris* 22 (1996): 17–32.

6. Richard Crangle, "'Next Slide Please': The Lantern Lecture in Britain, 1890–1910", in *The Sounds of Early Cinema*, ed. Richard Abel and Rick Altman (Bloomington: Indiana University Press, 2001), 46–7.

7. The AHRC funded project "Moving and Projected Image Entertainments in the South West, 1840–1914", led by Dr John Plunkett and myself, has sought to broaden our understanding of image-led public entertainments both geographically and chronologically. The locations studied within this project are: Bristol, Plymouth, Exeter, Torquay, Barnstaple, Penzance, Sidmouth, and Weston-super-Mare, a range of cities, towns, coastal resorts, and villages which has demonstrated the range of entertainments and exhibition practices at work across urban, rural, and provincial settlements.

8. For an extended treatment of Lacasse's view of the lecturer as "between tradition and modernity", and as the mediator of increasingly centralized film institutions for regional communities, see Germain Lacasse, *Le Bonimenteur de Vues Animées. Le Cinéma Muet entre Tradition et Modernité* (Paris: Méridiens Klincksieck, 2000), 183–96.

9. Jonathan Crary, *Suspensions of Perception: Attention, Spectacle, and Modern Culture* (Cambridge, MA: MIT Press, 1999).

10. Ibid., 47.

11. Ibid., 77.

12. T. Perkins, "Our Lantern Lectures", *Optical Magic Lantern and Photographic Enlarger*, Jan. 1902, 105.

13. See, for example: Andrew Comstock and James Allan Mair, *The Model Elocutionist: A Manual of Instruction in Vocal Gymnastics and Gesture* (London: William Collins, 1874); George L. Raymond, *The Orator's Manual: A Practical and Philosophical Treatise on Vocal Culture, Emphasis, and Gesture*, 3rd edn. (New York and London: Putnam's, 1910), first publ. 1879; and Charles Hartley, *How to Speak Well in Public and Private* (London: Groombridge, 1884).

14. James Albert Winans, *Public Speaking: Principles and Practice* (Ithaca, NY: Sewell, 1915), 63. His chief source was Edward Bradford Titchener, *A Primer of Psychology* (New York: MacMillan, 1898), 73–94.

15. Ibid., 64–5.

16. Ibid., 65

17. Titchener, *A Primer of Psychology*, 77.

18. Charles Musser, "A Cinema of Contemplation, a Cinema of Discernment: Spectatorship, Intertextuality and Attractions in the 1890s", in *The Cinema of Attractions Reloaded*, ed. Strauven, 159–79; Kember, *Marketing Modernity*, 13–40; Ben Singer, "The Ambimodernity of Early Cinema: Problems and Paradoxes in the Film-and-Modernity Discourse", in *Film 1900: Technology, Perception, Culture*, ed. Annemone Ligensa and Klaus Kreimeier (New Barnet: John Libbey, 2009), 37–52; Daniel Biltereyst, Richard Maltby, and Philippe Meers, "Cinema, Audiences and Modernity: An Introduction", in *Cinema, Audiences and Modernity: New Perspectives on European Cinema History*, ed. Daniel Biltereyst, Richard Maltby, and Philippe Meers (London: Routledge, 2012), 1–16.

19. See *Optical Lantern and Cinematograph Journal*, Sept. 1905, 170.

20. Martin Hewitt, "Beyond Scientific Spectacle: Image and Word in Nineteenth-Century Popular Lecturing", in *Popular Exhibitions, Science and Showmanship, 1840–1914*, ed. Joe Kember, John Plunkett, and Jill A. Sullivan (London: Pickering and Chatto, 2012), 79–96.

21. For some details of frequency of Sunday lectures using film in London venues, see Tony Fletcher, "Sunday and Holy Days", in *Networks of Entertainment: Early Film Distribution, 1895–1915*, ed. Frank Kessler and Nanna Verhoeff (Eastleigh: John Libbey, 2007), 236–7.

22. On Hibbert, See n.a., *The Showman*, 22 Mar. 1901, 168; on Malden, see n.a., "A Successful Living Picture Lecture", in *Optical Lantern and Cinematograph Journal*, May 1906, 93.

23. I am grateful to Rosalind Leveridge, PhD researcher for the project "Moving and Projected Images in the South West, 1840–1914", for providing information concerning lectures in Torquay.

24. "'Savage' Europe", *Torquay Directory and South Devon Journal*, 21 Mar. 1906, 3.

25. "Midst Arctic Snows", *Torquay Directory and South Devon Journal*, 10 Feb. 1909, 3.

26. "'Savage' Europe", *Torquay Directory and South Devon Journal*, 21 Mar. 1906, 3.

27. "Through Savage Europe", *Torquay Times*, 28 Mar. 1906, 6.

28. *Arthur B. Malden and his Cinema Travelogues*. I am grateful to Tony Fletcher, who has kindly given me a copy of this pamphlet.

29. On Urban's educational output, see Luke McKernan, "'Something More than a Mere Picture Show': Charles Urban and the Early Non-Fiction Film in Great Britain and America, 1897–1925" (PhD. diss., Birkbeck, University of London, 2004).

30. T. Perkins, "Our Lantern Lectures", *Optical Magic Lantern and Photographic Enlarger*, Jan. 1902, 105.

31. *Newton and Co's Catalogue of Lantern Slides (Pt II)* (London: Newton, [n.d.]), vii.

32. W. T. Stead, "The Church's Picture Galleries: A Plea for Special Sunday Cinemas", *Review of Reviews* 46/275 (Nov. 1912): 534.

33. "Questions Worth Answering", *The Bioscope*, 17 Dec. 1908, 21.

34. *The Era*, 3060, 15 May 1897, 27.

35. John A. Prestwich, "How to Give a Good Cinematograph Show", *The Showman*, 6 Sept. 1901, 571.

36. "At England's Home of Mystery", *The Showman*, 26 April 1901, 265.

37. "William Clark", *The Showman*, 1 Feb. 1901, 78; Lily May Richards, *Biography of William Haggar* (unpublished manuscript, National Fairground Archive, Sheffield), 16.

38. "Animated Pictures and Elocution", *The Showman*, 20 Sept. 1901, 24.

39. "Mr James Styles—Describer", *The World's Fair*, 24 Sept. 1910, 14.

40. See Jeffrey Klenotic, "'The Sensational Acme of Realism': 'Talker' Pictures as Early Cinema Sound Practice", in *The Sounds of Early Cinema*, ed. Abel and Altman, 156–66.

41. "The Bioscope Parliament", *The Bioscope*, 21 Jan. 1909, 23.

42. See Hudson John Powell, *Poole's Myriorama!: A Story of Travelling Panorama Showmen* (Bradford-on-Avon: ELSP, 2002).

43. For example, see "Poole's Myriorama", *Western Figaro*, 9 July 1897, 14.

44. "'Globe Choir' at the Mechanics' Institute", *Western Figaro*, 2 Mar. 1900, 12.

45. *Optical Magic Lantern and Photographic Enlarger*, Dec. 1899, 143.

46. Jon Burrows, "*West is Best!*; or, What we can Learn from Bournemouth", *Early Popular Visual Culture* 8/4 (2010): 351–62; Vanessa Toulmin, "Cuckoo in the Nest: Edwardian Itinerant Exhibition Practices and the Transition to Cinema in the United Kingdom from 1901 to 1906", *The Moving Image* 10/1 (2010): 52–79.

47. André Gaudreault and Jean Châteauvert, "The Noises of Spectators, or the Spectator as Additive to the Spectacle", in *Sounds of Early Cinema*, ed. Abel and Altman, 183–91.

48. *Western Daily Mercury*, 26 Nov. 1901, 4.

49. "Animated Pictures at St James's Hall", *Western Figaro*, 25 Oct. 1901, 15.

50. *The Era*, 5 July 1899.

51. "St. James' Hall", *Western Figaro*, 2 Aug. 1901, 18.

52. "St. James' Hall", *Western Figaro*, 24 May 1901, 6.

53. "Death of a Popular Lecturer", *The Bioscope*, 27 Jan. 1910, 13.

54. For accounts of the brief 1908–9 resurgence of lecturing in the United Kingdom, see Joe Kember, "'Go thou and do likewise': Advice to Lantern and Film Lecturers in the Trade Press, 1897–1909", *Early Popular Visual Culture* 8/4 (2010): 419–30. For an account of the debate in the 1908–9 trade press, see Kember, *Marketing Modernity*, 80–83.

2

"Now, where were we?": Ideal and Actual Early Cinema Lecturing
Practices in Britain, Germany and the United States

Judith Buchanan

What is cinema? –
"the offspring of technological curiosity and showmanship"

F. E. Sparshott, "Basic Film Aesthetics"[1]

1890S TRAVELLING FILM SHOWS

In 1896–7, British film pioneer Cecil Hepworth was setting out on his career by touring the country with a travelling show of projected pictures. His programme line-up,
as he later reported, was distinctly modest: "half a dozen throw-out forty-foot films
of R. W. Paul's and about a hundred lantern slides of my own."[2] In order to make his
"six miserable little films" fill up the available time, Hepworth became adept at the
patter of a showman: "talking through my hat", as he self-deprecatingly described
it. One of the time-filling strategies he deployed was to freeze the projection at a
moment that would leave the characters "in peculiarly awkward attitudes" on the
screen and then stage humorous arguments with them from his own, more vibrant,
position on the floor.[3] Positing himself as impish interlocutor *with* his images in this
way enabled Hepworth to trade on the comic disparities inherent in this allegedly
interactive engagement. In the service of the broader show, the films acted partly as a

technologically novel, and innovatively employed, prop. The one-way performance transaction staged by Hepworth would, therefore, have had the effect of emphasizing the live-ness of the containing act within which the films were being showcased.

Hepworth further reports that before the start of one of his touring shows, a member of the local clergy asked to see the list of pictures to be exhibited. Unfortunately, one title struck him as potentially corrupting: a hand-coloured film of Loïe Fuller ("La Loïe") performing her famously exotic serpentine dance. Concerned for the spiritual welfare of his "flock", the parson requested that this film be omitted from the programme.[4] Hepworth had a problem: keen though he was to avert unnecessary opposition from the voices of establishment respectability, he was nonetheless unable, at such short notice, to excise one film from his continuously spliced reel. Struck just in time by what he termed a "brainwave", Hepworth announced the film in question to the assembled audience not as an exotic dance performed by a well-known music hall artiste (which, in truth, it was), but rather as "Salome Dancing before Herod" (which, thus billed, it naturally now became in the minds of this particular audience). Having been introduced in these newly biblical terms, Ms Fuller then twirled and swirled her copious yards of fabric in mesmerizing spirals of cloth on the screen, just as she had in all her many previous screen outings before she expediently "became" Salome.

And how did this potentially suspect film play to its morally scrupulous audience? Hepworth's barely suppressed glee is evident in the report he supplies:

> Everyone was delighted. Especially the parson. He said in his nice little speech afterwards that he thought it was a particularly happy idea to introduce a little touch of Bible history into an otherwise wholly secular entertainment.[5]

As Hepworth had correctly predicted, the broader biblical narrative context—absent, for obvious reasons, from the film itself, but now implicitly conjured in the interpretive space around the frame by the contextualizing (re-)description opportunistically offered of it—was sufficient to license (and even commend) this particular voyeuristic cinematic pleasure to this particular audience. Remaking the film's cultural charge, moral flavour, and social acceptability by the simple act of renaming was a noteworthy achievement. This was film not merely being accompanied, but authored by an analogue speech act.

So much for Hepworth's tale. But was it his? Despite the confident sense of ownership with which he narrates the Salome incident, and the air of self-congratulation for a stylishly nonchalant rescue that underpins his account, the same anecdote, or one extremely like it, was in broader circulation in reports on the early moving picture showmen in Britain. As Joe Kember has helpfully documented, it was a yarn that was promiscuously appropriated. Not only, therefore, did Hepworth claim it

for his own, but in 1898 it was also attributed to an anonymous "professor" (a standard sobriquet for film showmen), and in subsequent accounts separately to travelling showmen William Haggar and Randall Williams.[6] Whichever dancer it was
whose film performance was actually considered suspect, and whichever showman
(if any) it was who then amusingly rebranded her in the moment of exhibition, the
recurrence of the tale across multiple reports testifies to how the early British film
industry wished to perceive of itself: as adaptable according to the conditions of
exhibition and fronted by men with an imperturbable and quick-thinking commitment to the success of the show. Those seeking to characterize the improvisatory
character of the 1890s film shows, and the ready wit and sangfroid of the showmen
who ran them, therefore reached gratefully, and repeatedly, for an entertaining anecdote to illustrate that.

Among those forging their way in the nascent American moving picture industry
at the same time, and similarly giving touring exhibitions, were two Englishmen,
Albert E. Smith and J. Stuart Blackton. As part of their show, Blackton would
deliver a rabble-rousing lecture, similarly designed not so much to accompany the
event (which might misleadingly imply a hierarchy in which the lecture was lesser
partner), as to drive it. As Smith subsequently recalled, they often began their show
by projecting the first frame of their most popular film, *The Black Diamond Express*,
as a frozen still.[7] This opening image showed that favourite trope of early cinema,
a steam train heading apparently straight for the camera. Blackton the impresario
(or "terroristic mood setter", as Smith colourfully tagged him) would then work the
audience's anticipation in the following terms:

> Ladies and gentlemen, you are now gazing upon a photograph of the famous
> Black Diamond Express. In just a moment, a cataclysmic moment, my friends,
> a moment without equal in the history of our times, you will see this train
> take life in a marvelous and most astounding manner. It will rush toward you,
> belching smoke and fire from its monstrous iron throat ...[8]

The register employed is uncompromising showmanship: the audience's appetite
is whetted and the ensuing collective gasp all but assured. Here were a couple of
entrepreneurs with a consciously employed instinct for selling their product, for
generating in their audience a sense both of wonder at the novelty of the hard-
ware and of communal privilege at seeing it showcased. And, like Hepworth in his
talking-back-to-the-screen antics, they used the drama of the human voice, their
foreknowledge of the films, and the vital immediacy of their own presence in the
exhibition space to draw from their projected images the greatest possible impact
for their audience.[9]

Hepworth's and Smith's memorial accounts are instructive, reminding us, as they do, of the live showmanship that, as Sparshott asserts, was crucially part of cinema's origins and early identity.[10] In their drama, variety, dependence on interjections from a live master of ceremonies, and style of appeals to their audience, very early moving picture shows on both sides of the Atlantic drew discernibly not only upon the subjects but also the exhibition conventions of British music hall and American vaudeville. And, indeed, they were quickly themselves absorbed into such shows, the cinematograph adding to the line-up of variety acts. The role of the picture-showman for very early cinema, who introduced the pictures and supplied the continuity links for the programme as a whole, would in due course cede to the role of the film lecturer employed to provide sustained explanatory or contextualizing commentary upon the images for an individual, longer narrative film sitting within a varied moving picture programme. And for both—the early showman-lecturer whose films, in effect, illustrated his act and the later lecturer there, unambiguously, at the service of the pictures—the provenance of this live figure speaking to the images lies not only in variety theatre but also in magic lantern shows.

THE "PRESENTNESS" OF THE LECTURER
IN LANTERN AND PICTURE SHOWS

The magic lantern was not a medium, and not conceived as a medium, in which the visual material of the slides had been expected to function autonomously. The presence of a lecturer for slide shows had, therefore, always been both necessary and assumed. Ranging from the flippantly jocular to the designedly edifying and educative, lantern lectures were sometimes offered by the lanternist himself from his slide-loading position by his lamp, sometimes by a separate lecturer at the front of the hall. In some cases the lecture had been scripted ahead of time; in others it was completely extemporized in the moment of delivery. Some scripted talks could be purchased directly from the slide manufacturers to accompany particular slide sequences, as a ready-made fillip to the lanternist's fluency of delivery; others were composed by the lanternist himself in order best to enliven and elucidate his own assembled slide set. Being personally present in the space of the audience, and able to determine the sequence, speed, and linguistic context in which he "released" his slides to the assembled crowd naturally imbued a lantern lecturer with a keen control of the event.

At more formal lantern shows, the lecturer would speak from the front of the hall while a separate lantern operator was responsible for changing the slides on cue. For such events, the smooth flow of the programme was always, inevitably, potentially susceptible to mini-disruptions through lapses in communicative fluency between lecturer and operator. Indeed, one British slide manufacturer, York and Sons, stated explicitly that it was to guard against the "awkward pause [at slide-changing moments] that so often spoils the smoothness of the whole entertainment" that it had inserted slide-changing marks into its published lantern scripts.[11] This, it hoped, would aid the lecturer in communicating seamlessly and consistently with the slide operator. Whether the slide change happened with greater or less fluency, though, at lantern shows, it was still squarely in the gift of the lecturer to determine the pace of the presentation by calling, or signalling, for the slide change at the moment that suited his own scripted or improvisatory lecturing purposes.

One of the defining features of lantern exhibition was, therefore, that no show had a fixed tonal character but was rather made, and remade, on each occasion by a lanternist's deft management of the technology and/or rhetorical dexterity in mediating engagingly between his slides and his audience. The supremacy of the live performance and the degree of engaging charisma with which the talk was delivered was always, and necessarily, the central animating force of a lantern show.[12] In the 1889 debut issue of the British publication *The Optical Magic and Lantern Journal and Photographic Enlarger*, Henry Cooper made the case:

> The lecture must be the backbone of the entertainment. The slides may be as good as possible, the lenses of the best construction, but if the description of the pictures be faulty, they will avail nothing to satisfy modern taste.[13]

Five years later in the same publication, Amy Johnson reasserted the position:

> let the slides of some interesting story be passed through the lantern in succession without a word of context, what is the result?—Weariness and yawning. Here is the secret, then—the story behind.[14]

It was, definitively, the live lecture, with the slides in supporting role, that formed "the backbone of the entertainment" and the success of the show therefore depended principally upon the quality of the lecturer.

Importing a version of this lecturing figure—so fundamental to the identity of a lantern show—to very early moving picture shows perpetuated the taste for an intimate, collaborative relationship between projected images and spoken words as a dominant feature of the show. The images themselves were not, at this stage in the film industry's history, offered as communicatively complete in themselves. Injecting a live speech element to proceedings therefore tempered any potential impression of cinema as an entirely pre-packaged phenomenon whose formal characteristics were all fully determined ahead of time, and which then simply played out mechanically, indifferent to its audience, in the exhibition moment. As Norman King has argued, a live commentary included as part of a film exhibition "actualised the image and, merging with it, emphasised the presentness of the performance and of the audience", so encouraging "a sense of immediacy and participation".[15]

At a lantern show, this sense of immediacy and participation could never have been in doubt. There, a dexterous lanternist in control of his own projections could dwell upon, or move swiftly on from, any slide he chose at any speed he chose; reprise any slide or sequence that had proved particularly popular, or likely to garner a laugh a second time around; omit any likely to cause offence or play less well to the particular community; and adjust his patter accordingly. And at a solo-presented early picture show, such as those given by Hepworth in the 1890s, where the showman-projectionist was himself partly improvising his way through his programme of short films in response to the dynamics within the exhibition hall (such as the presence of an over-scrupulous parson or the need to freeze the frame and stage a mock-argument with on screen characters to fill up the available time), the experience for an audience must have been similarly involved and involving.

It is now a critical given that the developmental phases of the film industry were far from definitive, discrete, or uniform across local and national contexts.[16] In broad terms, though, it was after 1907 that the pictures produced became longer, narrative-driven story films (*c.*1000-foot one-reelers and then "lengthy" two- and three-reelers).[17] And, by the same token, it was in this same period that narratives became correspondingly more complex in character line-ups, structure, progress, and outworking in order to make use of the newly available footage. But complexity also bred confusion in some cases, and the enhanced complexity of the stories provoked the call for the clarification of obscure plots and action that was not autonomously communicative.[18] It was this appeal for narrative clarification that helped usher in what Charles Musser has called the "craze"[19] for employing a "narrator", "lecturer", or "explainer" in those European and American picture houses that could afford such a thing—a craze most systematically indulged between 1907 and 1912.

The lecturer, in this period, was typically a hired employee separate from the projectionist. As a consequence, the relationships between lecturer and pictures, and between lecturer and audience, were necessarily adjusted. Since the projectionist at a moving picture show was tasked to crank through the programme of projections, as best he could, at a more or less regular speed,[20] the lecturer, where present, was correspondingly tasked to keep in time with this projection speed, matching the timing of his talk to the unspooling images as precisely as possible. Unlike his lantern counterpart, therefore, the moving picture lecturer needed to accommodate his own pace of delivery to the speed of the projection over which he had no control. The shifts in dominant style of film production and dominant mode of exhibition also, therefore, signalled a related shift in the hierarchical balance between lecture (where present) and picture. Whereas in the days of the early cinematograph showmen, the pictures had acted, in effect, as wondrous and arresting illustrative accompaniment for a lecture, in the more systematically industrialized transitional era (*c.*1907–12) the lecture was now commissioned as an accompanying aid to making sense of the pictures. The pictures had therefore usurped the lecture as the principal engine of the event to become the dominant partner in the pictures–words collaborative engagement.[21]

In those cases where the newly adjusted, triangulated relationship between players on the screen, lecturer, and picture-goers worked well, the lecturer's mediating presence could provide a more intimate conduit into the subject viewed, helping to set the scene, sketch the history, voice the parts, and make the drama *live* in ways sensitively attuned to the artistry of the production, the twists and turns of the developing story, and the interpretive needs of the particular assembled audience.[22] Most of all, he could smooth over narrative ellipses and the stop-start progress of successive *tableaux* by weaving a series of on screen "moments" into a continuous narrative and so the succession of scenes into a cohesive fictional world. Where it worked less well, however, the lecturer's mediating presence could prove an active impediment to an appreciation of the production—his "presentness," in King's terms, then becoming too conspicuous, an obtrusive obstacle to an audience's enjoyment of the pictures. In what follows, I examine the debates conducted in the British and American trade press about the correct delivery of a moving picture lecture, and the value of moving picture lectures per se. And then, as a check to map against the regular statement of vigorously promoted lecturing ideals, I discuss one rare surviving example of a transcript for a lecture as it was actually delivered by a particular lecturer facing a particular audience at a particular historical showing.

MOVING PICTURE LECTURERS: IDEAL AND ACTUAL PRACTICES

Since there was general agreement that the form a lecture took could decisively affect an audience's experience of the films viewed, commentators were keen to establish a set of performance benchmarks to which lecturers should aspire. In August 1908, with characteristic clarity and emphasis, W. Stephen Bush—the prominent American commentator on the movies and himself a lecturer available for hire on the East Coast—laid out the ground rules as he saw them:

> That a good, descriptive and well-delivered lecture is as much appreciated by the people as the picture itself is too plain a truth to need elaboration. What, then, are the requirements of such a lecture? What are the requisite qualifications

of the lecturer? An easy and perfect command of the English language is the first essential requirement. A clear, resonant voice, trained in public speaking, is the next. Some skill in elocution, rising, when occasion offers, to the heights of eloquence, is likewise indispensable.... [T]he average moving picture audience [is]... remarkably quick-witted and critical enough to detect in a moment the difference between a "barker" and a good speaker with scholarly attainments. They always enjoy hearing good and correct English. They are eager to learn and swift to appreciate. The great art of the lecturer consists in making the picture plain and at the same time attractive. To achieve this, his language, while absolutely correct and free from the slightest blemish of slang or vulgarity, should be plain and simple. There are points of power and beauty in very many pictures, which appeal strongly to any artistic temperament, and to bring these out forcefully and effectively is the business of the lecturer.[23]

The ideal lecturer of Bush's description is, self-evidently, a man of taste and erudition and this vision of the refinement of the lecturer was in tune with the industry's burgeoning "uplift movement" as it was to find increasingly insistent expression over the next few years on both sides of the Atlantic. Who the lecturer was, and the air of cultured sophistication his presence could bring to the moving picture show, could help to assert the educative and edifying tone of the industry more generally. In effect, therefore, the lecturer was invited to fulfil a double role, combining the functional requirement to clarify a particular film with the symbolic requirement to legitimize the event of its exhibition.

Just five months after the appearance of this compressed instruction manual for the picture lecturer, James Clancy published an opinion piece on the same subject which constituted a noticeable adjustment of Bush's position:

In regard to lecturing upon reels, it will always be a success, providing it is handled in the proper manner and the lecturer uses judgment in his language. If he will use plain, every-day English, and not words which he does not know the meaning of himself, and that the audience will not be compelled to have a dictionary beside them to find out what he is talking about, he will find that they will give him their undivided attention. If the lecturer will go right on with his lecture and not stop until he has finished he will find the applause of the audience will show him that they are satisfied with his efforts.[24]

Whereas Clancy wanted the tone of the lecturer to meet the people where they were, and in their own idiom, Bush wanted it to elevate them to a higher plane by offering them a rhetorical and elocutionary ideal. It was, in fact, part of Bush's

ongoing agenda to argue for the linguistic, moral, and social elevation and gentrifi-
cation of the movies—and, as a direct consequence, of those who frequented them.
In pursuit of both social and commercial ends, in 1910, he himself published the
scripts for two of his own film lectures for two recently released Pathé films, *The
Birth of Jesus* and *La grande bretèche* (adapted from Balzac's novel).[25] Following his
lead by adopting his published script would ensure that lecturers were functioning
at a suitably learned level to serve the best interests, as Bush perceived them, of the
individual film, the local audience, and the cultural standing of the industry more
generally.

As part of this same project to ensure the respectability of the medium, the
moving picture lecturer needed to be distinguished from other types of showmen.
André Gaudreault has shown how a lecturer's *élocution soignée* (meticulous, or educated, style of speech) was taken as a mark of his cultivation and, crucially, part of
what set him apart from those working in other exhibition arenas with rougher
accents, less polished styles of delivery, and less elevated pools of reference.[26] Bush's
own warnings about the pitfalls to be avoided in this respect had been expressed
with typical forthrightness:

> Never shout, and avoid as the most fatal fault of all the "barker" style.... The
> style infringes on the ancient copyright of the man who describes the charms
> of the living skeleton and the bearded lady.[27]

The comparative reference in this final sentence is, of course, to the low-life pur-
veyor of freak shows at fairgrounds and Bush was clear about how moving picture lecturers should be culturally positioned relative to this cheaply conjured foil:
they needed to ensure they could not be aligned with fairground barkers in style
or tone, in order to place some status-confirming distance between legitimate cinematograph shows in venues with cultural aspirations on the one hand and the
more socially suspect wares of fairgrounds and other exhibition spaces of dubious
repute on the other.

Finding appropriately qualified lecturers able to satisfy demand without lowering the tone proved problematic in Britain also. In February 1909, the British trade
paper *The Bioscope* made this contribution to the debate:

> There is much to be said in favour of the lecturer if he is competent, if speaking
> to pictures is with him more of a hobby than a duty, and if he has a sympathetic
> voice. But there are plenty of lecturers who are calculated to make any audi-
> ence feel very ill in bed, and the supply of good men is by no means equal to
> the demand.[28]

A lecturer, depending on his competence or otherwise, self-evidently had the potential to make or mar a picture show. While the taste for accompanying a selected film
from each programme with a lecture remained modish in both Europe and America,
the anxiety about the vulnerability of a film exhibition to the local particularities of
the lecturer's skill continued to be expressed. An article from *Moving Picture World*
in 1911 entitled "Lecture it right or not at all" that complained about lecturers who
obscured the sense of a picture and confused the audience, testified to this anxiety:[29]
for as long as lecturers were a key part of the exhibition conventions, the reputation
of the industry as a whole would remain troublingly dependent on the vagaries and
unregulatable quality of local delivery.

What that local delivery might actually have been like, however, is, in almost all
cases, now lost to us. Dutch early film historian Ruud Visschedijk paints a despond-
ent picture of the available evidence in this respect:

> few traces remain of the lecturer's work. The lectures which accompanied films
> were not recorded, either by the lecturer himself, or anyone else; they vanished
> as they were spoken. Film historians arrived too late: the lecturers themselves
> had already passed away from this mortal stage, and historians were restricted
> to second or even third hand sources.[30]

Into this sparsely populated landscape of historical materials, however, it is possible
to insert one vibrant piece of first-hand empirical data.

As a quirky gift to posterity, in 1912 a German academic linguist, Professor
Dr Sellmann, sat through a screening of a film of *Othello* in Berlin, faithfully tran-
scribing what the live lecturer said, including all asides and vocal peculiarities of
phrase, dialect, and accent. He published the full transcript as part of an essay entitled "Literatur und Kinematograph" in *Eckart—Ein Deutsches Literaturblatt*.[31] This
is, as far as I am aware, a unique document in silent cinema history. Other lecture
scripts survive—indeed many were published in the trade press partly as advance
advertising for the release of the film itself.[32] But I know of no other that records in
detail not what was meant to be said, or even scripted to be said, but what actually
was said. Lecturers in picture houses across the world will have run into awkward-
ness as they attempted to explicate films they had not seen, or did not themselves
understand, or as they responded to unforeseen occurrences within the auditorium:
departures from the script must have been frequent, and both witty asides and
toe-curling gaffes plentiful. The sheer rate at which new films had to be digested
and "explained" by lecturers in the busiest lecturing years, 1908–11, must, inevitably,
have strained their capacity to read source novels and plays at sufficient speed to
make sense of the narratively compressed film and prepare a clarifying account of

its action.[33] The improvisatory, effortful, embarrassing and/or brilliant lectures that emerged from the particularities of these conditions are, however, largely unrecoverable at this remove. The way in which Sellmann's colourfully detailed transcription of one lecturer's performance at one show in 1912 plunges us back vividly into the imperfect, but real and contingent circumstances of the moment, therefore, offers us unique retrospective access in this respect.

The (unnamed) lecturer himself was evidently a gruff Berliner who made no effort to elevate his colloquial tone or smooth out his accent for his current role as the interpreter of Shakespeare. With the social anthropologist's relish about the low-life colour to which he was being exposed, Sellmann reported that his subject spoke fluently in an "unverfälschtem Mulackstraßendialekt". This was an authentic (*unverfälschtem*) dialect of the Mulackstrasse area of Berlin—a rough working-class quarter then both economically deprived and socially suspect. A free translation of "unverfälschtem Mulackstraßendialekt" that attempts to capture the flavour of the social condescension implicit in Sellmann's phrase might, therefore, be "an authentic guttersnipe dialect of working-class Berlin".[34]

The lecturer's choice of vocabulary, as recorded by Sellmann, is folksy and of-the-people and his style of delivery ostentatiously offhand. In fact, so idiomatically local is it throughout that it reads almost as a willful rejection of all attempts to harness a cultured linguistic register (Gaudreault's *élocution soignée*) for such lectures. His commentary was not only delivered in a thick Berlin accent (conscientiously rendered in Sellmann's transcript) but punctuated throughout by both proverbial sayings and slightly tetchy asides to the audience as he attempted to retain some crowd control.

In acknowledgement of the distinctive "unverfälschtem Mulackstraßendialekt" flavour of the original, in the sample, translated sections of Sellmann's transcript that follow, I reach for a linguistic register of a comparably rich patina in English:

Othello, a Moor, has 'ad many great victories and returns 'ome. 'Ere 'e finds that 'is beloved—excuse me, man in't second row there, could yer stand up and let the pretty lady through—so, 'e finds that a certain Mr Roderigo is after 'er, big time, which prompts the black to lose 'is rag with jealousy.—Madam, I'd ask yer to please keep that child quiet, if yer don't mind. Now then, jealous is what Mr Iago is an' all, and 'e stirs up Othello mightily, and what you see 'ere, folks, is the big jealousy scene of all the main characters....

Now just look at how the black watches 'is pretty wife 'ere. You can see that—(man in the front right there: smoking's not allowed in 'ere, so would yer mind...?)—now, where were we? Oh yes, that the jealousy of the Moor 'as reached boiling point, which bears out the old adage: jealousy is a passion which keenly seeks out its own suffering. So now 'e just lets rip at 'er an' drags 'er out of 'er sweet slumber. Look now—she's protesting 'er innocence. But what does the black monster do? (I 'ave to insist on silence for this gripping section of the action. If it's a laugh y're wanting, I'd thank yer t' go over t' Luna Park instead.) So what does 'e do? 'E strangles the loveliest creature the world 'as ever seen. Take a look at this now: one last spasm, see, an' now she's dead.[35]

As an accidentally entertaining sideshow, such a lecture might well have had its idiosyncratic appeal. As a potential aid in drawing out the poetry or pathos of the dramatic moment, or even in helping make sense of the story, however, it must surely have come up short. Auditorium conditions were, it seems, far from optimal for the appreciation of the picture: late arrivals, noisy children, unlicensed smoking, inopportune laughing—and all capped by an interventionist lecturer trying to control the inconsiderate, expel the unruly, and micro-manage the community while simultaneously delivering his thunderingly insensitive account of the story ("Take a look at this now: one last spasm, see, an' now she's dead"; "Sehn se, jetzt zuckt se noch een Mal un nu is se dod.")

Needless to say, a disruptively noisy movie-going experience was far from particular to working-class Berlin in this period. Rather, it was characteristic of all urban movie theatres at the "livelier" end of town. In recalling his own early movie-going experiences in the East End of London before and during the First World War, for example, it was the noise of the audience that cartoonist Harry Blacker remembered most forcibly:

A perpetual buzz of conversation mingled with the crackle of peanut shells that littered the floor like snow in winter. Every step in any direction crunched…Nearby, children were reading the titles out loud for the benefit of their foreign parents. Some even translated the words directly into Yiddish. Babies cried, kids were slapped, and an endless procession to the "ladies and gents" was greeted by outraged cries of "Siddown." Only the screen was silent.[36]

Faced with such a hubbub, it must have been tough for a lecturer to "go right on with his lecture and not stop until he has finished", as Clancy had idealistically advocated.[37] Certainly, the Berlin lecturer is repeatedly ambushed by contingencies that cause him to check his stride:

excuse me, man in't second row there, could yer stand up and let the pretty lady through?…Madam, I'd ask yer to please keep that child quiet, if yer don't mind.…If it's a laugh y're wanting, I'd thank yer t' go over t' Luna Park instead. [*Jehn Se doch in'n Lunapark, wenn Se lachen wollen!*][38]

Since there were no German releases of *Othello* that we know of between 1909 and 1912, we may safely assume that the film Sellmann saw in Berlin in 1912 was a non-German production of the English drama—and quite possibly the Italian version from Rome-based company Film d'Arte Italiana that had been doing its unhurried distribution rounds on the European circuit on and off since 1909.[39] The threat to expel disruptive patrons from a culturally ranging experience of this sort back onto the streets and other amusements of Berlin[40] therefore incidentally encoded a competitive assertion of cinema's cosmopolitan capital that chimed with contemporary claims of cinema's global reach and fluency in crossing borders untrammeled by linguistic or cultural difference.

The irony of this is, of course, that every word that emerged from this particular lecturer's mouth, the dialect in which it was delivered and the regular alerts he made throughout to the precise conditions and people within the auditorium, indelibly inflected this particular movie-going experience with the temporally specific and the irrefutably local. The lecturer's conspicuous presence, distinctive commentary, and pronounced accent inevitably ensured that this film, whatever its actual cinematic provenance, was now emphatically coloured by, and absorbed into, the cultural landscape of Mulackstrasse.

*

In early May 1913, in a spirit of cross-cultural exploration, W. Stephen Bush visited London as part of his tour "inspecting productions and making a study of the European market generally". His commission was to "contribute some interesting stories upon the various phases of the motion picture business in Europe" for the *Moving Picture World*.[41] In despatches home, Bush commented on the British film industry with characteristic diligence: he discussed ticket pricing, cinema furnishings, relative investment levels for picture production and cinema buildings, orchestral accompaniment, the exhibitor's role in programming, the British taste for American pictures, projection quality, socially differentiated cinemas, the rate of programme rotation, the role of educational films in British society, and the nature of the film stock.[42] Had Bush encountered a moving picture lecture on the London leg of his trip, it would surely have featured in his comprehensive account of British exhibition practices. The fact that he makes no mention of lectures in London in May 1913 may, therefore, be taken as an indication of how quickly the once-popular practice had fallen into abeyance.

By 1913, moving picture lecturing was on the wane in mainstream exhibition practice and had, moreover, by then more or less been dropped from discussions on exhibition practices in the trade presses of both Britain and the United States.[43] If brief, however, the flourishing of this practice had certainly been vigorous. It was only five years earlier, in August 1908, for example, that Bush had himself predicted that "the time is surely coming when the good lecture will be as much a part of the successful moving picture theater as the lamp, the lens and the carbons".[44] The terms in which he had couched this claim were as strategically conceived as they were overblown. Adding the figure of the lecturer to the line-up of the material components of cinematic exhibition (lamp, lens, carbons) had constituted a deliberate attempt to absorb him into the necessary mechanisms of moving picture exhibition. Bush's rallying call was that the lecturer, thus packaged, should be thought of not as an optional add-on to the show, but as a defining part of the material paraphernalia that made the show possible. As history was to show, Bush had got this one wrong and by 1913 other narrative, aesthetic, performance, and commercial agendas had combined to configure the presence of a lecturer a symbolic admission that the cinematic images themselves lacked sufficient clarity or eloquence to be able to communicate without live linguistic supplementation. Popular as he once had been, and as necessary as some had wanted to depict him, the figure had become, in effect, an industry anachronism. Though he continued to ply his trade in some corners of the British film industry for years to come, in mainstream practice he had become yesterday's man.

Films that needed no supernumerary narrative strategies to tell their stories were now part of progressive cinema, shaping the future of production by privileging visual communicative autonomy. And, significantly, serving up lecture-free moving picture programmes liberated cinema from some of its more embedded relationships to the local. As André Gaudreault and Germain Lacasse have argued:

> These agents of the word [i.e., moving picture lecturers] contaminated the images to some degree, appropriating them in order to write them into a narrative able to accommodate itself to, and integrate itself into, the specific culture of its spectator; they became part of an account that could strike the spectator as familiar, one that made this new territory opening up before him still accessible to him.[45]

With the excision from the picture show of the live commentary that influentially inflected, or even "contaminated", the images, intervening in their engagements with the public in order to reconfigure the "new territory" (*nouvel espace*) of the screen in terms culturally accessible to the spectator, a film's fate in reception needed no longer depend upon the brilliance, hopelessness, or simply the cultural specificity of a local lecturer. Without his mediating presence, cinema could therefore become a more homogenized product across its myriad showings in different venues.[46] Eliminating this figure from the line-up of cinema's "necessary things" (lamp, lens, carbons) therefore helped refine the exhibition conditions in ways that allowed cinema to find undiluted and forcible expression for a globalizing capitalist modernity. Even the campaign for the erudition and eloquence of the moving picture lecturer, as ardently advocated in the trade press of both Britain and the United States, and the publication of set lectures to accompany particular films, had, in effect, contributed to the drive for the streamlining and systematizing of the cinematic product, a desire to control not only its projected substance but also its style of exhibition and mode of reception. What an encounter with any "ordinary" lecturer of the period must do, as our irritable Berliner symptomatically illustrates, is remind us how emphatically a live figure rooted in the specifics of his own space and moment may be gloriously resistant to, and disruptive of, just such attempts to homogenize the picture-going experience.

NOTES

1. F. E. Sparshott, "Basic Film Aesthetics", *Journal of Aesthetic Education* 5/2 (1971): 31.

2. Cecil M Hepworth, "Those Were the Days", in *Penguin Film Review* 6 (1948). Reprinted in Harry M. Geduld, ed., *Film Makers on Film Making* (Harmondsworth: Penguin, 1967), 43.

3. Ibid.

4. Ibid., 45.

5. Ibid.

6. The anecdote was attributed to the anonymous "professor" in an 1898 issue of *Photographic News* and to Haggar and Williams in subsequent accounts by their daughter and great grand-daughter respectively. See Joe Kember, *Marketing Modernity: Victorian Popular Shows and Early Cinema* (Exeter: University of Exeter Press, 2009), 90–91.

7. Smith and Blackton's travelling shows were mini-variety events, incorporating short films purchased from other producers (including Edison's *The Black Diamond Express*), shorts they had made themselves and Blackton's own live act as a cartoonist.

8. Albert E. Smith with Phil A. Koury, *Two Reels and a Crank: From Nickelodeon to Picture Palace* (Garden City: Doubleday, 1952), 39.

9. The international profitability of Vitagraph, the production company Smith and Blackton went on to found, testifies to their success in reading the market.

10. Sparshott, "Basic Film Aesthetics", 31.

11. "Preliminary Hints to Amateur Lecturers", in *The Human Body or the House We Live In* (London: York, c.1890), flyleaf. Quoted in Richard Crangle, "'Next Slide Please': The Lantern Lecture in Britain, 1890–1910", in *The Sounds of Early Cinema*, ed. Richard Abel and Rick Altman (Bloomington: Indiana University Press, 2001), 45.

12. On lantern lectures in Britain 1890–1910, see Crangle, "'Next Slide Please'". On lecturing styles in nineteenth-century Britain to accompany Shakespearean slide sequences, see Judith Buchanan, "Shakespeare and the Magic Lantern", *Shakespeare Survey* 62 (2009): 191–210.

13. *Optical Magic Lantern Journal and Photographic Enlarger* (hereafter, *OMLJPE*), 15 June 1889, 8.

14. Amy Johnson, "Is the Lantern Played Out? No", *OMLJPE*, 1 Dec. 1894, 208–9 (9).

15. Norman King, "The Sound of Silents", *Screen* 25/3 (1984): 15.

16. See, for example, Ben Brewster, "Periodization of Early Cinema", in *American Cinema's Transitional Era: Audiences, Institutions, Practices*, ed. Charlie Keil and Shelley Stamp (Berkeley: University of California Press, 2004), 66–75.

17. Run at 16 fps (an average early cinema projection speed), a one-reeler represented about thirteen minutes' projection time.

18. See Van C. Lee, "The Value of a Lecture", *Moving Picture World* (hereafter, *MPW*), 22 Feb. 1908, 93; and Eileen Bowser, *The Transformation of Cinema, 1907–1915* (Berkeley: University of California Press, 1990), 54.

19. Charles Musser, "The Nickelodeon Era Begins: Establishing the Framework for Hollywood's Mode of Representation", in *Early Cinema: Space, Frame, Narrative*, ed. Thomas Elsaesser with Adam Barker (London: BFI, 1990), 264.

20. On variable and actual projection speeds in the era, see Kevin Brownlow, "Silent Films—What Was the Right Speed?", in *Early Cinema*, ed. Elsaesser, 282–90.

21. In French, this shift is usefully communicated through differentiated vocabulary: a *conférencier* being a lecturer who selects images to illustrate his talk, a *bonimenteur* an explainer of and interpreter for a film already constituted. See André Gaudreault with Jean-Pierre Sirois-Trahan, "Le retour du [bonimenteur] refoulé… (où serait-ce le bonisseur-conférencier, le commentateur, le conférencier, le présentateur ou le 'speacher'?)", *Iris* 22 (Autumn 1996): 17–32.

22. An alternative strategy was to employ actors behind the screen vocalizing the parts: space prohibits discussion of this alternative vocal exhibition practice here.

23. W. Stephen Bush, "Lectures on Moving Pictures", *MPW*, 22 Aug. 1908, 136–7.

24. James Clancy, "The Human Voice as a Factor in the Moving Picture Show", *MPW*, 30 Jan. 1909, 115.

25. W. Stephen Bush, "Special Lectures on Notable Films", *MPW*, 8 Jan. 1910, 19.

26. André Gaudreault and Germain Lacasse, "Le bonimenteur de vues animées (1895–1930)", GRAFICS website: http://cri.histart.umontreal.ca/grafics/fr/bonimenteur.asp.

27. Bush, "Lectures on Moving Pictures", 137.

28. *The Bioscope*, 25 Feb. 1909, 3.

29. *MPW*, 29 April 1911, 943.

30. Ruud Visschedijk, "Introduction" to Max Nabarro, "This is my life", *Iris* 22 (Autumn, 1996): 183.

31. The 1912 lecture-transcript is quoted in full (in "Berlin-German") in Steffen Wolf, "Geschichte der Shakespeare-Verfilmungen (1899–1964)", in *Shakespeare im Film*, ed. Max Lippmann (Wiesbaden: Deutsches Institut für Filmkunde, 1964), 15–32.

32. See, for example, Herbert Reynolds, "Aural Gratification with Kalem Films: A Case History of Music, Lectures and Sound Effects, 1907–1917", *Film History* 12/4 (2000): 417–42, esp. 421–2.

33. See, for example, Rick Altman's account of the exhausting lecturing rate of one lecturer in Providence across 1908 and 1909; Altman, *Silent Film Sound* (New York: Columbia University Press, 2004), 141.

34. With grateful thanks to Kostja New in helping catch the tone of this Berlin German.

35. Quoted (in German) in *Shakespeare im Film*, ed. Lippmann, 19–20.

36. Harry Blacker, *Just Like It Was: Memoirs of the Mittel East* (London: Vallentine, Mitchell, 1974), 27–28. Quoted in Luke McKernan, "'Only the Screen Was Silent…': Memories of Children's Cinema-Going in London before the First World War", *Film Studies* 10 (2007): 9.

37. Clancy, "Human Voice", 115.

38. This lecturer may also have been theatre manager of this picture house, thus avoiding the need to drain precious business resource by paying an additional salary for a lecturer. Such role doubling would help explain his managerial approach to the organization of his auditorium,

heightened interest in audience behaviour, and sketchy grasp of the plot of *Othello*. On such role doubling, see Bowser, *Transformation of Cinema*, 19.

39. On the film, see Judith Buchanan, *Shakespeare on Silent Film: An Excellent Dumb Discourse* (Cambridge: Cambridge University Press, 2009), 88–104.

40. Luna Park, opened in Berlin's Halensee district in 1909, was Europe's then largest amusement park. See Claudia Puttkammer and Sacha Szabo, *Gruß aus dem Luna-Park. Eine Archäologie des Vergnügens. Freizeit- und Vergnügungsparks Anfang des zwanzigsten Jahrhunderts* (Berlin: Wissenschaftlicher Verlag Berlin, 2007).

41. "Facts and Comments", *MPW*, 3 May 1913, 463.

42. "Yankee Films Abroad: An Interesting Budget of Information on Picture Conditions in Great Britain", *MPW*, 10 May 1913, 573–4.

43. Despite this general trend see, however, chapters 3 and 4 in this volume.

44. Bush, "Lectures on Moving Pictures", 137.

45. André Gaudreault and Germain Lacasse, "Editorial: Le bonimenteur de vues animées", *Iris* 22 (Autumn 1996): 6. My translation.

46. The eradication of the live lecturer's particularizing and localizing effect, once his role became defunct, did not, of course, similarly eradicate the comparable effects of the musical accompaniment. It would take the coming of commercial synchronized sound to achieve this.

3

Eric Williams: Speaking to Pictures

Stephen Bottomore

DURING THE PAST couple of decades film scholars have been exploring neglected aspects of sound practices in early cinema. In addition to unearthing information about mechanical sync-sound systems, a number of historians—most notably Rick Altman—have shown that live sound was often a significant feature of film shows in the pioneering period, and manifested itself in surprisingly diverse ways.[1] One might classify these live audio practices under three broad headings: instrumental music, voices, and effects. One finds, for example, many kinds of music played along with films; voice accompaniment as narration, recitation, song and live lip-syncing of on screen actors; and all sorts of sound effects produced by multi-effect machines and individual "noisemakers".[2]

These live-sound practices were found in various different countries, from Europe to the Americas to the Far East, but no nation exhibited more diversity in this respect than Britain.[3] An "experimental" era for live audio lasted quite a long time in British cinema, well into the 1910s, when one might have expected film presentation practices to "settle down," as production and exhibition generally became more standardized.

In this chapter I will concentrate on the work of just one of these live sound pioneers, Eric Williams, who recited poems and other texts to films which he himself made and starred in. Williams's name crops up quite frequently in the British film trade press from 1911 and into the First World War years, yet he has received little historical attention.[4]

THE LIVE VOICE AND THE SCREEN

From the earliest days of screen images, there has been vocal accompaniment. It would be a rare lantern slide show in the nineteenth century without some kind of accompanying lecture, as Joe Kember details in chapter 1 of this volume. Although one can distinguish many kinds of lantern exhibitions, most such shows fall into two broad categories, depending whether the image or the spoken text is the starting point. In the first case, "image primacy", the showman takes an existing series of slides and weaves appropriate words around those, while in the second case, "word primacy", he/she chooses an existing text and builds the images on that.[5] An example of the first would be a travelogue in which the lecturer (say Burton Holmes) selects slides of the places he has visited and writes his lecture around these; an example of the latter would be a slide set based on an existing famous ballad (e.g., a George Sims life-model set).

In early "live voice" cinema there were instances of both approaches, with either the film or the text being the starting point. As far as the "image primacy" category goes, the early era is full of examples of existing "off the shelf" films being shown while a lecturer in the auditorium attempted to explain the images to the audience. In some cases this went further, and dramatic films were post-synced or "voiced" by performers behind the screen, to simulate the mute talking of actors on screen. Exponents of this technique included the Humanovo and Actologue companies in the United States, *benshi* in Japan, and various showmen in Britain including Nix Webber and Dove Paterson, the latter's career discussed in chapter 4 by Trevor Griffiths.[6] A slight variation on this "image primacy" category would be film lectures in which the lecturer himself chose the film clips, and then wrote a text around them.[7]

Examples of the other approach, "word primacy"—where an existing written text is the foundation, and images are filmed to match that text—are more diverse, with both songs and spoken examples. Films were made from the late 1890s to be shown while particular pre-existing songs were sung: including *Simon the Cellarer* (Sealy, 1899), R. W. Paul's "songs with animated illustrations" (see Ian Christie, chapter 5 of this volume, for more details), and Edison's "picture songs" such as *The Astor Tramp* (both 1899).[8] There are other examples too.[9]

Generally coming a little later, one finds instances of the *spoken*, rather than sung, word as the primary source, with films made specially to accompany a written text. There are some doubtful claims here,[10] but specially made films to go with poems were definitely the basis of a system called Kinemapoems in 1913 (see below),[11] and Clarendon Speaking Pictures also made their own films to go with existing texts. They developed a mechanical device to scroll the script for a narrator (behind screen), to maintain synchronization with the unspooling of the film.[12]

Instances of "live voice" cinema continued during the First World War. For example, in mid-1915 a couple of films were made by the B & C Voxograph company to be voiced by offstage reciters; soon after that Orpheus Song Films produced four scenes to be accompanied by live singers; and in late 1916, the so-called Popular Song Favourites involved a similar scheme of live accompaniment.[13]

In at least one case neither the text nor the film took precedence: both were specially created. The artist in question was Harry Hemsley, a music hall performer who specialized in impersonating children's voices. He made films to show as part of his live act, such as *In and Out of the Picture* of October 1914. These film and live presentations were known as "synchronized speaking", and involved the live lip-syncing of characters on screen, and a close choreography between the action of Hemsley on screen and Hemsley in the auditorium (passing objects from screen-self to real-self, for example).[14]

Eric Williams therefore emerged at a time of quite significant experimentation in the relationship between the human voice and the new moving pictures. While Williams fits into our category of "word primacy", the particularities of his technique, as we shall see, separate him somewhat from all the cases mentioned above.

BEGINNINGS: *A BALLAD OF SPLENDID SILENCE*

Eric Williams (see Figure 3.1) started out as an actor in stock at the Theatre Royal, Brighton, appearing with several famed stage stars, before turning to stage recitation, sometimes called "elocution" at that time, as a career.[15] He was certainly reciting by 1908 because he performed to a group of war veterans that year, and one of the attendees recalled this "admirable recital of Mr. Eric Williams," noting that the recitations consisted of selections from *Julius Caesar*, *Hamlet*, and *The Surgeon's Child*, among others.[16] Williams would later make several of these texts into films.

It is likely that during his time as an "elocutionist", before he turned to film, Williams showed magic lantern slides while he spoke, for that was certainly a standard technique for lecturing. This seems to have been the assumption of one trade journal reporter who, when Williams started to use films, noted that he would lecture with films "instead of employing ordinary lantern slides", confirming the close perceived similarities between these two visual media.[17]

If Williams was not the first to recite poems and the like while appropriate films were screened, film reciting was nevertheless probably his own idea.[18] It was in 1911 when, as he put it, "I launched my boat on the seething waters of the film industry", first airing his film and recitation technique at an audition at the London Hippodrome.[19] Then, having convinced at least one theatre proprietor, he began performances in earnest in March 1911, appearing for a week at the Alexandra Theatre, Stoke Newington, reciting to his specially made film, *A Ballad of Splendid Silence*.[20]

MR. ERIC WILLIAMS.

TWO YEARS ago the KINEMATOGRAPH WEEKLY was the first to draw attention to a new phase of art in conjunction with the kinematograph film by the publication of an article on " Reciting to Pictures " from the pen of Mr. Eric Williams, its inventor. Since then others have entered the field with various kinds of ' speaking pictures,' but the pioneer of this form of entertainment has gone steadily on his way, producing new subjects, and always improving upon his earlier efforts.

FIGURE 3.1 Williams was profiled in several articles in the trade press. *Kinematograph and Lantern Weekly*, 5 November 1914: 43.

This was based on a poem, written by E. Nesbit, commemorating a patriotic hero of the 1848 Hungarian revolution, Ferencz Renyi.[21] It included such stirring lines as:

He loved the Spirit of Freedom,
He hated his country's wrongs.
He told the patriots' stories,
And he sang the patriots' songs.

The film which Williams showed as he recited the poem (a "Bioscope recital" someone called it) had been made for him by Barker Motion Photography Ltd. A trade journal noted that this "picture play" was "acted by the Alexandra Stock Company, with Mr. Williams himself as 'Renyi', the hero, and numerous auxiliaries" [i.e., extras]. It would therefore seem to have been some kind of coproduction with the Alexandra Theatre, particularly as he recited at that theatre to the finished film.[22] Subsequently Williams took this film recitation on a provincial tour of cinemas/ theatres, and such personal tours would become his regular practice.[23]

THE SURGEON'S CHILD

By the following year, 1912, Williams had another film ready, *The Surgeon's Child* (see Table 3.1 below) made for him by the Crystal Film Co., and again based on a poem, a standard piece for reciters from the late 1880s by popular author and lyricist Frederick Weatherly.[24] Again the film featured Williams himself as a main character, the coachman who tells the story: about how a doctor leaves his fatally ill daughter at Christmas to save a shipwrecked crew, with the coachman's help. This long ballad poem of about 130 lines would have taken Williams some ten minutes to perform. It was probably his most successful production. In September at Kensington Picture Palace he recited the poem as the film was shown, and an additional element was included in the form of a specially composed piano accompaniment by a "Mr. Platto". A trade writer, describing the act as a "bioscope scena", reported that the spectators "were almost boisterously enthusiastic", and described the performance as follows:

> Mr. Williams recites, whilst a film, in which he himself appears, illustrates the story visually. One sees the actor in his character as an old coachman on the screen, and one hears his voice, perfectly synchronised with the picture for the most part, emerging from the darkness—it is, indeed, almost an uncanny sensation to listen to what is, apparently, a real, live "talking picture." It is an admirable idea, and Mr. Williams has made a distinct success of it.[25]

He presented the same film at the Majestic Picturedrome in central London a couple of weeks later, with a similar press verdict of "excellent".[26] The next month, such was the interest in his work that the *Kinematograph and Lantern Weekly* published an article by Williams in which, as well as thanking the theatre proprietors who'd booked his act, he gave some more details of *The Surgeon's Child*. His film featured several characters: a country doctor and his wife, their sick child, a coachman "who has been in the family for many years" (played by Williams), and a group of village yokels. The scenes consisted of:

> a taproom of a village inn, exterior and hall, interior of the doctor's house, the bed-room of the sick child, exciting drives to and from a wreck, the sea shore with wreckage and dead bodies washed up on to the rocks, with a picturesque

TABLE 3.1 Eric Williams's film recitations (known as "speaking pictures").

Film title	Recited text	Details	Date
A Ballad of Splendid Silence	Poem by E. Nesbit	EW as Renyi. p: Barker. Gifford says 1913/2.	1911
The Surgeon's Child	Poem by Frederick Edward Weatherly	EW as the Coachman. p: Crystal Film Co. d: Harry Thurston Harris.	1912/8
Fra Giacomo; or The Count's Revenge	Poem by Robert Buchanan	EW as the Count. p: Searchlight. Sometimes wrongly cited as "Fra Giacone."	1913/1
[Uncle Podger] Hanging a Picture	From J. K. Jerome's *Three Men in a Boat*	EW as Uncle Podger. Gifford says 1915/1.	1913/1
Hubert and Arthur	The prison cell scene from Shakespeare's *King John*	EW as Hubert. Gifford says 1914/9.	1913/7
Preparing for the Duel	From Sheridan's *The Rivals*	EW as Lucius O'Trigger. p: Gaumont. Gifford says 1914/9.	1913/7
The Lifeboat	Ballad by George R. Sims	EW as the The Lifeboatman.	1914/4
The Charge of the Light Brigade	Poem by Alfred Lord Tennyson	Film by Edison	1914/9
Hamlet	Shakespeare	EW as Hamlet.	1914/9
England's Warrior King	From Shakespeare's *Henry V*	EW as Henry V. p: Yorkshire Cinematograph Co. Featuring men of the Royal Scots Greys.	1915/7
The Fireman's Wedding	Poem by W.A. Eaton	EW as Artizan. p: Barker.	1918/8
Brutus and Cassius	From Shakespeare's *Julius Caesar*	EW as Brutus. d: Marshall Moore. Filmed in August 1914?	1918/8
A Christmas Story	Poem by Frederick Edward Weatherly	approx 1000 ft	1918/11

group of fishermen and the doctor and coachman in attendance, the arrival home from the wreck just in time to witness the crisis of the child's illness successfully passed and the certainty of recovery assured. The story closes with a return to the tap-room, where the beautiful moral of the story is driven home by the old coachman.[27]

From this it seems that *The Surgeon's Child* was a fully visualized, multi-scene film with a complete cast of actors (though sadly we don't know where it was shot). In the same article Williams specified some "fundamental principles" on which the success of his "reciting to pictures" technique was based:

> Firstly, the characters in the story chosen must be popular charac-
> ters…Secondly, the story must be capable of successful pictorial illustration,
> with sufficient variety in the series of pictures to avoid the smallest suggestion
> of monotony.… [Thirdly] the reciter must act in his own pictures, or he will
> miss the magnetic influence absolutely necessary to attain success. Hence the
> reciter must be a good actor, too.[28]

He added, as a fourth principle, that "the value of appropriate music cannot be over-estimated", and paid tribute to the conductor at the Majestic, a "Mr. Wertheimer" (probably Wertheim, see below). The job of film reciting was hard work, Williams emphasized—he sometimes did three performances in a day[29]—and he advised that reciting was not suitable for anyone who was not physically strong:

> The difficulties of synchronisation are great and the physical disadvantage
> under which one has to work in the less fashionable picture theatres, crowded,
> hot and full of smoke, are often distressing and demand more than ordinary
> resource and reserve of lung power. Anything halting or weak on the part of
> the performer would inevitably result in disastrous failure and a great disap-
> pointment to all concerned. On the other hand, for the experienced and well
> seasoned elocutionist and actor, a fine field of really artistic work is opening
> up, and I feel not unnaturally proud to have pointed the way.[30]

TOURING

Through the winter of 1912–13 Williams was touring Britain with his films, includ-ing performing in London.[31] By this time his shows were sometimes being called "bioscope ballads".[32] He was making new films too, and appeared in (and recited to) a version of *Fra Giacomo*, based on a first-person narrative poem by Robert Buchanan about a man who has been cuckolded by a priest and takes his revenge. This heavy drama was contrasted by Williams in another film he had made by this time, *Hanging a Picture*, a section from Jerome K. Jerome's comic novel *Three Men in a Boat*. In early 1913, at the Majestic in central London, Williams presented all four of his "bioscope ballads" to date—accompanied not by piano but by an orches-tra, the music specially arranged by a respected classical instrumentalist, Siegfried Wertheim.[33] The employment of Wertheim and the use of an orchestra suggest that Williams was doing well financially by this stage.

In April 1913 Williams completed a six-month tour for two of the major cinema chains in Britain: Cinema House, Ltd. and Electric Theatres (1908) Ltd.[34] In subsequent tours he repeated this arrangement, appearing at a chain of theatres, travelling from one of their venues to another over a period of several weeks. During the spring Williams made two more films, these produced by Gaumont, and the company trumpeted the news in their house journal, the *Gaumont Weekly*, calling his works by yet another name, "biograph stories". Gaumont announced that previews would take place in early August of these new films, entitled *Hubert and Arthur* and *Preparing for the Duel*—the one from Shakespeare's *King John* and the other from Sheridan's *The Rivals*.[35]

In September Williams was on the road again, to Manchester and other provincial cities, also Edinburgh, and then back to London, in theatres run by London and Provincial Cinematograph Theatres Ltd.[36] This was yet another chain of theatres, different from the two he had worked with earlier in the year, which suggests that by now he was widely known among several major exhibition chains in Britain. Rivals were hot on his heels though: Kinemapoems was using virtually his same technique, though lacking a front man of Williams's prominence. Williams responded, claiming his own priority in "reciting to pictures".[37]

In any case, his success seemed unaffected by competition, and in early 1914 the trade press reported that he was already being rebooked for the next season, from autumn through the winter (see Figure 3.2). Such booking so far ahead suggests he was indeed sought after by theatre proprietors as a popular attraction.[38] And he was already busy enough in the early part of the year: having finished touring in Manchester and the North, he continued in March in Surrey and the South.[39] The South was in fact more like "home territory" than the North, for Williams was based in Maida Vale, London, and by the end of the year in Windsor.[40] The latter address was at a fine location, just next to Home Park and within half a kilometre of Windsor Castle, which again suggests that he was thriving, and financially fairly well off at this point.

SUCCESS

Some of Williams's greatest popular successes were indeed achieved in the south of England. In the spring of 1914 he was booked by yet another circuit, Central Halls, which controlled a dozen theatres, and in March he appeared at one of these, Central Hall Picture Palace, Upper Tooting Road, in South West London, where the show was advertised as "the real human voice". The *Kinematograph and Lantern Weekly* reported that when the audience heard "the impressive tones of the artiste" during the projection of *The Surgeon's Child* they were held in "rapt attention" throughout

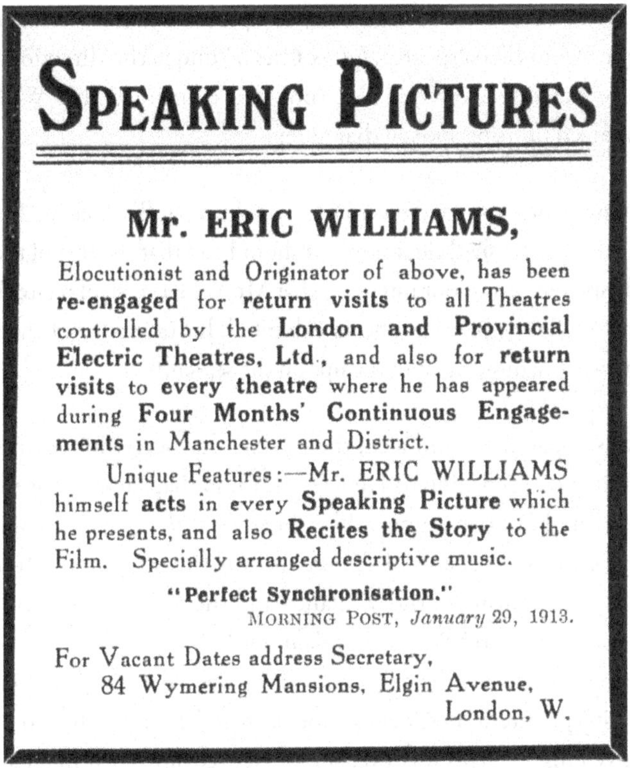

SPEAKING PICTURES

Mr. ERIC WILLIAMS,

Elocutionist and Originator of above, has been **re-engaged** for **return visits** to all Theatres controlled by the **London and Provincial Electric Theatres, Ltd.**, and also for **return visits** to **every theatre** where he has appeared during **Four Months' Continuous Engagements** in Manchester and District.

Unique Features:—Mr. ERIC WILLIAMS himself **acts** in every **Speaking Picture** which he presents, and also **Recites the Story** to the Film. Specially arranged descriptive music.

"Perfect Synchronisation."
MORNING POST, *January* 29, 1913.

For Vacant Dates address Secretary,
84 Wymering Mansions, Elgin Avenue,
London, W.

FIGURE 3.2. Advertisement for Eric Williams's "Speaking Pictures", noting that he appeared in the films and then spoke lip-sync in the theatre. *Kinematograph and Lantern Weekly*, 5 February 1914: 83.

the performance, and "vociferous applause greeted its close. Mr Williams, indeed, scored a triumphant success."[41]

About a week later in east London at Central Hall Picture House, Catford, he presented *The Surgeon's Child* for the one thousandth time, and as a tribute after the performance a certain Councillor Prior on behalf of the theatre proprietors made a presentation to Williams of a souvenir portrait of himself in a large solid silver and oak frame.[42] In May at the Central Hall in Watford a trade writer observed of Williams's recitations that "the tense attention given to them indicated to what a degree the reality of the 'human voice' grips interest", and that the performances were attracting large audiences.[43]

For two weeks in June Williams was at the prestigious Grand Opera House, Middlesbrough, and was joined by one J. C. Padden, who lectured to a film entitled *His Guiding Star*.[44] There are no details, but it seems likely this was an existing commercially released film,[45] and Padden therefore was probably not seen as a rival by Williams, but rather as a lesser attraction on the bill, a mere film lecturer.

Williams continued touring through the summer of 1914 in the north of England and Scotland, attracting large audiences to the stuffy picture palaces despite the hot weather that year.[46] He had not neglected new production, however, and arranged two film scenes from Shakespeare's *Julius Caesar*, under the direction of Marshall Moore. Moore was interviewed at this time and confirmed that Williams's technique still involved miming spoken dialogue:

> Early in August I propose to film certain scenes from "Julius Caesar" for Mr. Eric Williams, the distinguished elocutionist. I should add that the text of these scenes will be fully spoken, as it is our intention that Mr. Williams shall recite the appropriate words while the picture is being exhibited, his utterance of the lines synchronising with the movement of the lips on the screen.[47]

The film was apparently produced, though the first screenings of it seem not to have been until 1918, according to Denis Gifford. Perhaps it did not turn out well, and was only brought out at a time of film shortage at the end of the war? Williams might also have made a version of *Hamlet* at this time, reports Gifford.[48] By late August 1914 he was touring in the Midlands and the South again, and this despite the fact that the First World War had broken out.[49]

In early September, during the first weeks of the war, he was in London to premiere his latest speaking picture at the Chelsea Cinema, King's Road, with accompaniment of "fine descriptive music".[50] This was a version of George Sims's sentimental ballad "The Lifeboat", for which Williams had bought the rights the previous winter.[51] It is a longish ballad of over a hundred lines, which would take about ten minutes to recite, so the film would have been about the same length (less than a reel). The ballad—with a similar plot to Williams's earlier film *The Surgeon's Child*—is an account by a lifeboat man of his going out one stormy night to rescue survivors from a sunken ship, while his wife lies dying at home, crying out for their long-lost son. A few lines will give a flavour:

> You've heard of the Royal Helen, the ship as was wrecked last year?
> Yon be the rock she struck on—the boat as went out be here;
> The night as she struck was reckoned the worst as ever we had,
> And this is a coast in winter where the weather be awful bad.

Typically of Sims, the ballad has a driving narrative, with no need for any visual aid or illustration, and it is not clear what visuals the accompanying film by Williams would have included, apart from the obvious seas and lifeboats; all we know is that Williams starred as the lifeboat man, and the film was made with the assistance of the Royal National Lifeboat Institution. Williams presented it several times, with his usual polish and well-rehearsed timing: for the Chelsea premiere it was reported that he narrated the new film in "perfect synchronization, without mechanical assistance of any kind".[52] Later that month he was presenting the film in Birmingham. Interestingly, at this same performance he also narrated to an Edison film, *The Charge of the Light Brigade* (directed by J. S. Dawley, 1912).[53] This was a departure for Williams, to narrate a film he hadn't made. Perhaps he just wanted to screen a suitably patriotic and military subject in the early days of the war.

Through September and to the end of the year he was booked all over London and the Midlands, and then in the North, many of these bookings being return visits.[54] By the end of 1914 he had been touring through Britain for two and a half years without a break.[55] I have scarcely traced him in the following years, though he certainly made some appearances.[56] Apparently he also released some more films, according to Gifford, who lists one title in 1915 and three in 1918: a couple of Shakespeare recitation films, *England's Warrior King* and *Brutus and Cassius* (the latter, mentioned earlier, from *Julius Caesar*), and two films based on poems, *The Fireman's Wedding* and *A Christmas Story* (the second by Weatherly again). Apart from one mention of him helping to put on an entertainment for wounded troops in 1919, I have found little information about what became of Williams after the First World War.[57]

Given that Williams made several films—I have identified about a dozen productions (see Table 3.1)—is it possible that any of these survive? It seems unlikely; indeed less likely than for almost any other kinds of film made in this period. The reason is that while for most commercial films many prints were run from the negative to project in different cinemas, in the case of Williams's productions far fewer prints would be needed: because he appeared during the projection of the film, in principle only a single print would ever have been required (though perhaps he would have had other copies as a backup). So unless Williams or his descendants or the production company themselves kept these few copies (or the negative), or donated them to an archive, it is improbable that any still survives.[58]

THE OLD AND THE NEW

One might well ask what was the "draw" or appeal of Williams, this rather oddball live performer, in an era of machine-made entertainment? There is no doubt that he did appeal to audiences: contemporary reports in the trade press often use terms such as "vociferous reception" in describing reactions to his performances, and he was repeatedly booked by cinema chains and was featured in numerous individual halls and theatres. And yet this was a time when the lecturer was generally disappearing from film venues, and self-narrated feature films were fast arriving on the scene. How could a live performer survive against the tide of this increasingly standardized film product, which needed no voice to tell its tale?

Williams may have prevailed by appealing to audiences through a combination of *tradition* and *novelty*, the old and the new. Tradition came in the form of his live recitation of stirring or sentimental tales—a type of performance which many in the audience would know and love of old. Even in this era of picture palaces and gramophones and other mechanical marvels, there was still an interest in, and place for, live events. Concerts, plays, and lectures were still popular in the 1910s, and, as indicated at the start of this article, many exhibitions of lectured films, song films and so on took place. Such events were obviously *live*, and Williams's considerable appeal might partly have been that he fitted into this existing and ongoing tradition: he offered the well-recognized "warmth" of a live recitation, albeit coupled to the new medium of film. This vocal presence had a recognized power, as the enthusiastic audience reaction to Williams and his ilk demonstrated.[59]

Williams's other main appeal was the factor of novelty. His system of "reciting to pictures" was certainly distinctive, based on three novel features: the production of custom-made films, the appearance of a narrator/main character in both film and live on stage, and lip-syncing of the main character. On the first point, Williams almost always made the films specially for his own recitations, and this differentiated him from most other film-voicing or film-recitation acts, which generally used existing off-the-shelf films.

Secondly, Williams appeared in the films himself, and narrated in-person on stage to his own image. As stated in his ads, "the reciter acts in his own film". This was in contrast to other live-voice film acts, which mostly didn't make their own films, and even if they did, the live voices would come from anonymous actors behind the screen.[60] In short, these other acts did not have what we might call a "duplication factor", with the same person on screen and live in the theatre. The trade press pinpointed this as Williams's special quality:

> The unique feature of Mr. E. Williams' performance is that he not only recites the particular story or selection which he presents on the screen, but he also himself acts the principal character in the pictures, and thus the audience is, for the first time, brought face to face with the personality of the actor in the film during the actual representation.[61]

It is not quite clear whether the audience could actually see Williams reciting live while his screen image was projected. Some reports mention his voice "emerging from the darkness", which suggests that the live Williams was not illuminated during the projection. On the other hand, film lecturers in this era were sometimes seen dimly next to the screen.[62] In any case it would seem that he was introduced in person at some time during the performance, so the audience would be told and would recognize that the live presenter was the same man who appeared on screen. The above phrase, "face to face with the personality of the actor", suggests that everyone knew that Williams was performing both in-person and on screen.

It may be that this in-person quality of Williams's act was strengthened by the fact that some of his poems and readings were in the first person, or were from one person's point of view: he was telling a personal story, with himself both on the screen and actually present in theatre. Perhaps a form of *identification* (as film theorists would later call it) was taking place here, between spectators and the live/screen reciter?

A third appealing aspect of Williams's act was that he recited in close synchronization with the film, and often he actually read the words in lip-sync with himself on screen. A *Morning Post* writer praised this "perfect synchronisation",[63] which was also highlighted by the aforementioned Councillor Prior when introducing Williams for his special Catford show:

> [Prior] ... congratulated Mr. Williams upon the originality of his idea in applying reciting to pictures, and the clever and entirely successful way in which it had been carried out. What struck him most was the absolute synchronisation of the words which were being spoken by the reciter to the lips of the figures on the screen, which lent such realism to the whole performance. [64]

Therefore, to conclude, Williams's success may be attributed to the fact that he offered audiences three novelty factors: a specially made film in which he starred, a live presence on stage next to the film image, and the "trick" of lip-syncing with the original dialogue. While some other live-voice film acts might have had two of these factors, no-one else had all three. Williams was therefore an especially original turn, and one whose appeal was grounded in the traditional pull of a live performance. But he was just one pioneer in live sound among several others, and his system—unique as it was—was of course not one which had much of a future in the classical narrative cinema as it developed. Nevertheless, he is an interesting figure, who exemplifies the importance of live sound in the early years of the British cinema, and who shows us once again how full of experimentation these early film years really were.

NOTES

1. Rick Altman, *Silent Film Sound* (New York: Columbia University Press, 2004). See also two collections of papers of the 1998 Domitor Conference: *The Sounds of Early Cinema*, ed. Richard Abel and Rick Altman (Bloomington: Indiana University Press, 2001); "Global Experiments in Early Synchronous Sound", ed. Richard Abel and Rick Altman, *Film History* 11/4 (special issue) (1999).

2. See, for example, my own published research on the latter: Stephen Bottomore, "An International Survey of Sound Effects in Early Cinema", *Film History* 11/4 (1999): 485–498; and "The Story of Percy Peashaker: Debates about Sound Effects in the Early Cinema", in *Sounds of Early Cinema*, ed. Abel and Altman, 129–142.

3. My claim is based on examples of sound practices I have seen described in issues of early trade journals from Britain, the United States, France, Germany, Italy, and elsewhere. British diversity in this respect was perhaps partially an inheritance of the country's rich lantern culture.

4. For example, Eric Williams goes unrecorded in Rachael Low's general history of British cinema. Tony Fletcher mentions Williams in his "Sound before Blackmail (1929)", in *The Showman, the Spectacle and the Two-Minute Silence: Performing British Cinema before 1930*, ed. Alan Burton and Laraine Porter (Trowbridge: Flicks Books, 2001), 6–7. Williams is also briefly mentioned in some local histories of British cinema; and is listed in Denis Gifford, *The British Film Catalogue*, Vol. 1: *Fiction Film, 1895–1994*. (London: Fitzroy Dearborn, 2000) and in Denis Gifford, *Books and Plays in Films, 1896–1915: Literary, Theatrical and Artistic Sources of the First Twenty Years of Motion Pictures* (London: Mansell, 1991).

5. This is a useful distinction which both Altman and André Gaudreault have referred to. Altman, *Silent Film Sound*, 141; Gaudreault: presentation at Domitor conference, 2010.

6. And one might mention the little known Elocution Films and Voiced Films. See *The Bioscope*, 1 Oct. 1914, 84.

7. Examples of this include war correspondents and travellers, such as Frederic Villiers and R. G. Knowles, or professional travelogue lecturers, such as Burton Holmes.

8. See Paul's November 1901 catalogue and Edison's March 1900 catalogue.

9. For example, *Little Jim* (Gaumont catalogue, Nov. 1902), Clarendon's *The Mistletoe Bough* (Gaumont catalogue, Christmas 1904), and in Brazil the so-called "falantes e cantantes". See *Archivos de la Filmoteca* 28, Feb. 1998: 138–9. Fregoli experimented with a screen/voice combination in the 1890s: see Mario Verdone, *Gli Intellettuali e Il Cinema* (Roma: Bulzoni, 1982), 23.

10. For example, Harry Hinton, an ex-stage actor and his wife, Marie Bennett, recited to films from 1909 or 1910, headlined as "Biodrama", and at the Shepherd's Bush Empire, Hinton and Bennett reportedly "held the audience spell bound" and gained "hearty applause". See *Kinematograph and Lantern Weekly* (hereafter *KLW*), 7 April 1910, 1215; "Pictures that talk", *Bioscope*, 14 April 1910, 19. They claimed they produced their own films, (*Bioscope*, 28 April 1910, 55.) but the main film mentioned is Griffith's *The Convict's Sacrifice* (Biograph, 1909), so their claim is doubtful. Also it seems they might not have originated this system (see letters in *Bioscope*, 21 and 28 April 1910); and see the claim by Madge Clements, stating she read texts to films for Will's Picture Co. as early as 1905. *KLW*, 7 April 1910, 1215; letter in *KLW*, 5 May 1910, 1461.

11. *Illustrated Films Monthly*, Jan. 1914, 275.

12. For more on Clarendon Speaking Pictures see *Cinema News and Property Gazette* (hereafter, *Cinema*), 2 April 1914, 23; 11 Dec. 1913, 32; *KLW*, 9 Oct. 1913, 2537; *KLW*, 26 Mar. 1914, 89.

13. Gifford, *British Film Catalogue*: film numbers 5506–07, 5745, 6157.

14. Hemsley is mentioned in the trade press and in Patrick Loobey, *Cinemas and Theatres of Wandsworth and Battersea* (Stroud: Tempus, 2004), 67.

15. *KLW*, 18 Dec, 1913, 3, 5. A colleague later claimed that in his early days Williams had been headmaster of Worthing Collegiate School. See Low Warren, *The Film Game* (London: T. Werner Laurie, 1937), 180.

16. This was at Ramsgate on 28 September: Williams also recited "The Charge of the Light Brigade", "The Address of Henry V to his Soldiers before Harfleur", and some humorous pieces. See Henry M. Vibart, *The Life of General Sir Harry N. D. Prendergast* (London: Eveleigh Nash, 1914), 407. Shakespeare was often recited in this era. *The Showman* (20 Sept. 1901, 24) reported that one "elocutionist and actor" recited the bard's plays with "limelight views". It is possible that this was Bransby Williams, who performed sketches of Shylock, Hamlet, and Henry V (see a report from the Stratford Empire in *The Era*, 10 Sept. 1903, 21). Bransby and Eric Williams may have been related.

17. *KLW*, 13 April 1911, 1565. There was later a similar confusion when it was reported that he would appear in "illustrated songs"—before that was corrected to "speaking pictures": *Bioscope*, 22 Jan. 1914, 307.

18. David R. Williams suggests that he had earlier worked with another film reciter, Harry Hinton, but I have seen no contemporary evidence for that. See Williams, *Cinema in Leicester, 1896–1931* (Loughborough: Heart of Albion Press, 1993), 101. And see note 9.

19. *KLW*, 18 Dec. 1913, 3, 5; Eric Williams, "Reciting to pictures", *Bioscope*, 7 Nov. 1912, 231.

20. *KLW*, 11 Dec. 1913, 6.

21. Written *c*.1886, the correct title of the poem is "The Ballad of Splendid Silence". It is about 140 lines long and is collected in E. Nesbit, *Ballads and Lyrics of Socialism, 1883–1908* (London: Fabian Society, 1908). It was made into a feature film in 1914 entitled *The Ordeal*.

22. *KLW*, 13 April 1911, 1565.

23. *KLW*, 22 June 1911, 297.

24. "The Surgeon's Child" (apparently based on a real incident) is mentioned in Rupert Garry, *Elocution, Voice and Gesture* (London: Bemrose, 1888) and printed in Robert D. Blackman, *Voice, Speech and Gesture* (Edinburgh: John Grant, 1908), 396–403. Frederick Edward Weatherly (1848–1929), an English lawyer, songwriter, and author, was most renowned for writing the famous ballad "Danny Boy".

25. *Bioscope*, 19 Sept. 1912, 847. Another trade paper also noticed the "enthusiastic applause": *KLW*, 19 Sept. 1912, 1503.

26. *KLW*, 3 Oct. 1912, 1651. The Majestic was in Tottenham Court Road.

27. Eric Williams, "Reciting to pictures", *Bioscope*, 7 Nov. 1912, 231. Williams is described in the byline as, "the well-known elocutionist".

28. Ibid.

29. For an Edinburgh booking he appeared at 3.30, 8.30, and 10.30: *Bioscope*, 16 Oct. 1913, 229.

30. Ibid.

31. *KLW*, 5 Dec. 1912, 619.

32. *Bioscope*, 30 Jan. 1913, 321.

33. *KLW*, 30 Jan. 1913, 1351–52. Siegfried L. Wertheim had appeared in London with the Hambourg Quartet (*Times*, 18 April 1907, 10; 24 Oct. 1907, 10) and then as viola soloist (*Times*, 11 Dec. 1909, 4; 13 Dec. 1909, 10). His playing was praised by *The Times*'s critic ("Mr. Wertheim's recital", *Times*, 15 Dec. 1909, 10). Wertheim does not feature in *The New Grove Dictionary of Music and Musicians*, 2nd edition (2001), the *Répertoire International de Littérature Musicale* (RILM), or the *International Index to Music Periodicals*.

34. *KLW*, 24 April 1913, 3.

35. *Gaumont Weekly*, 31 July 1913, 4; *KLW*, 24 April 1913, 3.

36. *KLW*, 18 Sept. 1913, 2164, which stated that the music was arranged for piano or orchestra. *Bioscope*, 25 Sept. 1913, 985; 16 Oct. 1913, 229.

37. *KLW*, 11 Dec. 1913, 6.

38. *Bioscope*, 29 Jan. 1914, 423; 12 Feb. 1914, 633; *KLW*, 5 Feb. 1914, 83; 26 Feb. 1914, 11.

39. *Bioscope*, 12 Mar. 1914, 1145; 12 Mar. 1914, 1119; 19 Mar. 1914, 1325.

40. His address in various ads at the time was given as 84 Wymering Mansions, Elgin Avenue, London. At the end of the year his new address was given as: 16 Park Street, Windsor, Berkshire. *KLW*, 3 Dec. 1914, xlvii.

41. *KLW*, 26 Mar. 1914, 27, 29. The report noted that Williams was booked for practically every week until the end of the year.

42. The audience too received souvenirs. *KLW*, 9 April 1914, 29. The report added that Williams was appearing at the twelve theatres of the Central Halls circuit until the end of May.

43. *Bioscope*, 21 May 1914, 829.

44. *Bioscope*, 18 June 1914, 1224; *Cinema*, 11 June 1914, 31. *KLW*, 11 June 1914, 28, notes that Williams has a repertoire of five films with two more in preparation.

45. I can find no films of exactly this title, but a Selig film, *His Guiding Spirit*, was released in early 1914. Perhaps the reviewer made a slight mistake with the title, or quoted a British release title.

46. *Bioscope*, 9 July 1914, 199 and 138.

47. *Cinema*, 23 July 1914, 47. This is an interview with Moore, who claims he had been connected with Irving, Tree, Augustus Harris, and only now was starting to make films (though he added that even on stage he was always concerned with *action* telling the story).

48. Gifford, *British Film Catalogue*: film number 04903.

49. *Bioscope*, 27 Aug. 1914, 853.

50. *Film Censor*, 9 Sept. 1914, 3b; *Bioscope*, 10 Sept. 1914, 937; *KLW*, 10 Sept. 1914, 58.

51. *KLW*, 8 Jan. 1914, 32a; *Illustrated Films Monthly*, Feb. 1914, 338; *Bioscope*, 9 April 1914, 217. The trade press reported from March that Williams's next tour would include "The Lifeboat". *Bioscope*, 12 Mar. 1914, 1145. The poem is in George Robert Sims, *The Lifeboat, and Other Poems* (London: J. P. Fuller, 1883).

52. *KLW*, 10 Sept. 1914, 58.

53. *KLW*, 1 Oct. 1914, 11; *Bioscope*, 1 Oct. 1914, 11.

54. *KLW*, 24 Sept. 1914, xlv; 8 Oct. 1914, xxxv.

55. *Bioscope*, 29 Oct. 1914, 399.

56. *KLW*, 1 April 1915, 414 reports the actor-elocutionist's performance at the Electric Pavilion cinema, Edgware Road (London).

57. *Times*, 2 Sept. 1919, 8. Incidentally, Williams is not the "writer of verse" who published volumes of poetry in 1924 and 1927. See also *KLW*, 7 Feb 1918, n.p. Ball finds *Hubert and Arthur* and *England's Warrior King* being screened as late as 1919. The latter film, from Shakespeare's *Henry V*, was shot in York with Williams in the lead role and troops as the rest of the cast. See Robert Hamilton Ball, *Shakespeare on Silent Film: A Strange Eventful History* (London: Allen and Unwin, 1968), 164, 343–44; and Warren, *The Film Game*.

58. None of these films is listed in the British Film Institute's online Film & TV Database.

59. The live voice still had the edge, some believed, even when mechanical sync-sound systems were already available and in use. One company which made films for live-voiced shows stated: "You cannot tug at the strings of emotion through a metal gramophone" (though the later triumph of the talkies would seem to contradict this opinion!). *KLW*, 21 May 1914, 19: advertisement for Clarendon Speaking Pictures.

60. Altman, *Sounds of Early Cinema*, 166, uses the phrase "voices behind the screen" as a section subtitle.

61. *Bioscope*, 12 Mar. 1914, 1145.

62. For example, see the image of a film lecturer with pointer in *The Sphere*, 12 April 1913.

63. *Morning Post*, 29 Jan. 1913, cited in *KLW*, 5 Feb. 1914, 83.

64. *Bioscope*, 9 April 1914, 217.

4

Sounding Scottish: Sound Practices and Silent Cinema in Scotland

Trevor Griffiths

INTRODUCTION

For the better part of two decades, at a time when the silent film was increasingly recognized and valued as a distinct cultural form, picture-goers in Aberdeen in the north-east of Scotland experienced a particular form of "sound cinema". This involved "elocutionists", often husband and wife, "speaking to" the images shown from behind the screen, frequently lacing their dialogue with references to the immediate and the local. It was an approach unknown elsewhere in Scotland and, although documented elsewhere in Britain, lingered far longer in Scotland than it did in England and Wales. The principal purpose of this chapter is to explain the emergence and longevity of this practice. In doing so, particular use is made of the financial and administrative records of individual cinemas, exploring the choices available to managers as they decided on modes of presentation. To clarify the context, the discussion first considers the broader pattern of sonic provision across Scotland more generally. Elocutionism as practised in Aberdeen was one of a variety of approaches to applying the human voice in support of film, and these methods are briefly examined to provide a sense both of the wider performing tradition within which "speaking to" pictures emerged and of the expectations audiences may have had as to the function of sound in supporting the moving image. As a prelude to that, some reflections on the geographical focus of this chapter are pertinent.

Cinema's attraction for Scots was peculiarly intense. Surveys undertaken close to the height of the medium's popularity around mid-century found a greater density of cinemas and cinema seats in Scotland than across Britain as a whole. In 1951, whereas in England there were 12.2 people per seat, the figure for Scotland was 8.6. Not only that, those seats were filled more regularly, with an average of thirty-six visits a year compared to twenty-eight for Britain more generally. In certain settings, enthusiasm was even more pronounced, Glaswegians and those living in towns with a population of between 50,000 and 100,000 seeing the insides of picture houses fifty-one times on average in the year to March 1951.[1] Indications are, even if statistical verification is often lacking, that this deep engagement with the motion picture extended back to cinema's earliest years. When the English exhibitor Albany Ward planned a tour of Scotland towards the end of the nineteenth century, he was warned away from Edinburgh, on the grounds that the capital was over-endowed with moving picture shows.[2] Equally, in the first wave of cinema building in the years leading up to the First World War, Scottish capital flowed readily into the industry, to the extent that by the summer of 1913, Glasgow had eighty-five venues licensed for shows under the 1909 Cinematograph Act.[3] Cinema put down roots that were both deep and extensive, so that when war came, moving pictures were a presence not only in the larger urban centres, but in over sixty settlements with populations of fewer than 5,000 each, extending down to the Inverness-shire village of Beauly, population 882, where films were shown at the local Phipp's Hall.[4]

Cinema's ability to root itself in population centres of markedly varying size inevitably necessitated differing approaches to matters of presentation. So, when D. W. Griffith's epic *The Birth of a Nation* made its Edinburgh debut at the city's Royal Lyceum Theatre in July 1916, it was supported by a symphony orchestra of twenty-eight, to which were added cannonade effects for the battle scenes.[5] Two years later, a much abbreviated print of the film was being handled by Tom Gilbert, who combined distribution activities with an exhibition business that took in small halls in villages across southern Fife. In one of these the accompaniment was entrusted to a part-time pianist aged fourteen, who was said to extemporise his own material.[6]

Exhibition strategies endeavoured to tailor a product increasingly subject to the homogenizing influences of international systems of production and distribution, to particular, often highly localized tastes. Yet information on the methods used is notoriously uneven. While trade publications gave extensive attention to the practices of showmanship, these tended to concentrate on one-off campaigns designed to give business a short-term boost. By contrast, more everyday approaches to film exhibition pass largely without comment. Listings of film programmes in local newspapers rarely give intimation of the nature of any accompaniment to the images being projected, and even where mention is made of specific contributions, their role in the entertainment is seldom elucidated. As a result, a rounded discussion of sound in the exhibition of early Scottish cinema remains impracticable.

Yet documentation exists which enables us to offer informed reflections on the pattern of provision, and in particular to identify points at which practice may have differed markedly from that observed elsewhere. The most significant variation appears to have centred on the use of speech. Long an important accompaniment to visual forms of entertainment, in this context the human voice was capable of fulfilling diverse functions, offering enlightenment through learned discourse or amusement by enlivening the narrative flow, as discussed in Joe Kember's chapter.[7] In parts of Scotland, the latter role was exploited with an enthusiasm that, in its degree and its duration, appears to have been unique. Here, the reportage of the trade and mainstream press may be supplemented by surviving business records, a perspective of some value given the wider economic instability which characterized long periods of the silent era and which at particular points of crisis, such as the inflationary spiral of the First World War and the sharp contraction shortly following the Armistice, would exert a powerful influence over managerial thinking.[8] Yet the insights afforded by the business perspective remain, in many respects, incomplete.

Other forces were also at play in shaping exhibition practices: the legal and regulatory context set by the licensing policies of local authorities and, of rather greater moment, the preferences of picture-goers as communicated via the box office. The nature of the audience for silent film remains a matter for debate. One argument emphasizes how, over time, a largely proletarian amusement, which thrived in working-class milieux such as the fairground or the music hall, came to pitch its appeal increasingly at a more respectable, socially elevated clientele. A number of interrelated developments assisted this process: the emergence of lengthier, more complex film narratives, staged in dedicated venues that were subject to increasingly close regulation governing both the physical setting and the content of shows.[9] Yet the Scottish evidence suggests that this perspective stands in need of re-evaluation and that the development of sound practices and the organizational changes they accompanied may have been shaped more by a growing recognition of a hitherto under-appreciated audience that was substantially working class and in large part young. To begin with, however, a brief discussion of the place of music in silent cinema in Scotland provides a context for understanding the function of speech in the presentation of silent film.

LYRICAL INTERLUDE: THE PLACE OF MUSIC
IN SCOTTISH SILENT CINEMA

Business records convey the importance of sound to a show's commercial effective-ness, with music perhaps the most obvious element in this. As was the case elsewhere in Britain, at larger, better-appointed houses, much was made of music's capacity to secure the reputation of the business as a source of respectable, high-quality enter-tainment. The director of music played a key role, often charged with recruiting play-ers and with acquiring a suitable library of pieces to perform, and the prominence given in publicity to such figures highlights the weight music could carry in estab-lishing the relative standing of such venues. The Hillhead Picture Salon, for example, emphasized the employment of a German conductor in its early publicity, helping to establish its place as a centre of rational amusement in Glasgow's west end.[10]

Levels of pay mirrored with some accuracy the importance of the director to the overall functioning of the concern. At Aberdeen's Grand Central Picture House in the 1920s, the conductor received a salary of £260 a year, placing him second only to the manager on £312.[11] That music could be an important attraction in its own right was acknowledged by the directors of the Glasgow Cinema House, who, when confronted early in 1912 with evidence of slack business during afternoons, intro-duced an orchestra to supplement the piano, along with the offer of free cups of tea to all patrons in higher-priced seats in the balcony.[12] As this suggests, provision was often tailored to the needs of the audience and could vary through the day as levels of attendance fluctuated, as *The Bioscope*'s music correspondent found on a tour of houses in central Edinburgh in 1916 (see Table 4.1)[13]

The quality of instrumentation was also considered important.[14] If often far removed from the tinny upright of popular memory, the piano was a central element in the soundscape of early cinema, its ubiquity reflected in the comparatively modest

TABLE 4.1 Music at the Palace Cinema, Edinburgh, 1916

Time	Instrumentation
1 to 2 p.m.	One piano
2 to 3 p.m.	One piano and one violin
3 to 5 p.m.	Full orchestra (two pianos, two violins, one cello, one bass)
5 to 7 p.m.	Trio
7 to 10.10 p.m.	Full orchestra
10.10 to 10.30 p.m.	One piano

Source: The Bioscope, 31 August 1916: 816.

premium that came to attach to the pianist's art.[15] In planning a concert tour of small towns and villages across West Lothian and Lanarkshire in the late summer of 1903, Alexander Mathieson, an entertainments manager from Aberdeen, hired a pianist from Glasgow entertainment agent J. F. Calverto at a cost of £2 10s. a week to accompany both the live acts and the cinematograph which was to form the show's central attraction. By contrast, the services of a soprano commanded weekly payments of £3 10s.[16] The Cinema House in Glasgow relied on two female pianists to provide the music for less popular afternoon shows, for which they received a modest 30s. a week each in 1911. Four years later, at the Star Picture House in Aberdeen, the wage paid to the one female pianist was even lower at 20s. a week.[17]

Within the context of performance, music, in common with other forms of sound, was carefully selected to enhance the desired effect of the images on show. This could be achieved through the employment of apposite melodies, or the use of performers who themselves appeared or were similar to those depicted on the screen.[18] At a children's entertainment organized by Sir William and Lady Brooks in January 1898 at the Forest of Glen Tana near Aberdeen, footage of the Gordon Highlanders, a staple of programmes offered by local exhibitor William Walker, was accompanied by a performance of the song "Jessie's Dream".[19] Similarly, at the entertainment provided by directors of the Great North of Scotland Railway Co. for their employees, held in Aberdeen's Music Hall in March 1898, images of the Gordon Highlanders were accompanied by a piper and drummer from the regiment.[20] The effect was to add to the sense of verisimilitude which exhibitors of silent film so often strove to achieve. So, the presence of the pipes and drums of the Gordon Highlanders at a concert given by the Blairgowrie Lodge of Shepherds Friendly Society in February 1899 was felt to provide "additional realism" to the show, especially when combined with Scottish pictures.[21]

With the onset of war from 1914, opportunities to revisit music's capacity to inspire patriotic feeling within an overall aesthetic of realism once more presented themselves. In the summer of 1915, Dove Paterson, a cinema proprietor in Aberdeen to whose career we will return, commenced a tour of villages across Aberdeenshire and neighbouring counties. His aim was to boost recruitment as the first flush of enthusiasm for voluntary enlistment abated towards the end of the first year of the war or, as he himself put it rather more pithily, to undertake "Slacker Sweeping with the Cinema". To this end, a show was mounted which, in echoes of earlier itinerant ventures, included a two-reel film of the Gordon Highlanders in camp at Bedford, the effect of which was heightened by accompaniment provided by the regimental pipe major.[22]

In Scotland, as elsewhere, then, music assumed a variety of forms and fulfilled diverse functions for early exhibitors, its precise role determined by the particular financial and aesthetic demands of the performance. This perspective is also of value when we turn to consider the uses to which speech was put in film shows during the silent era. It was here that cinema's links to earlier forms of visual representation were most apparent.

SPEAKING TO PICTURES IN SCOTLAND

For nineteenth-century audiences, the distinction between the polite, embodying ideas of rationality based upon the pursuit of intellectual and physical improvement, and the popular, while clear in theory was less distinct in practice. Agencies of social and moral uplift, including missionary and temperance societies, had long used the techniques of popular entertainment to promote their ends, enlivening their meetings through dramatic tales of personal conversion or poetic recitations by reformed drunkards.[23] Equally, visual entertainments were frequently promoted as vehicles of enlightenment and uplift. As Joe Kember has demonstrated, the precise balance between education and entertainment was often articulated through speech and the figure of the "lecturer". If the term suggests a didactic role, its application to differing modes of exposition also conveys the often flexible role assumed by the spoken word.[24] This section explores that diversity, moving from speech as a means of communicating factual information to its function as a facet of the entertainment itself.

The conventional function of the lecturer in offering a learned and informed discourse, was evident from cinema's earliest times and drew upon exhibitors' links with the magic lantern trade. For William Walker and Co., of Aberdeen, the cinematograph was the latest phase in a logical business progression that had gone from dealing in educational books, to the hire of lantern slides and their use in public shows. Unsurprisingly, then, Walker's early film exhibitions in and around Aberdeen also included lectures, such as "A Night with Charles Dickens", delivered in November 1896 by a lecturer at the city's university, supported by 160 "Electro-Drama Illustrations".[25] More typical, perhaps, were the discourses on travel and topical events offered by Mr Hamish Beveridge, who appeared as part of Walker's party from 1896, speaking on two sites of British military endeavour: the Transvaal and the Sudan.[26]

The learned disquisition based on specific areas of expertise retained a particular utility at times of great public moment. For example, in May 1910, under the auspices of T. J. West, Edinburgh audiences witnessed an exhibition of still and animated photographs marking the life of the late Edward VII. Their guide was the former London County Councillor, director of the Tropical Institute at Liverpool University, and Irish peer, William Geoffrey Bouchard de Montmorency, sixth Viscount Mountmorres. Although fulfilling the role of film "lecturer" represented but a short phase in an otherwise varied public career that would later see his expository skills applied on an altogether higher plane in the service of the church, Mountmorres returned to Edinburgh the following year, this time on his own account, to front a show on the life of the newly crowned George V. *The Scotsman* made much of the presence of a figure of such comparatively high social standing in a setting increasingly associated with the entertainment of the masses and was drawn to comment at unusual length on Mountmorres's performance, noting with approval that he did

> not allow the pictures to speak for themselves. He possess [*sic*] the gift of vivid description, and his running commentary on every depicted item in the lives of the King, the Queen, the Prince of Wales, and Princess Mary is not only happily phrased, but always interesting and instructive.[27]

In the copy accompanying his performance, the threefold repetition of his name gave some indication of the value that attached, from a commercial perspective, to the figure of the lecturer.

The point is perhaps exemplified best through the figure of the same T. J. West, who first comes to our attention in February 1898 as a "lecturer" associated with the recently formed Modern Marvel Co. Ltd, based in Edinburgh. In its published objects, the company declared its aim to be to "give scientific demonstrations", while committing itself also "To provide and promote entertainments in public and in private" and "To exploit scientific instruments and apparatus appropriate to the purpose of popular entertainment or technical education".[28] To this end, it offered programmes that aspired to be both educative and amusing. Among the films selected for exhibition in Edinburgh during the Christmas and New Year season of 1904–5 were travelogues of Palestine and Italy, along with a "sensational and fantastic" picture, depicting *A Trip to the Sun*. In addition, audiences were given a demonstration of the properties of liquid air via the "magic kettle" which, among other things, turned grapes "as hard as bullets" and rendered India rubber "as brittle as glass". The owner of the kettle was "careful to explain that there was no trickery or conjuring about his exhibition; it was simply a scientific demonstration."[29] West's role appears to have been central and, in one of the rare direct references to his contribution, *The Scotsman* in 1901 had praised his "excellent description of the scenes and incidents projected on the screen [which] makes them very enjoyable." The more direct engagement with the audience which this implies signalled a departure from the formal function of the lecturer, a shift reflected in the description of West offered the following year as the Modern Marvel's "raconteur and manager".[30] In later years, the company and its manager would extend their activities to England and the wider empire, the latter providing the raw material for their exhibitions at the turn of the year in Edinburgh. The programme for 1905–6 thus included footage of West's tour of New Zealand, including scenes of "Maori Life and Customs", by which point the company was trumpeting West as "The Original and Acknowledged Entrepreneur of Cinematography in Edinburgh".[31]

For a show to be effective, it was important that both the material and the mode of delivery were adapted to the needs of the show and the expectations of the audience. As both changed, so styles of presentation were amended also, a point which becomes clear if we consider the career of one of the earliest cinema proprietors in Aberdeen, Dove Paterson. Prior to the cinematograph's debut in the north-east, Paterson had gained renown as a "reader" and "elocutionist". Indeed, at a Corporation Concert held in the local Burgh Hall in March 1896, he had been hailed as "the most accomplished elocutionist who had ever appeared in Montrose".[32] The term reflected an approach related to but distinct from that of the lecturer, involving recitations in which drama or humour was evoked through the realization of character. During the Boer War, Paterson drew praise for the power of his presentation of Kipling's "The Absent-Minded Beggar", the refrain of "Pass the hat for your credit's sake, and pay – pay – pay!" providing the occasion for a collection among the audience. By early December 1899, performances were said to have raised upwards of £100 for war charities.[33] Yet although Paterson shared the stage with most of the early local exhibitors, giving a recitation of "The Stowaway" in 1898 to the accompaniment of lantern slides supplied by William Walker, he appears not to have engaged at this time directly with the motion picture.[34] When he did seek to adapt his recital style, it was initially through the still photograph and the magic lantern and only in 1906, when he used the cinematograph to illustrate a "Pictorial Trip to Belgium", did he endeavour to link more systematically the spoken word with film.

In 1908 Paterson acquired the lease of the Gaiety Theatre in Aberdeen and sought to apply the elocutionist's skills honed on concert platforms over the years. As he explained to *Kinematograph Weekly* that same year, one of his key aims was to provide "an intelligent dialogue for every picture I show".[35] Some nineteen months later *The Bioscope* was drawn to comment on the principal attractions at the Gaiety, and made much of "the dramatic, picturesque, and illuminative comments and descriptions supplied by the master of ceremonies himself on the pictures as they pass."[36] To this point, the mode of presentation seemed wholly consistent with Paterson's roots in the arts of elocution and concert management. The most significant departure occurred later that year, with the employment of a female elocutionist, Ms Marie Pascoe. Paterson had occasionally shared the stage with his son, "little Leo", but the employment of a female voice now signalled a shift from the use of speech to describe images to the development of dialogue as a means of expounding the narrative. It is from this point that the practice that would become familiar to Aberdeen audiences of "speaking to" pictures from behind the screen appears to have become regularized. Paterson and Ms Pascoe married early in 1911, continuing to "speak to" the pictures thereafter. *The Bioscope*'s Scottish correspondent, drawn to comment in October 1912 on the Gaiety's success, remarked that it was "often hard to say which attracts the crowds, the elocutionary efforts of Mr and Mrs Paterson, or the pictures".[37] When, in the following year, Paterson acquired another Aberdeen cinema, the Coliseum, he and Marie switched their efforts to the new house. However, speaking continued at the Gaiety, the voices supplied by another husband-and-wife team.[38]

Paterson's idea was also taken up by the Aberdeen Picture Palaces Co. Ltd, which operated two houses from 1911: the Star Picture Palace and the Globe. At the former, located in what had been the city's East End Mission, the company's managing director, Bert Gates, spoke to the pictures, accompanied by his wife, Nellie. Like Paterson, Gates came to moving pictures following a career on the concert platform, appearing alongside Nellie in comic sketches, many of which he wrote himself. Transferring the site of their entertainments from the stage to the screen may have appeared a natural progression, particularly given the success enjoyed by the Patersons.[39]

The use of dialogue did not preclude the provision of music. Indeed, in his interview with *Kinematograph Weekly*, Paterson was keen to emphasize that "The best possible music by the best possible musicians accompanies all my pictures."[40] At the Star, support was provided by a piano and a Kino Symphonola phonograph, acquired in 1913 for the substantial sum of £85. Despite this, the value that each business attached to music and speech, and the comparative rarity of the skills demanded of practitioners, was reflected in the higher rates of pay commanded by elocutionists. In 1915 Gates took on a female elocutionist at a weekly rate of 30s., fully fifty per cent more than the Star's pianist was paid.[41] The premium commanded by an effective speaker reflected more than anything, perhaps, the importance placed on embedding the films within an aesthetic of realism. Paterson, for example, was insistent, as had been William Walker before him, that at no point should the presentation's hold be broken by a lapse into silence. So, in the breaks between subjects, still slides would be exhibited to musical accompaniment. At the Star, the Gates' elocutionary endeavours were supplemented by a box of stage effects acquired for £5 in 1913. These added a further touch of verisimilitude to the presentation of subjects such as *Neath the Lion's Paw*, heralded as "The Greatest Animal Drama Ever Seen", at which the audience was assured "You will actually hear the lions roar".[42]

Two further features of the practice of "speaking to" pictures merit comment. First, it does not appear to have travelled much if at all beyond Aberdeen. Shortly after concluding his drive to sweep up local slackers in 1915, Paterson appeared with his wife at Glasgow's St Andrew's Hall. Their attempts to give voice to the pictures offered local audiences, in the view of *The Bioscope*, a "new idea in cinema entertainment", and one which did not appear to catch on. In 1921 the local trade paper, *The Scottish Kinema Record*, reported a survey of Glasgow cinema managers which concluded that "there is little chance of 'talking pictures' ever being a popular proposition", the perception being that local cinema-goers preferred silence over speech.[43] Secondly, although localized, the practice endured to a degree which, whether viewed in national or international terms, seems unusual, if not unique. Although dialogue was extensively employed in the first decade of the century, such experiments proved, in most cases, short lived. In the United States, the use of acting troupes to "voice" the films was quickly abandoned, due to cost and the problem of effective synchronization of sound and image.[44] In Aberdeen, by contrast, the innovation credited to Paterson endured for much of the remainder of the silent era and was only finally abandoned in 1926.

THE ENDURING APPEAL OF THE ELOCUTIONIST EXPLAINED

In explaining the emergence and persistence of such local peculiarities in practice, a variety of potential influences may be identified, ranging from the political and economic to the cultural. To take each in turn, the regulatory framework within which Scottish cinema developed from its earliest days was the product of a highly localized system of urban governance. Licensing powers were exercised according to a series of, mostly local, Police Acts, so that the conditions governing shows could vary from place to place. In most smaller burghs, authority was vested in magistrates' committees by the 1892 Burgh Police (Scotland) Act, while in the larger centres of Edinburgh, Dundee, Glasgow, Aberdeen, and Greenock, regulation was shaped by a series of separate local measures.[45] The scope for local difference carried over into the period following the passage of the 1909 Cinematograph Act, as magistrates retained the right to add to the provisions set down by the Secretary of State for Scotland and to lay down conditions for each show.[46] In one respect, their work was complicated by the 1909 Act, which created a distinct set of regulations for one form of amusement that in practice shared many features common to other modes of entertainment. The cinematograph had long found a home on variety theatre bills, while picture houses were known to make regular use of live artistes at designated points in the programme. In December 1911 music hall proprietors across Glasgow petitioned the city's magistrates to urge adoption of a common system of licensing. As this threatened to extend the requirements for fire prevention to all parts of the building, picture house owners were keen to oppose a change that threatened markedly to increase their operating costs. They further urged that variety turns were only used to cover changes in film reels and were a preferred alternative to plunging auditoria into both silence and darkness, with all the moral hazards to which that gave rise.[47] Magistrates, however, voted to require that, where variety artistes were employed, full music hall licences be taken out. Proposals to place vocalists behind the screen, establishing some clear distinction from theatrical modes of presentation, failed to alter the decision. Strictly interpreted, it was pointed out, the change would prevent the use of lecturers, raconteurs, and the like to discourse on the scenes presented and would even act to discourage managers from addressing audiences directly. As one local newspaper had it, the effect would be to render the cinema "a voiceless entertainment".[48] That prospect proved fleeting, however. In September 1912, four months after the decision to impose full music hall conditions, the magistrates relented, not as a consequence of lobbying by the cinema trade, but from a recognition that the new conditions would effectively put an end to the staging of cheap Saturday concerts in halls owned by the City Corporation and thus would strike a blow against the promotion of rational uplift.[49]

The Glasgow experience suggests that the impact of the law on performance practice was at best limited. In Aberdeen, even before the passage of the 1909 Act, cinemas were required to operate under music hall licences, a position confirmed by the terms of the 1911 Aberdeen Corporation Act.[50] The costs imposed by the licence remained the same regardless of the character of entertainment on offer. In explaining the preference in some Aberdonian houses for dialogue and the location of speakers behind the screen, we must look beyond the regulatory regime.

Seemingly, an altogether more powerful influence on managerial preferences was the financial context within which businesses operated. The two decades separating the emergence of dedicated picture houses from the coming of sound film were among the most economically volatile of the twentieth century.[51] The fortunes of one concern, the Dunfermline Cinema House, Ltd, for which accounts exist from just before the outbreak of war through the remainder of the silent era, illustrate the kind of shifts to which the exhibition business as a whole was vulnerable, and help to clarify the context within which decisions over performance practice were taken (see Table 4.2).

The accompanying chart places these years within the longer-term trading performance of the company and points up the unusual volatility of cinema finances in the silent period (see Chart 4.1).

In the first wave of picture house building from 1910, many businesses sought to maximize their appeal by keeping prices low, an approach necessitating that costs be minimized if profitability were to be maintained. This was most effectively achieved, as the promoters of the Scottish Electric Picture Palaces, Ltd, explained, by limiting the number of front-of-house staff and, more especially, the hiring of live artistes.[52] The decision of management at Aberdeen's Star Picture Palace to underscore pictures through a combination of speech and the Kino Symphonola may be seen to

TABLE 4.2 Dunfermline Cinema House, trading performance, 1914–1930.

Year	Profit/Loss
1914–15	£2,435 12s. 4d.
1915–16	£2,761 16s. 4d.
1916–17	£826 11s. 11d.
1917–18	£1,335 18s. 4d.
1918–19	£3,506 12s. 1d.
1919–20	£4,078 9s. 7d.
1920–1	£4,164 13s. 2d.
1921–2	−£241 15s.
1922–3	−£1,168 10s.
1923–4	£423 18s. 6d.
1924–5	£1,556 11s. 3d.
1925–6	£699 8s. 3d.
1926–7	£669 14s. 10d.
1927–8	£1,223 8s. 5d.
1928–9	£1,323 14s. 6d.
1929–30	£1,947 8s. 7d.

Source: NAS, BT2/8516/18–34, Dunfermline Cinema House, Ltd, Balance Sheets, 5 May 1915 – 21 March 1930.

have been informed by similar calculations. The one-off payment of £85 for the Symphonola in 1913, service charges aside, contrasted with a weekly outlay of £8 5s. at more prestigious houses, such as Glasgow's Cinema House, where five musicians (two pianists, one cellist, and two violinists) were employed from 1911.[53] After a matter of weeks, the Symphonola would, purely from a business perspective, more than justify itself. Nevertheless, arrangements at the Star were subject to constant review and in 1916, prompted by enhanced competition from a nearby house, the decision was taken to replace elocutionists with variety acts backed by an orchestra, at an estimated additional cost of £16 to £21 a week. Recent losses at the Star had served to convince Gates "that speaking to the Pictures had now ceased to be effective".[54] The change, however, proved short lived. Within two months, the decision was taken to downsize the musical accompaniment from an orchestra to a pianist and, barely four months after Gates had declared dialogue obsolete, directors opted to restore the practice. Depressed trade in the third year of the war made this an inauspicious point at which to take on additional costs, so that, although the introduction of variety immediately boosted takings by an estimated £30 a week, enthusiasm quickly waned and losses resumed. Reviewing the year's operations to April 1917, directors

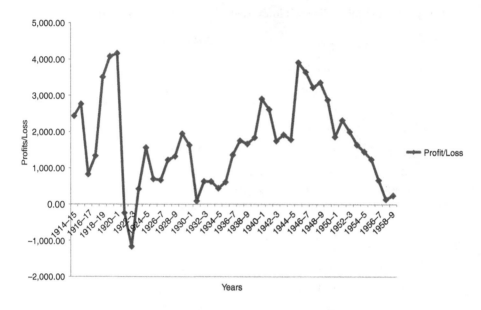

CHART 4.1 Dunfermline Cinema House, profit and loss account, 1914–1959.
SOURCE: NAS, BT2/8516/18–72, BALANCE SHEETS, 5 MAY 1915 – 21 MARCH 1959.

noted an overall deficit of £80 2s. 8½d., which, along with the war and the introduction of entertainment tax, they ascribed to "the experiment of variety shows, the latter having proved a distinct failure financially".[55] There is also evidence that, by the war's end, audiences had become less tolerant of many of the live acts hired to fill out programmes. While observed to be quiet and attentive during the films, they were seen to become increasingly rowdy when variety acts appeared. In defiance of familiar stereotypes, Aberdeen cinema-goers even vented their displeasure by hurling pennies at the performers.[56]

In some quarters, opinion had also hardened against the practice of speaking to pictures, to the extent that, in November 1920, directors of the Aberdeen Picture Palaces, Ltd, decided to end the use of elocutionists at houses in the more affluent west end of the city. The move was endorsed by the local correspondent of the trade paper *The Scottish Kinema Record*, who a year earlier had noted the continued popularity of the practice among local picture-goers: "I must say that the audience that requires dialogue to a picture nowadays seems to me to be lacking in intelligence."[57] This is suggestive of a fracturing in the local "taste community" along lines of socio-economic status, as speaking to pictures continued in halls located in poorer districts further east.[58] Other factors, it may be noted, also contributed to the change, which occurred at a time of rapidly escalating costs, with cinemas faced with growing obligations covering the burden of local taxation, the hire of films, and the employment of musicians.[59] Yet burgeoning receipts, reflecting high levels of attendance, enabled such obligations to be met without undue difficulty. Prosperity thus enabled many houses to consider augmenting their musical provision in this period, introducing wider and more varied orchestral combinations. It was at this point that the Picturedrome in Aberdeen, another of the houses run by the Aberdeen Picture Palaces, Ltd, opted to install an orchestra.[60]

If the improved financial context proved an important enabling factor, facilitating the greater use of music over speech, responses to the subsequent deterioration in the trading performance suggest that the fate of the elocutionists rested on more than calculations of cost alone. From the second half of 1920, profit margins were seriously squeezed, more especially in halls where orchestras now performed in place of the spoken word. In two consecutive trading years, the highest profits at all the houses run by the Aberdeen Picture Palaces, Ltd, were recorded at the Star, where speaking to pictures continued (see Table 4.3):

Yet at no point did the growing pressure on balance sheets persuade the company to restore dialogue at its other theatres. Indications are that such a mode of presentation was deemed increasingly outmoded, particularly for the wealthier clientele of the west end. By 1926 that perception had gained sufficient ground to call into question the operation of elocutionists even at the Star. At a time when profit margins more generally were recovering from the slump of the early 1920s, that house's financial performance worsened markedly, as net drawings contracted sharply over the financial year 1925–6. The board needed no further persuasion that the practice of speaking to pictures no longer enthralled local cinema-goers. The decision was thus taken to replace elocutionists with an orchestra.[61] Yet the subsequent financial history of the Star suggests that directors may, in this case, have acted in advance of audience opinion. Certainly, the belief that an orchestra would prove a better draw than dialogue was not borne out by returns at the box office. As the following table

TABLE 4.3 Aberdeen Picture Palaces, Ltd, profits (February–September).

	1921	1922
Star	£1,068 1s. 1½d.	£1,105 5s. 3d.
Globe	£283 – 5½d.	£263 17s. 1½d.
Picturedrome	£139 17s. 8d.	£414 7s. 5½d.
Playhouse	–	£387 10s. 6d.
King's	£ 714 16s. 11d.	£882 18s. ½d.

Source: Cinema Museum, Aberdeen Picture Palaces, Ltd, Minute Book, February 1913–September 1922, Meeting of Directors, 12 September 1922.

indicates, once amounts due under entertainments tax are eliminated, takings continued to decline through the remainder of the silent era (see Table 4.4)

Despite the antipathy thus registered against the change in exhibition practice, consideration was not given to reinstating speech at the Star in the late 1920s. As far as management was concerned, "speaking to" pictures had had its day.

That the Star's patrons were not, it would appear, of the same mind has much to tell us about the appeal of speech locally and its role in consolidating cinema's rise to popularity. As practised by Bert and Nellie Gates, at least, dialogue was used to root the films in a sense of the immediate. The concern was not just to explain the basics of the plot, but also to incorporate easily recognizable references to local events and personalities.[62] It is conceivable that, with time, this approach could, with certain audiences, come to seem petty and parochial and this may help to explain the turn against speech in the years after the First World War. Despite that, its importance in generating enthusiasm for cinema in its early phase cannot be gainsaid and indeed is revealing as to the nature of the industry's appeal at a key stage in its development.

As indicated earlier, the rise of the dedicated picture house is often interpreted as a pitch for a more respectable, affluent clientele, and the construction of halls along leading thoroughfares, such as Edinburgh's Princes Street, Glasgow's Sauchiehall Street, and Aberdeen's Union Street, suggests that this view is not entirely without validity.[63] Yet when rationalizing building plans, company promoters emphasized the ability of businesses to reach out to a new mass audience. The Scottish Electric Picture Palaces, Ltd, launched in 1910, the same year in which "speaking to" pictures debuted at Aberdeen's Gaiety Theatre, justified its plans to construct eight halls across west-central Scotland by noting "an increasing demand for these entertainments, which can be provided to the public at admission charges well within the means of all."[64] With seats invariably cheaper than those available in variety theatres, the picture house had the capacity to exploit a growing taste for amusements among those with limited spending power. The location of halls maximized this potential. So the

TABLE 4.4 Star Picture Palace, Aberdeen, net drawings, 1924–1930

Financial Year	Net Drawings
1924–5	£7,559 1s. 5d.
1925–6	£6,536 11s. 7d.
1926–7	£5,869 2s.
1927–8	£5,450 2s. 1d.
1928–9	£5,183 6s. 5d.
1929–30	£5,558 12s. 11d.

Source: Cinema Museum, Aberdeen Picture Palaces, Ltd, Accounts.

houses projected by the Scottish Electric Picture Palaces, Ltd, were situated close to major transport arteries with sizeable clusters of working-class housing nearby. As the company's architect assured potential investors, "The inhabitants of these centres are composed mostly of the classes which, experience shows, will liberally patronise Cinematograph Theatres, and for which at present no such popular forms of entertainment have been provided."[65] The strength of working-class demand for commercial amusements had been demonstrated during the cyclical downturn of 1908–9 when, despite reduced activity across many leading industries, business for most popular recreations remained robust.[66]

The decision of elocutionists in Aberdeen to retreat behind the screen and to "speak to" pictures in a manner markedly at variance from many earlier lecturing traditions may thus be plausibly linked to growing recognition of the commercial potential inherent in the new mass market for amusements. A further feature of this new audience was its comparative youth. The presence of large numbers of children at moving picture shows first began to excite comment around the time of the emergence of the earliest dedicated cinemas. In October 1910 Glasgow's parish council approached the city's magistrates to express its alarm at the impact of exhibitions, mounted in the east end of the city, on the young.[67] In the north-east also, ticket sales to children were key to the prosperity of houses in the poorer districts, so that one of the first moves to restore prosperity following the increase in entertainments tax in 1931 was a reduction in prices for children. The impact was immediate, with a significant increase in the number of seats filled.[68] However indirect, this evidence from a later decade suggests that exhibition strategies were determined by the need to satisfy the particular needs of an audience that was predominantly poor and young.

CONCLUSION

In summary then, sound practices proved markedly adaptable to the changing needs of the industry and the singular career of the Aberdeen elocutionists suggests that this mutability was maintained throughout the remainder of the silent era. It also serves as a reminder that, while often seen as the epitome of modern "mass" culture, capable of generating standardized images of appeal to audiences regardless of physical distance and cultural difference, moving pictures substantially based their initial appeal on the reproduction of the local and the familiar. This has most often been traced through the production of the local topical, which gave a familiar inflexion to the most varied and exotic bill of fare.[69] In explaining his approach to film exhibition, Dove Paterson placed importance on the securing of a regular supply of subjects of local interest.[70] Speech, whether the expository efforts of lecturers or the dialogue supplied by elocutionists, worked towards the same end, eliding the distance separating life in urban Scotland from images culled from far-flung parts of the world. Rather than offering an "escape" to an alternative reality, cinema through the efforts of the elocutionists was brought close to home and embedded in the familiar, and it is in this as much as in its comparative cheapness that its enduring appeal for audiences and managements alike resided.

NOTES

1. H. E. Browning and A. A. Sorrell, "Cinemas and Cinema-Going in Great Britain", *Journal of the Royal Statistical Society*, Series A (General), 117/2 (1954), 137–8.

2. I am grateful to Patricia Cook for this information, see also Patricia Cook, "Albany Ward and the Development of Cinema Exhibition in England", *Film History* 20/3 (2008): 294–307.

3. Glasgow City Archives, D-OPW 61/5, List of Premises Licensed under the Cinematograph Act, 12 July 1913.

4. Nicholas Hiley, "'Nothing More Than a "Craze"': Cinema Building in Britain from 1909 to 1914", in *Young and Innocent? The Cinema in Britain, 1896–1930*, ed. Andrew Higson (Exeter: University of Exeter Press, 2002), 111–27; *The Kinematograph Year Book Diary and Directory* (London: Kinematograph and Lantern Weekly, 1915; 1916).

5. *The Scotsman*, 10 July 1916, 1; 11 July 1916, 7.

6. National Archives of Scotland (hereafter NAS), SC36/79/18, Letter Book of Thomas Gilbert [catalogued as Letter Book of Glasgow Film Services, Ltd], 29 July 1918, Gilbert to D. Fraser of Fraser and Carmichael, Dunfermline; 2 Dec. 1918, Gilbert to Hall Keeper, Leslie; 11 Oct. 1920, Gilbert to Performing Right Society, London.

7. See also Joe Kember, *Marketing Modernity: Victorian Popular Shows and Early Cinema* (Exeter: University of Exeter Press, 2009), chapter 2.

8. David Greasley and Les Oxley, "Discontinuities in Competitiveness: The Impact of the First World War on British industry", *Economic History Review* 2nd series, 49/1 (1996), 82–100; Peter Dewey, *War and Progress. Britain, 1914–1945* (Harlow: Longman, 1997), chapter 2; Derek H. Aldcroft, *The British Economy between the Wars* (Oxford: Philip Allan, 1983), chapter 2.

9. For example, see Lise Shapiro Sanders, "'Indecent Incentives to Vice': Regulating Films and Audience Behaviour from the 1890s to the 1910s", in Andrew Higson, ed., *Young and Innocent?* 97–110; Andrew Shail, "'A Distinct Advance in Society': Early Cinema's 'Proletarian Public Sphere' and Isolated Spectatorship in the UK, 1911–18", *Journal of British Cinema and Television* 3/2 (2006): 209–28; Stuart Hanson, *From Silent Screen to Multi-Screen: A History of Cinema Exhibition in Britain since 1896* (Manchester: Manchester University Press, 2007), 25–9.

10. *The Entertainer, Theatrical, Vaudeville, Musical, Social and Athletic* 4 Oct. 1913: 14 (hereafter, *Entertainer*).

11. Cinema Museum, Lambeth, James F. Donald (Cinemas), Ltd, Grand Central Picture House, Employees, Schedule E Returns, 1927–8; see also Cinema House, Employer's Schedule E Returns, 1927–8; Scottish Screen Archive (hereafter SSA), 5/22/3, The Glasgow Picture House, Ltd, Minute Book, Meeting of Directors, 28 Dec. 1911.

12. SSA, 5/22/3, The Glasgow Picture House, Ltd, Minute Book, Meetings of Directors, 5 Feb., 20 Feb. 1912; the "tendency to use sound to spruce up the program" is noted in Rick Altman,

Silent Film Sound (New York: Columbia University Press, 2004), 124. See also Davison's chapter in this volume for further discussion of orchestra augmentation at the Cinema House, and rates of pay for cinema musicians more generally.

13. A similar practice was encountered at the nearby King's Cinema, *Bioscope*, 31 Aug. 1916, 817; see also SSA, 5/22/3, Meetings of Directors, 27 Nov. 1911; 28 Dec. 1911.

14. Such halls included the Cinema House in central Glasgow, where a Fiedler grand priced at £51 to £60 was installed in 1911. SSA, 5/22/3, Meetings of Directors, 14 Nov. 1911.

15. Cyril Ehrlich, *The Piano: A History* (London: Dent, 1976); Derek Scott, *The Singing Bourgeois: Songs of the Victorian Drawing Room and Parlour* (Milton Keynes: Open University Press, 1989), chapter 2.

16. NAS, CS248/4062, Copy Correspondence IC, Alexander Mathieson and J. F. Calverto, 29 August 1903, Calverto to Mathieson.

17. SSA, 5/22/3, Meetings of Directors, 27 Nov.; 5 Dec. 1911; Cinema Museum, Aberdeen Picture Palaces, Ltd, Minute Book, Feb. 1913 – Sept. 1922, Meeting of Directors, 14 April 1915. See Davison, chapter 13 in this volume, for more on the cost of musicians in the period.

18. See Stephen Bottomore, chapter 1 in this volume, on Eric Williams for a detailed discussion of an "elocutionist" who recited to films in which he himself appeared.

19. *Aberdeen Weekly Journal*, 5 Jan. 1898, 6 (hereafter *AWJ*). An image of the sheet music cover for this song is available online at: https://jscholarship.library.jhu.edu/bitstream/handle/1774.2/20850/014.029.000.webimage.JPEG?sequence=9 [accessed 3 August 2012].

20. *Aberdeen Journal* (hereafter *AJ*), 4 Mar. 1898, 6; see also 31 Oct. 1898, 7.

21. *AJ*, 16 Feb. 1899, 4.

22. *Bioscope*, 8 July 1915, 189; 22 July 1915, 393; 29 July 1915, 501.

23. Robert J. Morris, "Leisure, Entertainment and the Associational Culture of British Towns, 1800–1900" (unpublished paper, 1996); "Clubs, Societies and Associations", in *The Cambridge Social History of Britain, 1750–1950*. Vol. 3: *Social Agencies and Institutions*, ed. F. Michael L. Thompson (Cambridge: Cambridge University Press, 1990), 395–443.

24. Kember, *Marketing Modernity*, 50–8. See also Judith Buchanan, chapter 2 in this volume.

25. For Walker, see B. H. Gates, "Cinema in Aberdeen", in *Educational Film Bulletin* 33 (Sept. 1946): 16–17; Michael Thomson, *Silver Screen in the Silver City: A History of Cinemas in Aberdeen, 1896–1987* (Aberdeen: Aberdeen University Press, 1988), 7–8; *AJ*, 16 Nov. 1896, 1.

26. *AJ*, 8 Dec. 1896, 5; 11 Feb. 1899, 1.

27. *Scotsman*, 11 July 1911, 10; 27 May 1910, 1; *Who Was Who, 1929–40* (London: Adam and Charles Black, 1967 ed.), 977.

28. NAS, BT2/3449/1, The Modern Marvel Co. Ltd, Memorandum of Association; 5, Summary of Capital and Shares, 21 Feb. 1898.

29. *Scotsman*, 27 Dec. 1904, 5; 3 Jan. 1905, 1; 10 Jan. 1905, 8.

30. *Scotsman*, 15 Jan. 1901, 9; 11 Feb. 1902, 5.

31. Jon Burrows, "*West is Best!*; or What We Can Learn from Bournemouth", *Early Popular Visual Culture* 8/4 (Nov. 2010): 351–62; *Scotsman*, 26 Dec. 1905, 4; 1 Jan. 1907, 1.

32. *AJ*, 16 Mar. 1896, 6.

33. *AJ*, 14 Nov. 1899, 4; 8 Dec. 1899, 4.

34. *AJ*, 4 May 1898, 6; 21 Jan. 1899, 1; 14 Nov. 1899, 4.

35. *Kinematograph and Lantern Weekly*, 2 July 1908, cited in Thomson, *Silver Screen*, 36; *Bioscope*, 7 Oct. 1909: 71; B. H. Gates, "Cinema in Aberdeen".

36. *Bioscope*, 27 Jan. 1910, 33.

37. *Bioscope*, 10 Oct. 1912, 87; 22 Sept. 1910, 15; 23 Feb. 1911, 57; on Leo, *AJ*, 16 Nov. 1899, 7.

38. *Bioscope*, 14 Aug. 1913, 475; Thomson, *Silver Screen*, 70.

39. Thomson, *Silver Screen*, 52–3.

40. Thomson, *Silver Screen*, 37.

41. Cinema Museum, Aberdeen Picture Palaces, Ltd, Minute Book, Feb. 1913 – Sept. 1922, Meeting of Directors, 21 Aug. 1913; 14 April 1915; 14 July 1915.

42. Thomson, *Silver Screen*, 36–7, 55; for Walker's practice, see *AJ*, 30 Sept. 1899, 6; Cinema Museum, Aberdeen Pictures Palaces, Ltd, Minute Book, Feb. 1913 – Sept. 1922, Meeting of Directors, 21 Aug. 1913.

43. *Bioscope*, 16 Sept. 1915, 1283; *The Scottish Kinema Record* (the title of *The Entertainer* from the edition dated 22 May 1920, hereafter *SKR*), 10 Sept. 1921, 1.

44. Altman, *Silent Film Sound*, chapter 9.

45. Glasgow City Archives, RU4/2/15, Rutherglen, Cinematograph Act, 1909, Scottish Office to Town Clerk, County Clerk, Clerk of the Peace, 19 June 1935; John Lindsay, *Corporation of Glasgow. Review of Municipal Government in Glasgow* (Glasgow: William Hodge, 1909); Robert J. Morris, "Urbanisation and Scotland", in *People and Society in Scotland*. Vol. 2: *1830–1914*, ed. W. Hamish Fraser and Robert J. Morris (Edinburgh: John Donald, 1990), 73–102.

46. Glasgow City Archives, MP41/106, Memorandum by the Town Clerk on the Cinematograph Act, 1909, and relative regulations made by the Secretary for Scotland on 10th March 1910.

47. *Bioscope*, 28 Dec. 1911, 909; 22 Feb. 1912, 517; 4 April 1912, 55; 18 April 1912, 179.

48. *Bioscope*, 16 May 1912, 481; 23 May 1912, 557 (citing an unnamed Glasgow newspaper).

49. *Bioscope*, 26 Sept. 1912, 925; Elspeth King, "Popular Culture in Glasgow", in *The Working Class in Glasgow, 1750–1914*, ed. R. A. Cage (Beckenham: Croom Helm, 1987), 142–87; Paul Maloney, *Scotland and the Music Hall, 1850–1914* (Manchester: Manchester University Press, 2003), 191.

50. *Bioscope*, 23 Sept. 1909, 19–21; Glasgow City Archive, RU4/2/15, Rutherglen, Cinematograph Act, 1909, Town Clerk, Aberdeen to Town Clerk, Rutherglen, 27 Jan. 1933.

51. *Entertainer*, 4 Oct. 1913, 13; *Kinematograph Year Book,* 1921 (London: Kinematograph Weekly), 13; 1923 (London: Kinematograph Weekly), 3.

52. SSA, 5/8/23, Green Family Collection, Prospectus, Scottish Electric Picture Palaces, Ltd (1910).

53. Cinema Museum, Aberdeen Picture Palaces, Ltd, Minute Book, Feb. 1913 – Sept.1922, Meeting of Directors, 21 Aug. 1913; SSA, 5/22/3, Glasgow Picture House, Ltd, Minute Book, Meeting of Directors, 5 Dec. 1911.

54. Cinema Museum, Aberdeen Picture Palaces, Ltd, Minute Book, Feb. 1913 – Sept. 1922, Meetings of Directors, 12 July 1916; 13 Oct. 1916.

55. Cinema Museum, Aberdeen Picture Palaces, Ltd, Minute Book, Feb. 1913 – Sept. 1922, Meetings of Directors, 9 Aug. 1916; 19 Sept. 1916; 4 April 1917.

56. *Entertainer*, 17 May 1919, 10; see also, 8 Nov. 1919, 12; 15 Nov. 1919, 12.

57. *Entertainer*, 19 July 1919: 8; *SKR*, 27 Nov. 1920, 16.

58. Sue Harper, "A Lower Middle-Class Taste-Community in the 1930s: Admissions Figures at the Regent Cinema, Portsmouth, UK", *Historical Journal of Film, Radio and Television* 24/4 (2006): 565–87.

59. *Entertainer*, 6 Dec. 1919, 9; on the issue of municipal rates, see SSA, 5/11/17, Cinematograph Exhibitors' Association, Edinburgh and East of Scotland Section, Minute Book, Meeting at Princes Cinema, 23 Sept. 1919. For more on the costs associated with musicians, see Davison, chapter 13 in this volume.

60. *Entertainer*, 15 Nov. 1919, 11.

61. Cinema Museum, Aberdeen Picture Palaces, Ltd, Minute Book, Oct. 1922 – Oct. 1930, Meetings of Directors, 18 Feb. 1926; 8 June 1926.

62. Thomson, *Silver Screen*, 55.

63. *Bioscope* 26 March 1914, 1420; 1 Jan. 1914, 17, for the opening of the Palace on Princes Street.

64. SSA, 5/8/23, Green Family Collection, Scottish Electric Picture Palaces, Ltd (1910), Prospectus.

65. Ibid.

66. *Evening Times*, 17 Aug. 1908, 4.

67. GCA, Glasgow Corporation, Magistrates' Committee Minutes, April to November 1910, 27 Oct. 1910.

68. Cinema Museum, Aberdeen Picture Palaces, Ltd, Minute Book, 6 Nov. 1930 – 15 Nov. 1934, Meetings of Directors, 25 Sept. 1931; 9 Oct. 1931; 8 Dec. 1932; 13 Oct. 1933; 6 Nov. 1933.

69. Leo Charney and Vanessa R. Schwartz, ed. "Introduction", *Cinema and the Invention of Modern Life* (Berkeley, Los Angeles, London: University of California Press, 1995), 1–12; Vanessa Toulmin, "'Local films for local people': Travelling Showmen and the Commissioning of Local Films in Great Britain, 1900–1902", *Film History* 13/2 (2001): 118–37; Vanessa Toulmin and Martin Loiperdinger, "Is It You? Recognition, Representation and Response in Relation to the Local Film", *Film History* 17/1 (2005): 7–18.

70. Thomson, *Silver Screen*, 36.

PART TWO

Accompanying Pictures

5

"Suitable Music": Accompaniment Practice in Early London Screen
Exhibition from R. W. Paul to the Picture Palaces

Ian Christie

I WANT TO pose, and partially answer, the basic question: what evidence do we have of
accompaniment practice for early film screenings in Britain, and specifically in London,
before the mid-1910s? There have been for some time two main assumptions about
accompaniment in the early years of moving pictures. The most common is that "the
silents were never silent", which has been challenged by the claim that they *were* frequently unaccompanied, at least before about 1908.[1] This latter view was advanced by
Rick Altman in his controversial 1997 paper, "The Silence of the Silents", arguing that
many, if not most, early film shows only had music *between* rather that accompanying
films.[2] But rather than start from either of these assumptions, I want to marshal what
evidence is available, and to look specifically at London, bearing in mind that practices
may very well have been different in other cities and countries.

Immediately, we have to address the issues of prevailing practices and tradition,
and of incomplete evidence. In terms of tradition, we can look back to the earliest self-proclaimed "moving pictures" in London: the Eidophusikon of Philippe
de Loutherbourg. According to an advertisement in the *Daily Universal Register*
of 1 March 1786, this entertainment offered five items: Aurora, Sunset, A Storm
and Moon Light, ending with "a Grand Conclusive Scene", illustrating an episode
from Milton's *Paradise Lost*, with Satan reviewing his troops before the Palace of
Pandemonium.[3] The advertisement also stated that these would be given "with suitable accompaniment". A handbill for the Eidophusikon from the same year refers to
"the usual accompaniments" for the "Grand Scene from Milton".[4]

Despite various appreciative comments from those who saw De Loutherbourg's shows, the only evidence of what the accompaniment might have been is the *Daily Universal Register* advertisement's reference to "English readings and recitals" that will be given while scenery is being changed, and a harpsichord visible in Edward Burney's 1782 watercolour of the Eidophusikon.[5] Iain McCalman notes that "between scenes, painted transparencies served as curtain drops, and Mr and Mrs Michael Arne entertained the audience with violin music and song."[6] This might suggest that the main purpose of the readings and music was to "cover" the scene changes, much as Altman has claimed music was used to bridge across reel changes in early cinema exhibition. Certainly there were sound effects, since De Loutherbourg was already recognized for his mastery of "the picturesque of sound" in his stage work for David Garrick. Ephraim Hardcastle's recollection of attending the Eidophusikon goes into considerable detail on how De Loutherbourg enhanced his vividly realized "moving pictures".[7]

Throughout the following century, three important trends would have a bearing on the place of music in relation to spectacle. One was the return of "incidental" music to the English stage. Although theatre music had been commonplace in seventeenth-century London, with Henry Purcell writing music for over forty plays in the 1690s, musical fashion favoured operas and masques during the eighteenth century, with Thomas Arne and Handel among the most popular composers in Britain.[8] But by the mid-nineteenth century, as the London theatre turned towards spectacle, incidental music became fashionable. An early example of the spectacle melodramas that would come to dominate Victorian popular theatre was *The Cataract of the Ganges*, staged at Drury Lane in 1823. The stage directions called for

A field of battle near Ahmedabad by moonlight.... After overture descriptive of a battle, the curtain rises and discovers wounded, dead and dying [...]. Music expresses the groans of the wounded and dying, the retreat of the Mahomedan army at a distance...[9]

By the mid-century, descriptive and evocative music had become integral, not only for melodrama, but for the spectacular staging of classic works. Madame Vestris's *Midsummer Night's Dream* at Covent Garden in 1840 featured extensive musical accompaniment and ballets, using Mendelssohn's music.[10] And for his *Faust* at the Lyceum Theatre in 1885, Henry Irving increased the size of his usual orchestra to place even greater emphasis on the role of music, heard continuously throughout the performance.[11]

Another trend of the early nineteenth century was the rise of Romantic programme music. Again, there had been instances of narrative and scene painting in seventeenth- and eighteenth-century music—Kuhnau's Biblical Sonatas and various "effects" in the symphonies of Haydn come to mind. But from Beethoven's "Pastoral" (Sixth) Symphony onwards, by way of his *Battle Symphony* and Tchaikovsky's *1812 Overture*, through Liszt's symphonic poems and piano landscapes, there was a growing recognition of the descriptive and evocative potential of music. And much of this would later be recycled in pot-pourri film accompaniment during the 1910s and 1920s.

This last was an international trend, as was the emergence of popular music-based "variety" entertainment aimed at a wider social spectrum than the audience for concert music. The success of such entertainment soon prompted building on a lavish scale, with London music halls leading the way, and often providing a model—as in the case of the Folies Bergère in Paris being inspired by the Moorish Alhambra in London. In post-Civil War America, the new vaudeville theatres catered for family audiences by prohibiting alcohol and stressing wholesome performances—very different from the raffish atmosphere of London's rapidly expanding network of music halls. The music halls and their equivalents became the first regular exhibition sites for film, and so their existing practices became the earliest conventions for film presentation.

This strongly suggests that moving picture shows at the Empire and the Alhambra, the two Leicester Square music halls which were first to present this novelty, had musical accompaniment from the outset. According to various accounts, the Paris Lumière show that began at the end of 1895 had piano accompaniment; and the London Lumière debut at the Polytechnic on 20 February 1896 is reported to have been accompanied by a harmonium.[12] Although early Lumière Cinématographe shows at the Empire began in the Grand Foyer during the afternoons in March 1896, and may not have been accompanied, these proved so popular that they soon moved into the main theatre, and a playbill dated 8 March states that "a selection of music will be played under the direction of Mr George Byng."[13]

In the case of Robert Paul's rival Theatrograph, there are two valuable reviews that give some insight into just what early accompaniments were providing. Paul's Theatrograph made its debut at the Egyptian Hall on 19 March 1896, introduced by the magician Nevil Maskelyne, and a review from a month later reported

The first moving scene announced by Mr Nevil Maskelyne is a band practice. The music of the march that one may imagine is being played is given on the pianoforte by Mr F. Cramer.[14]

The other items in this programme of Edison Kinetoscope subjects—Highland dancers, a Serpentine dance, and boxing cats—all suggest that Mr Cramer would have supplied appropriate music that "one may imagine". When Paul was booked by the Empire's near neighbour in Leicester Square, the Alhambra music hall, his projector was renamed The Animatograph, and began a two-year run on 25 March 1896. There is no reference to musical accompaniment until June, when Paul filmed the Derby being won by Persimmon, a horse belonging to the Prince of Wales. Having captured the finish of the race and taken his film back to London for overnight processing, Paul was able to present it on the following evening at the Alhambra, where

> an enormous audience...witnessed the Prince's Derby, all to themselves amidst wild enthusiasm, which all but drowned the strains of "God Bless the Prince of Wales," as played by the splendid orchestra.[15]

Another account describes the same film being shown at the Canterbury music hall, also "to the strains of 'God Bless the Prince of Wales,'" and at both venues it was apparently encored.[16]

These appear to be the only contemporary accounts of film screenings in London before 1900 that specifically refer to musical accompaniment. But they all indicate what seems to have been a normal practice in venues where music normally accompanied most performance. Is it imaginable that the Alhambra's orchestra, used to playing for a wide range of acts on the programme, would have played *only* for this single film, lasting less than a minute, and forming part of a series that normally included up to twenty titles? The "Persimmon" case rather implies that such accompaniment was routine; and that it was likely to be based on verbal/title association, as Altman has suggested.[17] It implies that early London film shows would follow the conventions of the place of exhibition. Where an orchestra was present, there would be "normal" accompaniment, most likely based on subject or title "cueing"—so that, for instance, another film by Paul of Henley Regatta would most likely have been accompanied by a relevant boating song, while mention of the sea might have invited such staples as "Heart of Oak" (1759), or "A Life on the Ocean Wave" (1838), or even something from the recent Gilbert and Sullivan operetta *The Pirates of Penzance* (1880).

Many early films were in fact based on, and no doubt suggested by, popular songs. When the Alhambra manager invited Paul to add a fictional film to his repertoire in April 1896, the subject chosen, *The Soldier's Courtship*, seems to have been inspired by the popular figure of "Tommy Atkins", celebrated in a recent music hall song, "Private Tommy Atkins".[18] It seems very likely, especially given the participatory habits of music hall audiences, that this would have been accompanied by the song's music, which the audience would have then taken up. An even clearer example of a film suggested by a song is Paul's *Come Along, Do* (1898), in which an elderly couple are first seen outside an art exhibition, then inside the man is seen staring at a nude female statue, while his wife tries to pull him away.[19]

This has attracted attention as the earliest example known in film making of two spatially distinct shots being joined to tell a story. But equally significant is the film's complex genealogy, stretching back some thirty-five years to a painting that narrativized and mocked the controversy caused by John Gibson's nude sculpture *Tinted Venus*, when this was exhibited at the 1862 International Exhibition. A song quickly appeared, using the same title and illustrated by a near-copy of the painting, with the refrain "Come along do / What are you staring at? / You ought to know better—so come along do".[20] In the 1870s, the anecdote was realized as a photographic stereo card, which was later republished in the 1890s, and presumably formed the immediate basis of Paul's filmed realization. This chain inevitably recalls Martin Meisel's influential study of "realization" in nineteenth-century culture, whereby novels gave rise to illustrations, which in turn could become the basis of stage versions.[21] In the case of *Come Along Do*, a statue gives rise to an ironic anecdote, which mutates through four different media, acquiring in the process both a visual/dramatic form and a musical narrative, as a song by Walter Burnot and Jesse Williams—which are likely to have been available to both exhibitors and audiences for the film. In short, it is more than likely that screenings of the film would have prompted a knowing accompanist to "quote" the song.[22]

Evidence of the kind of context in which early film screening took place beyond music halls comes from reports of a mixed lantern slide and film presentation in the London district of Muswell Hill in December 1899, soon after the outbreak of the Anglo-Boer War.[23] Billed as "A Trip to the Transvaal", this was a lantern lecture held to raise money towards building a new church in this developing suburb. It was given by a Mr Salmond, who had travelled widely in Southern Africa before the outbreak of the war, possibly as a missionary, in view of the venue for the lecture. In addition to the usual lantern slides, at least six films were shown, all apparently drawn from the Warwick Trading Company's extensive catalogue of non-fiction subjects. Four of the films dealt with a ship's launch, the embarkation of passengers, departure and on-board games; and two showed Cape Town. All dated from before the outbreak of war, although it was clearly this that had given the "trip" topical appeal.

What makes this suburban occasion—no doubt typical of many, as films began to be shown in community halls—particularly interesting in relation to musical accompaniment is a report of Mr Salmond performing two songs.[24] These are not identified, so we have no way of knowing if they were in any way related to the subject of the lecture. Perhaps more likely, in view of the setting, is that they were "sacred songs" from the repertoire that was already common at Nonconformist church social events.[25] Nor do we know if the Presbyterian hall had a piano or the increasingly popular harmonium, which was common in such halls and could have been used to accompany Mr Salmond—and potentially also his slides and films. Live musical performance was indeed an integral part of much Victorian and Edwardian sociality. So rather than ask *if* films were accompanied, it may make more historical sense to ask: why would they *not* be?

The magic lantern show was an important tradition which "incubated" moving picture exhibition in early hybrid or composite performances. Lantern shows took place in a wide variety of settings, ranging from the purely domestic to increasingly large halls, as new illuminants appeared in the later nineteenth century. Most lantern shows were broadly informative or educational, and therefore relied on the lecturer's voice alone.[26] But many "life model" lantern narratives had accompanying dramatic texts for recitation, often in verse, and would certainly have been accompanied by music performed on whatever instruments were available.[27] London's most elaborate lantern shows, known as "dissolving views", were given throughout the mid-nineteenth century at the Royal Polytechnic in Regent Street—which would also house the first Lumière demonstration in February 1896—and these routinely had elaborate musical accompaniment, serving to emphasize their pictorial and "aesthetic" content.[28]

We have one retrospective account of how such a composite slide and film show was presented with musical accompaniment. Cecil Hepworth was the son of a noted lanternist, T. C. Hepworth, and entered the film business in 1896, initially as an exhibitor. He continued as a director and producer until the 1920s, and published his memoirs in 1951.[29] Here he recalled "a little series" shown during the mid-1890s

> which always went down very well indeed. It was called The Storm and consisted of half a dozen slides and one forty-foot film. My sister Effie was a very good pianist and she travelled with me on most of these jaunts. The sequence opened with a calm and peaceful picture of the sea and sky. Soft and gentle music (Schumann, I think). That changed to another seascape, though the clouds looked a little more interesting and the music quickened a bit. At each change the inevitability of a coming gale became more insistent and the music more threatening; until the storm broke with an exciting film, of dashing waves bursting into the entrance of a cave, with wild music (by Jensen, I think).[30]

Martin Miller Marks has analysed this account from a musical standpoint, suggesting that Effie Hepworth may have played "in an improvisatory fashion", to link the composed pieces she was drawing upon.[31] Like other commentators on Hepworth's recollection, however, he does not identify the film, which was almost certainly Paul's

Sea Cave Near Lisbon, the most widely admired of his 1896 series *A Tour Through Spain and Portugal*.[32]

After the first appearance of this series at the Alhambra, in October 1896, reviews described the *Sea Cave* as "a picture of real beauty" and "one of the most remarkable effects produced by any of the 'graphies' yet put forward".[33] Hepworth reveals that it could be used in quite a different way, to create the climax in a pictorial sequence, with still images as it were "breaking into movement". This not only suggests a continuity with the picturesque tradition that De Loutherbourg had helped inaugurate through his stage work and the Eidophusikon; it also draws attention to the influence of Symbolist culture at the *fin de siècle*, in which sound, word, and image were closely intertwined, often to synaesthetic effect. A celebrated Russian music critic's reaction to his first experience of the Lumière film of children diving into the sea was to recall the musical representation of a similar effect: "And then to watch the sea moving just a few feet away from our chairs—Mendelssohn's *Meerstille!*—yet this silvery movement produces a music of its own."[34] Moving images, whether or not audibly accompanied, could create "music of movement", just as the music of such Symbolist composers as Debussy and Skryabin aspired to evoke images, colours, and even perfumes.

There is further scattered evidence of early moving pictures being associated with contemporary music making. During the second season of the popular Promenade Concerts at London's new orchestral concert venue, Queen's Hall in Langham Place, in September 1896, the magician David Devant showed Paul's Animated Photographs as an interval attraction in the upstairs 500-seat Small Hall, normally devoted to chamber music.[35] There is no mention of any musical accompaniment to Devant's shows, and there may well not have been any, since this was an interval in an orchestral concert, but the association between these pioneering concerts and the new experience seems significant.[36] However, the documented relationship that developed over the next ten years seems to have been less one of music accompanying film than the reverse. In 1907 Covent Garden Royal Opera House was reported to be using both lantern slides and, for the first time, film in its new production of Wagner's *Ring of the Nibelungen*. The film of the "Ride of the Valkyries", taken during a special rehearsal in Surrey, was, according to the *Kinematograph and Lantern Weekly*, "generally admitted to be better than the old method" of presenting this popular episode from *The Valkyrie*.[37]

In spite of the evocative associations between movement and music, the most obvious pattern was more or less literal illustration. Slides based on the stories told by popular songs, as well as those providing the words to be sung, were a familiar feature of the lantern repertoire. Why not, then, use film to bring familiar songs to life? The first to attempt this in England seems to have been Lewis Sealy, a pioneer exhibitor who later became an actor in America. Early in 1899, with the help of Esme Collings, Sealy filmed "dramatizations" of two songs, "Tomorrow Will be Friday" and "Simon the Cellarer", and the latter was released in January as three films corresponding to each of the three verses, described as "the latest sensation".[38] A trade journal review praised the films, noting that "when coupled with the singing of the song [they form] a spectacle which is of great interest".[39]

Robert Paul was quick to adopt this new form, introducing four contrasting "songs with animated illustrations" in his 1901 catalogue, "on the basis of a large amount of experiment and trial".[40] The songs are each characterized differently:

"'Arry on the Steamboat"—a coster song[41]
"Britain's Tribute to Her Sons"—a patriotic song
"Ora Pro Nobis"—a sentimental song
"The Waif and the Wizard"—a descriptive song

Three of these were existing songs, two associated with relatively well-known performers,[42] while "Britain's Tribute" was announced with some fanfare as "a grand patriotic song…Specially written and composed for R. W. Paul" by Clarence Hunt, with music by Frank Byng. Byng is described as "of the Strand Theatre", where he was presumably music director or conductor[43]; and his association with Paul had started a year earlier when he arranged a special score for *Army Life* in 1900.

This ambitious documentary series, subtitled "How Soldiers Are Made", consisted of twenty-one parts that covered the experience of joining up and "training in the various branches of the service".[44] Paul launched it at a special screening at the Alhambra on 18 September 1900, with an invited audience of officers, Chelsea Pensioners, and schoolboys. Backed and facilitated by the army's adjutant-general, it was no doubt seen as a useful stimulus to recruitment as the South African war entered its second year. But it also seems to have been a distinctly personal project for Paul, whose brothers were serving in the City Imperial Volunteers and who acted as his own cameraman for the series. The 1901 catalogue offered illustrated brochures for sale and twelve-sheet posters to promote what was the longest film of the period, at nearly fifty minutes. A compilation of "suitable music" was part of the exhibition strategy proposed, "suitable for Sunday evening exhibition, with or without a lecturer".

In this, as with the "animated songs", Paul seems to have been an innovator. The song films are said to illustrate the songs' incidents word for word, and are contrasted with "phonograph accompaniment of the picture of a figure on stage".[45] Clearly Paul envisaged live performance as an attraction, or a necessity, since phonograph technology at this time made filling any large space difficult, and he promised future illustrated songs: "Particulars of new Christmas, Temperance and Religious Films, now in hand, will be announced shortly". That these failed to appear suggests that the "refined" audiences for which they were apparently intended had not responded or not been reached. However, one of Paul's other productions in 1901 pointed towards a new direction: *The Magic Sword* was billed as a "medieval mystery" and uses stop-motion and multiple-exposure to reproduce on film the kind of magic spectacle normally associated with pantomime.[46] There is no reference to any special music offered to accompany it, but its genre strongly suggests that Paul was aiming to provide a form of "remediated" pantomime, for which music would have been expected.[47] His other major production of late 1901, a multi-scene adaptation of Dickens's *A Christmas Carol*, entitled *Scrooge, or Marley's Ghost*, also made use of the studio's growing skill with trick-film effects, and had its premiere in the Promenade Concert interval at the Queen's Hall in January 1902.

If Paul's proposed series did not find takers in 1901, "illustrated songs" would become the staple repertoire of various proprietary systems for synchronizing recordings and films that appeared during the first decade of the 1900s, and their use for at least one item on the typical programme of seven to ten short films seems to have been widespread throughout Britain. These systems included the Vivaphone, developed by Hepworth in 1907, and Walturdaw's Cinematophone, launched in the same year.[48] Leon Gaumont had launched his Chronophone in 1902, but it was not until Gaumont introduced the Elgéphone in 1906, driven by compressed air, that the company's *phonoscènes* attracted substantial audiences.[49] In London, they enjoyed a successful run at the Hippodrome during 1906–7 under the anglicized name "Chronomegaphone". When Gilbert and Sullivan's popular *Mikado* was temporarily banned from performance in 1907, to avoid giving offence to visiting Japanese diplomats, Walturdaw issued a set of twelve Cinematophone numbers from it, while the trade press optimistically suggested that "people will flock to hear the opera by cinematophone now that they cannot see it on stage".[50]

Reports in the "Round the Shows" pages of the *Kinematograph and Lantern Weekly* trade journal regularly note the inclusion of "songs by the Cinephone". This was a relatively simple device, developed by the pioneer cameraman and producer Will Barker, and patented by Warwick in 1909. According to a present-day Australian collector, who owns one:

Barker placed the playback gramophone in the corner of the shot with a speed indicator clearly in view while the players mouthed to the playing record. Later, when the film was shown to an audience, an identical gramophone, also with an indicator, was placed on the stage. The projectionist had a control dial for the gramophone and all he had to do was ride herd on matching the two indicators. With the aid of a quick starting double spring projector, he could have the show in sync during the head leader and before the first image. The whole thing depended on the projectionist's skill.[51]

Despite, or perhaps because of, the performative element in presentation, Cinephone items on the programme were always said to be "well received", although they continued to be supplemented by live "illustrated songs" and variety acts. There are also occasional tantalizing references to more ambitious presentations, such as a "patriotic song scena 'Invasion,' illustrated by lantern slides" in 1909, which indicate that picture houses were still offering hybrid programmes of entertainment.[52]

But were the other films that made up the bulk of these programmes being accompanied? There is intermittent evidence from "Round the Shows" that the bedrock of successful exhibition in this period was a capable improvising pianist. According to an experienced manager, quoted in 1909:

> too much importance cannot be attached to the music, and therefore it is necessary to have a competent pianist who knows how to improvise and "fit in" as the phases of the pictures change.[53]

This would suggest that such accompaniment was widespread, if not universal; although Jon Burrows has argued that trade press exhortation represented a "blip" or aspiration against the reality of many exhibitors offering either only phonograph accompaniment or none at all.[54] Much reporting of the period is simply silent on the issue of music. For instance, the opening of the new 900-seat Brixton Cinematograph Theatre in March 1911, part of "the ever-widening circle of Mr Montagu A. Pyke's high-class picture theatres", was greeted by *Kinematograph and Lantern Weekly* with a description of every aspect of the new cinema—except whether music accompanied the "full two hours' show". It seems highly unlikely that such a performance was viewed in silence, but we simply do not know what form or scale of accompaniment was usual in Pyke's cinemas. However, a year later, *The Bioscope* reported that "the Islington Picture Palace has made a substantial addition, with an orchestra of five instrumentalists".[55] Does this mean that this small theatre, seating just 120, had none before, or only a pianist?[56] We cannot be sure. As Annette Davison also explores in chapter 13 in this volume, costs were a constant concern, even if, according to *The Bioscope*, a pianist was paid rather less than the projectionist in 1912, and in some cases less than £2 per week. Yet on the supply side, sheet music albums of suitable mood and genre music began to appear with increasing frequency from 1909, along with advice columns in trade journals, and more comprehensive manuals, such as W. Tyacke George's *Playing to Pictures* (1912).[57]

Perhaps even more than music, sound effects played an important part in early film exhibition, as Stephen Bottomore has demonstrated, with the pianist often supplemented by a percussionist, who became responsible for a growing range of specialized effects. Effects machines began to appear around 1909, to automate what had become a demanding and expensive performance routine.[58] Electric pianos also came on the market, as a means of economically providing "up to date" music in cinemas,[59] while in America, theatre or "unit" organs offered a versatile range of orchestral timbres and sound effects.[60] Amid all this technological innovation in an increasingly competitive marketplace, producers began to intervene in the chaotic variety of performance practices—in the case of Edison and Vitagraph, issuing their own recommendations for suitable accompaniment.[61] The Film d'Art company in France had led the way in 1908 by commissioning a small orchestral score from the doyen of French composers, Camille Saint-Saëns, for their debut production, L'Assassinat du duc de Guise, although there is no evidence that this was used after its premiere. But Pathé's takeover of Film d'Art triggered an international movement that promoted cultural and historical subjects, and, together with the rise of the Italian "epic", this undoubtedly helped promote a more "symphonic" style of accompaniment.[62]

The seating capacity of new cinemas was also increasing, which called for more volume and perhaps variety in accompaniment. Super productions such as Cabiria and The Birth of a Nation (both of which reached Britain in 1915) were shown at the Royal Albert Hall, and certainly had full-scale orchestral accompaniment with prepared scores accompanying both films. British "features" aspiring to the same scale, such as The Battle of Waterloo (1913) and Barnaby Rudge (1915), would no doubt have met audiences' rising expectations that accompaniment would match spectacle. The earliest British medley or compilation score that has been reconstructed and performed from an original set of musical suggestions was prepared for The Battle of the Somme (1916), an official chronicle that proved unexpectedly popular in the months after the battle.[63] Using a variety of traditional and contemporary melodies, this confirms that close matching of mood was not expected in 1916.

The British film and music press have traditionally been regarded as taking little interest in cinema music during the "silent" period, which has perhaps encouraged the belief that the British public was similarly indifferent. But there are in fact many clues scattered throughout the trade papers of the 1910s and 1920s, which are beginning to be gathered and interpreted and which suggest that good local practice was appreciated. An example of this exists in the form of a report of the presentation of Griffith's Way Down East in 1923 at the Tower Cinema in Peckham, which reveals that the intricate leitmotif style then favoured in Hollywood was not necessarily appreciated in a London cinema. Albert Marchbank, conductor of the Tower cinema orchestra, took it upon himself to replace the supplied score by William Frederick

Peters and Louis Silvers with his own, combining sound and visual effects with music in a performance that evidently thrilled the *American Organist* correspondent:

> The storm music provided the greatest sensation, and this, together with the wonderful effects supplied with the film, absolutely brought the house down. There were, for instance, realistic lightning effects for which a special electric installation had been laid on. This lightning, Mr Marchmont—like Zeus—controlled (from the organ), evoking thunderous replies form the lower regions of the orchestra. There were also ice-breaking machines, waterfall, rain wind effects and what not. All these effects, manipulated in the right way, combined with the wonderful setting of the music, as a musical illustration of the drama on the screen ...[64]

As described, this accompaniment somewhat recalls both De Loutherbourg's Eidophusikon and the era of "sensation" melodrama, to which Griffith's film properly belonged. In this sense, it would have been completely idiomatic, evoking the theatrical thrill of melodrama at Drury Lane a quarter of a century earlier. Such highly integrated performances may have been exceptional—the writer claims, in what is surely an exaggeration, that "thousands of people had to be turned away from the Tower in Peckham" once the reputation of the show spread—but there is anecdotal and local press evidence that novel accompaniment could constitute a strong attraction.[65] Yet there were undoubtedly contrary views. In America, Vachel Lindsay argued in 1915 that "the *perfect* photoplay gathering place would have no sound but the hum of the conversing audience";[66] while in Britain, the heroine of D. H. Lawrence's novel *The Lost Girl* reaches her lowest ebb playing for a "picture show" in a Midlands town, where she discovers that "pictures don't have any life except in the people who watch them".[67] For Lindsay and Lawrence, both romantic conservatives, the fusion of moving pictures and music that had created a deeply attractive new audiovisual form by the mid-teens was a threat, to be resisted. Yet for the mass audience, it had clearly become addictive.

The emergence of "screen history" as a wider disciplinary frame than "film studies" suggests that the "early silent era" of cinema in Britain can usefully be seen as part of a continuum reaching back to the eighteenth century, with underlying practices and conventions often continuing into new technological regimes. Understanding contexts of presentation is vital, and believing in the "specificity" of the medium fatal. Within this continuum, mediated drama—or what the theatre historian Christopher Baugh has called "technology-driven entertainment"—has been constantly refashioned, or "remediated", to maintain its appeal in a highly competitive market. Lacking confidence in the native quality of both music and film, British critics have consistently tended to underestimate the achievements of their compatriots, even though there is much to rediscover, and, no doubt, to celebrate.

NOTES

1. Like many early-cinema researchers, I am indebted to Stephen Bottomore, who laid the empirical foundations for much that has been attempted later—including this essay. He recalls the nostrum that "the silents were never silent" (originally attributed to Irving Thalberg) in his pioneering essay, "An International Survey of Sound Effects in Early Cinema", *Film History* 11/4 (1999): 485–98.

2. Rick Altman, "The Silence of the Silents", *Musical Quarterly* 80/4 (1996): 648–718. Altman reiterated this claim in his contribution to the 1998 Domitor Conference in Washington. See his notes on "The Living Nickelodeon", in the conference proceedings: *The Sounds of Early Cinema*, ed. Richard Abel and Rick Altman (Bloomington: Indiana University Press, 2001), 232–40.

3. The *Register* was the forerunner of *The Times*, which it became in 1790.

4. Reproduced in Richard Altick, *The Shows of London: A Panoramic History of Exhibitions, 1600–1862* (Cambridge, MA: Belknap Press, 1978, 142)..

5. Edward Francis Burney, *The Eidophusikon Showing Satan arraying his Troups on the Banks of a Fiery Lake with the Raising of Pandemonium from Milton*, 1782.

6. Iain McCalman, "The Virtual Infernal: Philippe de Loutherbourg, William Beckford and the Spectacle of the Sublime", *Romanticism on the Net* 46 (May 2007): http://www.erudit.org/revue/ron/2007/v/n46/016129ar.html. [Jan. 1, 2011]. See also: Christopher Baugh, "Philippe de Loutherbourg: Technology-Driven Entertainment and Spectacle in the Late Eighteenth Century", *Huntington Library Quarterly* 70/2 (June 2007): 251–68.

7. Ephraim Hardcastle, *Wine and Walnuts* (London: Longman, Hurst, Rees, Orme, 1824), 297.

8. Only the "patent theatres" could put on spoken drama, so other venues resorted to mime accompanied by music. Michael R. Booth, *Victorian Spectacular Theatre, 1850–1910* (London: Routledge & Kegan Paul, 1981), 60.

9. Quoted by Booth, *Victorian Spectacular Theatre*, 62.

10. Only the overture would have been available at this date, written as a concert work in 1826, since Mendelssohn did not write the rest of his incidental music for the play until 1842.

11. Booth, *Victorian Spectacular Theatre*, 97.

12. Countless texts on early cinema, film, and music refer to the Lumière presentation on 28 December 1895 in Paris being accompanied by a pianist, although the evidence for this is, at best, debatable. Certainly the "pianist-composer" Émile Maraval accompanied later screenings, but it seems unlikely that he was present on this occasion. See Thierry Lecointe, "La sonorisation des séances Lumière en 1896 et 1897", *1895. Mille huit cent quatre-vingt-quinze* 52, 2007, available online at: http://1895.revues.org/1022 [accessed 3 August 2012]. The report of harmonium accompaniment at the London Lumière shows is quoted in Roger Manvell and John Huntley, *The Technique of Film Music* (London: Focal Press, 1957), 211, and seems to have originated with Hepworth's memoir, *Came the Dawn: Memories of a Film Pioneer* (London: Phoenix House, 1951).

13. Manvell and Huntley, *Technique of Film Music*, 17. Strictly speaking, this does not confirm that the music *accompanied* the films, but we might wonder what its relationship was if not to accompany them?

14. *Era*, 18 April 1896, 16; quoted in John Barnes, *The Beginnings of the Cinema in England, 1894–1901*, Vol. 1: *1894–1896* (Exeter: University of Exeter Press, 1998), 134, 136.

15. *Strand Magazine*, Aug. 1896; quoted Barnes, *Beginnings of Cinema*, Vol. 1, 130.

16. Canterbury report, *Era*, 6 June 1896, 16.

17. Altman, "The Living Nickelodeon", 234.

18. "Private Tommy Atkins", with lyrics by Henry Hamilton and music by S. Potter, was published in 1893, possibly inspired by Rudyard Kipling's invocation of the typical solider in his 1892 ballad "Tommy". Although the 1896 film made no specific reference to "Tommy Atkins", when Paul remade it in 1898, he titled the new film *Tommy Atkins in the Park*.

19. The second shot is lost, but its contents are known from frame stills printed in Paul's catalogue.

20. I am grateful to David Robinson for first introducing me to this history and subsequently supplying detailed references from his collection.

21. Martin Meisel, *Realizations: Narrative, Pictorial, and Theatrical Arts in Nineteenth-Century England*, (Princeton: Princeton University Press, 1983).

22. As Stephen Horne does in his accompaniment to the film on the DVD *R. W. Paul: The Collected Films, 1895–1908* (London: British Film Institute, 2006).

23. Described in greater detail in my article, "The Anglo-Boer War in North London: A Micro-Study", in *Picture Perfect: Landscape, Place and Travel in British Cinema before 1930*, ed. Laraine Porter and Bryony Dixon (Exeter: University of Exeter Press, 2007), 82–91.

24. *Wood Green Weekly Herald*, 9 December 1899, 5.

25. Many of these were collected in Ira D. Sankey's *Sacred Songs and Solos* (1873), published after the American evangelical singer had first visited Britain, and which has remained a popular source of quasi-religious music.

26. For an overview of magic lantern lecture practice, see Richard Crangle, "'Next Slide Please': The Lantern Lecture in Britain, 1890–1910", in *Sounds of Early Cinema*, ed. Abel and Altman, 39–47.

27. A practice revived in the annual shows given by Jeremy Brooker, Stephen Horne, and the author at Birkbeck College, University of London, since 2006.

28. For details of the Polytechnic's practice, I am indebted to Jeremy Brooker's PhD research on the history of the Royal Polytechnic, "The Temple of Minerva: Magic and the Magic Lantern at the Royal Polytechnic Institution, 1837–1900", PhD diss., Birkbeck College, University of London, 2012.

29. Hepworth, *Came the Dawn*.

30. Hepworth, *Came the Dawn*, 31–2.

31. Martin Miller Marks, *Music and the Silent Film: Contexts and Case Studies, 1895–1924* (New York: Oxford University Press, 1997), 247.

32. A sequence of eighteen films shot by Henry Short for Paul in August to September 1896, and premiered on 22 October at the Alhambra. For details, see Barnes, *Beginnings of Cinema*, Vol. 1, 256–8.

33. *Daily Telegraph*, 23 Oct. 1896; *Morning Post*, 23 Oct. 1896. The latter comment refers to the profusion of terms being used for moving pictures, often mocked in the contemporary press.

34. Vladimir Stasov, writing to his brother after attending a screening with the composer Glazunov on 30 May 1896, printed in *Iskusstvo kino*, 1957, quoted in Jay Leyda, *Kino: A History of the Russian and Soviet Film* (London: Allen and Unwin, 1960), 18.

35. Reported by John Barnes in a photocopied addendum to Vol. 1 of his *Beginnings of Cinema in England*, with a reproduction of the original handbill from the Barnes Collection, 136a. See also *Era*, 12 Sept. 1896; 19 Sept. 1896.

36. The 1896 Promenade Concert handbill also advertises a new "piano resonator", with an endorsement by the famous Polish virtuoso Paderewski.

37. *Kinematograph and Lantern Weekly* (hereafter, *KLW*), 6 June 1907, 54. Covent Garden's performance history records that there were additional performances of *The Valkyrie* in 1908, outside the then-yearly *Ring* cycle.

38. *Simon the Cellarer* was advertised by Philipp Wolff in *The Era* on 21 Jan. 1899. Details in John Barnes, *The Beginnings of Cinema in England, 1894–1901*. Vol. 4: *1899* (Exeter: University of Exeter Press, 1996). 29–31, 307.

39. *Optical and Magic Lantern Journal*, 10/117 (Feb. 1899), 118. Cited in Barnes, *Beginnings of Cinema in England*, Vol. 4, 31.

40. Robert W. Paul, 1901 Catalogue, 10.

41. "Coster" is an abbreviation for costermonger, or street-seller of fruit and vegetables in the Victorian era. By the late nineteenth century, the "coster" was famous for his street cries and songs, and as a music hall character, notably performed by stars such as Albert Chevalier and Gus Elen. On costermongers, see Henry Mayhew, *London Labour and the London Poor (1851)*, ed. Victor Neuburg (London: Penguin, 1985), 12–14. See also Derek Scott, chapter 10 in this volume.

42. I am grateful to David Robinson for identifying these three songs and their authors. "'Arry on the Steamboat" (*c.*1895), with words by Harry Grattan and music by Albert Maurice, was sung by E. J. Lonnen (1860–1901), a performer in stage musicals, who seems to have done music hall work as well. "The Waif and the Wizard" was written in 1898 by Edward Kent, who also performed it, and was taken up by Mel B. Spurr (1852–1904), "pre-eminent society entertainer at the piano". "Ora Pro Nobis", music by M. Piccolomini with words by A. Horspool, was popular from the 1880s to the First World War. Copies of all three are in the British Library.

43. The Royal Strand Theatre, as it then was, had had a chequered history throughout the nineteenth century, being rebuilt a number of times, before a musical, *A Chinese Honeymoon*, settled in for a record run of 1075 performances, after which the theatre was demolished and its site used for the Aldwych underground station.

44. Only one of these parts is currently known to exist, but a detailed programme brochure illustrates the whole series.

45. Of these, only *The Waif and the Wizard* film survives, in part. For this fragment, see *R. W. Paul: The Collected Films* DVD.

46. See my detailed discussion of this film in "*The Magic Sword*: Genealogy of an English Trick Film", *Film History* 16/2 (April 2004): 163–71.

47. On the concept of "remediation", see Jay David Bolter and Richard Grusin, *Remediation: Understanding New Media* (Boston: MIT Press, 2000).

48. Other synchronization systems in use in Britain included the Filmophone, Replicaphone, the Simplex, and the Appollogramophone. See Rachael Low, *The History of the British Film, 1906–1914* (London: Allen and Unwin, 1949), 265–9.

49. Laurent Mannoni, "Phonoscènes", in *Encyclopaedia of Early Cinema*, ed. Richard Abel (Abingdon: Routledge, 2005), 518.

50. *KLW*, 16 May 1907, 10.

51. See the archive of the ABC *Collectors* series, available online at http://www.abc.net.au/tv/collectors/showandtell/archive/s2082210.htm [accessed 3 August 2012].

52. At the St James's Hall, Kingston, *KLW*, 1 April 1909, 1365.

53. Mr J. S. Bainton, who has had thirteen years experience in "kinematography" after previous "connection with lantern shows, etc.", quoted in *KLW*, 6 May 1909, 1556.

54. See Jon Burrows, chapter 6 in this volume.

55. *Bioscope*, 7 Mar. 1912, 663.

56. Information on the Islington Picture Palace from The London Project database, part of the London Screen Study Centre, based at Birkbeck College's Centre for Film and Media Research, available online at http://londonfilm.bbk.ac.uk/view/venue/?id=581 [accessed 3 August 2012].

57. W. Tyacke George, *Playing to Pictures: A Guide for Pianists and Conductors of Motion Picture Theatres* (London: Kinematograph Weekly, 1912). For a recent survey of this evolution, see Julie Hubbert, ed., *Celluloid Symphonies: Texts and Contexts in Film Music History* (Berkeley: University of California Press, 2011).

58. Bottomore, "An International Survey of Sound Effects in Early Cinema".

59. See, for instance, an advertisement by the Harper Electric Piano Company, *KLW*, 1 April 1909, 1366.

60. Robert Hope-Jones was an English organ builder who developed the "unit orchestra" electric organ in the 1890s, before emigrating to the United States in 1903, where he eventually joined the Wurlitzer company in 1910 and began to install organs in cinemas as well as churches from 1911 onwards. See, Q. David Bowers, *Nickelodeon Theatres and their Music* (New York: Vestal Press, 1986), 180. Although Low refers to "an outburst of organs, zithers and bells from about 1910", it is not clear how many of these expensive instruments were installed in British cinemas; and most would have been substantially later. Low, *The History of the British Film, 1906–1914*, 286.

61. Gillian Anderson, *Music for Silent Films, 1894–1929: A Guide* (Washington: Library of Congress, 1988), xxix.

62. Ambrosio's *The Last Days of Pompeii* was advertised on its premiere run at the West End Cinema in 1913 as being accompanied by "full orchestra, with specially arranged music". *Times*, 6 Oct. 1913.

63. Performances of the original compilation by J. Morton Hutcheson have been given by Stephen Horne and John Sweeney. See Toby Haggith, "Reconstructing the Musical Arrangement for *The Battle of the Somme* (1916)", *Film History* 14/1 (2002): 11–24.

64. M. M. Hansford, "Picturegraphs", *American Organist*, 6/24 (1923), 234; quoted in Anderson, *Music for Silent Films*, xxxvii. The author appears to have been a regular contributor to this journal, and was presumably American, as well as an organist.

65. In North London, a 1913 advertisement for the East Finchley Picturedrome announced "the special engagement of the 'Nella' Bijou Orchestra, conducted by Mrs Cecil Allen", *Finchley Press*, 3 Jan. 1913, 11; and later in the same year, the rival Finchley Rink Cinema advertised a film of Max Reinhardt's great stage success, *The Miracle*, as "with chorus", *Finchley Press*, 5 Dec. 1913, 11.

66. Vachel Lindsay, *The Art of the Moving Picture* (New York: Macmillan, 1915), 189.

67. Lawrence began what became *The Lost Girl* in 1913, and his account of the "Woodhouse" variety show "going over" to showing only films is likely to have been based on his own observation of the that period. D. H. Lawrence, *The Lost Girl* (1920) (New York: Penguin, 1995), 116.

6

The Art of *Not* "Playing to Pictures" in British Cinemas, 1906–1914

Jon Burrows

MOST COMMERCIAL EXHIBITIONS today of 35mm silent era film prints feature live musical accompaniment provided by a lone pianist. In a majority of such cases this music is improvised. The pianists don't typically use composed scores; they don't usually get any rehearsal time with a film—they have to carefully watch it as it is projected and extemporize accordingly. There are still occasional silent film presentations in the twenty-first century which feature orchestral accompaniment, presenting a specially composed score. This doesn't happen as a matter of course, however, because it takes months, even years sometimes, to either adapt an existing score for use with a particular surviving print, or to compose something original from scratch. And extensive rehearsal time is necessary to get things right; it is a very laborious and expensive process. A single improvisational pianist—and there are still a small number of sufficiently gifted individuals around who specialize in this kind of work—represents the logical and practical option for most present day silent film screenings.

If there is a single, dominant assumption about pre-First World War silent film music in Britain, it is that this situation also pertained when the very first cinemas were established in this country: "The important music of the period was that of the piano, and it was here that artistic intentions were most clearly expressed."[1] This constitutes Rachael Low's chief reflection on sound accompaniment in her 1949 study of the British film industry between 1906 and 1914, which is still the standard work on the subject. Her claim seems to have a credible basis in fact. Nearly all of the very earliest articles in the film industry trade press on the subject of what constitutes the best form of musical accompaniment for films identify the lone pianist as the model to adopt. More specifically, they argue that the ideal film music is that provided by pianists with a talent for paying careful attention to the films being accompanied and improvising in tandem with unfolding narrative action. So we find many arguments made along the following lines throughout 1909 and 1910—the years in which cinemas started to appear in Britain in very significant numbers:

> In order to keep strictly in harmony with the pictures, it is the master mind which must act or perform, and that directly, and not through the medium of others...hence the most satisfactory instrument under these conditions would be the piano...[T]he music should, as it were, synchronize with the pictures...Hence the one mind and the one instrument is the only perfect way out of the difficulty.[2]

> The essential points in a good picture-pianist are tact, ability to play with proper affinity to the picture, quickness of perception and unobtrusiveness.[3]

One discovers the most elaborate expressions of this view in a series of five articles on "The Art of Playing to the Pictures", written in early 1910 by Bert Vipond (the pseudonym of a Yorkshire cinema pianist called Brian Lawrence). Vipond tells us that "The art of playing to the pictures consists in providing music which gives harmonised expression to the scenes and passions displayed in them.... Therefore, it is the improviser and man with a memory for melody who will best fill the position."[4] Furthermore,

> He should never assert himself, never obtrude on the attention of the audience...To be able to improvise aptly and well is a necessary accomplishment for the picture pianist to have. A first class man can sit at the piano and improvise all through the performance, and no one in the house will know that he has done so....He has done his work well, and he has influenced the audience without their being aware of it.[5]

This describes exactly the same philosophy which the very best improvisational pianists try to abide by today. The emphasis on the passive unobtrusiveness of the music also echoes the dominant rule which film music composers have been expected to abide by for much of the sound era, so it seems as if the fundamental principles of matching music to image were grasped almost immediately, right at the point when cinema first emerged as a true mass medium.

This version of events also appears to be absolutely consistent with what Rick Altman sees as the dominant and most persistent trend in thinking about silent film music in the United States from the later years of the first decade of the 1900s. According to Altman, in his groundbreaking study of silent film accompaniment in the United States, the American film industry strove, through the medium of its trade press advice columns, to divest musicians of the relative prominence and autonomy they enjoyed when the very first cinemas or nickelodeons were opened in America, between 1905 and 1908, and to make them occupy instead a subordinate position in relation to the projected image, whereby they would "invisibly" support the goal of efficient storytelling. Altman notes that the earliest nickelodeon musicians had regularly upstaged narrative meaning by playing well-known compositions in their entirety, but he explains how they were subsequently pressurized throughout the 1910s to ignore traditional principles of musical logic and respond obediently and immediately to the dictates of narrative logic instead.[6]

In what follows, I am going to argue that this conception of film music did not win the day in British cinemas during the same period. It seems to me that the valorization of the lone improvisational pianist that we get from some commentators in late 1909 and early 1910 essentially represents a blip, the exception rather than the rule. The most compelling evidence available suggests, as I interpret it, that close musical synchronization with the image was never widely or consistently pursued as standard practice at any time within the first eight years of the permanent picture theatre. During the early 1910s, when this new form of entertainment firmly established itself as a prominent feature of the urban landscape, cinema managers practised a philosophy which defined the principles of good film music as practically identical to the traditional principles of concert music.

I have been led to this conclusion partly by looking closely at the cinema licensing records of the London County Council (LCC). These provide a lot of detailed and systematic empirical evidence about musical accompaniment practices in cinemas within the county of London—what we now call inner London—an area with a population of four and a half million people and 314 cinemas by the end of 1914. LCC records are particularly useful when it comes to documenting cinemas in existence from January 1910 onwards, which is when the first piece of national legislation concerned with cinema, the 1909 Cinematograph Act, came into law. This was an Act which determined that nobody could put on a public film show without getting a licence from the local authorities and then abiding by the terms of that licence.[7] The LCC records preserved at the London Metropolitan Archives provide important and unique information about every cinema in London that was granted a licence from 1910 onwards.

There is quite a lot of revealing information about exhibition practices at cinemas in London before 1910 which can be traced as well, though. Before the 1909 Cinematograph Act was passed, local councils like the LCC had relatively little power to control how film shows were conducted, which greatly concerned and frustrated them. Other than standard building regulations, the one legal mechanism which had some degree of potential applicability to the first cinemas was the 1751 Disorderly Houses Act, which ensured that places of entertainment in which performed music played a substantial part were regulated by local councils through the requirement that all such venues needed to secure a licence to present said music. Before 1910 the only way in which the LCC could try to make cinemas conform to the safety regulations it applied to other places of entertainment was to determine if music formed a substantial part of film shows and if they could thus be prosecuted for operating without a music licence. Between 1907 and 1909 the Metropolitan Police compiled observational reports on unlicensed film shows that featured some form of musical accompaniment in order to ascertain if they could be charged with conducting their business illegally. The LCC's solicitors then made an assessment as to whether a case could be made; the criterion they applied was that any music featured had to be directly relevant to the films, so that it could be said to materially enhance the presentation and thus constitute a substantial rather than a subsidiary part of the performance.

The significant thing to note here is that, despite the LCC's obsessive surveillance of the earliest cinemas, only a tiny handful of them were found to feature a type of music that gave any credible hope of making a successful prosecution—that is, they found precious little evidence that there was *any* meaningful relationship between sound and image in the overwhelming majority of the earliest cinemas. In February 1908 the LCC compiled a list of details about thirty-six unlicensed film shows as part of the paperwork it submitted to the Home Office in the hope of persuading the government to introduce cinematograph legislation.[8] Sixteen of these shows featured no form of musical accompaniment whatsoever. Fifteen supplied music via some form of mechanical device—gramophone players, automatic pianos, and barrel organs—and would thus be unable to provide tight synchronization with individual films. Of the remaining five which employed either a piano or an orchestra, three were venues which held film shows only one night a week. This leaves us with two full-time cinemas which had conventional pianos. LCC inspectors' reports tell us that at the first of these, the New Egyptian Hall, Piccadilly, "a piano was played at intervals, but the music bore no relation to the pictures shown".[9] The other cinema at 63 Whitechapel Road was a converted shop, which a subsequent police inspection found to be in possession of a piano, but no pianist; a notice was displayed which invited members of the audience to play instead if they wished.[10]

Between 1907 and 1909 the LCC could identify only three unlicensed cinemas in London which were felt to be vulnerable to prosecution on the basis that they featured music which formed a significant part of the entertainment; we can uncover a significant amount of further information about musical practices in these venues because the Council took all three of them to court. The first of the prosecutions was something of a red herring. In October 1908 the Camden Theatre was found guilty of staging a musical entertainment without the necessary licence. This was a legitimate theatre which had lost its licence to stage plays, and had temporarily switched to films instead. The music which accompanied the screenings was provided by an automatic piano and thus was not tightly synchronized to the content of the films, but the manager of the theatre had advertised the show on playbills as "a combination of the latest developments in animated pictures, combined with music and effects", and the prosecution successfully argued that this was an admission that the music was intended as a substantial part of the entertainment.[11] Other film shows featuring mechanical pianos were careful to avoid this mistake in future.

The second court case involved the Electric Theatre at Wilton Road, Victoria. The cinema employed a human pianist, but evidence presented at the hearing in July 1909 was deemed by the magistrate presiding to establish that "there was no co-relation between the pictures and the music…[. O]ne of the witnesses [testified] that the film depicting Morris Beff Co.'s Team of Horses on Show was shown to a set of lancers [i.e., square-dance music], and that The Next Door Neighbours Quarreling [*sic*] was accompanied by a set of quadrilles!"[12]

The third and final case, in September 1909, involved another human pianist at the King's Hall, Tooting, and did result in a successful prosecution. Although the manager of the cinema maintained that it was in fact "absolutely impossible to play music to suit all the pictures", one of the witnesses called by the prosecution revealed that during a show he had attended, the actuality film *Bleriot Flies Across the Channel* (Pathé, 1909) was accompanied by the pianist's rendition of "See the Conquering Hero Comes", from Handel's oratorio *Judas Maccabaeus*. The evidence was deemed sufficient to prove that the music had constituted a material "enhancement" of the screening.[13]

A census of film shows undertaken by the police on 15 December 1909 identified 112 full-time cinemas in London that were open for business on this day.[14] Of these, a mere sixteen were in possession of a music licence—twelve of these having been secured only the previous month. So just fourteen per cent of London cinemas had any legal right to synchronize music and image before 1910, and it would seem, putting aside the ingenuity of the LCC's solicitors, that none of the unlicensed shows made any sustained or meaningful attempt to break the law and carefully co-ordinate music and films.

When the Cinematograph Act passed into law in 1910, the film trade was greatly perturbed to find that the Act did not contain a single clause that made any reference to music; the level of frustration and anxiety on this front is evidenced by a cartoon published in *The Bioscope* in April 1910 (see Figure 6.1). This meant that

FIGURE 6.1 A trade paper cartoonist's response to the lack of any reference to music in the 1909 Cinematograph Act. *The Bioscope*, 14 April 1910, 55.

even having acquired a cinematograph licence, a show might still be vulnerable to prosecution if it provided suitable musical accompaniment. In an attempt to avoid confusion around this issue, the LCC passed a resolution in February 1910:

> That no action be taken for the present as regards the performance of music in conjunction with cinematograph exhibitions in premises which are not licensed for music but are licensed under the Cinematograph Act, 1909, *provided that the only instrument employed is a piano (mechanical or otherwise), and that the music is kept quite a subsidiary part of the entertainment.*[15] [emphasis added]

In practice, the LCC gave up on trying to prosecute any use of piano music that directly complemented the pictures—if the only instrument used was a piano, then cinemas were left in peace, irrespective of whether it was technically a subsidiary or meaningful part of the show. The LCC turned its attention instead to venues without a music licence that used more than one instrument. In October 1910, for example, the council stopped a show at the Kensington Picture Theatre from proceeding because it had been advertised as a special performance featuring a small orchestra.[16] The Putney Bridge Cinematograph Theatre was similarly given a stern warning about its future conduct in May 1911 when a rival cinema owner in the district reported that his competitor had been supplementing piano music with a violin.[17]

Despite the covert easing of restrictions around piano music, it would appear that many cinemas, whether through fear, or ingrained habit, or sheer indifference to the idea of complementary synchronization, continued to abjure any attempt at matching the music to the films. For example, the Electro Theatre De Luxe in Battersea installed an automatic piano for its opening in 1910 rather than hiring a musician,[18] and such devices continued to be vigorously promoted to the trade throughout 1910.[19] Even more surprisingly, the Cinema de Paris, which was located in the heart of the West End, off Leicester Square, accompanied its films with gramophone records when it opened in 1910. One journalist who visited it was greatly impressed to find that three private boxes were provided for fashionable patrons—a striking new development in early cinema architecture—but simultaneously bemused to hear a gramophone recording of Enrico Caruso singing "Canio's Lament" from Leoncavallo's opera *Pagliacci* being played alongside a Pathé film about cocoa plantations.[20]

I think it is these kinds of practices that commentators like Bert Vipond were responding to in promoting improvisational pianists as the ideal asset for every picture theatre. There was a degree of consensus among trade commentators that phonographs and automatic pianos were not suitable accoutrements for putting on the best possible show, so, momentarily, the lone pianist was perceived as a superior alternative. However, one finds a very different kind of advice being disseminated in the trade press from late 1911 onwards. Andrew Higson rightly points out in chapter 7 of this volume that there is a marked lack of consistency across these types of sources, but there were distinctive new trends in thinking that became especially fashionable, and were advanced with particular conviction, at specific chronological junctures. *Picture Theatre News* declared in December 1911 that "'Vamping' and 'improvising' should be sternly suppressed".[21] When the *Kinematograph and Lantern Weekly* established its first regular column on film music, "The Picture Pianist", in August 1912, it consistently expounded the same message that pianists shouldn't improvise in greater detail:

> Is there any reason why [in providing music] the picture should be considered exclusively and all other factors in the situation ignored?... I think there is only one way, and that is by playing attractive and melodious music, in fact, music that would be acceptable without the picture. I am quite aware that at times it is impossible to do this and suit the picture...[22]

> I will admit that the [extemporisation] method suits the picture. That is all I will admit, for I cannot see how such a method is likely to be satisfactory to the audience, and I think that every reader who gives the matter fair consideration will agree.... [I]t is bad policy to ignore the audience and adhere too slavishly to the picture. To employ the species of "extemporisation" under discussion means that we are not considering the audience. I will explain why. The most ardent devotees of this musical jugglery must admit that it necessitates the chopping to pieces of good compositions. If the public know and appreciate a composition they naturally wish to hear it in its entirety.... The man who tickles the ears of the public by presenting them with a bundle of scraps may sometimes earn a passing compliment for his "smart" way of introducing them, but from a musical point of view his performance will not bear criticism.[23]

This is obviously a complete refutation of the notion previously propounded that traditional concepts of musical unity had to be abandoned in order to bend and subordinate the accompaniment to the film. The key question is: was it accompanied by a corresponding shift in actual practice? In 1913 this column was renamed "Picture Theatre Music" (the removal of the piano from the column title being accompanied by its replacement in the illustrated logo by wind, string, and percussion instruments) and was henceforth written by William Tyacke George. George was the musical director at the King's Hall cinema in Shepherd's Bush, where he ran a small orchestra. In 1912 he wrote a short instruction manual on film music called *Playing to Pictures*, in which he argued that pianists who claimed to be able to offer improvised accompaniment were liars and "charlatans"; although the book makes allowances for the fact that there are cinemas where "the pianist is the only musician that can be afforded", much of the advice provided is predominantly intended for conductors of "small bands".[24] By September 1913 George was claiming in his weekly column that "At the present time there are so many miniature orchestras attached to picture theatres that it is the rule rather than the exception to advertise a band of some sort as an attraction."[25]

This is not at all what received wisdom leads us to expect at this chronological juncture. Accompaniment by orchestra is traditionally not thought to have been a ubiquitous practice until the 1920s. So, is there any truth in this claim? For London at least, the LCC's licensing records can tell us the answer. As explained earlier, following the introduction of the Cinematograph Act, if a cinema wanted to feature more elaborate musical accompaniment than a lone piano it still had to obtain a music licence. With a small handful of exceptions, music licences awarded to cinemas in London during this period had a restrictive covenant which permitted the venue to present *instrumental* music only in conjunction with the films rather than as separate live acts, as a result of extensive lobbying by the Entertainments Protection Association which didn't want cinemas to encroach on the terrain of music halls.[26] Therefore, the number of music licences awarded to cinemas effectively tells us the number of cinemas which employed some form of orchestra, for at least part of the year. At the start of 1912, ninety-seven (or forty-two per cent) of the 229 cinemas in London had been granted a music licence.[27] At the start of 1913 there were 271 full-time cinemas in London, and 135—that is fifty per cent—had music licences.[28] By the end of 1914 there were 314 cinemas open in London and 180, or fifty-seven per cent, of these had music licences.[29] So, George's extraordinary claim is actually true as far as the capital is concerned: there were as many cinemas using orchestras as venues solely reliant upon lone pianists by the end of 1912, and the former were in the majority by the middle of 1913.

What the trade called an "orchestra" is somewhat different to the conventional understanding of the term. It typically consisted of five to seven instruments made up of combinations such as the following:

- Electric Palace, Clapham: cello, three violins, bass, piano, organ[30]
- The Imperial, Highbury: violin, cello, organ, piano, drums[31]
- Pyke's Cinematograph Theatre, Piccadilly Circus: two violins, cello, bass, piano[32]
- Palladium Playhouse, Brixton: four violins, cello, bass, flute, clarinet, piano, organ, drums[33]
- "Golden Domes" Picture Theatre, Camberwell: piano, organ, cello, double bass, two violins, clarinet[34]

The trend stimulated some music publishers to offer sheet music which provided special arrangements for this hitherto unusual form of "miniature orchestra".[35] An indication of how necessary and desirable orchestral accompaniment to films was perceived to be can be found in the details of an appeal mounted in 1914 by the Apollo Picture Theatre in Stoke Newington against the LCC's decision not to award it a music licence (Stoke Newington Borough Council had successfully opposed its application on the basis that the volume of music provided by an orchestra would be audible during the services at a nearby church):

> It is now over two months since we opened the [cinema], and, I am sorry to state, it is not a success. The building is palatial, the furnishings are most luxurious, the pictures the finest to be had, but the one drawback to our success is that the piano which we use fails to fill the hall or even make an impression on the public. I mention this with the hope that you will see fit to allow us to play with just 3 or 4 string instruments, no band of the West End order, but just to accompany the pictures and enable us to please our patrons.... [I]t hurts very much when we get letters from would-be patrons, who praise our hall and its maginficence but tell us point blank that they will not give us their patronage, since we cannot give them any music, to enliven the dreariness of sitting through a programme of pictures.[36]

This widespread adoption of orchestral accompaniment comes much earlier than previous accounts suggest: before the predomination of feature films; before distributors began preparing and circulating specially compiled or original musical scores in any significant numbers; before the timetable for changing cinema programmes was arranged to allow musicians to get meaningful rehearsal time with a new release. A band of several musicians cannot improvise together in harmony in spontaneous response to the film projected before them. It therefore becomes vital to ask if these small orchestras somehow found another way of playing music that was tightly synchronized with narrative development. Most of the anecdotal evidence available suggests that usually they didn't even try to follow the action of the film. Musical selections were chosen which were felt to be complementary to the general subject of the picture but—it would seem—efforts at synchronization went no further. The *Kinematograph and Lantern Weekly*'s "Stroller" observed that "Much though an orchestra may be preferable to a pianoforte accompaniment, it has its shortcomings and is characterised by some irregularities...[which come] about chiefly through the conductor or leader following his music instead of, as a competent pianist does, watching the picture."[37] The complaint below from an unnamed British scriptwriter is a typical comment upon the standard practice:

In some of the cinemas having orchestras of four to seven pieces there is a tendency to play music that is absolutely not suited to the requirements of the pictures shown, and to arrange their musical programme as a sort of counter-attraction. This is particularly noticeable when, for instance, the orchestra starts in some battle scene with a piece like "Light Cavalry Overture," and keeps right on playing it through the subsequent action, even though it runs through dainty love scenes, and ends abruptly in the scene where the heroine's mother dies. If the piece is popular and well played, part of the audience will appreciate it—perhaps in a part of the picture where the interest should be most intense.[38]

Some orchestral musicians responded bullishly to criticisms like this, defending their approach on the grounds that it made both musical and commercial sense. For example, a Miss M. Taylor wrote the following letter to *The Cinema*'s music columnist:

I am a member of a ladies' orchestra employed in a leading picture theatre. We show excellent pictures, and play the best of music. Moreover, we play it just as it is written—just as the composer intended it should be played, so far as lies in our power. I do not believe in cutting or slashing good music just because some parts of it do not happen to be in keeping with certain scenes on the screen. Of course, we try in a general way to choose music which will harmonise with the picture, but if the finale of an overture comes in the middle of a picture, we play it there. Our manager is making a feature of his orchestra, and the patrons of the theatre come to hear the music as well as to see the pictures. In fact, I know the orchestra is sometimes more appreciated than the pictures.[39]

Echoing the sentiments of the proprietors of the Apollo Picture Theatre, Stoke Newington, quoted above, A. J. Roberts, the musical director of the orchestra at the Hampstead Picture Playhouse, went so far as to claim that music was now "The Main Attraction" and that the provision of good concert music would insure cinemas against an inevitable decline in the appeal of moving pictures:

I deny at once that the picture is as indispensable to the music as the music is to the picture.... Pictures may come and pictures may go, but music goes on for ever, and wise is the management who builds its house upon the proven rock of public evidence, and not upon the shifting sands of a public craze.[40]

Did audiences really find this form of accompaniment appealing? This is a question one can never answer satisfactorily, but there are interesting accounts of how some patrons responded. The following passage is an extract from an article documenting the author's experience at a "first-class cinema in one of our largest cities", which was showing a film adapted from the play *Don Cesar de Bazan*, which was also the inspiration for a nineteenth-century William Wallace opera called *Maritana*. The orchestra at the cinema thought it appropriate to play the music from *Maritana*:

> The story followed the same lines as you find in the *libretto* of the opera: every opening was offered to the musicians therefore. To prepare himself for his task the conductor—an Englishman with a German *nom-de-baton*—had furnished his colleagues with somebody or other's *selections* from Wallace's setting; and when the picture commenced the copy was played religiously through to the end and then *da capo*. The result was as humorous as it was hideous. In the scene where the happy gitana is seen telling the fortunes of the people in the street, the little band thundered forth "Let me like a soldier fall"—a bit anomalous, to say the least of it. "Alas! those chimes" made a sort of humanising synchronisation with the duel episode, and the festive *mise en scene* of the ball was attended by the strains of "There is a flower that bloometh." The roof of every kinema covers a multitude of solecisms such as these.... [Yet] my clever companions seemed satisfied, and the morning paper next day referred to the sympathetic musical treatment this particular film received. A Maritana play with Maritana music! *Que voulez-vous?*... The significant fact remains that a thousand people sat and actually listened and enjoyed the *melange*. If they had been stupidly apathetic there might be some sort of hope for them even yet, but they were not.[41]

Clearly, the development of silent film accompaniment in the 1900s and early 1910s was not predominantly guided by concerns to ensure careful synchronization and to enhance the explication of narrative content. The accuracy of the account I have provided here is confirmed by a short historical overview provided in a 1914 article by "Musicus", the editor of *The Cinema*'s regular music page, which effectively writes my summation for me:

> [T]he present trend in the majority of cases seems to be toward straight "concert music" regardless of its fitness for the show—i.e. the picture.... When music was first introduced into the picture theatre any old thing would do—a mechanical instrument playing popular junk or a strong-arm piano player likewise playing popular songs. Then the popular demand for more suitable picture music made itself felt, and pianists began "working up" their pictures; rather crudely in some instances, still a great step forward. The popular taste now

demands that the musical accompaniment shall advance as well as the theatre and the pictures shown therein. Hence the increasing numbers of orchestras and pipe-organs. Having got them, the managers (and musicians also) naturally want the public to know it, so they are giving the aforesaid public the best music in their repertoire—concert music; nobody seems to care whether it is consistent with the pictured scenes any more than they cared seven or eight years ago. Here and there a few voices are crying out in the wilderness in protest of the standard overture that ends in the middle of a pathetic scene.... Some leaders here and there adapt their music to their pictures, and choose numbers in keeping with the show. There are more who do not. But for all that, it is a great stride forward.[42]

This outlines exactly the same three-phased pattern of trends that I have identified from surviving empirical sources: a reliance upon automatic machines in the very earliest years of the permanent picture theatre, followed by a growing tendency to employ human pianists, which was itself quickly succeeded by a fashion for installing miniature orchestras playing "concert music" that was only loosely matched to film content. The improvisational pianist who is clearly best equipped to meet the ideal of invisible and subservient accompaniment achieves primacy for only a fleeting moment within this narrative. Despite the note of exasperation from "Musicus" as to the frequent clumsiness of standard musical practices on the eve of the First World War, he nonetheless concludes that the mini-orchestras represent "a great stride forward". Irrespective of the frequently surreal and ridiculous consequences, this was presumably still perceived to be an advantageous development because it represented a meaningful elevation in the cultural status and social address of the cinema theatre.

NOTES

1. Rachael Low, *The History of the British Film, 1906–1914* (London: Allen and Unwin, 1949), 268.

2. J. Hay Taylor, "Music and the Pictures", *Kinematograph and Lantern Weekly* (hereafter, *KLW*), 14 Oct. 1909, 1123.

3. "A Pioneer Picture Pianist", *KLW*, 28 Oct. 1909, 1260.

4. Bert Vipond, "The Art of Playing to Pictures No. I—Introduction", *KLW*, 24 Feb. 1910, 885.

5. Bert Vipond, "The Art of Playing to Pictures No. IV—Hints to Picture Pianists", *KLW*, 17 Mar. 1910, 1053.

6. Rick Altman, *Silent Film Sound* (New York: Columbia University Press, 2004), 231–46.

7. For a detailed account of the introduction of the 1909 Cinematograph Act, see Jon Burrows, "Penny Pleasures: Film Exhibition in London during the Nickelodeon Era, 1906–1914", *Film History* 16/1 (2004), 66–71, 82–86.

8. "Deputation on Cinematograph Exhibitions 28 February 1908", National Archives (NA)/ HO 45/10376/161425.

9. Minutes of meeting of Theatres and Music Halls Committee, 3 March 1909, LCC/ MIN/10730.

10. Notes by PC George Jordan, "H" Division, Arbour Square Station, 27 March 1909, NA/ MEPO 2/9172, File 590446/5.

11. "County of London Sessions", *The Times*, 28 Oct. 1908, 4.

12. "Motion Pictures v. Music Halls", *KLW*, 15 July 1909, 447.

13. LCC/MIN/10837; *Morning Advertiser*, 11 Sept. 1909.

14. General papers of Theatres and Music Halls Committee, 15 Dec. 1909, LCC/MIN/10933.

15. Minutes of meeting of Theatres and Music Halls Committee, 23 Feb. 1910, LCC/ MIN/10731.

16. General papers of Theatres and Music Halls Committee, 19 Oct. 1910, LCC/MIN/10941.

17. General papers of Theatres and Music Halls Committee, 24 June 1911, LCC/MIN/10949; minutes of the Theatres and Music Halls Committee, 1911, LCC/MIN/10732.

18. *Picture Theatre News*, 26 Feb. 1910, 16.

19. See, for example, *KLW*, 6 Jan. 1910, 505; 27 Oct. 1910. Rick Altman has documented the fact that dual-roll automatic pianos became available in the mid-1910s, and that these permitted rapid switches between musical selections, "thus facilitating appropriate changes of musical atmosphere" (Altman, *Silent Film Sound*, 325–6). The automatic pianos that I refer to in this essay did *not* possess this facility.

20. *KLW*, 14 April 1910, 1265.

21. "Music in Picture Theatres", *Picture Theatre News*, 27 Dec. 1911, 4.

22. Henry A. Watson, "The Picture Pianist", *KLW*, 29 Aug. 1912, 1245.

23. *KLW*, 7 Nov. 1912, 224.

24. W. Tyacke George, *Playing to Pictures: A Guide for Pianists and Conductors of Motion Picture Theatres* (London: Kinematograph Weekly, 1912), 29, 49.

25. W. Tyacke George, "Picture Theatre Music", *KLW*, 4 Sept. 1913, 1973. It should be acknowledged here that there was one trade paper musical advice column in this period—*The Bioscope*'s anonymously authored "The Picture Pianist"—which did steadfastly continue to restrict itself to discussion of piano accompaniment and to strongly advocate improvisation; see, for example, "The Picture Pianist", *Bioscope*, 10 Oct. 1912, 125. However, the column was pointedly criticized by some readers for ignoring the increasing use of small orchestras (e.g., 22 May 1913, 557), and although it did belatedly acknowledge their increasing popularity and prominence as a distinct attraction (e.g., 15 Jan. 1914, 240), it is perhaps indicative of how "out of touch" this particular writer was perceived to be that he/she was permanently dropped in April 1914.

26. Minutes of meeting of Theatres and Music Halls Committee, 10 Nov. 1911, LCC/ MIN/10732. This covenant was strictly enforced: for example, in February 1912 the Queen's Hall Picture Theatre in Peckham was threatened with the withdrawal of its music licence when it was found to be booking comedians and singers as well as films—see general papers of Theatres and Music Halls Committee, 28 Feb. 1912, LCC/MIN/10958. In May 1913 the proprietor of the King's Hall cinema in Tooting, another music licence holder, was refused permission to employ four vocalists hidden from view to accompany an unspecified film adaptation of the Faust legend—see general papers of Theatres and Music Halls Committee, 11 June 1913, LCC/MIN/10970, and minutes of the Theatres and Music Halls Committee, LCC/MIN/10734.

27. Figures derived from LCC/MIN/10732 and LCC MIN/10733.

28. LCC/MIN/10733, LCC/MIN/10734.

29. General papers of Theatres and Music Halls Committee, 23 Dec. 1914, LCC/MIN/10983.

30. "Among the Cinemas", *Cinema News and Property Gazette* (hereafter, *Cinema*), 8 Jan. 1913, 7.

31. *Cinema*, 5 Feb. 1913, 13.

32. *Cinema*, 26 Feb. 1913, 27.

33. *Cinema*, 9 April 1913, 13.

34. *Cinema*, 16 April 1914, 21.

35. *Cinema*, 14 May 1913, 31; 11 June 1914, 61.

36. General Papers of Theatres and Music Halls Committee, 4 Nov. 1914, LCC/MIN/10982.

37. *KLW*, 26 March 1914, 5.

38. "Music That Fits", *Cinema*, 21 May 1914, 60.

39. "Concert Music", *Cinema*, 19 Mar. 1914, 49.

40. "The Main Attraction", *Cinema*, 2 April 1914, 54. It was a not uncommon view in the 1910s that the appeal of moving images was just a passing craze that couldn't last—see Jon Burrows and Richard Brown, "Financing the Edwardian Cinema Boom, 1909–1914", *Historical Journal of Film, Radio and Television* 30/1 (March 2010): 2–4.

41. B. V., "The Orchestra and the Kinema", *KLW*, 29 Oct. 1914, 25.

42. "Musicus", "A Step Forward", *Cinema*, 12 Feb. 1914, 57.

7

"The efforts of the wretched pianist:"

Learning to Play to the Pictures in Britain, 1911–1913

Andrew Higson

IN 1912 WILLIAM TYACKE GEORGE, British picture pianist, musical director, and author of the manual *Playing to Pictures*, enthusiastically proclaimed,

> Science, brains and wealth have all contributed to make moving pictures the greatest marvel and blessing of the age!... From every point of view, whether artistic, scientific, or humanizing, nothing can compete, or hope to compete with pictures in motion.... One thing only can put the absolute finish on it, lift it altogether out of the sea of mechanical ingenuity and give it just that one touch to make it human—*beautiful music*![1]

Another experienced picture player, who was given a column in the leading British trade paper *Kinematograph and Lantern Weekly* in 1912, Henry A. Watson, less rhapsodically explained that

> the picture thrown silently through the darkened auditorium would give a very bald result without the assistance of some auxiliary effect. The auxiliary effect in universal use in the present day is music.... As the characters in a picture are not able to speak, it is the business of the pianist to provide a musical atmosphere to surround them and make them live.[2]

A year later, in 1913, another UK commentator, Colin Bennett, noted in his *A Handbook of Kinematography*, that:

> There is a certain part of the kinematograph entertainment which the average member of the audience takes no very particular notice of, and yet if it were absent he would notice it fast enough. This is the music which sometimes of better, sometimes of less quality, invariably accompanies the progress of the picture on the screen.[3]

Comments such as these suggest that musical accompaniment was a standard part of the UK cinema-going experience by 1913, but that its quality was uneven. The evidence of the trade press and various related publications of the period is that, as in the United States,[4] there was a developing concern in Britain about this unevenness of musical accompaniment in the period, and an effort to improve the quality of accompaniment in the context of the industry's bid for respectability. A letter to *Kinematograph and Lantern Weekly* in 1912, for instance, which initiated a lively debate over the following weeks, had the writer wondering

> whether any attention is paid by the proprietors or managers of some of our picturedromes to the musical part of their show.... In some of them, the music is abominable in every way; in fact, I often think the player or players have been "picked up" somewhere just to knock a bit of music (?) up to fill in.[5]

THE NATURE OF EVIDENCE: FICTION AND FACT

In looking at some of these debates and developments in Britain in the early 1910s, this chapter is very much a companion piece to Jon Burrows's preceding chapter in this volume and to the work of Rick Altman, Tim Anderson, and others concerning parallel debates and developments in the United States.[6] Burrows presents a wonderfully well-researched argument about musical accompaniment for films in London picture houses, challenging some of the received wisdom about such issues, demonstrating that trade papers and their writers had their own agendas and revealing the remarkable value of a range of other evidence from the period. Trade papers and "how to" manuals can provide important insights into contemporary debates about musical accompaniment, but Burrows uses other evidence to demonstrate the sort of musical experience film audiences in this period might actually have been accustomed to. His key sources are the cinema licensing records and related legal evidence in the archives of the London County Council.

Other historians, including Altman, have shown the value of cartoons, photographs, advertisements, letters, evidence of film music accompaniment cue-sheets and suggestions, as well as specially composed or compiled scores, journalistic accounts in the non-specialist press, reminiscence, and so on. Such work is part of the turn away from textual analysis as the defining characteristic of film studies towards a historicist emphasis on the empirical evidence of both production and reception.

Another source available to historians prepared to work in this way is contemporary fiction. That is to say, fiction can in certain cases provide factual evidence, as I want to suggest by looking at a short story published in *The Strand* magazine in 1912, "A Sense of Touch," written by Ernest Dunlop Swinton, under the pseudonym of "Ole Luk-Oie".[7] The story provides a very detailed albeit fictional account of a visit to a small cinema in London, ostensibly by a middle-class man unaccustomed to spending much time in such places: "The hall was very much the usual sort of place…long and narrow, with a floor sloping down from the back. In front of the screen…was an enclosed pit containing some artificial palms and tin hydrangeas, a piano and a harmonium."[8] The fictional visitor goes on to describe the experience of watching films in this space, commenting with a certain irony on the music being played and the quality of the musicianship. He notes, for instance, that "at the critical moment of a touching scene" in one film, the sentimental drama is accompanied by "the sound of soft, sad music, all on the black notes." In a war film, the cavalry is, as it were, stirred into action by "a trumpet-call on the harmonium, and away dashed the relief force of mounted men." At the climax of the film, as the hero completes his task, the music moves to "'They all love Jack,' an imitation of bagpipes on the harmonium, and 'Rule Britannia' from the combined orchestra."[9] A third film introduces

> a bit of the supernatural. I'm afraid I didn't notice what took place, so I'll spare you a description. I was entirely engrossed with the efforts of the wretched pianist to play *tremolo* for ten solid minutes. I think it was the ghost melody from "The Corsican Brothers" that she was struggling with, and the harmonium did not help one bit. The execution got slower and slower and more *staccato* as her hands grew tired, and at the end I am sure she was jabbing the notes with her aching fingers straight and stiff. Poor girl! What a life![10]

The story comes to a climax when some giant but extremely realistic insects on the screen burst "out of the picture, scrambling over the little well where the orchestra had previously been playing. I heard horny feet scratching over the polished top of the piano, and a great discordant *arpeggio* struck on the bass notes." All is brought to a conclusion when the storyteller reveals he had fallen asleep and been dreaming:

"One of the attendants was shaking me by the arm; the lights were up; the piano and harmonium were having the usual ding-dong race.... I rubbed my eyes."[11]

This is not journalistic reportage but fiction—yet it is still able to tell us a great deal about musical accompaniment, musicianship, instrumentation, and other sound effects for silent films in Britain in the early 1910s. Or at least, it is able to tell us about a certain middle-class perception of musical accompaniment in the cinema in this period, for both the diegetic storyteller and the author of the short story were solid, respectable middle-class commentators, with moving pictures presented in the story as a popular entertainment not really suitable for a discerning middle-class sensibility.[12]

In a sort of mockery of refined musical performance, "the wretched pianist" in the story is a mere girl, the "combined orchestra" seems to consist of just a piano and a harmonium, situated in a pit beneath the screen, and the music is thoroughly conventional—and therefore, for our storyteller, predictable—while the performance of the music fails to reach what the storyteller assumes to be acceptable professional standards.

The overly conventional predictability of the music is evident in the choice of tunes to be played—including the ghost theme from the well-known stage play *The Corsican Brothers* adapted by Dion Boucicault, "They All Love Jack", a popular song of the late nineteenth century, and the patriotic song "Rule Britannia" among the fare. The predictability of the music is evident too in its arrangement, with the harmonium imitating a trumpet and bagpipes at crucial moments. This sense of crass predictability is matched by what is presented as the impoverished manner and quality of the playing—the black notes for a sad, sentimental scene; ten solid minutes of tremolo for an exciting scene with tension, eventually played staccato, with straight, stiff fingers; the struggle the pianist has with *The Corsican Brothers*; and the "ding-dong race" between the piano and the harmonium at the end of the show.

THE DEBATE ABOUT PICTURE MUSIC, 1911–1913:
ESTABLISHING PROFESSIONAL STANDARDS

There is much here that is familiar from other evidence of the period—the arrangement of piano and harmonium in a pit beneath the screen,[13] the choice of music, the girl who tries hard but is not a brilliant musician—suggesting that we can treat the story as a reasonably insightful description of a certain experience of cinema-going in the period. The story is of course a piece of entertaining writing, at the heart of which is a blurring of reality and fantasy. The details of what is effectively middle-class concern about the nature and quality of the experience are incidental. But in the early 1910s, when the story was published, there was a far wider debate about the role that music might play in the cinema-going experience in Britain, in which this same concern was played out in a variety of forms.

That debate suggests that the early 1910s are a transitional period, with many involved in the film business working to professionalize musical accompaniment, and to formalize or codify what might count as good picture playing, in the context of more general efforts to standardize the experience of cinema-going. As Burrows's chapter also suggests, this was a period of change, uncertainty, and exploration. The evidence of the debate in the letters pages of the trade press, columns about the emerging profession of the cinema musician, "how to" manuals, and so on, is that considerable efforts were being made to establish a proper or appropriate manner of musical accompaniment for films, something that might rise above the efforts of the wretched pianist in the short story.

In their accounts of parallel developments in the United States, both Anderson and Altman note the ongoing shift from an attractionist aesthetic to one of narrative integration, from a period in which sound accompaniment to films took many divergent and inconsistent forms to one in which a certain type of film music became standard.[14] The new standard was about the narrational function of music in relation to film, rather than about a type of spectacular or sensationalist music or sound effects that might distract from the development of the storyline in the increasingly complex fiction films of the period.

While there are certain important differences between the United States and Britain in the way things unfolded, there is a great deal that is familiar too, not least in the role that the trade papers and professional manuals of the period adopted in relation to this process of standardization. Part of that role was about the perceived need to regulate audience behaviour in picture houses, to discourage boisterous, interactive audience behaviour, to encourage absorption in the development of characters and storylines, and to attract a particular type of middle-class audience. If this institutional or industrial goal was beginning to emerge in Britain in the period 1911–13, however, it was not yet as explicit as the equivalent debate in the United States; it was certainly some way from being achieved in the years before the First World War.

Trade papers in the United States and Britain initiated regular columns about musical accompaniment for films around the same period, although they seem unaware of each other's contributions. Manuals advising on music and other aspects of the exhibition experience also began to appear on both sides of the Atlantic around this time. The discourse that emerged was in both countries shaped by musicians, arrangers, conductors, and others commenting in these columns and manuals on what they saw as worst and best practice; and by film producers, film renters, and music publishers, who began to issue specially composed scores and compilations of musical suggestions deemed to be appropriate for film accompaniment, and to which the trade paper columnists frequently draw attention.

In late 1911, for instance, a series of letters appeared in one of the key British trade papers, *The Bioscope*, which then ran a fully-fledged article on "The Music of the Picture Theatre".[15] Early in 1912 another debate took place on the letters pages of the rival *Kinematograph and Lantern Weekly* (*KLW*). One of the letters in the latter publication was from W. Tyacke George, who had for some time worked as a cinema pianist and a conductor of a cinema orchestra.[16] George had in fact just written a sixty-four-page book, *Playing to Pictures*, which was brought out by the publishers of *KLW* around the same time, probably in March 1912.[17]

George's book was promoted as "a guide for Musicians and Conductors of Motion Picture Theatres, full of valuable, original advice for Pianists, Managers, and Proprietors".[18] Alongside sections on Music Arrangements, Classifying the Picture, The Art of Improvising, and How to Produce Effects were other sections on Music Licences and How to Obtain Them, Musicians' Salaries, How to Choose a Piano, and Musical Copyright, as well as lists of Music Publishers, Specially Written Music, Appropriate Music and Popular Songs.

A few months later, at the end of August 1912, *KLW* established a regular fortnightly column in its pages, entitled "The Picture Pianist".[19] This was written by Henry A. Watson, another contributor to the debate in the letters pages back at the start of the year and also an experienced picture house musician.[20] Watson's column presented what he regarded as the golden rules of musical accompaniment, and especially piano accompaniment for films: "it is my intention…to indicate what…the business of the picture pianist is, and what are the chief factors he should consider when playing to pictures."[21] Alongside this column another new one eventually appeared in *KLW*, called "Music Reviews and Notes", again written by George, which set out to review sheet music, and to recommend particular collections and pieces of music for the piano accompanist.[22]

PLAYING *TO* THE PICTURES

Contributors to the UK debate about musical accompaniment for moving pictures in the early 1910s were unable to agree on the most appropriate approach to musical accompaniment, with some arguing that good music in itself was sufficient, and others calling for music suited to the images on the screen. Even so, as in the United States, one strong line of argument in the trade press was that music should support rather than distract from what appeared on the screen. According to one writer, even if historically music had been introduced in the picture theatre "to liven things up a bit", it soon became good practice to play music "that was more or less appropriate to the picture".[23] The music selected, it was argued, "should never be so conspicuous as to take away from the interest of the picture".[24] Another picture pianist complained about accompaniment that included "selections that had no earthly relations to the pictures on the screen".[25] Yet another was critical of those musicians who seemed to believe that they were "the only person of importance in [the] show". She went on: "the music for pictures should be an accompaniment, sufficiently interesting to show patrons what the film is about, but not predominant. No one goes to hear pianoforte recitals at picture theatres. People cannot enjoy the pictures if the music is overpowering."[26]

A 1913 UK manual, meanwhile, "strongly advised that picture pianists bear in mind that their function is to follow, and not lead, the pictorial side of the entertainment."[27] "What is needed," argued another contributor to the debate, "is a thorough understanding between musician and picture, and the sooner it comes the better for the general public."[28] Henry Watson, in the first of his *KLW* columns about the work of the picture pianist, added a further dimension: "the picture," he agreed, "should be the principal consideration," but the pianist should also "arrange his music with the idea of suiting the picture, and pleasing the audience at one and the same time... by playing attractive and melodious music, in fact, music that would be perfectly acceptable without the picture."[29] A good film, on the other hand, could be "utterly ruined... by... inapt and inappropriate choice of music"[30]—and the letters pages of *KLW* are full of examples of such "incongruous music".[31] Another frequently noted fault was to allow the music to end before the close of the picture: "every pianist has a golden opportunity of proving himself an artiste by bringing picture and music to a simultaneous conclusion in a suitable and impressive climax."[32]

Such comments suggest that a sense of good practice was emerging in Britain, in theory, at least, in which the appropriateness of the music and its synchonicity with the pictures played a large role. This was frequently explained in terms of a distinction between playing *to* the pictures and playing *at* the pictures: "There can be but one satisfactory method of picture accompaniment, viz., that all music shall be so chosen or improvisation used so that it shall seem to be 'part of' or 'wedded to' the story the picture portrays, otherwise you play 'at' the picture rather than 'to' it."[33] The wretched pianist in the short story does of course endeavour to play *to* the pictures on the screen, to accompany them rather than compete with them, and to choose material appropriate to what is on the screen. Yet from the tenor of the debate in the British trade press and in manuals about film accompaniment in the period 1911–13, and from the other evidence that Jon Burrows presents, this practice was not always possible or even accepted by contemporary musicians or exhibitors. Judging by the research of Stephen Bottomore, the worst offenders in terms of playing *at* the pictures were perhaps the often extremely boisterous sound effects operators in some cinemas, who had fun making a lot of noise rather than producing something congruent with what was on the screen.[34]

THE QUESTION OF TECHNIQUE: TO IMPROVISE OR NOT?

Clearly a good number of cinemas in this period relied upon the efforts of a lone pianist. To be a "really good picture pianist," it was argued, one "must possess brilliant technique, an excellent memory, be able to play *without music*, to extemporise, and, above all, must be gifted with imagination and romance, and be well educated."[35] Or, as another commentator put it, the really good accompanist "would be able to improvise, read anything and everything from sight,... possess a wide and far-reaching memory and a sense of humour, and a rapid grasp of the situation."[36]

There were however competing views about the relative value of the ability of a pianist to improvise versus the capacity to draw on a library of sheet music or memory for appropriate tunes. Even where established tunes were recommended, there was a debate about the extent to which such music should be specially arranged for film accompaniment. One commentator, for instance, asked "how far should picture music take the form of actual tunes, and how far should it be considered as a mere following of the pictures and nothing more?" Answering his own question, this commentator responded that "it is both far cleverer and far more effective to make use of good published music, chosen with care, and when necessary, varied just sufficiently to fall in with the incidents and motions of the scene portrayed on the projection screen."[37]

In a similar vein, George argued that a small orchestra of good musicians, playing from a repertoire of music, rather than a pianist improvising, was the way forward—to which end what was needed was extensive music libraries in all good picture houses. Watson was more forthright in his condemnation of those pianists that indulged in

> a mass of insipid extemporization, which in the majority of cases is nothing but tap-room vamping.... Many people claim that this so-called extemporization suits the picture better than published compositions. This is entirely a fallacy. It may appear to suit the picture, but in reality... for the bulk of the time it is a characterless unmeaning succession of sounds with neither melody nor harmony to make it endurable.[38]

THE CHOICE OF INSTRUMENTS

The tenor of the debates of 1911–13 suggests that the piano was the most widely used form of musical accompaniment in picture houses, but that other instruments and combinations of instruments were used too, as Burrows's research also demonstrates. According to one commentator, "the piano is the most common, and... the most convenient, but an adroit player of the American organ [the harmonium] can produce sounds and effects of which a piano is incapable."[39] There were also evidently in late 1911 some very good "small orchestral combinations of four or five instruments" whose musical director carefully prepared the music to be played in order that it was able to "*illustrate* the picture".[40] Meanwhile, "at some of the large theatres 'converted' to pictures, a full orchestra of twelve to fourteen instrumental-ists may be heard."[41] Here, however, at least in this writer's experience, it seemed to be accepted that the orchestra would, "as a rule, make no attempt, and wisely so, to play *to* the picture except travel subjects".[42]

Another writer argues that orchestras are as a result rarely suitable for cinemas because they so rarely attempt to play *to* the pictures on the screen—although "a selec-tion of music by the orchestra between spools is very acceptable to an audience as a rule".[43] The perceived problem with orchestras is that

> it is impossible for more than one player to extemporise simultaneously. On the other hand, if set pieces are performed, however carefully selected, they will not absolutely synchronise with the changing sentiments of the actors por-trayed on the screen.... The only other alternative to set pieces would be to have special music composed for each film![44]

The fact that this latter sentence ends with an exclamation mark demonstrates just how unusual this was in 1912. The more general concern about the difficulties faced by orchestras was not however universally accepted, since for some "an orchestra can undoubtedly add to the charm of what is taking place on the magic screen".[45] On the other hand, as another commentator noted,

> only the largest halls can possibly bear the expense of even a small competent orchestra (as any but first rate are worse than useless), five being ample and more easily managed in quick changes than a larger number. Then, with a large classical and modern library, [and] careful study at the picture rehearsals, a result satisfactory to the average audience is attained.[46]

Alongside the piano and the small orchestra, the American organ or harmo-nium also commonly featured, though with all manner of brand names such as the Cinfonium and the Cinechordeon, effects machines such as the Allefex, and other more crude means of creating sound effects. It is not unusual to find commentators arguing that "the piano and the harmonium played together are the best substitute for an orchestra extant",[47] which of course is the combination described in the short story in the *Strand Magazine*.

THE PROBLEMS OF ECONOMICS

Evidently musical accompaniment varied enormously across different venues in Britain, depending on the quality of the musicians and the decisions of cinema managers or proprietors about hiring and salaries, a situation also explored in other chapters in this volume by Griffiths and Davison. On the one hand, this was a matter of how much cinema managers could afford to pay their musicians; on the other hand, many argued at the time that managers were being short-sighted by not investing more in the music, since it had such a profound effect on the cinema-going experience and therefore on the ability of cinemas to build and maintain their audiences. As W. Tyacke George put it, in an article entitled "The Neglect of Music in Picture Theatres", "money is poured like water in every other department needed to produce the film, but when the question of music is raised, the answer is 'Oh, anything will do!'".[48] There was evidently a concern to persuade managers to invest more in musical accompaniment, in the quality of the players, in collections of sheet music and in the piano and other equipment, if used, the argument being that such investment will reap benefits at the box office. As George commented, "with competition becoming keener daily, picture hall owners *will have to spend money on music* whether they like it or not!"[49]

With "picture pianists", it was suggested, "the division of first class, second class, and other classes is pretty much one of salary. A manager who wants a good pianist must be prepared to pay at least a reasonable price for his services."[50] Too often, however, as is evident from Davison's chapter as well, "picture theatre music is treated with contempt," with

shocking salaries offered to musicians. No competent self-respecting musician would entertain a salary below that of the municipal dustman! The class of musician most frequently found in our beautiful picture palaces are not musicians—but only punters or fakers, they would never remain in a decent band for two minutes.[51]

For some commentators, such as the storyteller in the *Strand Magazine*, matters of salary and quality were intimately linked to gender. One picture pianist, for instance, rather pompously made it clear that, in his view, male pianists were superior to female pianists:

playing to pictures is a branch of the musical profession by itself, and if proprietors will only stop the short-sighted policy of engaging young women at 15s. a week to attempt work that should be done by trained men for at least twice that sum, they will reap the benefit of their enterprise.[52]

Three weeks later, *The Bioscope* published letters from two female pianists, challenging the misogyny of the original correspondent.[53]

Contemporary commentators noted other factors that affected the ability of musicians to provide particular types of accompaniment: "it is unfair to expect a good result from such an artist unless he is allowed to see the pictures beforehand, or is provided with…adequate synopses of their plots or stories."[54] Such a practice was clearly by no means standard. Another pianist complained that he was never given a "preliminary view of the pictures I had to play to"; with a continuous show and two different programmes each week, "I found I had, on the spot, to invent two completely new programmes of music every week."[55] British cinema historian Rachael Low records that many pianists of this period earned insufficient money to buy new music and were given insufficient time to learn new pieces or to arrange music for a film show.[56] A good and well-resourced musical director or pianist would, however, be able to view the film in advance and/or consult a good synopsis, make notes about "the various emotions displayed by the actors, and the changes in the scenes", select appropriate pieces of music, or portions of music from a library or the repertoire of the musicians, and then arrange them to fit the timing of the action on the screen.[57] Even then, "it is absolutely essential for the pianist to have one eye on the picture", while she or he "must be allowed considerable liberty with regard to [the] tempo and expression" of the pieces selected for playing, for it is "impossible at times to follow the composer's directions exactly".[58]

SELECTING APPROPRIATE MUSIC

What was emerging as good practice in Britain, and in a very similar way in the United States, was hardly new. As the authors of an American film music manual published in 1920 suggested, a good model could be found in the close "welding of action and music" and the use of leitmotifs in opera.[59] An article published in Britain in 1911 meanwhile proposed another model in "the music of the old melodramas": "the 'slow music', the 'hurry', etc., are just what is required for pictures. Such collections of themes assist the picture without interrupting the action by attracting too much attention to the music."[60] A 1913 UK manual also suggested that, alongside more finished or complete pieces of music, "motion pictures cannot be played without a proper repertoire of incidental music": "hurry music…for fights, Indian attacks, duels, sword fights, etc., sentimental music for death scenes, despair, sadness, meditation, and special music for military, comic, love, exotic, racing, and a hundred other scenes too numerous to mention."[61]

Yet more complete pieces of music were also to be recommended, with the same 1913 manual recommending that "the basis of the stock repertory [should] be culled from the minor and more melodious classics".[62] Another experienced pianist recommended building up "a large classical and modern library", with "'light modern' published music for comedy and Mendelssohn or Chopin excerpts for travel and educational films".[63]

Another argued that, taking into account the composition of the audience, "the light music of today" is able to "suit almost every class of picture", not least because it is "easily understood", makes "a direct appeal to the ear", and does not "require a mighty intellect to understand [its] significance".[64] In addition, it was suggested, "classical selections from the compositions of the old masters" should be used sparingly, certainly not for contemporary drama, although they might be used for "historical or legendary pictures, or pictures, the plots of which are culled from early classical literature". Music hall refrains, on the other hand, might be used "for all kinds of bustling comic pictures".[65]

An editorial piece in *KLW* early in 1912 commented that the poor quality of music at many venues was due not so much to the ability of the pianist as to "the fact that the stock of music placed at his disposal is of a most meagre description" because "managers are apt to look upon the acquisition of sheet music as an expensive and to their mind useless item".[66] In an effort to remedy this problem, an increasing amount of effort was put into recommending and indeed publishing appropriate sheet music, usually at this stage in a generic sense, rather than recommending particular pieces of music for particular films. In the first of George's regular *KLW* columns reviewing sheet music, for instance, he drew attention to "a folio of music specially written for picture work", published by Francis and Day.[67] An earlier editorial piece in *KLW* had drawn readers' attention to some reasonably priced piano music collections published by Breitkopf and Härtel, including marches, waltzes, national dances, overtures, descriptive pieces, and so on: "pianists and leaders of orchestras would do well to get into communication with this firm".[68]

As Rachael Low notes, it was around this time that British producers and renters started to make suggestions as to appropriate music for particular films or to arrange specially composed scores.[69] In another of his *KLW* columns, for instance, George noted with surprisingly little fanfare a specially composed piano score produced by Pathé for their film *The God of the Sun*, its nineteen pages of music for sixty-five separate scenes making "the task of accompanying this film relatively easy". The rarity of such specially composed music at this time is confirmed by George's further comments:

> Messrs. Pathé Frères are to be complimented on their forethought to render their production still more effective. They evidently realise that music makes or mars a film, and mean taking no risks where their own work has been long and

costly. We wish "The God of the Sun" a brilliant success, and trust the union of picture and music may be only one of many on their part.[70]

CONCLUSIONS

The history of musical accompaniment for films has to be placed in the context of the history of the development of the film business and film culture. The efforts to "improve" the quality of picture playing, to standardize and professionalize picture playing, were clearly tied up with the development of longer narrative films, and with the move upmarket and the aspiration that cinema might become a respectable and solidly profitable cultural practice attracting a "discerning" audience. As Burrows makes clear, the history of music in picture houses was also shaped by moral and legal regulation and by competition with other strands of the entertainment business. An article in *The Times* in 1912, for instance, noted the competition for audiences between music hall and cinema, and the growth of music as an attraction in its own right in cinemas—not playing *to* the pictures, or playing *at* them, but in effect playing *beyond* them: "Films, however engrossing, do not appear to fully satisfy all the cravings of those who patronize the cinematograph shows. They want music as well, and when they have got instrumental music they want singing too."[71] Some audiences, it seems, did go to film shows to hear pianoforte recitals or to have a good sing-song, even if others in both Britain and the United States were discouraging this sort of distractive and/ or interactive musical performance.

The ostensible subject of the article in *The Times* was the effect of legal regulation on the types of entertainment and particularly music that were allowed in cinemas, the need for cinemas to acquire singing licences if they were to enter into that form of entertainment, but also the concern of music hall owners to limit such licensing. The debate about legality and competition was dressed up in the language of morality, however, and the professed desire to generate "healthy" entertainment.[72]

The debate in the trade press, the manuals and handbooks, and the evidence of contemporary fiction and licensing negotiations, establish that there was a wide range of different types of venues catering for different audiences in the 1911–13 period, with a similarly wide range of musical experiences. For many of the commentators, the ideal model was "a clean well-conducted theatre in a respectable quarter of the town," where a well-educated pianist could accompany the pictures with a repertoire of light modern and classical music.[73] Such theatres should allow and enable "a program of music carefully chosen by the pianist and in every way suitable to the pictures the individual pieces are intended to follow, since there is no doubt audiences are becoming daily more discriminating in such matters."[74] But there was no firm consensus as yet, with the lone pianist in some venues replaced by an orchestra, whose size and instrumentation changed from venue to venue. Nor was there yet a firm consensus about the benefits of improvisation versus specially written or arranged music, or about the need to produce music that enhanced the narrative, dramatic, thematic, or emotional qualities of the film. On the contrary, there were competing discourses in circulation, competing agendas and regulatory and industrial circumstances.

This was then still very much a period of transition in Britain, with a wide range of exhibition experiences in play, even if the debate in the trade press and elsewhere was beginning to identify a clear set of standards for musical accompaniment. As in the United States, there was an emerging professional consensus about the sort of musical accompaniment that was appropriate for the increasingly complex fiction films of the period, about what should be played when and how, about the different sorts of music demanded by different narrative genres, as well as by travel films and topicals. One cinema accompanist working in Britain in 1911 was very clear about the technique required by this sort of narrative playing: "to follow the pictures properly, one has to watch them continually, play first to this character, then to that one, and generally try to convey to the audience in music the meaning of every scene which appears."[75] As both Anderson and Altman note, this was to a large extent about using music to encourage narratively subtle readings of films, and in particular to shore up the narrative meanings intended by producers and/or publicists working for film renters, and thereby to regulate what happened in the cinema exhibition space.[76]

At this stage, the control of the musical aspects of the experience remained at the point of exhibition, but the emergence of specially composed film scores issued by producer-renters is indicative of a gradual shift of control away from the showman exhibitor. In due course, the wretched pianist in the less salubrious picture house was to be replaced by synchronized sound films whose music and other sound effects were controlled primarily by the studios. In the early 1910s, however, the goal was to encourage better picture playing and more accomplished and better-paid pianists and other musicians. It was evidently a slow process. Many of the concerns of the earlier period remained, as is clear from the opening statement of a manual for cinema pianists and organists published simultaneously in the United States and Britain in 1920:

That music is an invaluable and necessary aid to the success and enjoyment of moving pictures, is a fact which no one will deny. But the accompanying, or illustrating, music must be of the *right kind*, or else its very aim will be defeated. Unfortunately, the right kind of "picture music" is something that is not universally understood....[77]

NOTES

1. W. Tyacke George, "The Neglect of Music in Picture Theatres", *Kinematograph and Lantern Weekly* (henceforth *KLW*), 15 Feb. 1912, 869; I would like to thank Pierluigi Ercole for assisting with the research for this chapter, and Julie Brown and Annette Davison for their insightful comments and patience.

2. Henry A. Watson, "The Picture Pianist", *KLW*, 12 Sept. 1912, 1422.

3. Colin N. Bennett, *The Handbook of Kinematography* (London: Kinematograph Weekly, 1913), 277; reproduced in *A History of Early Film*, Vol. 2, ed. Stephen Herbert (London and New York: Routledge, 2000), 349.

4. On US debates and developments, see Rick Altman, *Silent Film Sound* (New York: Columbia University Press, 2004), 231–85; and Tim Anderson, "Reforming 'Jackass Music': The Problematic Aesthetics of Early American Film Music Accompaniment", *Cinema Journal* 37/1 (1997): 3–22.

5. Alexander Villiers, letter to *KLW*, 18 Jan. 1912, 637.

6. See Jon Burrows, chapter 6 in this volume; Altman, *Silent Film Sound*, 231–85; and Anderson, "Reforming 'Jackass Music'".

7. "Ole Luk-Oie", "A Sense of Touch", *The Strand*, 44 (Dec. 1912): 620–31. Reprinted in *Reading the Cinematograph: The Cinema in British Short Fiction, 1896–1912*, ed. Andrew Shail (Exeter: Exeter University Press, 2010), 219–39; all subsequent page references are to the reprint. See also my commentary on this short story, Andrew Higson, "A Visit to the Cinema in 1912: 'The Sense of Touch,'" also in Shail, *Reading the Cinematograph*, 240–56.

8. "Ole Luk-Oie", "A Sense of Touch", 221–2.

9. Ibid., 221, 223, 224.

10. Ibid., 225.

11. Ibid., 239.

12. See Higson, "A visit to the cinema in 1912."

13. According to a 1913 handbook "It is advisable to sink the piano in a well close to the picture." Bennett, *The Handbook of Kinematography*, 278 (reproduced in Herbert, *History of Early Film*, 350).

14. Altman, *Silent Film Sound*, 231–285; and Anderson, 'Reforming "Jackass Music"'.

15. See "A Pianist", "Music in Picture Theatres", letter to *The Bioscope*, 9 Nov. 1911, 435; Madge Clements and "Pianiste", "The Picture Pianist", letters to *The Bioscope*, 30 Nov. 1911, 631; and "Souffleur", "The Music of the Picture Theatre", *The Bioscope*, 14 Dec. 1911, 749. All are reproduced in Herbert, *History of Early Film*, 37–40.

16. See letter in *KLW*, 1 Dec. 1912, and advertisements in *KLW*, 21 Mar. 1912, 1158, and *Kinematograph Monthly Film Record*, 1 (May 1912), 100.

17. W. Tyacke George, *Playing to Pictures* (London: Kinematograph Weekly, 1912).

18. See, for example, advertisements in *KLW*, 21 Mar. 1912, 1158, and *Kinematograph Monthly Film Record*, 1 (May 1912), 100.

19. See, for example, Watson, "Picture Pianist", *KLW*, 29 Aug. 1912, 1245; 12 Sept. 1912, 1422; 26 Sept. 1912, 1592; 10 Oct. 1912, 1740; 24 Oct. 1912, 27.

20. See Henry A. Watson, letter to *KLW*, 22 Feb. 1912, 939.

21. Watson, "Picture Pianist", *KLW*, 29 Aug. 1912, 1245.

22. The first column was W. Tyacke George, "Music Reviews and Notes", *KLW*, 12 Sept. 1912, 1422–3; it then appeared fortnightly.

23. "Souffleur", "Music of the Picture Theatre", 749 (reproduced in Herbert, *History of Early Film*, 40).

24. Ibid.

25. "A Pianist", "Music in Picture Theatres", 435 (reproduced in Herbert, *History of Early Film*, 37).

26. Madge Clements, letter to *Bioscope*, 30 Nov. 1911, 631 (reproduced in Herbert, *History of Early Film*, 39).

27. Bennett, *Handbook of Kinematography*, 278 (reproduced in Herbert, *History of Early Film*, 350).

28. "One who knows his 'Biz'", letter to *KLW*, 1 Feb. 1912, 743.

29. Watson, "Picture Pianist", *KLW*, 29 Aug. 1912, 1245.

30. W. Tyacke George, letter to *KLW*, 1 Feb. 1912, 743.

31. See, for example, *KLW*, 18 Jan. 1912, 637; 1 Feb. 1912, 743; 8 Feb. 1912, 813; 15 Feb. 1912, 880–81; and 22 Feb. 1912, 937–9; the quotation is from *KLW*, 18 Jan. 1912, 637.

32. Watson, "Picture Pianist", *KLW*, 24 Oct. 1912, 27.

33. Arthur W. Owen, letter to *KLW*, 22 Feb. 1912, 939; see also, for example, Alexander Villiers, letter to *KLW*, 18 Jan. 1912, 637.

34. See Stephen Bottomore, "The Story of Percy Peashaker: Debates about Sound Effects in the Early Cinema", in *The Sounds of Early Cinema*, ed. Richard Abel and Rick Altman (Bloomington: Indiana University Press, 2001), 129–42; several of Bottomore's examples are from UK sources (as with the cartoon on p. 139), although his chapter also deals with US and other European developments; see also Frederick A. Talbot, *Moving Pictures: How They are Made and Worked* (London: William Heinemann, 1912), 139–40.

35. "A Pianist", "Music in Picture Theatres", 435 (reproduced in Herbert, *History of Early Film*, 37).

36. "Souffleur", "Music of the Picture Theatre", 749 (reproduced in Herbert, *History of Early Film*, 40).

37. Bennett, *The Handbook of Kinematography*, 278 (reproduced in Herbert, *History of Early Film*, 350).

38. Watson, "Picture Pianist", *KLW*, 29 Aug. 1912, 1245. For the American trade press response to improvisation as a practice, see Anderson, "Reforming 'Jackass Music'", 17.

39. "Souffleur", "Music of the Picture Theatre", 749 (reproduced in Herbert, *History of Early Film*, 40).

40. Ibid.

41. Ibid.

42. Ibid.

43. Alexander Villiers, letter to *KLW*, 18 Jan. 1912, 637.

44. Herbert Hodder, letter to *KLW*, 15 Feb. 1912, 880.

45. Tom Vaisey, letter to *KLW*, 22 Feb. 1912, 937.

46. Arthur W. Owen, letter to *KLW*, 22 Feb. 1912, 939.

47. Herbert Hodder, letter to *KLW*, 15 Feb. 1912, 880.

48. George, "The Neglect of Music in Picture Theatres", 869.

49. W. Tyacke George, letter to *KLW*, 1 Feb. 1912, 743.

50. Bennett, *Handbook of Kinematography*, 277 (reproduced in Herbert, *History of Early Film*, 349); see also Watson, "Picture Pianist", *KLW*, 29 August 1912, 1245.

51. W. Tyacke George, letter to *KLW*, 1 Feb. 1912, 743.

52. "A Pianist", letter to *The Bioscope*, 9 Nov. 1911, 437 (reproduced in Herbert, *History of Early Film*, 38).

53. See Madge Clements and "Pianiste", "The Picture Pianist", 631 (reproduced in Herbert, *History of Early Film*, 39).

54. "Souffleur", "Music of the Picture Theatre", 749 (reproduced in Herbert, *History of Early Film*, 40).

55. "A Pianist", "Music in Picture Theatres", 435 (reproduced in Herbert, *History of Early Film*, 37).

56. Rachael Low, *The History of the British Film, 1906–1914* (London: Allen and Unwin, 1949), 268.

57. "Souffleur", "Music of the Picture Theatre", 749 (reproduced in Herbert, *History of Early Film*, 40).

58. Watson, "Picture Pianist", *KLW*, 29 Aug. 1912, 1245.

59. Edith Lang and George West, *Musical Accompaniment of Moving Pictures: A Practical Manual for Pianists and Organists and an Exposition of the Principles Underlying the Musical Interpretation of Moving Pictures* (Boston: The Boston Music Company, and London: Winthrop Rogers, 1920), 6.

60. "Souffleur", "Music of the Picture Theatre", 749 (reproduced in Herbert, *History of Early Film*, 40).

61. Bennett, *Handbook of Kinematography*, 279–80 (reproduced in Herbert, *History of Early Film*, 351–2).

62. Ibid., 278 (reproduced in Herbert, *History of Early Film*, 350).

63. Arthur W. Owen, letter to *KLW*, 22 February 1912, 939.

64. Watson, "Picture Pianist", *KLW*, 12 Sept. 1912, 1422.

65. Watson, "Picture Pianist", *KLW*, 26 Sept. 1912, 1592.

66. Anon., "Music and the pictures", *KLW*, 1 Feb. 1912, 737.

67. W. Tyacke George, "Music Reviews and Notes", *KLW*, 12 Sept. 1912, 1422.

68. Ibid.; for a discussion of a similar range of musical recommendations in the United States, see Altman, *Silent Film Sound*, 258–69.

69. Low, *History of the British Film*, 269.

70. W. Tyacke George, "Kinematograph Music: Reviews and Notes", *KLW*, 10 Oct. 1912, 1741. In the same column, George also noted that Excelsior had produced sheet music to be played synchronously with its recent production, *Turkey Trot*; see also an advertisement for this "dancing film", *KLW*, 26 Sept. 1912, 1592. See Stephen Bottomore, chapter 9 in this volume, on Selsior's dance films for more on Excelsior and the *Turkey Trot*. More research is needed to determine when specially composed film scores began to circulate in Britain; for instance, were earlier Pathé films circulated with specially written scores in Britain? Films d'art, financially supported by Pathé, were certainly issuing such scores in France from 1908; see, for example, Altman, *Silent Film Sound*, 251–2.

71. Anon., "Cinematograph Shows", *Times*, 30 Nov. 1912, 7; see also Anon., "Music at picture theatres", *Times*, 15 Nov. 1912, 3.

72. See Anon., "Cinematograph Shows", 7.

73. Watson, "Picture Pianist", *KLW*, 12 Sept. 1912, 1422.

74. Bennett, *Handbook of Kinematography*, 278 (reproduced in Herbert, *History of Early Film*, 350).

75. "A Pianist", "Music in Picture Theatres", 435 (reproduced in Herbert, *History of Early Film*, 37).

76. See Anderson, "Reforming 'Jackass Music'", 17; and Altman, *Silent Film Sound*, 239–46.

77. Lang and West, *Musical Accompaniment of Moving Pictures*, 1.

8

The Reception of British Exhibition Practices in *Moving Picture World*, 1907–1914

James Buhler

FOUNDED IN MARCH 1907 by James P. Chalmers, Jr, *Moving Picture World* was the leading film industry trade paper for North America almost from its inception until the early 1920s. Aimed primarily at exhibitors in the United States, the paper distinguished itself by remaining neutral in the long legal battle between the Motion Picture Patents Company and the independent producers and by its sustained commitment to cultural uplift, to elevating the status of the entertainment presented in the moving picture houses of the United States and, to a lesser extent, Canada. As a trade paper, *Moving Picture World* specialized in reporting industry news such as acquisitions, travels of film company executives, regulations, and court cases affecting the industry, along with announcements of new theatres, brief reviews of recent film releases, and general advice for exhibitors and operators. But the paper also devoted extensive space to articles on improving the quality of the films on the programme, on rebutting widespread criticism especially by general newspapers, politicians and clergy of moving picture houses as disreputable, and on strategies for enhancing the theatrical experience—notably by investing in the musical portion of the programme—in order to attract better paying audiences.

Before 1910 exhibition practices in Britain were rarely mentioned in the pages of *Moving Picture World*. Given that exhibition conditions in places such as France and Australia were paid considerably more attention in these years, it might be thought that this neglect was due in some measure to the fact that British regulation for film exhibition, or rather for obtaining a music licence, particularly in London, was peculiar when measured against the situation in the United States, making formal comparisons unproductive.[1] The few comments on British exhibition that appear before 1910 invariably comment that the picture houses were not well developed, especially as compared to the United States and France. In the inaugural "Our London Letter" from 24 August 1907, for instance, the correspondent made the following observation:

> There are very few cinematograph theaters in England of the sort which are so common in France and America, but things are mending in this particular. Hale's Tours opened a place in Oxford street [*sic*] in October last as an experiment and instantly scored such an enormous success that they have since opened close upon a dozen other shows in London and the provinces. The show which they gave at first for 6d. (12c.) was a very poor one, but it has since been improved and they are taking films of their own which should further add to their success.[2]

In September of that same year *Moving Picture World* carried an item reprinted from *Kinematograph Weekly* complaining about the lack of "living picture exhibitions" in London compared to other cities of the world. Although the article admitted that few if any theatres in the world surpassed those of the West End, "the West End is not London, and the great bulk of Londoners have neither the means nor the time to visit the places of amusement there."[3] The report also noted that the situation in London was strange because motion picture houses were relatively common elsewhere in the country. Patronage in the few London suburban cinemas, the author claimed, was strong, and the provinces had "many permanent shows.... The latter, in many cases, are kept going for practically the whole of the year, on a smaller population, and in the face of a greater competition, from theaters, music halls, and other picture shows, that a great number of London suburbs possess."[4] London in 1907 was portrayed as not having many theatres specializing in screening motion pictures, and an editor of *Moving Picture World* added a comment: "This seems like a good chance for some of America's surplus cash with enterprise."[5]

Will G. Barker, at the time managing director of the Warwick Trading Company, was clearly impressed with the sheer number of nickelodeons in Chicago and New York during his autumn 1907 trip through the United States and Canada. In December of that year, after his return to London, *Moving Picture World* reprinted a long article from *Show World*, in which Barker had published an account of his trip.[6] "I came down to Chicago, and here I find the moving picture theater at its

very highest. I am given to understand there are about two hundred such places of
entertainment in Chicago, and I do not know of any other city in the world that can
boast of so many."[7] He also compared the type of film entertainment available in the
United States with that available in England.

> In England we try to make them an animated newspaper, and show the stay-
> at-home Englishman the wonders of the world. We are endeavoring to make
> cinematography take its proper place in the world, namely, to convey truth-
> fully, without any garnishing, the true state of things and manner and customs,
> etc.[8]

Here, I insert a brief caveat, which will be apparent to anyone who has spent time
with trade publications. We should be under no illusion that accounts such as
Barker's represent actual practice in England—or anywhere else. A paper such as
Moving Picture World did not simply publish a range of opinions but selected what
its editors saw as in the interest of the business—its business—and accounts such
as Barker's always need to be evaluated in terms of whatever polemical point—or
business interest—an author is trying to defend as well as the aims of the trade publication.[9] In this case, it is certainly relevant to note that at this time Barker specialized in nonfiction films and that he was trying to break through the cartel of film
manufacturers that controlled the American market. I mention this caveat because
throughout my chapter I will present and summarize a number of claims made in
American trade papers about British practice, but my interest is not so much to eval-
uate those claims for what they reveal about that British practice as it is to examine
them for what they reveal about how American practices were being defined and
refined (whether by example or counterexample). Consequently, sometimes it seems
that English audiences love American films; at other times the English like nothing
better than educational films. At the point when the coverage of London theatres
was at its apex, 1911–13, accounts of London exhibition rarely failed to mention that
theatres there did not use vaudeville; reports frequently noted the ubiquitous use of
orchestras; and they also continually pointed out the higher pricing scale. *Moving
Picture World* publicized the views of Barker in the article cited above because he
was making the case for film as the basis for a respectable and edifying entertainment, important concerns for the paper.

  Moving Picture World would press this case again in May 1908, tying a somewhat
stodgy technique that was thought to inhere in British film to a seriousness of purpose. In the passage that I will cite, Europe as a whole is mentioned, but the title
of the article—"British Achievements with Motion Pictures"—and the drift of the
argument suggest that the primary focus was Britain:

Europe, while being far behind this country in the mechanical end of the moving picture industry, has regarded [the moving picture] far more seriously and placed it on a higher plane. At the present time the British Government has under consideration the advisability of forming a department, with a large staff of experts, for the exact chronicling, by means of moving photographs, of all important public events.[10]

For better or worse this notion of respectability would come to define and (safely) limit the appeal of British film for several years: British filmmakers were inevitably praised by *Moving Picture World* for their educational subjects and the moral uprightness of their fiction films, but the films were also criticized for lagging behind the competition in terms of narrative construction and even technical photographic excellence. I. W. Ullman, an executive for the Film Import and Trading Company, summarized the perception in April 1909: "England is not, by any means as far advanced as she might be. The insularity and conservatism of the people operates against the production of moving picture plays by English firms which are acceptable by the people of other countries."[11] Although from a technical standpoint of making clear and steady pictures—an important aesthetic criterion of the time—English films were on par with films from other countries, Ullman found the films lagging in terms of drama and scenic interest. He ended on a hopeful note, however, stating that "the English manufacturers are waking up to the needs of the situation, both as regards the quality of the picture and the commercial way of handling them."[12] An article from December 1911 was even more blunt: "There is little danger of moral corruption in English films, but they are so uniformly and ineffably stupid as a rule, that they never, or hardly ever, leave Great Britain. With all their pro-British patriotism even the Canadians cannot stand them."[13]

As British films developed a reputation in the *Moving Picture World*, well earned or not, for stodginess and insipidity in all but nonfiction genres, British exhibition, especially in London, followed quite the opposite trajectory and was quickly receiving extensive praise. This is all the more remarkable for the relatively late entry in the field. In early 1908, at least three years after the nickelodeon boom had started in the United States, one English correspondent reported rapid growth of small theatres, particularly in London. He wrote:

The latest development of trade in England seems to be on the lines of street shows, so common in America and on the Continent. Quite a host of these shops, charging from 1d. to 3d. admission, have sprung up in London, and the L. C. C., scared by the fact that they do not apply for a license for music and are so under no control, at its last meeting agreed to send a deputation to the home secretary (Mr. H. Gladstone), urging that a license should be necessary for this class of entertainment, many of which are by no means too safe.[14]

Jon Burrows discusses the spurt of small shows at this time in the first of his "Penny Pleasures" articles, confirming and extending earlier historians' speculation that the Cinematograph Act of 1909 had been enacted largely in reaction to the rise (and lack of regulation) of these small shows, which were analogous to the American nickelodeons.[15] In that same report cited above, the English correspondent also noted the proliferation of motion picture exhibition options available in London at much higher prices. Pathé had recently opened the New Egyptian Hall in Piccadilly, and the author was impressed that a patron could, "by payment of 1s., sit and look at an exhibition of their pictures for as long as he likes and without extra charge, enjoying tea in a basement fitted out as a Japanese tea shop."[16]

Nevertheless, at this point the proliferation of theatres was such that it could evidently still pass virtually undetected by visitors. In March 1908 Albert E. Smith of the Vitagraph Company, recently returned from a European trip, still saw England as a marginal film market, due to excessive regulation of theatres, and he pointed to Paris as the leading world city for film exhibition.

> England is yet far behind [the other counties in Europe]. I did not have time to visit other cities there, but in London the few theaters that have overcome the very strict municipal ordinances are prospering. But Paris is where you want to go to see motion pictures in perfection! Perfect as to photographic quality, steadiness and freedom from flicker. The theaters are neat and attractive and the admission prices far above those in this country. Imagine the public here flocking to the theatoriums at 40 cents per head![17]

An interviewer then incredulously interjected: "But do not these places also present strong vaudeville attractions?" Smith answered: "Oh no! Just a straight picture show, although some have the chronophone and nearly all have high-class music."[18]

Smith's comments on vaudeville and music are prescient. In early 1908 vaudeville was not yet an object of regular derision in the American trade press, although it soon would be, and music, outside the illustrated song, was rarely mentioned in any substantive fashion. Both topics would receive much attention over the coming years, and *Moving Picture World* would use foreign exhibition practices—after 1910 particularly those of London—to make the case for the viability of a more expensive motion picture theatre that featured music and eschewed vaudeville.

By October of 1908 *Moving Picture World* reprinted an item from the *New York Herald* that proclaimed the success of a two-hour talking picture presentation in

London. What is pertinent for the argument at hand is not the presence of the talking pictures, which were all the rage at the time, but an offhand comment in the preamble to the story, which declared that "moving picture shows are as common in England nowadays as they are in America."[19] Even so, Lux Graphicus, a pseudonym for Thomas Bedding, editor and regular columnist at *Moving Picture World* as well as an English expatriate,[20] could still report in June 1909 that "a friend writes me this week that the moving picture theater in Britain has become a craze."[21] If the moving pictures had indeed "become a craze", the situation was also much less than ideal for the exhibitors. One American attempting to run a show wrote to *Moving Picture World* in August to complain that: "The picture business is in rather an unsettled condition at present, owing to the fact that the L. C. C. are about to bring out some new regulations which will make a big change in the whole business."[22]

In the first of a pair of articles recording his observations on American moving picture theatres, Fred Marriott remarked in July 1909 that the theatres in New York were nicer than equivalent ones in London: "Paying a very moderate entrance fee I was surprised to find a nicely appointed little theater, nicely carpeted, 'where soft the footsteps fall.'"[23] He was also surprised by the continuous show, which he said was not common in England, as well as the constitution of the audience. "The idea of an all-day show has not caught on with us in England as it appears to have done in a very marked degree here and in the States, and the absence of the ladies and their youthful offspring and the substitution of obvious men struck me very forcibly." On the other hand, Marriott observed that the illustrated song was common in London. "The songs, together with the accompaniment on the piano, as in London, were appropriate to the subjects on the screen and well rendered." When he wrote again in October, having now visited other parts of the country, Marriott pointed to what from his perspective were the confusing semiotics of the American moving picture theatre, especially the strikingly ostentatious combination of exterior lighting and interior gilding. In Detroit, he noted one theatre

in particular more representing a small Opera House, with its gilded boxes, than a "Nickelodeon." In England this gorgeous electrically lighted display is rather regarded as an indication of the "penny gaff," than of the more refined class of entertainment, such as one usually finds in your moving picture resorts. The Majestic, at Detroit, is a comfortable house not on the theater or opera principle, but the seating accommodation is ample and the pictures excellent. It is spoilt, however, by the introduction of the most commonplace vaudeville entertainment.[24]

Marriott's attack on vaudeville, which consumed about a third of the article, was in the autumn of 1909 already becoming a common theme of articles on exhibition reform in *Moving Picture World*, and it would become one of the principal points of comparison between American and British exhibition practices.

Almost exactly a year later in October 1910 Josephine Clement, the well-regarded manager of Keith's Bijou Theatre in Boston, differentiated American from British and Australian audiences in moving picture houses on the basis of their interest in vaudeville.[25]

> On the vexed question of vaudeville, Mrs. Clement seemed to be of the opinion that high-class vaudeville did not hurt the picture. Vaudeville of this kind in her view was called for, simply because the picture itself was hardly strong enough to attract the public. The pay box tells a story which admits of no refutation. Many houses we know rely almost exclusively upon the picture, but, generally speaking, the American public differs from English, Australian and other publics, in that it will not stand for the picture alone. But then we all know that Americans like change, variety and plenty for their money.[26]

Vaudeville, Clement claimed, found a home in American theatres because of the nature of the audience. She suggested that British audiences were attracted to a more unified or at least a more consistent form of entertainment, whereas Americans preferred variety. A similar point was made by Lux Graphicus, who cited a quip by an English actor that Americans "take their pleasures quickly and in tabloid doses".[27] And R. W. Hulbert, a Canadian working in the film business, likewise drew on this difference in an interview reprinted by *Moving Picture World* from *The Bioscope* in February 1910. Comparing what he saw as the respective flaws in Canadian and British practices, Hulbert pointed to the tedium of the British programme as opposed to the tendency to race through the films of the Canadian programme.

> So far as the English picture palace program is concerned, your English program is very good, but it seems a little too long and tedious at times. In Canada the length of the program depends on the price charged for admission. We show either two or three reels. We get so many people who want to see the show that there is a tendency now to rush the pictures through too quickly, giving them too jerky a movement.[28]

The Canadian practice and priorities were closer to those that prevailed in the United States than in London, which was, in the wake of the Cinematograph Act, seeing a large number of relatively opulent theatres dedicated to the moving picture opening. Hulbert's principal point of comparison was a visit to the Theatre de Luxe in the

Strand, which he noted presented an entertainment that was "a little more elaborate than shows in Canada". He observed a number of other relevant distinctions:

> We do not allow smoking, for instance, and none of our lady patrons retain their headgear whilst in the theater. It is a recognized thing for all ladies to remove their hats. In some places they come to the picture theater, dressed as for the ordinary theater, with no head covering beyond a fascinator or shawl. Then, again, it would be difficult to find a picture theater in Canada that had not an inclined floor, no matter how small a place it is.[29]

Such differences in smoking policy and inclined floors were noted by several commentators and, according to the published accounts, many British theatres evidently encouraged eating and drinking by patrons in a way that was not yet common in American theatres,[30] perhaps because of the shorter programmes. Horace G. Plimpton, a manager at Edison, still noted the difference in April 1913 when he compared London theatres to those in New York:

> I visited a great many theaters in London and found that they were far superior to anything on this side. The English exhibitor provides for the comfort of his patrons to a remarkable degree.... The seats are large and comfortable; there is ample space between the rows so that one can pass those seated on either side without stepping on their toes. Most houses have a bar where refreshments can be obtained without leaving the house and, in many, tea is served at the usual hour. Smoking is also permitted. The prices obtained are much better than here. In all the houses I visited I found nothing that would correspond with the usual New York house.[31]

Just a week after having reprinted the interview with Hulbert in February 1910, *Moving Picture World* published a condensed version of another *Bioscope* article, this one a report on the opening of the Ealing Cinematograph Theatre in London. *Moving Picture World* was clearly impressed with the sumptuous description of the theatre in the report, as the paper introduced it with the following editorial note: "It will be seen that [the theatre] possesses many features not enjoyed by the average American moving picture theater". The article itself described the theatre as "a veritable palace of luxury, and admitted by those who have seen it and are in a position to compare it with others, to be the finest the world has yet seen." The article also gave a fairly extensive description of the music:

> There is no lack of music by which appropriate accompaniment are obtained to the pictures. Piano and organ are provided, and on the occasion of our visit

the music was tastefully and skilfully [*sic*] rendered in keeping with the subject of the pictures. In addition, one of Messrs. Keith, Prowse's splendid automatic pianos, which gives high-class selections, and one of Messrs. Hepworth's wonderful singing machines—the Vivaphone—have been installed.[32]

At the end of 1910 *Moving Picture World* reprinted yet another article from the British trade press, this time from the *Kinematograph Weekly*. In this article H. A. Browne confidently asserted the rapid advance of British theatres so that in his opinion they now stood well in front of American theatres. "In every town of any size in the United Kingdom to-day are picture houses, electric theaters, picture palaces, call them what you will, that are the last word in comfort, cleanliness and luxury. The pictures are as a general rule, well shown, carefully selected, and accompanied by a skillful pianist."[33] Whereas most of the theatres in Britain had been newly constructed specifically for exhibiting motion pictures, or at least had been thoroughly renovated, the American stock of theatres consisted, Browne claimed, primarily of hastily converted legitimate houses, "music halls, and buildings of various descriptions, which have not had a tithe of the money spent on their conversion that the English halls have spent on their erection and equipment." As a result in the United States spaces were not particularly well adapted for use in screening motion pictures. Browne then slyly extended his story of shoddy conversion to the quality of the show itself, where vaudeville on the programme (again) became a sign that the American shows were not well adapted to the proper display of motion pictures.

Then, again, the pictures are interspersed with vaudeville turns that are very far from first class. To be perfectly frank, they are usually "rotten," but I suppose his audience demands them, so he must have them. There is no doubt that the picture business on the other side is, as here, booming, but until the picture theater proprietors can get an open market in which to rent or purchase their films, they must be content to take a back seat when comparing their entertainment with that given in London.[34]

If the new London picture palaces did not, like their American counterparts, utilize vaudeville, they did by all accounts feature music on their programmes to a great extent. At least the suggestion that music could serve as an effective substitute for vaudeville was a case that *Moving Picture World* was intent on pressing, as it featured in accounts of exhibition practices in other countries besides England, and it accorded well with the paper's agenda of severing motion picture exhibition from vaudeville. In London, however, the turn against vaudeville seemed to have had less to do with the mixed programme as Browne insinuates, since it continued to work perfectly fine on music hall programmes, than with the fact that the picture palaces in particular were drawing their patrons primarily from those who would otherwise attend suburban evening concerts. This at least was the position articulated by A. E. Taylor, the English correspondent responsible for the recently reinstated "London Letter" in February 1911.

> Whilst the moving picture is gradually but surely ousting the variety hall and theater from popularity, it has also sounded the death knell of the evening concert in suburban London. This admission has been made by an authority on concerts in the metropolis. Personally I do not wonder at this for many of the so-called evening concerts were simply caterwauling displays, whereas at "the pictures" one is always certain of a programme well worth seeing. By the way, too, English people have a dislike for those picture shows which run variety turns, and do not care for the combination of the music hall and pictures at a picture theater. And yet they like pictures at the variety theater. Verily there is no accounting for taste.[35]

Over the next couple of years, *Moving Picture World* would endow London moving picture theatres, at least the large ones, with a strong reputation for music, and in particular the use of the orchestra. During this period, which coincided, hardly by chance, with the paper's attempt to define and codify institutional standards for film exhibition in the United States, London theatres and audiences commonly served as a means to measure the progress of American exhibition practices.[36] The inaugural reinstated "London Letter" stated the goals fairly forthrightly:

> I shall endeavor to give manufacturers, exhibitors and operators in the "New Country" a pen picture of matters appertaining to the industry in all its branches in the "Old Country," in the hope that what I am able to tell them will make for that goal which we all have at heart, the uplifting of the picture and the cementing of friendly relations between those whose lot it is to be connected with film producing or picture projection in England and America.[37]

At the same time, to establish the London exhibition practices as the ideal toward which American practice should aspire, it was necessary to recognize and recount the disappearance of the small theatres, whatever the reality. In April 1912 the author of the "London Letter" obliged by writing the obituary of the small house:

> The day of the little moving picture here has passed. The shop or similar sized small building hastily converted into a "theater" is passing away, no matter how low the prices of admission are. The money is being made in the specially built, comfortable, roomy buildings with handsome entrance lobbies where queues

can wait in comfort. Simplicity is the note of the internal decorations, and such little incidental comforts as free tea and coffee are not neglected.[38]

Statements like this one marking the passing of the small theatre are always suspicious, nowhere more so than when they fit clear ideological agendas. And other evidence in the paper suggests that small houses continued to be viable in England, if in a less prominent way, much as they were in the United States.[39] According to a long report in *Moving Picture World*, the British International Kinematograph Exhibition held in March 1913 featured a competition in improvisatory piano accompaniment, hardly the practice one would expect to find in a large theatre with an orchestra, even if a pianist might spell the orchestra for a dinner show. More tellingly, the report also mentioned a number of exhibits featuring labour-saving mechanical devices for producing music and sound, devices that would be almost useless in larger theatres. As the author astutely observed:

It would seem from the many mechanical musical instruments shown at Olympia that, so far as the smaller shows are concerned, the orchestra will soon be swept out of existence. A most ingenious contrivance which attracted endless attention was a violin-playing instrument. The sceptic showman will ask "How can a machine draw a bow across a fiddle with accurate musical expression." That is not the point. The violin plays the bow, the latter remaining stationary throughout. The invention consists of a three-legged frame to which is attached three violins, close together and all in line. Across the three is stretched a huge bow and when the motor is set going and the sound regulator fed with paper music rools [*sic*] the three play together. Pneumatic stops regulate the strings instead of fingers.... Combinations of pianos, organs, orchestrions and violins were [also] exhibited by the dozen and all were under electric control, compact, and regulated on the press-the-button principle.[40]

The report certainly implied that small shows were under some competitive pressure from the larger theatres in terms of music. Yet the fact that such mechanical musical instruments and sound-effects cabinets were abundant at the exhibition suggests that either the small theatres had somehow regained their health in the succeeding year or, more probably, they had not in fact faded to the extent that the correspondent of the "London Letter" had implied. In any case, at the time of the exhibition, the small theatre seemed to remain a viable market.

In early 1912 *Moving Picture World* carried an item that recognized improvements in American theatres, while acknowledging that most houses lagged behind the practices in countries such as England.

[T]he average moving picture theater of the United States is by no means in keeping with the demands of the time. Structurally, the great majority of such houses are two years or more behind the progress of the moving pictures. They are small, cheap-looking and uninviting. They have served their day. During 1911 quite a number of fine, modern structures have been erected for the exclusive use of moving pictures. They are the vanguard.[41]

Characteristically, W. Stephen Bush gave the most articulate account along these lines. In the spring of 1913 Bush embarked on a long tour of Europe, looking into both the exhibition and production sides of the business in the major European countries. He summarized the situation in England by explicitly contrasting the strength of the exhibition sector with the weakness of the production sector. "While through the lack of financial support, English film making enterprises languish like an exotic plant on unfriendly soil, the city is dotted with modern superb moving picture theaters."[42] Bush was particularly impressed with the music in one London theatre, which he represented as the norm for London rather than extraordinary.

At 10 o'clock the house was crowded. The seating capacity was only 800, but that is good enough with such a scale of prices [which started at 1s. and ranged upward from there]. The furnishings were of a high order throughout. There was an invisible orchestra, which played music suitable to the pictures. Please take that word "suitable" in its actual, and not in its American or Pickwickian sense. No doubt the music had been carefully rehearsed, as it invariably struck home at the psychological moments. I have a painful recollection of an orchestra in New York engaged in an effort to follow the pictures with suitable music, and frequently coming to a dead stop at precisely the wrong moment, closing, for instance, with a crashing finale just a minute before the climax of the play on the screen. The highest price in the New York theater was 15 cents. I will leave it to the reader to draw his own conclusions. I characterized the program as moderately good, and barring the luxurious surroundings, the splendid music and the perfect management, I have seen moving picture entertainments at home a grade better than this, and charging no more than 10 cents. Again I leave the reader to draw his own conclusions which lie on the surface.[43]

Fittingly, Bush's trip to Europe represents the final phase of intense interest in London exhibition before the 1913 arrival in New York of Samuel Rothapfel, the most important manager and impresario of picture palaces in the United States from this moment until he was forced out of Radio City Music Hall in 1934.[44]

In fact, *Moving Picture World* featured details of British exhibition practices as well as those of other countries much less frequently through the end of 1913 and in 1914, where I ended my survey. Already in the second half of 1913, "Foreign Trade Notes", which had replaced the "London Letter" in 1912, focussed more on issues of production and distribution than had been the case from 1910 to 1913. In some respects this recapitulated the situation from the years before 1910, when reports from foreign correspondents, interviews with visiting foreign film company executives and with American executives who had recently been abroad, and reprints from foreign newspapers and trade journals tended to remark on the level of interest of a country's population in film, whether the audiences liked American films, how the film companies of that country saw the American market, and so forth. The articles seemed designed, in other words, to report on the sort of economic activity that would be of direct interest to Americans engaged in the film business.

Perhaps Rothapfel's arrival, coupled with the rapid proliferation of elaborate theatres in the city,[45] was sufficient that the editors of the *Moving Picture World* no longer felt that they needed to look abroad to find the future of film exhibition. Rothapfel had quickly advanced through theatres in the Upper Midwest, most notably in Minneapolis, Milwaukee, and Chicago, and moved to New York City in 1913. He managed a series of increasingly elaborate theatres in the city, many built to his specification, and his shows, which always put a premium on music—including as large an orchestra as the theatre could support—set the standard for film exhibition in the United States for the remainder of the silent era. Certainly Rothapfel received regular and lavish praise from the paper, including a highly complimentary feature article by Bush, who explicitly placed Rothapfel's work at the Regent above what he had just recently heard in London: "For the first time in this country," Bush wrote, "I was made aware of the possibilities of the music. I had thought until then that London and Berlin had wrought wonders with motion picture music but I confess that at the Regent Theater [*sic*] a very high standard has been set."[46] In that same issue, an interview with B. Nichols, a London film distributer, had noted "the increasing number of handsome houses going up in New York. Your local exhibitors should be very grateful to the late Mayor Gaynor for making possible the erection of more adequate places of exhibition, but I refer more particularly to the still larger houses that class under the regular theater laws. For many years New York was far behind London, but they are making up for it now."[47] In early 1914 Rothapfel had also travelled to Europe, "to look over the exhibition field in various countries" in anticipation of the opening of the new Strand Theatre, which he had been hired to manage, so the editors may well have felt that he had the issue in hand.[48] When Rothapfel returned from his trip, *Moving Picture World* reported that he "declined to join the chorus of praise for European methods of presentation and frankly declares that 'we have nothing to learn.' Mr. Rothapfel spent a few days in London, in Paris and Berlin, and in none of these cities was he at all impressed with the achievements in the presentation of motion pictures."[49] With respect to music, he was willing to concede only that the standard in the general house in European cities might be higher, "but we have houses on this side that far surpass their best in the matter of music". Although Rothapfel remembered his impressions somewhat differently when he returned to London in February 1923 and addressed exhibitors there, back in America in March 1914 he reported that the best American theatres were already the best in the world, and henceforth writers in *Moving Picture World* would cite the theatres of London and other European cities primarily to encourage exhibitors to raise their prices so they could afford to elevate the general level of show.[50]

Or perhaps the reason *Moving Picture World* moved away from closely observing exhibition trends in England and other countries was that the rise of the multireel feature made foreign films more competitive on the American market and disrupted the established distribution and production system. It fractured the just recently stabilized exhibition system in ways that made it inconvenient to overtly hold up highly capitalized foreign exhibition systems as a model for small American exhibitors, who were themselves being increasingly marginalized by large, highly capitalized theatrical concerns investing in the combination of multireel features and lavish theatres. At one point attempting to cajole exhibitors into embracing multireel features and more adventuresome programming, rather than simply playing what the exchanges were sending out, Bush made the highly dubious assertion that "the owners of the great and successful kinema theatres in London and Berlin are self-made men".[51] In general, however, Bush was sensitive to the problems of the small exhibitors and apt to want to help them negotiate the transformation that the introduction of the multireel feature was having on the business. He recognized more clearly than most that the uplift that his paper understood as advantageous to the industry as a whole also favoured the large theatrical concerns and was likely to make it extremely difficult for the small exhibitors to continue the success that they enjoyed when the single reel was the basis of the industry.[52] Increasingly it was clear that elaborate music and other accoutrements of luxury would also be used by the large theatrical concerns to force a stratification of the market, leaving only marginal sectors, such as impoverished ghettos and small towns, to the small exhibitor. Whatever the reason for the shift in reporting, London exhibition, which had served as *Moving Picture World*'s most prominent model for American exhibition from 1910 to 1913, ceased to receive much more than passing mention after 1914.

NOTES

1. On music licensing in London, see Jon Burrows, chapter 6 in this volume.

2. Our Own Correspondent, "Our London Letter", *Moving Picture World* (hereafter, *MPW*), 24 Aug. 1907, 390.

3. "London As a Field for Kinematograph Enterprise—Who Will Cultivate It?" *MPW*, 21 Sept. 1907, 454–5.

4. Ibid, 455.

5. Ibid.

6. For background on Barker during this period, see Rachael Low and Roger Manvell, *The History of the British Film: 1896–1906* (London: Allen and Unwin, 1948), 15. Barker left Warwick at the end of 1909 to set up his own production company, Barker Motion Photography Ltd, which specialized in elaborate dramatic films. His most notable early success was *Henry VIII* (1911). For an overview of this phase of Barker's career, see Low, *The History of the British Film, 1906–1914* (London: Allen and Unwin, 1949), 45–7, 94–6; and Brian McFarlane, "Barker, William George (1868–1951)", *Oxford Dictionary of National Biography* (Oxford: Oxford University Press, Oct 2006); online edn, Jan 2010, http://www.oxforddnb.com/view/article/95007 [accessed 3 Aug 2012].

7. "Will G. Barker on Moving Pictures", *MPW*, 21 Dec. 1907, 689.

8. Ibid, 690.

9. On distortions of trade papers, see Eileen Bowser, *The Transformation of Cinema, 1907–1915* (New York: Scribner, 1990), 121. Noël Burch likewise argues the trade papers' mission was fundamentally ideological; see his *Life to Those Shadows*, trans. and ed. Ben Brewster (Berkeley: University of California Press, 1990), 126. See also Jon Burrows and Julie Brown, chapters 6 and 11 respectively in this volume.

10. "British Achievements with Moving Pictures", *MPW*, 30 May 1908, 476.

11. "The Moving Picture in Europe and America", *MPW*, 24 April, 1909, 512.

12. Ibid.

13. "The Dangers of the Foreign Market", *MPW*, 16 Dec. 1911, 878.

14. "Foreign News and Notes: From Our English Correspondent", *MPW*, 22 Feb. 1908, 139.

15. Jon Burrows, "Penny Pleasures [I]: Film Exhibition in London during the Nickelodeon Era, 1906–1914", *Film History* 16/1 (2004): 82–6. See also David R. Williams, "The 'Cinematograph Act' of 1909: An Introduction to the Impetus behind the Legislation and Some Early Effects", *Film History* 9/4 (1997): 341–50.

16. "Foreign News and Notes: From Our English Correspondent", *MPW*, 22 Feb. 1908, 139.

17. "Interviews with F. S. A. Members and Others", *MPW*, 28 Mar. 1908, 260.

18. Ibid.

19. "Motion Picture Show in London", *MPW*, 10 Oct. 1908, 281.

20. Bowser identifies Lux Graphicus as Bedding's pseudonym in *The Transformation of Cinema*, 83.

21. Lux Graphicus, "On the Screen", *MPW*, 12 June 1909, 793.

22. F. W. Swett, "An American Exhibitor in London", *MPW*, 28 Aug. 1909, 284.

23. Fred Marriott, "An English View of the American Moving Picture", *MPW*, 24 July 1909, 116.

24. Fred Marriott, "Some Impressions of the Moving Picture in St. Louis, Detroit and Buffalo", *MPW*, 2 Oct. 1909, 446.

25. According to Marianne Triponi, common use of the spelling "theatre" in the names of American picture palaces reflected these venues' quests for legitimacy; see Triponi, "The New Ironwood Theatre in Context: Movie Palace as Symbol", *Journal of American Culture* 13/4 (1990): 2.

26. "Mrs. Clement and Her Work", *MPW*, 15 Oct. 1910, 859.

27. Lux Graphicus, "On the Screen", *MPW*, 20 Aug. 1910, 405.

28. "The Picture Business in Canada", *MPW*, 19 Feb. 1910, 254.

29. Ibid.

30. See, for instance, "The Motion Picture in European Countries", *MPW*, 10 Feb. 1912, 494.

31. "Plimpton back from Europe", *MPW*, 12 April 1913, 144.

32. "A London Moving Picture House De Luxe", *MPW*, 26 Feb. 1910, 293.

33. H. A. Browne, "American Versus English Films", *MPW*, 24 Dec. 1910, 1483.

34. Ibid.

35. A. E. Taylor, "London Letter", *MPW*, 18 Feb. 1911, 355.

36. On the building of American theaters in this period, see Bowser, *The Transformation of Cinema*, 121–36; and Lary May, *Screening Out the Past: The Birth of Mass Culture and the Motion Picture Industry* (New York: Oxford University Press, 1980), 147–66.

37. A. E. Taylor, "London Letter", *MPW*, 11 Feb. 1911, 295.

38. "London Letter", *MPW*, 13 April 1912, 124.

39. According to Bowser, "the old-style nickelodeons continued to exist in large numbers, particularly in urban ghettos, and some of them far past 1915" (*Transformation of Cinema*, 121). For a careful analysis of the change from small to large theaters during the mid-1910s based on a difference of programming, see Ben Singer, "Feature Films, Variety Programs, and the Crisis of the Small Exhibitor", in *American Cinema's Transitional Era: Audiences, Institutions, Practices*, ed. Charlie Keil and Shelley Stamp (Berkeley: University of California Press, 2004), 76–100. For the situation in London, see Burrows, "Penny Pleasures [I]", passim, and Nicholas Hiley, "Nothing More Than a 'Craze': Cinema Building in Britain from 1909 to 1914", in *Young and Innocent? The Cinema in Britain 1896–1930*, ed. Andrew Higson (Exeter: University of Exeter Press, 2002), 111–27.

40. "British Trade Exhibition", *MPW*, 19 April 1913, 259.

41. "Achievements of 'Nineteen-Eleven'", *MPW*, 13 Jan. 1912.

42. W. Stephen Bush, "Yankee Films Abroad", *MPW*, 10 May 1913, 573.

43. Ibid. American theatres at the time often advertised as accompanying films with "suitable music". Bush believed that most American theatres were not in fact using suitable music, that "suitable music" had devolved into a mere advertising slogan in America, and he was impressed that in London "suitable music" retained its actual meaning.

44. For more on Rothapfel, see Rick Altman, *Silent Film Sound* (New York: Columbia University Press, 2004), 290–92; Ben M. Hall, *The Best Remaining Seats: The Golden Age of the Movie Palace* (New York: Clarkson N. Potter, 1961); Martin Miller Marks, *Music and the Silent Film: Contexts and Case Studies, 1895–1924* (New York: Oxford University Press, 1997), 92–8. Ross Melnick's *American Showman: Samuel "Roxy" Rothafel and the Birth of the Entertainment Industry* (New York: Columbia University Press, 2012) is the most comprehensive account of Rothapfel's career, but it appeared after this chapter went into production. Rothapfel dropped the "p" in the spelling of his name around June 1920. For more on this, see chapter 11, note 7.

45. *Moving Picture World* devoted extensive coverage to the Regent (before Rothapfel moved to the Strand) and, in 1914, the openings of both the Vitagraph Theatre ("Vitagraph Picture

Theater", *MPW* 14 Feb. 1914, 786–87) and the Strand (W. Stephen Bush, "The Opening of the Strand", *MPW*, 18 April 1914, 371).

46. W. Stephen Bush, "The Theatre of Realization", *MPW*, 15 Nov. 1913, 714.

47. Epes Winthrop Sargeant, "B. Nichols Talks", *MPW*, 15 Nov. 1913, 721.

48. "Rothapfel Sails for Europe", *MPW*, 24 Jan. 1914, 398. On the other hand, *Moving Picture World*'s effective long-term training of its readership is illustrated by a letter to Clarence E. Sinn published that same week that contrasted the music in New York to that of London:

> how much longer we will have to be tortured by incompetent pianists and cheap orchestras before the producers and exhibitors will realize that the public is getting disgusted with the musical setting offered daily in the principal theaters here in New York. In London and on the continent managers appreciate the value of the complement of fine music and are employing large orchestras that play good music, intelligently chosen and synchronized with the picture. (H. J. G., cited by Clarence E. Sinn, "Music for the Picture", *MPW*, 15 Nov. 1913, 725).

49. "Rothapfel Back From Europe", *MPW*, 21 Mar. 1914, 526.

50. See, for instance, W. Stephen Bush, "Is the 'Nickel Show' on the Wane", *MPW*, 28 Feb. 1914, 1065; Jas. S. McQuade, "Chicago Letter", *MPW*, 28 Feb. 1914, 1092; and W. Stephen Bush, "Quality's Deadliest Foe", *MPW*, 21 Mar. 1914, 1504. Bush had been advocating for higher prices since 1908, see "The Coming Ten and Twenty Cent Moving Picture Theater", *MPW*, 29 Aug. 1908, 152–3. On the campaign to raise prices during this period, see Robert C. Allen, "Manhattan Myopia; or Oh! Iowa!" *Cinema Journal* 35/3 (1996): 75–103; on audience resistance to the campaign, see Michael G. Aronson, "The Wrong Kind of Nickel Madness: Pricing Problems for Pittsburgh Nickelodeons", *Cinema Journal* 42/1 (2002): 71–96. For more on Rothapfel and a discussion of his report to London exhibitors in 1923, see Julie Brown, chapter 11 this volume.

51. W. Stephen Bush, "The Day of the Expert", *MPW*, 7 Mar. 1914, 1213.

52. See, for instance, W. Stephen Bush, "Gradations of Service", *MPW*, 2 May 1914, 645.

PART THREE

Performance in Cinemas

9

Selsior Dancing Films, 1912–1917

Stephen Bottomore

IN THE COUPLE of years up to the First World War, a film company in London called Selsior made over a dozen charming little films of dances. These films had a gimmick, which was to include the image of a conductor in one side of the frame, to enable a live orchestra in the theatre to keep time with the filmed dancers. Selsior productions were therefore live events and filmed acts rather than conventional film stories, and were an enjoyable novelty for cinema audiences.

The Selsior company did quite well for a while, under managing director and founder Oszkár Rausch, an Austro-Hungarian émigré inventor (see Figure 9.1), but then things went wrong. Rausch had borrowed money for his business, and, pursued by creditors, in the spring of 1914 he resigned from Selsior; and then when war broke out he was interned as an alien-enemy, to face misery in a British prisoner-of-war camp. What makes this story even more poignant is that apparently none of Rausch's Selsior dance films survive. The films would have been a fine testament to the fertile brain of this interesting man, as well as a reminder of the merry side of life before the war. But although the films themselves are not preserved, articles and pictorial advertisements from the trade press disclose many details about these fun-filled movies and give us a good idea of how they looked, and I use this material as the basis of my chapter. By way of an introduction, I will briefly outline the wider context of dance and early film.

FIGURE 9.1   Oszkár János Rausch (b.1884) invented and developed the Selsior system. *The Picturegoer*, 22 November 1913: 214.

DANCE, MUSIC AND EARLY FILM

From the beginnings of moving pictures (even in Muybridge's work) dance has been a frequent and appealing subject.[1] This is scarcely surprising: movies needed movement, and dance *is* organized movement. One of the earliest film catalogues from 1894, listing Edison films made for the kinetoscope, includes an entire section for the genre "Dances".[2] This preoccupation with things terpsichorean lasted some years at the turn of the century—this being an era of dance crazes[3]—and films were made of all kinds of dances: ballet, traditional, popular, Serpentine, clog and speciality, folk, modern, and so on. There were literally dozens of early films made of or about dancing (and even films to teach it). For example, about half of Gaumont's 1900–1902 releases were dance films,[4] while over two hundred dance-related titles were released in the United States just for the period to 1910 (according to the American Film Institute catalogue).[5]

As with live dance, where one had screen dancing one usually had a musical accompaniment too. But here a problem arose: how to get the music to fit, to synchronize with the film. Of course the musicians could just improvise (or "vamp" as they said at the time), but that might be imprecise, depending on the skills of the players. Another approach was to link the film projector mechanically or otherwise with a phonograph, and systems such as Cinephone with its on screen dial were developed; but such systems were not perfect and often went out of sync, and anyway the phonograph sound was "tinny" and not loud enough. A live orchestra sounded much better, but how could one possibly synchronize a group of live musicians in the theatre with the projected film?

Some people came up with the idea of photographing an image of the conductor on one side of the film, and then this "virtual conductor" would in effect "conduct" the orchestra in the hall where the movie was showing. Probably the first to do this was the Italian quick-change artist Leopoldo Fregoli around the turn of the century. He made a film in which he impersonated various famous conductors and composers, such as Rossini, in the act of conducting an orchestra: the live theatre orchestra could then play the original music in time with the filmed musicians.[6] Another early instance came in 1905 in the United States from a troupe calling itself the "Spook Minstrels", consisting of actors and musicians in the theatre who accompanied specially made films in which an on screen conductor helped keep them in time.[7]

A more sophisticated system was invented by a German, Jakob Beck, who applied for a patent in his own country in 1911, and in Britain, France, and the United States in the next two years.[8] This involved using a mirror to reflect a small image of the conductor or "band master", located in an orchestra pit, onto the side of the film, while the main subjects (dancers or the like) were filmed on stage. Variations on this were developed in succeeding years, with additional features: one system in 1914 had an insert image of the score of the sheet music, presumably scrolling down for the players to follow; and other systems had an image of a metronome on the film (all these systems included the conductor's image too).[9] One should also not forget the Dirigentenfilm system, developed by Oskar Messter and Giuseppe Becce in 1914, whereby only the conductor was filmed, his moving image later being projected for musicians: the aim was to allow famous conductors to direct large orchestras without being present in the flesh.[10] Bolesław Matuszewski back in 1898 also suggested filming great conductors (and indeed dances) to preserve their techniques for posterity, offering as example the famed conductor Felix Weingartner—who was later filmed for Dirigentenfilm.[11]

SELSIOR AND OSZKÁR RAUSCH

But what of the Selsior system? When I first came across illustrated advertisements for Selsior in the trade press I thought it might be based on the Beck system of similar date, using a mirror during filming, but actually I found it used a simpler approach. According to Rausch's patent of January 1913, the conductor simply stood in the foreground, with the dancers beyond, and both were filmed in one shot (see Figure 9.2).[12] So in Selsior films the conductor appeared superimposed on the dance scenes (whereas using a mirror the conductor would appear in a separate inset frame, not superimposed on the scene of the dancers).

FIGURE 9.2 In Selsior productions the conductor was filmed in the same shot as the dancers, even in an exterior location as here for *Way Down the Mississippi*. *The Cinema*, 11 December 1913: 79.

During the shooting of a Selsior film the conductor would stand in the side of shot and conduct an off screen pianist who played the music for the dancers on set. Then subsequently in cinemas the theatre musicians would play the same sheet music, while the screen dancers went through their steps. Selsior boasted that its films could be shown in any theatre "without apparatus of any kind", because by watching the on screen conductor the theatre musicians would keep in synchronization.[13] An *Evening Standard* journalist gave a succinct explanation:

> A film in which the conductor in the picture actually directs the living orchestra of the theatre, and makes it keep time with the dancers in the film. The effect is most realistic, and the result is that perfect synchronisation of music and dancing which has hitherto defied all efforts to accompany pictures of dancing.[14]

Selsior's inventor, Oszkár János Rausch (which he anglicized to Oscar John Raush), was born in Budapest on 22 May 1884 and brought up in Vienna.[15] In the early years of the new century he went to Switzerland and Egypt, and then to the United States at the beginning of 1908, where he worked as an engineer near Jersey City until 1910.[16] He arrived in Britain in September of that year, sold a couple of his patents to Dixon and Co., and was appointed consulting engineer with the company, where he stayed for eighteen months.[17] At that point, with great enterprise, he started out on his own as a film producer.

In an interview Rausch stated that he'd been interested in cinema since visiting France and the United States, and seeing the flourishing state of the film business.[18] He realized the need for a sync system for dance performance films when he visited a picture house and noticed that the orchestra's accompaniment for a dance sequence, as he put it, "did not go at all well with that part of the film".[19] He came up with the idea for an on screen conductor and established Selsior in Soho, London.[20] He became managing director with two Germans, Alfred and Otto Liebmann, as directors, and there were a number of mostly German shareholders.[21] Selsior's first films were shot by September 1912 and were shown specially for the press with a live musical accompaniment. A trade writer was there, and noted:

> The musician was rending the air to time beaten by a conductor whose only existence was in the film. There is a fascination about the picture which makes a unique film, and one exhibitors should on no account miss.... At last it can be truthfully asserted that there is something new in films.[22]

The film referred to was Selsior's first effort, entitled *The Turkey Trot*, the name of a popular dance of the day, performed by Joe Bissett and Enid Sellers.[23] The music was "Everybody's Doing It" and "Alexander's Ragtime Band", both current hits by Irving Berlin, and the on screen conductor was an established name from the music hall, George K. Hatley of the Holborn Empire. This film was 300 feet long, so would have run about five minutes. Subsequent Selsior productions were between five and eight minutes. They usually depicted popular dances of the day, often performed by well-known dancers, for as Rausch stated, "I have made a point of securing dancers well known to the public and of real ability. I think this is good from a 'billing' point of view, too."[24]

Selsior films were hired to theatres as special attractions, each costing between about £3 and £8 rental for a week, which included special posters and sheet music for that particular film.[25] This was the same music which the dancers had actually danced to when filmed[26]—so the theatre orchestra, or solo pianist, simply had to play this score, while keeping one eye on the baton of the screen conductor, and that should ensure synchronization. Historian Gillian Anderson has pointed out that one potential sync problem with a Selsior performance would be if the film broke and frames were lost, so making the screen conductor get ahead of the theatre musicians. However, it seems the system generally worked well according to trade press writers of the time: one stated that the Selsior "system of synchronisation" was "as effective as it is novel", and this writer was sufficiently impressed to predict that these films might become "a permanency" in cinema programmes.[27]

The Turkey Trot and the next two Selsior films were based on ragtime rhythms, a very popular musical style of the time (and perhaps the most important genre of Edwardian popular music, say historians).[28] There was *Ragtime Texas Tommy*, again with music by Irving Berlin,[29] and then *Ragtime à la Carte*. The latter film was screened at (among other venues) a leading cinema in London, the Majestic in Tottenham Court Road, and was hugely popular, being rebooked because, "the audience went frantic with delight, and accorded this subject vociferous applause" (see Figure 9.3).[30]

FIGURE 9.3 *Ragtime à la Carte* proved hugely popular when screened at leading cinemas like the Majestic in Tottenham Court Road, London. *The Cinema News and Property Gazette*, 9 April 1913: 30.

SELSIOR DANCING FILMS ACHIEVE SUCCESS

It seems that at this point in early 1913 Selsior was involved in some kind of coproduction with the Kinematograph Trading Co., and four further films were released not credited to Selsior, though these were alike in other respects, being similar-length popular dance films with the conductor appearing in the foreground. The titles were *Bunny Hug* and *Argentine Tango*, both danced by George Grossmith and Phyllis Dare;[31] and *It's Ragtime*.[32] Then in May 1913 came *Always Gay*, also known as *The Evening News Waltz* (from the composition of that title), danced by Vera Maxwell and Jack Jarrott, with Archibald Joyce conducting "in the picture".[33]

In the late spring of 1913 Rausch made a change to procedure, deciding to have the music for his films specially composed. He brought in a skilled musical arranger, Guy Jones, who is credited as composer for the next half-dozen Selsior films, from the summer to the autumn of 1913.[34] The first Jones-composed film was *The Tango Waltz*, danced by Norah Walker and Ernest Belcher, which proved so popular it "had to be screened twice in succession" at one West End venue (see Figure 9.4).[35]

Soon after that came *Way Down the Mississippi*, again composed by Jones, which was something new for Selsior in that it was shot outdoors. It featured Nat Lewis and John Roker (with banjo as "Uncle Tom"), and included a comedy story element; it was said to be one of the most successful of its films.[36] The same cast of Lewis and Roker appeared a couple of months later in Selsior's *The Tramp's Dream*, along with "the four Selsior kiddies" as elves (it became a pattern at Selsior to have four supporting players).[37]

That same summer the company made a film featuring its biggest star so far, the comedy dancer Fanny Fields. For well over a decade, Fields had been a major music hall star in Britain, and this was apparently her only appearance in films. She starred with four other performers, "the four little Dutchmen", of whom Selsior said: "quaint and snappy in action, and will hold any audience".[38] This latter statement proved true, and the film was encored when shown at the Majestic.[39] (The Fields film was an occasion for another sales opportunity too, for exhibitors could sell the sheet music to their audiences at sixpence a copy.[40]) The two remaining Selsior productions with music by Guy Jones were *The Empire Glide* and *The Cowboy Twist*. The first featured starlets from London's Empire Theatre known as "the four Empire beauties";[41] while *The Cowboy Twist* featured a pair of dancers, Rosie Sloman and Harry Perry.[42]

Through the winter of 1913–14 Selsior made four more films.[43] Two of these starred an actress called Mercy Manners: *The Spanish-American Quickstep* was described as full of "movement and vim", and co-starred four other attractive

FIGURE 9.4 *The Tango Waltz* was another hit, and dancer Ernest Belcher later became a leading choreographer in Hollywood. *The Cinema News and Property Gazette*, 20 November 1913: 12.

actresses;[44] *By the Sea* featured Manners and "the Empire girls" again, and a silly-ass character or "knut", complete with monocle, who eventually walks off with the girls (see Figure 9.5). One reviewer called it "a capital little film", with "charming ladies tripping the light fantastic, in perfect synchronism with the music.... A tasty little dish just in time for the summer season."[45]

The other two films from this time, *The Society Tango*[46] and *The Maxixe Brasilienne* were it seems straightforward dance performance films, featuring amateur dance champions R. L. Leonard and Amélie de S–, who were described as the "greatest tangoists ever".[47] Selsior's publicity added that Amélie de S– was "a well-known continental lady who does not wish her name to transpire".[48] *The Society Tango* was available hand-coloured. Rausch also had another ambitious production either under way or planned at this time, *Cinema Revue*, starring Daisy James among a claimed cast of fifty (see Figure 9.6).[49]

FIGURE 9.5 *By the Sea* was a typically jolly Selsior title, but by this time Rausch was in financial trouble and this film was distributed by Walturdaw. *Walturdaw Weekly Budget*, 7 July 1914: 181.

AND THEN CAME 1914

At this point, by my count, Selsior had released thirteen films under its brand name (see Table 9.1).[50] With that it seems production came to an end, even though the company seemed to be doing well and was even developing foreign markets.[51] Rausch himself was trying to start other companies, but it seems that these plans went nowhere because he was in financial trouble by this stage.[52] Rausch resigned as managing director of Selsior in May 1914.[53] The reason would appear to be that at about that time he was sued for unpaid debts, for although Selsior had been successful

FIGURE 9.6 Three films advertised by Selsior in its heyday: *The Society Tango*, *The Spanish-American Quickstep*, and the planned *Cinema Revue*. *Kinematograph and Lantern Weekly*, 19 February 1914: 80.

for the past year, Rausch himself had been borrowing money for some time, and was declared bankrupt in December.[54] He owed over £358 to nineteen creditors, the bulk of it to money lenders, but also to film and other companies. Although in his bankruptcy hearing he declared that "my failure is due entirely to the War and to the alien enemy restrictions", that statement was somewhat disingenuous, for he had been sued three months *before* the First World War began.[55] In fact, it is plain that Rausch was the architect of his own financial failure—though the war then added immeasurably to his misery.

Rausch was from Austria-Hungary, which was at war with Britain from 12 August 1914, and "alien-enemies" were soon under suspicion and subject to control: Rausch himself registered as an alien-enemy in September.[56] He was interned by the British authorities at Knockaloe Camp on the Isle of Man by the following year. His fellow directors Alfred and Otto Liebmann were also interned, but not at Knockaloe: they

TABLE 9.1 Filmography of Selsior films

Title	Month/Year	Performers	Conductor	Music	Feet	Comments
The Turkey Trot: Everybody's Doing It	Sept. 1912	Joe Bissett, Enid Sellers	George K. Hatley	Irving Berlin	300	distr: New Century
Ragtime Texas Tommy	Sept. 1912	Harry Perry, Millicent Ray		Irving Berlin	350	
Ragtime à la Carte	Jan.? 1913	Joe Bissett, Enid Sellers			?	
The Tango Waltz	June 1913	Ernest Belcher, Norah Walker	George K. Hatley	Guy Jones	550 or 300	distr: Gaumont
Happy Fanny Fields and the Four Little Dutchmen	July 1913	Fanny Fields and "the four little Dutchmen"	George K. Hatley	Guy Jones	450 or 400	distr: Gaumont?
Way Down the Mississippi	July 1913	John Roker, Nat Lewis "and the four Selsior kiddies"	George K. Hatley	Guy Jones	450 or 500	
The Empire Glide	Aug. 1913	"The four Empire beauties"	George K. Hatley	Guy Jones	500	
The Tramp's Dream	Sept. 1913	John Roker, Nat Lewis	George K. Hatley	Guy Jones	500	
The Cowboy Twist	Oct. 1913	Rosie Sloman, Harry Perry		Guy Jones	500	
The Spanish-American Quickstep	Nov. 1913	Mercy Manners and four "variety girls"			500	
The Society Tango	Feb. 1914	R. L. Leonard, Amélie de S–			500	in colour
The Maxixe Brasilienne	Mar. 1914	R. L. Leonard, Amélie de S–			500	
By the Sea	Apr. 1914	Mercy Manners and "the Empire girls"			350	distr: Walturdaw

presumably had more financial means, so were sent to a camp at Wakefield which was for better-off internees.[57]

Rausch became sick with rheumatism and catarrh, and was not permitted to see a doctor at Knockaloe, according to his brother (probably still in Austria) who complained about this to the authorities in Vienna. The Austrian authorities in January 1916 contacted the British Foreign Office (via the US embassy), and the complaint was investigated.[58] Rausch was pronounced fit in April, so could not be transferred, let alone released, and there was a similar conclusion the following year. It is likely that Rausch was still in Knockaloe in 1918.[59] I have however not managed to trace him after the war.

As to the Selsior company itself, while the directors had been incarcerated, the films continued to be distributed by others, including Walturdaw.[60] In 1917 a dozen Selsior films were available from the Sherwood Exclusive Film Agency of London. Their ads, headed "Selsior dancing films", stated patriotically that the films were "made in England by British Artistes", and there was no mention of the Germanic names of Rausch or Liebmann (see Figure 9.7).[61] I have not found out if Selsior films were still distributed after the war, nor have I discovered what happened to Rausch, and whether he returned to Hungary or the United States—or indeed if he even survived the war.[62] However, I have traced some of the other personnel who took part in these films, who had notable careers before and/or after their Selsior work.

Fanny Fields was, of course, already a major music hall star when she appeared for Selsior. Harry Perry and Rosie Sloman, the dancers in Selsior's *The Cowboy Twist*, were instrumentalists with the well-known group "the Ragtime six": in the 1920s, Sloman, under the name of "Jenny Golder", became a sensation on the Paris musical stage.[63] Guy Jones continued after the war as a top musical arranger, working on popular melodies and musicals, including Noel Coward's *Cavalcade*. Perhaps the most successful of all was Ernest Belcher (1882–1973), co-star of Selsior's *Tango Waltz*, and a skilled classical dancer. In 1914 he moved to the United States and became one of the leading choreographers for Hollywood films from the late 1910s, and a celebrated dance teacher in Los Angeles, training such stars as Cyd Charisse, Rita Hayworth, and many others.[64]

SELSIOR AND "ATTRACTIONS"

The Selsior films themselves, as mentioned, all seem to have disappeared. A shame, for they were an interesting experiment: interesting not least, I think, for film historiographical reasons. Tom Gunning writes that films of dances were "one of the most stable genres" up to about 1904, usually presented much like music hall turns with one dance being one film. Then film style evolved, and in cinema after 1904, though dance remained an important theme, it became just one element within the plot of a film.[65]

┌───┐

─ Something different that will fill your Theatre ─

GREAT SUCCESS OF THE

SELSIOR DANCING FILMS.

We are re-issuing the following subjects—

Way Down the Mississippi.	**Happy Fanny Fields.**
The Empire Glide.	**The Tango Waltz.**
The Society Tango.	**Ragtime Texas Tommy.**
Spanish-American Quickstep.	**By the Sea.**
Maxixe Brasilienne.	**The Tramp's Dream.**

Ragtime a la Carte.

Approx. 300-400 ft. each.   These films are made in England by British Artistes and every subject is an artistic production.

Write for full particulars of these Novelties.

> The synchronism is assured by the movements of the conductor, who is seen wielding his baton in the left hand corner of the picture. Specially composed music is issued with each film and any pianist or orchestra may render the accompaniment with perfect accuracy without any preparation or rehearsal.

THESE POWERFUL ATTRACTIONS MEAN MONEY FOR THE EXHIBITOR.
WHAT ABOUT YOUR TOWN ?
We are renting these films at LOW PRICES which include music and posters.

SEND FOR NEW LIST OF OVER 100 GOOD EXCLUSIVES AT BOTTOM PRICES
SEXTON BLAKE AND BRITAIN'S SECRET TREATY.
A great three-reeler.   Re-issue with NEW COPIES.
LIEUT. ROSE AND THE STOLEN BULLION.
London and the South.   (New Copies.)
THE CALL of the MOTHERLAND   **THE ARM OF THE LAW.**
THE EMIGRANT'S PERIL.   **A VOICE FROM THE SEA.**
And Many Others.

Sherwood Exclusive Film Agency,

STANLEY HOUSE, 8 & 9 SHERWOOD STREET, LONDON, W.   Telephone— GERRARD 414 8

└───┘

FIGURE 9.7   During the war Selsior films were distributed as all-British productions, with no mention of Rausch. *Kinematograph and Lantern Weekly*, 8 February 1917: 68.

So one might say that these Selsior films were a kind of throwback to a decade earlier and the presentational "cinema of attractions" style (using this term to contrast with "the classical Hollywood cinema,"[66] which drew spectators into a hermetic narrative). Even people of the time seemed to regard Selsior films as more like *acts* than typical films. One commentator stated in 1914: "there is no attempt at making a story of it; just the dance and nothing more."[67] Indeed, so much did Selsior films resemble *live* stage acts that, as I've mentioned above, spectators would call for encores. *The Picturegoer* stated: "These pictures are already so popular that more often than not they are actually encored and have to be repeated, for all the world as if they were a legitimate music-hall turn."[68]

Actually one could even argue that Selsior's films were more like music hall turns (and more "attraction like") than earlier dance films because, with the conductor in shot, viewers had a greater sense of being shown a live act (see, for instance, Figure 9.8).

October 22, 1913.   Supplement to THE CINEMA.   71

HAPPY FANNY FIELDS' FAREWELL.

EXHIBITORS,—Are you aware that Happy Fanny Fields is making her farewell this week at the Coliseum, London, and sails for America on November 6? This talented artiste will be seen no more on the Variety Stage, BUT SHE CAN BE SEEN ON YOUR SCREEN by booking the Selsior Dancing Film,

HAPPY FANNY FIELDS
and The Four Little Dutchmen.

£8
per week.
Including Posters.

£8
per week.
Including Posters.

THE ONLY FILM EVER TAKEN OF ENGLAND'S GREATEST COMEDIENNE

NOTICE.—Selsior Productions are the only **Dancing Films** which are produced and exhibited in a manner (**Protected under the Patent Act, 1907**) ensuring perfect synchronism between music and dancers.

SELSIOR, Ltd.,
Cinematograph Producers and Music Publishers,
3, Denman Street, Piccadilly Circus, London, W.
Tel. REGENT 1450.

Selsior Film
TRADE MARK

FIGURE 9.8 Selsior films, starring well-known performers like "Happy" Fanny Fields, resembled music hall acts with the conductor included in shot. *The Cinema News and Property Gazette*, 22 October 1913: 71.

The Selsior system was unusual in this respect, compared with some other sync sound systems which tried to hide their means of synchronization, lest the "mechanism" draw attention to itself and spoil the illusion.[69] The Jakob Beck patent, for example, recommended that the inset image of the conductor in the corner of the frame should be visible only to the theatre orchestra behind the screen, and that this corner of the image should be "covered by a suitable partition" in the theatre so as to hide it from the audience.[70] Thus an audience for a Beck film would see only the film itself and hear the music, but would not see the inset conductor.[71]

By contrast, Rausch was unabashed about showing his conductor to the audience. Why? Simply because Rausch believed that, while audiences didn't like seeing mechanical synchronization devices (e.g., the dial for the Cinephone), they *did* like seeing a human conductor in the picture. As he stated in his patent:

> Films so produced will be found to be much more appreciated and attractive to an audience than those on which a mechanical pointer arm or like device appears on each picture as the conductor will also appeal to the audience as well as to the pianist or orchestra....[72]

In short, Rausch thought that the conductor was more than a mere means of synchronization, and was an attraction in himself or herself, being *added value*, just as in live theatre. Indeed Selsior's publicity extolled the "star quality" of its conductors, such as George Hatley from the Holborn Empire, one of London's leading music halls. And the conductors *were* noticed: for example, one viewer wrote that in a particular Selsior film the conductor "works himself into a fine frenzy".[73] The conductor, therefore, as well as the dancers—as well as the live music—together made Selsior films the treat that they were.

In conclusion, the Selsior performance films suggest to me that, even as late as the First World War when "the classical Hollywood cinema" had become dominant, films as *turns* or *attractions* could still have considerable appeal. I suspect that these films even today would be enjoyable, featuring as they did some of the top musicians, conductors, and entertainers of the Edwardian era, presenting themselves directly to the camera. One can only hope that one or more of these lost Selsior films will someday be found, so that we too can experience the attraction.

NOTES

1. Muybridge's "woman dancing" sequence of 1893 shows a Miss Larrigan dancing.

2. This catalogue is reprinted in *Victorian Film Catalogues: A Facsimile Collection*, prepared for publication by Stephen Herbert, Colin Harding, and Simon Popple (London: Projection Box, 1996).

3. A dance craze spread through America and Europe from about 1911 and into the war years. David Nasaw, *Going Out: The Rise and Fall of Public Amusements* (Cambridge, MA: Harvard University Press, 1999), chapter 9.

4. Richard Abel's estimate, cited in Tom Gunning's entry on "Dance films" in *Encyclopedia of Early Cinema*, ed. Richard Abel (London: Routledge, 2005).

5. See www.afi.com.

6. Apparently the orchestra appearing in the film was the Alhambra Orchestra. See John Barnes, *The Beginnings of the Cinema in England, 1894–1901*, Vol. 3: *1898: The Rise of the Photoplay* (Exeter: University of Exeter Press, 1996), 12–15, 184.

7. Rick Altman, *Silent Film Sound* (New York: Columbia University Press, 2004), 109–11. It was reported that the synchronization sometimes didn't work very well.

8. See "Latest inventions", *The Bioscope*, 1 August 1912, 345. The US patent details are: J. Beck, "Method of obtaining synchronism between a kinematographic performance and an acoustic accompaniment thereof", number 1,069,221, applied 26 Feb. 1912, accepted 5 Aug. 1913. See www. espacenet.com for European patent details.

9. The score invention was by P. P. Benedetti of Rio de Janeiro: *Bioscope*, 21 May 1914, 853. The metronome system was by Beck in 1917: see Michael Wedel, "Messter's 'Silent' Heirs: Sync Systems of the German Music Film, 1914–1929", *Film History* 11/4 (1999), 464–76. A metronome was also used in the "film opera" system: *Scientific American Monthly* (June 1920), 521. Grimoin-Sanson made a film in 1920, *Le Comte de Griolet*, incorporating the conductor's baton at bottom of frame: see Raoul Grimoin-Sanson, *Le Film de Ma Vie* (Paris: Henry Parville, 1926), 161–8: including a frame still. One could also mention Luscombe's animated conductor films in the 1920s.

10. The conductor was filmed from two angles. See Harald Pulch, "Messters Experiment der Dirigentenfilme" [conductor films], *KINtop* 3 (1994): 53–64; and see Albert Narath, "Oskar Messter and his Work", in *A Technological History of Motion Pictures and Television*, ed. Raymond Fielding (Berkeley: University of California Press, 1967): 109–17. This cites patent 293573, 4 Nov. 1913; there were subsequent patents up to 1919. Also see reports in *New York Times*, 3 May 1914, 2; *Bioscope*, 18 June 1914, 1263; *Film Censor*, 1 July 1914, 2e; and Alfred Lorenz, "Der gefilmte Kapellmeister", *Neue Zeitschrift fur Musik* 81/26 (1914), 377–8. The system was in use in the United States in 1916: see *Popular Mechanics* 26 (1916), 653.

11. See chapter "Various uses of cinematography", in Bolesław Matuszewski, *La Photographie Animée: Ce Qu'elle Est; Ce Qu'elle Doit Être* (Paris: Noizette, 1898), 48–9.

12. The only complication was that in order to avoid the cameraman being tempted to crank in time to the music played on set and keep him cranking at a standard rate, he was to listen to a loud clockwork metronome-type device, and/or have his ears blocked. See British patent no. 1728: applied 21 Jan. 1913, accepted 15 Jan. 1914 under the anglicized name of "Raush" (in advertisements Selsior rightly claimed to be "protected under the patent act, 1907"). Incidentally, Rausch specifically states that his own system is better than Beck's mirror system. Rausch applied for a trademark for "Selsior Film" in January 1913, granted as no. 348,958: see *Trade Marks Journal*, 5 Mar. 1913, 351.

13. This claim appears in several of its advertisements, and it was stated that "any pianist or orchestra" could accompany in perfect accuracy "without any preparation or rehearsal". *Kinematograph and Lantern Weekly* (hereafter, *KLW*), 8 Feb. 1917, 68.

14. "Selsior Dancing Films: An Explanation", *Bioscope*, 7 Aug. 1913, xxxii.

15. "Preliminary examination of debtor", 16 Dec. 1914, among Rausch's bankruptcy papers in National Archives BT226/4258. Rausch states that he and his parents left for Vienna in 1886 where he remained some fifteen years. In the United States he made an initial application for naturalization, but for completion, a further application would have been required after three years, which he didn't do.

16. In "Preliminary examination of debtor" Rausch claims he arrived in the United States in 1907, but according to www.ellisisland.org, Oscar Rausch, a Magyar from Vienna, single, merchant, twenty-three years old arrived in the United States on 8 February 1908. Further details are: height 5 ft 6 inches; born Budapest; nearest relative, Oscar Rausch, Vienna. His passage was paid by his father; he had $60 on him and was going to see John A. Rausch, 610 Warren St, Syracuse.

17. He was on a reasonable salary, and Dixon's apparently did market his inventions. Rausch claimed that he had patented some kind of advertisement tape-making apparatus, and he applied

for a British patent, no. 20,301 (not issued) in September 1911 for a "photographic printing apparatus".

18. "Mr. O. J. Rausch", *Cinema News and Property Gazette* (hereafter, *Cinema*), 1 Jan. 1914, 85.

19. *Cinema*, 1 Jan. 1914, 85.

20. The company was registered 7 April 1913 at 3 Denman Street: *Bioscope*, 24 April 1913, 273; certificate of incorporation in BT 31/21359/128197. The London Project at http://londonfilm.bbk. ac.uk lists the addresses for Selsior, all in Soho: 3 Denman Street until January 1914; 16a Soho Square from January to July 1914; West End House, 3–6 Rupert Street from June 1914. The Soho Square address was announced as a new showroom in *The Bioscope*, 5 Feb. 1914, 524. Selsior was known as "Excelsior" in the early days at Denman Street, though when the Selsior name took over, Excelsior also continued, at 213 Shaftesbury Avenue. See the London Project, and *Bioscope*, 12 Sept. 1912, 773.

21. Selsior's shareholders were as follows on 18 July 1913 (see BT 31/21359/128197). Alfred and Otto Liebmann, who gave London addresses; Ernst Liebmann, who was a "merchant" of Mannheim, Germany (so one assumes all three Liebmanns were from there). Some other shareholders were also Mannheim merchants: Ludwig, Oscar, and Rudolf Adler, Alfred and Ernst Bodenheimer, Sally Haas, Heinrich Helwig, Adolf and Karl Mayer-Reinach, Philipp Reinhardt, Max Rose, Felix Traub; while Dr Eugen Weingart, also of Mannheim, was a barrister. Then from Wallington, Surrey, were Sidney Gillett (who was also assistant manager or secretary of Selsior) and Alan F. Harwar. Lastly, Henry Deacon Wood of 69 Alexandra Park Road, Muswell Hill, and Rausch himself of 26 Russell Chambers, Bury Street, London WC. This makes twenty shareholders in all of whom sixteen were from Mannheim. The figures show that Alfred Liebmann and Rausch were the largest shareholders.

22. *Cinema*, Sept. 1912, 2; *Bioscope*, 12 Sept. 1912, 773 states that this press show took place "Friday last".

23. *Bioscope*, 26 Sept. 1912, 923; 27 Feb. 1913, 621. *The Turkey Trot* is stated to be Selsior's first film in: "Dancing films", *Picturegoer*, 22 Nov. 1913, 214–15.

24. *Cinema*, 1 Jan. 1914, 85.

25. The price to hire a Selsior film varied depending on size of venue and newness of film. The highest price I have seen was £10, charged for an "artistically coloured" version of the *Society Tango*, *KLW*, 26 Feb. 1914, lix. Selsior used at least one travelling salesperson, Miss Dorothy Esworth (later managing director of the Pearl Film Co., a distributor) to visit cinema managers, trying to sell the films, *KLW*, 22 Oct. 1914, 73.

26. Selsior supplied piano music free, and charged 1s. 6d. for orchestrations. Also available were advertising postcards, printed with the name of the theatre, at 10s. for 500, *KLW*, 28 Aug. 1913, xlii.

27. *Kinematograph Year Book* for 1914, 27.

28. Ronald Pearsall, *Edwardian Popular Music* (Newton Abbot: David and Charles, 1975), 181.

29. *Bioscope*, 26 Sept. 1912, 923; 7 Nov. 1912, 391.

30. "How Ragtime Captured the Cinemas", *Cinema*, 9 April 1913, 30: based on an interview with Raush [*sic*]. The photograph in this article reveals that other films in the programme were *The Latent Spark* (American, 1913) and *Tigris* (Itala, 1913). The Majestic was at 36 Tottenham Court Road, where in 2012 the Odeon cinema stands.

31. These were released around February 1913, length 500 feet, with special music, and credited as the first productions of the Kinematograph Trading Co. See *Bioscope*, 6 Feb. 1913, 27; *Cinema*,

19 Feb. 1913, 397; *Kinetradogram*, 12 Feb. 1913. For more information about Dare, see "Phyllis Dare", *Silent Film Monthly*, Sept. 1997, 1–4.

32. *KLW*, 6 Feb. 1913, 1518: produced by the Kinematograph Trading Co.

33. Released by Hepworth, *Always Gay* was 250 ft long. The *Kinetradogram*, 28 May 1913, discusses this film and Kinematograph Trading Co.'s Grossmith/Dare films, which suggests they were all made by the same company.

34. Jones was a well-known arranger, with numerous credits to his name from the turn of the century.

35. Advertisememt for *The Tango Waltz*, *KLW*, 28 Aug. 1913, xlii. See also *Bioscope*, 10 July 1913, 113. The sheet music is excerpted in *Illustrated Films Monthly* (hereafter, *IFM*) Oct. 1913.

36. *Express Overseas Mail* (hereafter, *EOM*), Feb. 1914, 22.

37. *Bioscope*, 7 Aug. 1913, 395.

38. *Bioscope*, 17 July 1913, 217. See also *Cinema*, 23 July 1913, 39; *Bioscope*, 24 July 1913, 279.

39. "The Picture Pianist", *Bioscope*, 21 Aug. 1913, 593: this article added that screenings of *Way Down the Mississippi*, also at the Majestic, received "triumphant receptions" from audiences; see also *KLW*, 11 Sept. 1913, 2134.

40. The company also sold their music as general film accompaniment material. Selsior advertisement in W. Tyacke George, *Playing to Pictures: A Guide for Pianists and Conductors of Motion Picture Theatres*, 2nd edn (London: Heron, 1914).

41. *Cinema*, 27 Aug. 1913, 53; *KLW*, 25 Sept. 1913, 2282; *Cinema*, 11 Dec. 1913, ad.

42. *IFM*, Oct. 1913.

43. There is also a report, though no details, of Selsior making a sketch film about "bill-posting" for their planned film revue (see below): *KLW*, 26 Feb. 1914, lix.

44. *EOM*, Mar. 1914, 8. See also *Cinema*, 27 Nov. 1913, 29; *KLW*, 26 Mar. 1914, 70; 9 April 1914, 43.

45. *Cinematograph Exhibitors Mail*, 8 April 1914, 30: this writer called the "knut" a "typical seaside 'Johnny'". See also *KLW*, 23 April 1914, 64.

46. This is the second Tango title in the Selsior filmography, and was part of a tango trend of the time: dozens of films about this dance were produced.

47. The couple had won five competitions, including in Baden-Baden in 1913: *KLW*, 19 Feb. 1914, 80.

48. *KLW*, 26 Feb. 1914, lix; 5 Mar. 1914, 37.

49. Rausch discusses this big planned production in "How Ragtime Captured the Cinemas". The *Cinema Revue* film or series was promoted on the cover of *Illustrated Films Monthly* in January 1914. This magazine also promoted Selsior films on covers in September and December 1913.

50. In addition to thirteen titles credited to Selsior, four titles mentioned above seem to be Selsior productions but released by other companies such as Hepworth: *The Argentine Tango*, *The Bunny Hug*, *It's Ragtime*, and *Always Gay*; and Gifford lists two 300 ft films as Selsior's, but I can find no confirmation: *The Yankee Tangle* (October, 1912), with Ernest Belcher and Dorothy Grahame, and *The Manhattan Glide* (December 1912), with Joe Bissett and Enid Sellers. See Denis Gifford, *The British Film Catalogue*, Vol. 1: *Fiction Film, 1895–1994* (London: Fitzroy Dearborn, 2000).

51. It was announced Selsior had secured exhibition rights for three foreign territories and had one foreign agent. *KLW*, 9 April 1914, 35.

52. In "Preliminary examination of debtor" Rausch states that in 1914 he tried to float Cinema Club Ltd, Cinema Revue Ltd (see above), and planned Kinick Film Productions to attract capital from the public for film making.

53. *KLW*, 21 May 1914, 29. This noted that the company continued to produce and hire their films from 16a Soho Square. Selsior films were showcased in the *Walturdaw Weekly Budget* in June and July 1914 (magazine issues held in the Cinémathèque Canadienne, Montréal). Selsior business ceased from August according to Gillett's letter (see below).

54. With regard to Rausch's 1914 financial problems and bankruptcy, see BT 226/4258 and BT 221/1822. Proceedings were brought against him in May and a receiving order was made on 16 December 1914. The bankruptcy process continued until May 1915 at least.

55. "Preliminary examination of debtor", BT 226/4258.

56. He stated in "Preliminary Examination of Debtor" that he registered (with the name "Raush") on 30 September 1914 at "Vine Street", presumably the well-known Vine Street police station.

57. A document in BT 31/21359/128197 gives addresses of (former) Selsior directors as at 31 December 1915: Alfred and Otto Liebmann were at Lofthouse Park, Wakefield. In this same file, a letter from Sidney Gillett, Secretary of Selsior Ltd, to Companies Registration Office, 3 March 1916, states that the bulk of shareholders were "alien enemies".

58. The letter from Vienna was dated 31 January 1916. The National Archives, Foreign Office Files, FO 383/114; see also FO 383/115.

59. According to Foreign Office index cards (though I haven't traced the indexed documents) there was further correspondence in the next two years, including another mention in 1917 that the climate was not affecting Rausch's health (according to various accounts Knockaloe camp had a rather good health record).

60. There is a report of Selsior's "Spanish-American" film on a programme in La Scala, Glasgow: see *The Scotsman*, 5 Jan. 1915, 8.

61. Initially Sherwood reissued eleven of Selsior's total of thirteen films. *KLW*, 8 Feb. 1917, 68. Then *The Cowboy Twist* was added later in the year, making twelve reissued films. *Bioscope*, 13 Sept. 1917, 103. So the only credited title not to be re-released was *The Turkey Trot*. I have not systematically searched the trade press in the war years, and there might have been more convolutions to this post-Rausch history.

62. In response to my query, Günter Krenn of Filmarchiv Austria wrote in an email of 3 May 2011: "I couldn't find the name of your Mr. Rausch in the Austrian film industry. My Hungarian colleagues also found no evidence of his appearance."

63. With regard to Harry Perry and "the Ragtime Six", see the online resource http://harpguitars.net/blog/2010/09/"wilber"-wanted/ [accessed 3 August 2012]. Rosie Sloman was born 1894 (or 1896) in Kyneton, Australia, and educated in Britain (her mother's maiden name was Golder). See also www.udenap.org [11 March 2011].

64. A good account of Ernest Belcher is in: Naima Prevots, *Dancing in the Sun: Hollywood Choreographers, 1915–1937* (Ann Arbor: UMI, 1987). See also Larry Billman, *Film Choreographers and Dance Directors: an Illustrated Biographical Encyclopedia* (Jefferson, NC: McFarland, 1997), 22, 228–9.

65. Tom Gunning's entry on "Dance films", in Abel, *Encyclopedia of Early Cinema*, 163.

66. One might also use Noël Burch's term "institutional mode of representation".

67. *Cinematograph Exhibitors Mail*, 8 April 1914, 30. This was a slight exaggeration as some films, including the very one that the writer mentions, *By the Sea*, did have some narrative elements. Nevertheless, a Selsior film was basically a filmed act rather than a story.

68. "Dancing films", *Picturegoer*, 22 Nov. 1913, 214–15.

69. In some cases the synchronization device *was* a distraction. In the Cinephone sync system the film included a small image of a moving disc which had to be kept in exact step with a similar disc on a gramophone by the projectionist, and sometimes, wrote Cecil Hepworth, "the audience got so interested in watching his efforts that they forgot to listen". Quoted in John Scotland, *The Talkies* (London: Crosby Lockwood and Son, 1930), ix (Hepworth attributes the system to Barker). Thanks to Joe Kember for this information.

70. The Beck patent had the film projector also behind screen along with the orchestra.

71. Beck's American patent admits that in some cases the audience might be permitted to see the conductor's inset image, but the British patent doesn't allow for that. There are other examples in the early film era of live sound-making which was visible to the audience (such as sound effects making).

72. Rausch's patent no. 1728, 1913. I have corrected a misprint in the original which has "that" instead of "than".

73. This was in the *Bunny Hug* film. See *Kinetradogram*, 12 Feb. 1913, n.p. Incidentally, live conductors in cinemas too were sometimes objects of unusual interest. On one occasion in a Paris cinema "…so energetic was the conductor that the whole audience stood up to watch him, every eccentric movement of the bâton bringing forth peals of laughter, cries of derision, and loud clapping. People left their seats to get a better view…". *Bioscope*, 26 Sept. 1912, 957.

10

Song Performance in the Early Sound Shorts of British Pathé

Derek B. Scott

THIS CHAPTER IS concerned with the new demands, opportunities, and limitations of the medium of film as it attempted to capture theatrical performances in the early days of sound. During the early 1930s, it is interesting to see the impact on performers when they move from a theatre stage to a film studio and are faced with a camera instead of a live audience. As my case studies, I am choosing four Pathé musical shorts that are representative of three musical genres: music hall, operetta, and cabaret. The films I have chosen contain performances by the Cockney music hall comedian Gus Elen, the light operatic tenor Richard Tauber, and the cabaret artist Greta Keller. Musical shorts have been neglected by both film historians and musicologists, despite their value in capturing performances of the stars of a bygone age, some of whom do not appear in any other films.[1] In the case of Gus Elen, for example, we have a unique opportunity to watch one of the most acclaimed music hall stars of the 1890s, brought out of retirement specially to recreate his turns. Thanks to the funding of the digitization of the British Pathé archive by the UK National Lottery in 2002, the company's output became freely available for previewing online in 2010.[2]

British Pathé recorded many shorts of variety performers in the early years of sound. A brief history of Pathé will make clear the company's interests and the context of the films. Pathé Frères had set up in Paris in 1896 manufacturing cameras and projectors, but began to expand their business, moving into the production of records and films, and developing important markets in Britain, the United States,

Sweden, Russia, and Germany before the First World War.[3] Pathé opened a London office in 1902, and moved in 1910 to premises at 84 Wardour Street that included a small studio. Pathé had the novel idea of producing a newsreel to be shown before the feature film. These shorts were, from the first, designed to appeal to a broad range of film-goers. For example, *Pathé Gazette*, which began in Britain in 1910, included news items intended to appeal to young women. An advertisement headed "The Ladies!" was placed in *The Bioscope* in 1910, announcing that the Paris fashions would be making a weekly appearance in the Gazette.[4] The filming was from a single camera position in the early newsreels, and they were barely five minutes in duration (they became longer after the First World War), but their success with the public stimulated Pathé's interest in producing other shorts.

Music halls were important to the commercial interests of film pioneers in Britain in the very early years because these theatres were initially the primary venues where the films were shown.[5] In 1896 the Lumière show at the Empire, Leicester Square, generated an interest that quickly spread to other music halls. Something similar happened with vaudeville theatres in the United States. Pathé Cinematograph established a sales office in New York in 1904, and another in Chicago the following year.[6] In the summer of 1905 Harry Davis opened his nickelodeon in Pittsburgh, showing a continuous programme of moving pictures, and it was Pathé that Richard Abel identifies as the company that fueled the nickelodeon boom of 1905–6.[7] It is after the passing of this nickelodeon era that most histories of cinema choose to ignore short films.

Many of the early shorts, however, were not of music hall turns, even though they often fed off the existing entertainment found in the halls: Michael Chanan relates their use of simple stories to those already established in music hall sketches.[8] It should be remembered that both Charlie Chaplin and Stan Laurel began their careers in music hall.[9] Early films of variety turns were likely to be of jugglers, contortionists, and others who, unlike singers, did not require sound as an essential part of their performance. Some attempts were made in the early days to synchronize films of singers to a gramophone recording: Phono-Bio-Tableau Films, for instance, made an effort to do this with Vesta Tilley's "Algy, the Piccadilly Johnny" in 1900.[10] Other synchronized films of variety performers were made in the first decade of the century, using Léon Gaumont's sound-on-disc Chronophone (invented 1902) as well as a related technology, Cinematophone, developed by the Walturdaw Company in 1907. These sound films, however, enjoyed limited commercial success.

British filmmaker George Pearson, in his autobiography *Flashback*, describes the Pathé studio in London in 1912. He had to be content with a five-strong crew (cameraman, electrician, carpenter, scene painter, and handyman), and he found the methods there inflexible. The camera was fixed to the floor, and a chalk line was drawn to indicate to the actor that this was the point at which they would move out of frame (in other words, their feet would be chopped off).[11] It shows that Pathé conceived of the film set as a theatrical stage. It is evident that this remained the dominant concept for the shorts they filmed in Wardour Street in the early 1930s. One reason for the camera position being static in these early years was that it needed to be contained in a soundproofed booth to prevent the noise of its mechanism reaching the sensitive condenser microphone.[12] Cover shooting is a technique used to obtain differing shots when only one camera is available, and close examination shows that this is what has taken place in the Elen films I will be discussing. A tighter lens is fitted for a second take consisting of mid-shots, and Elen has been asked to repeat his performance as exactly as possible.

This contrasts with the studio Pathé had in upper Manhattan from September 1928 to December 1929, which was also used for shorts and newsreels.[13] Like the Wardour Street studio, it was cramped, but it did have three cameras positioned for multiple-camera shooting.[14] This technique was excellent for ensuring synchronization, but expensive because of the quantity of film reel it consumed. Everything had to be filmed at a single take, and if anything went wrong, a second whole take was necessary. Artists who had a fully worked-out routine were the easiest to work with. Disappointingly, but no doubt for financial reasons, the studio filmed chorus members from New York shows, rather than well-known stars. Pathé's American enterprise was bought by RKO Pictures in 1931 (and was acquired by Warner brothers in 1947).

In the 1920s the Pathé-Consortium was the leading French production company, and the reason for Hollywood's failure to achieve the same dominance in France as it had succeeded in doing in Britain.[15] Pathé-Natan (formed in 1929) was France's largest film production company during the period of conversion to sound. Pathé-Natan was keen on theatre adaptations, and signed up many well-known stage performers of the time. Yet most of the films were made solely for French consumption, and it did not produce dubbed versions for the international market. British Pathé therefore had an opportunity to follow suit and draw on the resources of the British stage and its performers. The course taken, however, was of necessity different in a major respect. After converting to sound in 1929, British Pathé did extend its range of interests to include entertainment and sport, but had sold its film studios at Alexandra Palace (dating from 1911) to Eastman Kodak in 1927, and was no longer in a position to make feature films.[16] In the early 1930s British Pathé was producing only shorts: the *Gazette*, *Pathétone Weekly*, *Pathé Pictorial*, and *Eve's Film Review*. Most of the musical items appeared in *Pathétone Weekly*. The filmed performances range from variety singers like Ella Shields to crooners like Al Bowlly. There are classical instrumentalists like violinist Albert Sandler, as well as dance bands, such as those led by

Billy Cotton and Jack Hylton.[17] Sometimes, as in the Richard Tauber short, which will be examined later, Pathé filmed artists who were involved in the many musical films that constituted an important part of the output of British film companies in the 1930s. These films accounted for around fifteen per cent of all films made in that decade, although, with the exception of Stephen Guy's research, the feature-length musicals have been as neglected as the musical shorts.[18]

Before discussing the shorts I have selected as case studies, it is helpful to bear in mind some significant differences between theatre and film. In the theatre the whole space of the action is seen, but the spectator's position and angle of vision is fixed. In film, Béla Balázs observes that four new devices take over: a scene can be broken into several shots; the spectator can be given a close-up; the angle of vision can be changed; and montage can be used.[19] In film, the camera does the focusing. Moreover, there is a need to consider the editing of shots, for example, the speed of change from one to another. There is a range of conventional shot positions, the most common being the long shot (the frame accommodates a standing actor and establishes the space of the scene), the mid-shot (head to waist, often used for two actors in the same scene), and the close-up (head and shoulders).

The theatre spectator can select a part of the scene to focus on, but a standard lens, such as those used in the 1930s, is of fixed focal length and simply transmits the whole.[20] The zoom lens, which offered a way round this problem, was not available until the late 1950s. A standard lens has a broad depth of field, enabling much of the scene to remain in focus, but not all of it will be of the same degree of sharpness (the wide-angle lens has the broadest depth of field). Tripods had been developed with swivelling heads so that a camera could sweep from one side of the scene to the other. The technique, known as "panoraming", was not used in the cramped conditions of the Pathé studio, but its effect can be seen in the *Pathétone* film of Edith Lorand and her Viennese Orchestra playing part of the *Blue Danube*. The camera moves left to right (and back again) across the orchestra.[21]

The relationship of the performer to the camera is important. If the performer sings to camera, this emphasizes the performance act, breaking with naturalistic illusion (in the manner of a Brechtian *Verfremdungseffekt*). There are many differences between working to camera and working with a live audience. A stage comedian can bring an audience into a confidence ("Don't tell the manager of this theatre, but…"), can chide an audience ("No, please, don't laugh"), and can let the audience feel it is dictating the course of the show ("OK, what do you want me to do now, then?"). In a variety theatre, a performer can turn unexpectedly to someone in the side stalls, or to a section of the audience in any part of the auditorium. Filmmakers like to edit shots; they do not like a performer suddenly deciding which camera to speak to. With these prefatory remarks in place, we can begin to examine in closer detail a selection of early shorts in which stage performers grapple with the changes demanded by the new medium.

ERNEST AUGUSTUS ELEN (1862–1940)

Ernest Augustus Elen, better known simply as Gus Elen was, and still is, often put forward as the "real" Cockney costermonger to Albert Chevalier's "sentimental" coster, as the "tough" and "true to life" character found selling vegetables from a cart on the streets of London.[22] Some years after his retirement he was brought into Pathé's Wardour Street studio in order to document some of his music hall performances in four shorts. I am devoting more time to Gus Elen than my other case studies, because he learned his craft on the music hall stage in the 1890s and was not filmed until he had reached the age of 69. He therefore illustrates the greatest contrast between the dictates of stage and film. The artificiality of the set used in these shorts indicates that the producer's intention was to evoke a theatrical performance. Elen's set solves the perspective problem of stage scenery by being of shallow depth, using house fronts to block out the distance from view. The street scene suggests little in terms of social context; it would have been better to suggest a poorer area of London associated with Elen's character.

Elen's costume indicates class position. He wears a characteristic hat for his performance: it works as a sign of the costermonger and, being pulled well to the side, a sign of the comedian also. In his *Pathétone* performance of "'Arf a Pint of Ale" (1931) he uses two more comic signs: a shambling walk and a pipe held upside down in his mouth.[23] Much of what Elen does during his performance is inessential to the song text: it is often illustrative on a very elementary level and, at times, even irrelevant to the song itself. He makes bread-cutting motions at "a crust of bread and cheese" and, for want of anything better to do, points to each finger in turn while listing his eating and drinking habits in the refrain. In another *Pathétone* short, "It's a Great Big Shame" (1932), a tale of a tall husband and tiny bullying wife, he imitates a hammer blow at "I'd let her know who's who", raises his thumb at the words "underneath her thumb", and makes hand and arm gestures indicating the size of the man and woman.[24] These songs, though complete in themselves, would be perceived to be lacking without such actions. The gestures are, therefore, a supplement in the Derridean sense, something that satisfies a lack in what is already self-sufficient.[25]

Elen's detailed notebook has survived, showing how carefully he worked out gestures and routines—"Business Make-ups", as he called them.[26] Stage movements can, of course, be timed with precision when accompanied by music. In the Pathé version of "It's a Great Big Shame", he reproduces the routine for this song exactly as he had written it down in his notebook many years earlier. His characteristic vocal delivery (little falsetto breaks in the voice before plunging down onto a melody note) also indicates a stylized performance. In fact, not even these cracks in the voice are left to be improvised, their precise locations are set down in his notes:

> When singing lines—at scrappin' 'e 'ad won some great renown.
> It took two coppers for to make 'im move along.
> And annover six to 'old the feller dow-own.
> *On word "renown" Jerk this out—latter part of word like double note*
> *(Re-now-own)—an extra Jerk out word (down)*[27]

Elen's use of an accent associated with a particular social group—the Cockney street vendors, or costermongers—is an example of what Erika Fischer-Lichte has termed a "paralinguistic sign".[28] Another paralinguistic sign operates on an individual level: it is the yodelling effect on the words "ain't" and "saint" in "It's a Great Big Shame" and on the word "ale" in "'Arf a Pint of Ale". This vocal device is associated with the particular stage persona Elen has constructed for himself. Gestures, movement, and the use of props can reinforce a musical sign, and vice versa. In "It's a Great Big Shame", a loud percussive chord reinforces a gesture: the striking of a hammer blow. We read Elen's facial expression as a comic mask rather than as evidence of hard-done-by misery. Elen is employing a mimic sign not so much to construct a miserable persona as a comic persona. Theatrical masks can take various forms: an actual mask, make-up, or a characteristic facial expression (Buster Keaton's blank expression, for instance).

The movements Elen makes to the music that comes between the verses of "'Arf a Pint of Ale" presuppose the stage space available in music halls, but here there are restrictions on what he can do. Elen's movements are not suited to the technology of early sound film, since they are at odds with the need to stay within the frame of the shot and to maintain a steady distance from the microphone. He has been given a loose frame in recognition of the problems in capturing his act in this new medium. At times Elen would no doubt have preferred to move further to the side or rear of the stage, but he cannot do so. On the music hall stage he had the option of walking to the side to address that section of the audience, but on film this would position him at the edge of the frame resulting in an odd-looking and unbalanced composition.

Elen needs to be aware at all times of the position of the microphone when moving around, and to be careful that his actions do not make too much noise, since the microphone will pick this up. Our ears are able to concentrate on particular sounds, but the aural selectivity that is possible in the theatre is not so easy to repeat when listening to a recording (bumps and creaks, for example, come across as exaggerated and irritating in films of live opera). The filming of Elen is restricted to long and mid-shots but, even so, there is a lack of realism in the sound. Elen gets bigger for the mid-shot, but the sound remains the same. In other words, the visual perspective changes, but the acoustic perspective remains the same.[29]

Elen uses the kinesic codes of music hall—grand gestures and vigorous movement. As such, they relate less to the "natural" expression of emotion called for by Constantin Stanislavski, who argued that actors should work to become the actual characters they are portraying by identifying with their roles psychologically.[30] Elen's performance is much closer to the stylized gestures associated with Vsevolod Meyerhold, who was attracted by techniques he witnessed in music hall, melodrama, and pantomime.[31] Note the exact repetition of gestures—the counting of the fingers, for example, in the chorus of "'Arf a Pint of Ale." Yet, in spite of this, the critical reception of Elen in the 1890s typically praises his performances as "authentic Cockney".

> Unlike his famous contemporary [Chevalier], Gus Elen devotes himself to the realistic side of the coster's life; he leaves the ideal severely alone and presents a plain, ungarnished portrayal of the coster as he really is, as he would be found at his work or in his home.[32]

After witnessing Elen's American debut at the New York Theatre, a reviewer commented that he delivered the Cockney working man on stage "very much as he is in his own environment". Elen offered the audience at the New York Theatre "true pictures" that seemed "built up from within, not merely pictorial representations".[33] It is significant that Elen's coster was recognizable as true to life by those living outside of London and unfamiliar with coster communities. Sixty years later, the abiding memory of Elen remained that he was "the real thing...not an actor impersonating a coster, but a real coster, or, at any rate, a real Cockney of the poor streets."[34] Colin MacInnes refers to Elen as a "genuine coster singer" and "everything Albert Chevalier wanted to be, and was not: a dyed-in-the-wool Cockney."[35] For those who chose to interpret Elen's stage persona as the real Cockney, the sign had, to borrow words from Umberto Eco, abolished "the distinction of the reference".[36]

Editing from long to mid-shot, as occurs in the Elen films, shifts the point of view and offers a substitute for the changes of eye focus made by theatre audiences. It is an indication, however, that the authority of the film camera overrides that of actors and viewers. In putting together a performance like this for *Pathétone Weekly*, it was crucial to use matched cutting and maintain continuity. The move from long to mid-shot had to follow logically, showing the action continuing but in more detail. The effect sought was the illusion of a natural and spontaneous performance, although it was actually a mixture of two takes. The lack of close-ups does have an effect on the impression the Elen films make, lessening his impact as an individual stage character, and adding emphasis to his class position, his socio-cultural identity as a Cockney, and his gender position as an upholder of patriarchal values. Elen is less a victim of camera work, however, than many others filmed under similar conditions. This is because his own star persona makes a significant contribution to the way his presence on stage is received.

Elen sings to an imagined audience, and his performance reinforces Marvin Carlson's contention that in theatre "the contribution of the audience" should be considered.[37] The refrain of "It's a Great Big Shame" is meant to be sung by the audience who, by participating in this way, turn into a modern equivalent of the classical Greek chorus, commenting on events. The audience adopts a moral stance, agreeing with the singer's opinions, and individuals are able to show the warmth of their support by the enthusiasm and volume of their singing. The musical structure of the songs calls for audience participation by preparing the way for a melodically infectious chorus with strong dominant harmony, just as Elen calls for vocal support with large encouraging gestures in the audience's direction (see Figures 10.1a and 10.1b).

Jacques Derrida has claimed that the West "has worked only for the erasure of the stage";[38] but, it is the refusal to erase the stage that causes Elen problems when being filmed. The whole conception of his performance relies on communication between clearly demarcated spaces for stage and audience. He "knows" where the audience is, even when, as in this film, the audience is not there. However, the lack of audience involvement (laughing, singing) evidently troubles him. Note how the text of "It's a Great Big Shame" implies a dialogue with the audience, upbraiding them in the first verse with the words, "Don't you think him dead because he ain't". At times, during "'Arf a Pint of Ale", Elen's struggle to address a single viewpoint collapses as he gives in to the temptation to address different parts of his imagined auditorium.

RICHARD TAUBER (BIRTH NAME RICHARD DENEMY, 1891–1948)

The next case study is different in many respects, not least because it was filmed at the studios of British International Pictures (BIP) in Elstree. A little background information is necessary to set the context. BIP were making determined efforts to compete with Hollywood at home and abroad, and had successfully attracted German director E. A. Dupont to work for them in 1926, the year after his huge international success with the film *Variété*. Further encouraging developments occurred in 1927, when the Cinematograph Films Act introduced quotas to foreign imports.[39] BIP moved rapidly to sound, "converting its studios and adopting a sound-film production schedule as fast as anyone".[40] In the early sound period, however, the mere filming of a performance often seemed to be regarded as sufficient

FIGURES 10.1A AND 10.1B Elen gestures to an absent audience for support in the chorus of "It's a Great Big Shame".

in itself. The reason Andy Medhurst gives for this is that "the main attraction was the 'magic' of the new technology itself".[41] In some respects, then, cinema took a backward step. Stephen Guy notes that the advent of sound technology caused filmmakers to revert to techniques and conventions established in stage productions, rather than to strive to open up new cinematic horizons.[42] *Elstree Calling* (directed by Adrian Brunel, 1930), for instance, was advertised as an "all-star vaudeville and revue entertainment". It mixed variety stars with those of revue and musical comedy, and it was the former who had the greatest difficulty with the new medium. They were used to addressing an audience directly with their gaze and gestures, so the only solution they could find when being filmed was to pretend an audience was present, or to gaze at the camera. Lily Morris appears in this film, and her performance is awkward in ways that are similar to her performances in Pathé shorts. A *Pathétone Weekly* of 1931, which shows her performing "The Old Apple Tree", has poor lip synchronization for the mid-shots and an odd composition during the final chorus because she has walked to the edge of the frame (although this is not entirely inappropriate since she is acting as if drunk).[43] Postsynchonization, or dubbing, was not used: the performance was shot with direct sound (recorded on the sound negative in the camera).[44] The mid-shots of Morris are a second take, and she has failed to reproduce her lip movements exactly as they were on the first take.

One type of musical film that did not rely on variety or revue was the adaptation of an operetta or Broadway musical. In many cases these adaptations were far from being filmed versions of the original stage productions: the music of more than one operetta might be included and the dialogue and narrative might change. About thirty British films made in the 1930s leaned heavily on Viennese operetta, and the fondness for this genre may have been partly motivated by the thought that there was a possibility of good returns from the European box office. *Blossom Time* of 1934 was a notable success, and even Alfred Hitchcock tried his hand that year with *Waltzes from Vienna*.

Blossom Time cost BIP much more than its other films, owing largely to the expensive sets and crowd scenes.[45] The director Paul Stein was Viennese, but had worked for five years in Hollywood.[46] Rachael Low has argued that the success of *Blossom Time* owed a great deal to the presence of the Austrian tenor Richard Tauber, hero of many a Franz Lehár operetta and the most famous star to work for BIP at that time. There was more in the way of mutual benefit than conflict of interest when it came to Pathé's musical short of Tauber rehearsing for this film, because the year previously Pathé had become part of the new holding company Associated British Picture Corporation, along with BIP and Associated British Cinemas (ABC).[47] The signing of what was, in effect, an international distribution pact with Pathé was one of many efforts to bolster the European industry against American competition. *Blossom Time* was a triumph commercially as well as being well received by the critics, and encouraged Stein to follow it up with *My Song Goes Round the World*, another film starring a famous tenor, this time Josef Schmidt.[48]

Before his appearance in Stein's film, Tauber had been playing the role of Franz Schubert in *Lilac Time* at the Aldwych Theatre, London, from 22 September to 21 October 1933. It was an arrangement by George Clutsam (to English lyrics by A. Ross) of Heinrich Berté's *Das Dreimäderlhaus*, an operetta based on Schubert's music. *Pathétone* had already filmed him during the Aldwych run, singing Schubert's

"Serenade" while sat at a grand piano centre stage.[49] Tauber was just the kind of star performer BPI needed to generate international interest: that interest is evident, for example, in there being a French *Pathé-Journal* short of him singing a song from *Lilac Time* in Brussels, which probably dates from late 1933.[50] The feature-length film based on the same stage work was given the title *Blossom Time*, the name by which the operetta was known in the United States.[51] Early into its production, a *Pathétone* short was made of Tauber and others rehearsing a scene at the BIP Studios. Thus we have a film of the making of a film, and this is something that the Pathé crew needed to make clear to the viewer.

At the side of the stage of a variety theatre, it was common to have a board announcing the various turns. It drew attention to the fact that one was about to witness a performance. In the *Pathétone* short, the inclusion of a brief example of Stein offering direction to the cast, and the showing of the camera at the beginning of Tauber's performance of "Once There Lived a Lady Fair", are the means of achieving a similar effect on film.[52] There is no suggestion that this is a distantiation device intended to subvert any impression of naturalistic illusion in the scene being played; quite the opposite, the intention here is to create the illusion of unmediated documentary realism.

Tauber's style of singing connotes an operatic musical idiom. His vocal timbre and wide dynamic range are part of a disciplined operatic technique. Another example is his use of the head voice in the conclusion to the song. Tauber's mimic and gestural signs also follow an operatic kinesic code rather than the illusionistic (or naturalistic) code adopted by the members of the drawing-room audience in the film: his gestures are theatrical, whereas theirs are economical. *Variety* remarked backhandedly of his acting in the film *Blossom Time* that it was "surprisingly good—for a world-famous tenor".[53] Jane Baxter, cast in the role of Vicki Wimpassinger, the object of Schubert's affection, was a glamorous film star of the 1930s, and she is careful to adopt the restrained kinesic code of cinema (she had appeared in several films already). Tauber is first and foremost a celebrated singer, and the song "Once There Lived a Lady Fair" proved a great success for him when he released a 78 rpm recording (CE 6480–2) in July 1934, the month after the *Pathétone* newsreel film was issued.

The Elen shorts contained shots only of him; the Tauber short makes use of additional shots. Intercutting is employed to show details of dramatic significance (the emotional impact his performance is having on the audience). These reaction shots would have been taken after the main event had been filmed. A camera can offer a subjective point of view, as occurs, for instance, when a shot of one character is taken from a position behind the shoulders of another character in the same scene (shot-reverse shot), but in the Tauber short, the singer is not seen from the point of view of a particular member of his audience, nor do we see any of them from his position at the piano. We gauge their reactions from the use of montage, which presents us with a sequence of different shots from which we interpret what is going on and build a picture of the whole (an idea of the space of the room, for instance). In one sense Tauber's audience "stands in" for us, the viewers of the film, since we have no presence in a film equivalent to that which we enjoy in a theatre. Christian Metz elaborates on this point, explaining that when "a character looks at another who is momentarily out-of-frame", the out-of-frame character has something in common with the film audience who is "looking at the screen".[54] Moreover, Tauber in *Blossom Time* is playing the role of Schubert, about whom the audience would already entertain certain knowledge and cultural associations. It is true that Tauber plays him as a middle-aged man who loses his sweetheart to a young officer, although the real Schubert died at the age of thirty-one. Such pedantic biographical detail does not, however, trouble the suspension of disbelief in any uncomfortable way.

GRETA KELLER (1903–1977)

My final case study is brief, and of a *Pathé Pictorial* of 1934, in which the Austrian cabaret artist Greta Keller (originally Margaretha Keller) sings "The Isle of Capri" accompanied at the piano by the song's composer, Wilhelm Grosz (1894–1939).[55] Greta Keller came to attention as a radio star in the 1930s, and toured internationally, singing as fluently in French and English as in German, and loading her low alto voice with an erotic charge. Before the *Anschluss* she moved to London, where this short film was made. She went on to establish her own club *Chez Greta* at the Palace Hotel, St Moritz, Switzerland, but also achieved stardom in New York.

In the Pathé short, the director introduces a technique not seen in the Elen or Tauber shorts. He makes the most of the new opportunities of the film medium by incorporating cutaway shots showing views of the Isle of Capri. These relate to the subject of the song and are intercut with Keller's singing, though they are not part of the scene of her performance, which is a domestic room. One feature that sheds light on the difficulty this seemingly relaxed singer has in tailoring her performance to the demands of film is the "emergency" shot of Will Grosz at the piano inserted towards the end. It has no dramatic significance, but a third take was clearly needed when it became apparent that there was a lack of continuity between two shots that were intended to connect (she may have moved an arm to a different position in the second take, for example).[56] After inserting the shot of Grosz playing the piano, the next shot of Keller can follow without any continuity problems. In filmed musical performance, the rhythm of the shots should ideally match the rhythm of the performance, and when that happens, as here, the finished result is such that only an experienced eye would pick up that there had been an error that had been patched

FIGURE 10.2 Greta Keller stares into the camera, while singing "The Isle of Capri".

over. It was fortunate that Grosz formed part of the diegesis, whereas the dance orchestra that is heard in this film is never seen.

Keller gives the impression of singing reflectively for herself, but she does turn her head and sing a little of the song directly to camera, albeit rather hesitantly (see Figure 10.2). In contrast to the "accidental" singing to camera that variety performers were prone to do, this action seems quite deliberate on Keller's part. As such, it breaks knowingly with the convention in classical continuity that the camera is not supposed to exist and, thus, must not be addressed. Keller appears to be consciously experimenting with a performance technique that would not be adopted in mainstream films for many years.

CONCLUSION

Each of the musical shorts I have discussed shows a singer confronting a new audio-visual medium and trying to mould their performances accordingly. Gus Elen sings to an audience that is not present in his films, but addresses this imagined audience directly. Richard Tauber, as Schubert, sings to a fictive audience, but his address is symbolic, being aimed indirectly at just one of them, his beloved. There is no suggestion, of course, that any of Tauber's audience would be welcome to join in with his singing, and the "art song" structure of the music does not invite participation. Elen is trying to adapt his performance to the demand that he stay in frame. Tauber does not have this problem being seated at a piano; yet, his theatrical style jars with the film-oriented acting of the rest of the cast. Moreover, his piano looks very much like a dummy. We never see the keyboard, which may be where the microphone is concealed, and his arm movements are oddly high (see Figure 10.3).

Greta Keller boldly directs some of her singing to camera, but has trouble keeping to exactly the same movements in different takes and so creates continuity problems for the editor. We have also seen how the authority and control of the performer, and that of the audience, were eroded in the new medium. For many years, song performance on film continued to offer a compromise between the competing dictates of different entertainment media, and variety performers continued to experience difficulty with the film medium. Andy Medhurst has linked the problems in finding "an adequate generic vehicle" for Gracie Fields to the fact that her early training was for the variety stage.[57] Many of Gracie Fields's films are, in Stephen Guy's words, "basically a series of linked sketches", even when they make efforts to be cinematic, as does *Sing as We Go* of 1934, with its complex narrative—the script was by J. B. Priestley—and use of montage.[58] Compromises continued into the later 1930s, as can be seen in the Crazy Gang's film *O-Kay for Sound* of 1937 where, in order to resolve the problems faced by performers trained in variety, the whole of the second half is constructed as a series of sketches. One of the best-known attempts to recreate the experience of music hall is *Champagne Charlie* of 1944 (directed by Alberto Cavalcanti), which stars Tommy Trinder as the Victorian *lion comique* George Leybourne. By the next decade, however, variety theatre and its associated performance practices had begun to wane, especially after the arrival of television into a multitude of homes, and filmmakers found they were finally able to develop fresh ideas about how to present music, song, and dance.

FIGURE 10.3 Richard Tauber playing the piano in "Once There Lived a Lady Fair".

NOTES

1. This is an appropriate point for me to thank the British Academy for an award that helped fund research undertaken at the British Film Institute. It is also the place to lament that all that exists in the BFI library of Elen's great rival Albert Chevalier is a collection of stills from lost (silent) films.

2. British Pathé historical archive, 1896–1976; available at http://www.britishpathe.com/ [accessed 3 August 2012].

3. See Marina Dahlquist, "Global versus Local: The Case of Pathé", *Film History* 17/1 (2005), 36; she cites the *Livres des Inventaires*, no. 4, 1911–1915, Collection Pathé, Paris.

4. *Bioscope*, 4 Aug. 1910, 12; reproduced in Stephen Bottomore, "Rediscovering Early Non-Fiction Film", *Film History* 13/2 (2001): 167.

5. Michael Chanan, *The Dream that Kicks: The Prehistory and Early Years of Cinema in Britain* (London: Routledge and Kegan Paul, 1980), 130.

6. Richard Abel, "'Pathé Goes to Town': French Films Create a Market for the Nickelodeon", *Cinema Journal* 35/1 (1995): 9.

7. Abel, "'Pathé Goes to Town'", 13–16.

8. Chanan, *The Dream that Kicks*, 133.

9. For an account of the influence of music hall on the cinema of Charlie Chaplin, see Frank Scheide, "The Influence of the English Music-Hall on Early Screen Acting", in *Moving Performance: British Stage and Screen, 1890s–1920s*, ed. Linda Fitzsimmons and Sarah Street (Trowbridge: Flicks Books, 2000), 75–8.

10. Andy Medhurst, "Music Hall and British Cinema", in *All Our Yesterdays: 90 Years of British Cinema*, ed. Charles Barr (London: BFI, 1986), 171. The actual title of the song is "Algy, or the Piccadilly Johnny with the Little Glass Eye". It was written and composed by Harry B. Norris.

11. George Pearson, *Flashback: The Autobiography of a British Film-maker* (London: Allen and Unwin, 1957). See Chanan, *The Dream That Kicks*, 250.

12. See Arthur Knight, "The Movies Learn to Talk: Ernst Lubitsch, René Clair, and Rouben Mamoulian", in *Film Sound: Theory and Practice*, ed. Elisabeth Weis and John Belton (New York: Columbia University Press, 1985), 215.

13. Richard Koszarski, "Laughter, Music and Tragedy at the New York Pathé Studio", *Film History* 14/1 (2002): 33. Pathé's main production studios were in Fort Lee, New Jersey (opened 1914).

14. See the diagram of the studio in Koszarski, "Laughter, Music and Tragedy", 36.

15. Jens Ulff-Møller, "Hollywood's 'Foreign War': The Effect of National Commercial Policy on the Emergence of the American Film Hegemony in France, 1920–1929", in *"Film Europe" and "Film America": Cinema, Commerce and Cultural Exchange, 1920–1939*, ed. Andrew Higson and Richard Maltby (Exeter: University of Exeter Press, 1999), 183–4.

16. Rachael Low, *The History of the British Film, 1929–1939: Film Making in 1930s Britain* (London: Allen and Unwin, 1985), 121.

17. Ella Shields performs "Sweet Adeline", PT 038 (issued 15 Dec. 1930); Al Bowlly sings "The Very Thought of You", PT 227 (issued 30 Jul. 1934); Albert Sandler plays Brahms's Hungarian Dance no. 5, PT 010 (issued 2 Jun. 1930).

18. Stephen Guy, "Calling All Stars: Musical Films in a Musical Decade", in *The Unknown 1930s: An Alternative History of the British Cinema, 1929–39*, ed. Jeffrey Richards (London: Tauris, 1998), 100.

19. Béla Balázs, *Theory of Film*, trans. Edith Bone (London: Dobson, 1952; originally published as *Filmkultúra*, Budapest: Szikra kiadás, 1948).

20. Marvin Carlson argues that "an important part of the unique power of the theatre" derives from "psychic polyphony—the simultaneous expression of a number of different psychic lines of action, allowing the spectator a choice of focus and a variety in the process of combination." *Theatre Semiotics: Signs of Life* (Bloomington: Indiana University Press, 1990), 101.

21. Issued 15/06/1931. PT 064. Location of performance unknown.

22. I discuss some of the problems with this view in *Sounds of the Metropolis: The 19th-Century Popular Music Revolution in London, New York, Paris, and Vienna* (New York: Oxford University Press, 2008), 171–95.

23. "'Arf a Pint of Ale" (words and music by Charles Tempest, 1905). *Pathétone* 85, issue date: 9 Nov. 1931. Preview available at: http://www.britishpathe.com/record.php?id=8938 [accessed 3 August 2012].

24. "It's a Great Big Shame! *Or*, I'm Blowed If 'E Can Call 'Isself 'Is Own" (words by Edgar Bateman, music by George Le Brunn, 1895). *Pathétone* 96, issue date: 26 Jan. 1932. Preview available at: http://www.britishpathe.com/record.php?id=8986 [accessed 3 August 2012]. Also available at: http://www.youtube.com/watch?v=Z9_YHS63hiw. [accessed 3 August 2012].

25. Alternatively, Elen's songs and his accompanying routines, may be regarded as examples of what Roman Ingarden terms *Haupttext* and *Nebentext*. The song sheet provides the *Haupttext*; the *Nebentext* is the mimetic action accompanying the song text. See Ingarden, *The Literary Work of Art*, trans. George G. Grabowicz (Evanston: Northwestern University Press, 3rd edn, 1973; originally published as *Das literarische Kunstwerk*, Halle [Saale]: Niemeyer, 1931).

26. See Adrian New, *The Times*, 19 Dec. 1970, reprinted in Benny Green, ed. *The Last Empires: A Music Hall Companion* (London: Pavilion Books, 1986), 119–23.

27. Elen's "Business Make-ups" book, quoted in Green, *Last Empires*, 122.

28. *The Semiotics of Theater*, trans. Jeremy Gaines and Doris L. Jones (Bloomington: Indiana University Press, 1992; originally published as *Semiotik des Theaters*, Tübingen: Gunter Narr Verlag, 1983), 14–16.

29. On the problems of scale-matching of voice and image in early sound film, see Charles O'Brien, *Cinema's Conversion to Sound: Technology and Film Style in France and the U.S.* (Bloomington: Indiana University Press, 2005), 97–102.

30. Constantin Stanislavski, *An Actor Prepares* [1936], trans. Elizabeth R. Hapgood [1948] (New York: Routledge, 1989), 139–208.

31. See Jonathan Pitches, *Vsevolod Meyerhold* (London: Routledge, 2003), 54.

32. *Nottingham Daily Express*, 12 Sept. 1899.

33. *New York Times*, 10 Sept. 1907, 7.

34. "Heyday of the Cockney Comedian", *Times*, 9 Jan. 1958, quoted in Ulrich Schneider, *Die Londoner Music Hall und ihre Songs, 1850–1920* (Tübingen: Niemeyer, 1984), 157.

35. *Sweet Saturday Night* (London: MacGibbon and Kee, 1967), 30 and 36.

36. *Travels in Hyperreality* (London: Pan, 1987), 7.

37. *Theatre Semiotics*, xii.

38. *Writing and Difference*, trans. A. Bass (Chicago: University of Chicago Press, 1978), 236.

39. Andrew Higson, "Polyglot Films for an International Market: E.A. Dupont, the British Film Industry, and the Idea of a European Cinema, 1926–1930", in *"Film Europe" and "Film America."* ed. Higson and Maltby, 275.

40. Ibid., 288.

41. Medhurst, "Music Hall and British Cinema", 173.

42. See Guy, "Calling All Stars", 117–18.

43. Issue Date: 25/05/1931. PT 061.

44. See Barry Salt on the early days of sound-on-film recording, in "Film Style and Technology in the Thirties: Sound", in *Film Sound*, ed. Weis and Belton, 37–43, at 42. There were still films being shot silently in 1931, however, to which sound was synchronized later (Carl Dreyer's *Vampyr* is an example).

45. Low, *History of the British Film, 1929–1939*, 123.

46. Roy Armes, *A Critical History of the British Cinema* (London: Secker and Warburg, 1978), 85.

47. Bill Bailleu and John Goodchild, *The British Film Business* (Chichester: John Wiley, 2002), 28.

48. This singer had made his reputation on radio, and his diminutive appearance on film had a negative effect, even though the shot man's struggle for recognition was built into the narrative.

49. *Pathétone Weekly* 184, release date 2 Oct. 1933. For all that it implied the scene was from the Aldwych, it looks as if it was filmed in the Pathé studio. Most of the film consists of a mid-shot of Tauber but from a position where his hands cannot be seen—a pity, because, in contrast to the short from *Blossom Time*, he is really playing the piano.

50. The date is estimated as 1933 by Pathé, and it is likely to have been late that year, after the production at the Aldwych closed. This musical short is available only at the BFI; it is not on British Pathé web site.

51. *Blossom Time* was Sigmund Romberg's arrangement of Heinrich Berté's *Das Dreimäderlhaus* (libretto by A. M. Willner and H. Reichert, premiered in Vienna in 1916). The film adaptation that appeared in 1934, despite being called *Blossom Time*, used Clutsam's musical arrangements.

52. "Once There Lived a Lady Fair" from *Blossom Time*, BIP Studios, Elstree. Pathétone 219, issue date: 14 Jun. 1934. Preview available at: http://www.britishpathe.com/record.php?id=9668 [accessed 3 August 2012]. Also available, with introductory matter cut, at: http://www.youtube.com/watch?v=hpZzAooPI6I [accessed 3 August 2012].

53. "Blossom Time", *Variety*, 24 July 1934, 14.

54. "The Imaginary Signifier", trans. Ben Brewster, *Screen* 16/2 (1975): 57.

55. "The Isle of Capri" (words and music by Wilhelm Grosz, 1934), Pathé Studio, London. *Pathé Pictorial* PSP 861, issue date: 4 Oct. 1934. Free preview available at: http://www.britishpathe.com/video/greta-keller-1/query/isle+of+capri [accessed 3 August 2012]. Also available at: http://www.youtube.com/watch?v=_5NojEJC6Gk [accessed 3 august 2012].

56. The mistake occurs at the line in the song referring to a "bright golden ring on her finger". She may have moved her hand differently to look at it, or perhaps had forgotten to put it on (the edit occurs just as she looks towards her hand).

57. Medhurst, "Music Hall and British Cinema", 176.

58. Guy, "Calling All Stars", 103. *Sing as We Go* was directed by Basil Dean.

11

Framing the Atmospheric Film Prologue in Britain, 1919–1926

Julie Brown

WHEN D. W. GRIFFITH'S *BROKEN BLOSSOMS* opened at the Alhambra Theatre in London for its "presentation run" on 15 March 1920, its elaborate, multi-sensory, Chinese-themed presentation sparked considerable trade interest.[1] According to its creator Robb Lawson, the live stage prologue

> employed nine actors who mimed a scene laid in a Buddhist Temple which was disclosed as the curtain rose to three notes of a gong. Perfume floated out to the auditorium from censers swung by Chinese incense bearers. After the preliminary action, a Chinese singer chanted a litany, standing in an amber spot light, and, with another note of the gong, the curtain fell to be followed immediately by the screening.[2]

Others noted that "priests were officiating in front of a dimly-lighted altar", and that within the cinema "female attendants were all dressed in Chinese garments, [while] red lamps gave a mysterious glow to the auditorium."[3] Mabel Poulton recalls miming the dying Lillian Gish in the temple.[4] Lawson described the elements of the presentation in an article in *The Bioscope* as having been similar to those used in New York, and an example of how an integrated approach to "special presentation" was a way of "preparing the minds of the audience to receive in the appropriate mood the story that is to be unfolded" in the ensuing feature film.[5] About a year earlier, in April 1919, an article by American Ernest A. Dench had already appeared in *Kinematograph and Lantern Weekly* reporting on atmospheric stage settings in New York—though not at that point prologues.[6] Dench described permanent and semi-permanent stage settings (an Italian pergola involving flower-entwined trellis work, for instance), "picturesque backgrounds", and colour lighting effects, and confidently asserted that approaches to atmosphere such as this, which go beyond "the picture itself" because "you must feel" the picture, come from New York: "S. L. Rothapfel, formerly in charge of the Rivoli, Rialto and Strand Theatres, New York City, is directly responsible for this advance in photoplay presentation."[7]

With the success of *Broken Blossoms*, promotion of special presentation, the creation of overall atmosphere, and the production of live stage prologues became a regular part of British trade paper discourse. *The Bioscope* featured several further articles in the second half of 1920; between August and December of the same year, *Kinematograph Weekly* reproduced a series of articles by Samuel ("Roxy") Rothafel from *Moving Picture World*; and from July 1921 *The Bioscope* ran a regular series on "exploitation" by Lawson himself.[8] Trade papers cited examples of good and bad prologue construction: both within and without dedicated "showmanship" columns short descriptions and/or photos—often apparently supplied to the paper by the cinema itself—were common. More conceptual essays of a page in length also occasionally featured, though rarely details such as drawings. Nevertheless, the prologue seemed to have arrived in Britain.

This 1920s industry discourse about cinematic atmosphere promoted an integrated system of exhibition and marketing which brought together many elements of exhibition practice that had already existed separately or in particular film contexts. The trade promoted increasingly integrated atmospheric techniques for presenting films; these might extend from themed decorations in cinema foyers and theatre spaces, to thematically costumed staff (house attendants, box office personnel, and even orchestral musicians), atmospheric—often dramatic—stage settings, atmospheric framings for the film screens themselves, special lighting effects, by the end of the twenties the very architecture of picture palace interiors and exteriors, and at the heart of it, an atmospherically conceived overall programme of entertainment.[9] Such a programme would involve appropriate atmospheric music accompanying the feature film, likely also an instrumental overture which set the programme mood, a live prologue immediately before the feature film, and potentially also other short films and stand-alone variety items which fit the overall programme theme. The film trade promoted the integration of these techniques as a way of facilitating the audience's immersion into the world of the feature film. It was an approach to film exhibition in which a thematically conceived show started well before the feature film itself, even before the mixed programme.[10] It started as customers walked towards the cinema's front door.

The live film prologue was an interesting part of this turn. It consisted of a theatrical and/or musical performance which bore a specific relation to the main feature
film and was promoted as a device to prepare the audience for the fictive world of
the feature film within an atmospherically conceived programme overall. In North
America, its development from the mid-teens through the twenties is closely associated not only with Rothafel and ex-theatre man D. W. Griffith, but also West
Coast showman Sid Grauman, whose prologue extravaganzas in Hollywood in
the late twenties sometimes involved up to one hundred stage extras.[11] During the
same period smaller theatre exhibitors nevertheless produced prologues on a different scale, often making use of local talent. As immortalized in Busby Berkeley's
Footlight Parade (1933), in the United States prologues even lingered into the thirties as touring phenomena, before eventually giving way to sound film.[12]

As the prologue entered British trade discourse in the early 1920s, there were no star
presenters of Rothafel's status, yet the nature of the prologues reported reflect types also
found in the United States.[13] They took a number of recognizable forms, some clearly
fundamentally musical, some in which music provided peripheral support, and some
without music. Prologues may have involved the film's theme song, have focussed on
dance, or have been structured around operatic selections or a scena.[14] *The Sea Hawk's*
trade-show screening at the Royal Albert Hall in 1924 was preceded by a prologue
which involved an extravagant staging, including a huge ship from which the film's
theme song was sung by a chorus of sailors. For *Her Reputation* (1924), which itself
involved cabaret scenes, the Pavilion, Cardiff, staged a lavish dance prologue which
involved a tango performed by two well-known dancers. For the 1922 Ernst Lubitsch
film *Passion* (1919), based on the adventures of Mme du Barry, the Scala Theatre,
London, had a tenor sing an altered version of the Flower Song from *Carmen*, with
words specially written for the occasion, which was then followed by a quartet from
Rigoletto.[15] Predominantly dramatic prologues, with secondary musical elements or
no music at all, included short pantomimes, short dramatic scenes (often re-enacting
a scene from the film itself, or a condensed version of the entire film narrative), and in
small venues, even simple monologues. The West End run of Cecil Hepworth's 1923
film of *Comin' Thro' the Rye* was preceded by a prologue which consisted of a synopsis
of the film's plot enacted in pantomime behind scrim screens and with harp musical
embellishments, though this was preceded by an orchestral overture consisting of Percy
Grainger's arrangement of the English folk song *Shepherd's Hey*, a choice atmospherically appropriate to the film's nostalgic portrayal of life in Victorian rural England;[16]
for D. W. Griffith's *Romance*, the Palace Theatre, London, presented a prologue written in blank verse and recited by a "prolocutor", concluding with a singer performing
"Connais-tu le pays" from *Mignon*.[17] Epilogues were also occasionally staged: at the
Alhambra, *Broken Blossoms* had both prologue and epilogue.

Although in smaller cinemas prologues tended to be created by the exhibitor himself, who might even appear in it, a small industry also emerged with specialist prologue creators offering their services. These ranged from small operators, such as "eminent Yorkshire vocalist" Francis Harris of Rotherham, to higher-profile individuals in London who also wrote columns in the trade papers (such as Lawson and H. F. Kessler-Howes), to theatrical agencies (see Figure 11.1).[18] As the prologue concept became more familiar some film companies also made specialists available to provide prologues, and enterprising individuals sometimes sought a renter's approval for their prologue in order to market it, and themselves, to cinemas. In August 1925 we read in *Kinematograph Weekly* that Yorkshire actor-entertainer,

FIGURE 11.1 Prologues and Vaudeville, Ltd, advertisement in *The Cinema News and Property Gazette*, 4 March 1926: 53.

Lister Reekie, had put together a prologue to the Jury-Metro-Goldwyn feature *He Who Gets Slapped* that had then been approved by the renters. The paper advises exhibitors to communicate with Mr Reekie if they are looking for a prologue.[19] By late 1926, however, Francis A. Mangan, Presentation Director of the Plaza Theatre, London, which opened earlier that year, emerged as something of a star prologue producer, inasmuch as his prologues were being regularly featured in *Kinematograph Weekly*. Originally from New York, Mangan had worked at the Capitol, Chicago, immediately before coming to London, and previously in Detroit, Cleveland, and

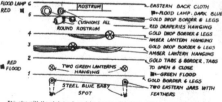

FIGURE 11.2   Feature article by Francis A. Mangan, "Presentation Director" of the Plaza Theatre, London. *Kinematograph Weekly*, 24 February 1927: 81.

Montreal.[20] In early 1927 *Kinematograph Weekly* ran a series of articles by Mangan, in which he described some of his prologues with the help not only of the ubiquitous photograph, but also of diagrams (see Figure 11.2).[21] For Kessler-Howes "Plaza prologues remain the best and most imaginative of their kind, little tabloid plays and scenas created with wonderful stage-craft."[22]

From 1920 through to 1926, the most elaborate prologues described in the film trade papers were one-off productions for evening trade showings for trade audiences and special guests only, of which the most extravagant were mounted in the cavernous Royal Albert Hall. On 29 January 1924, for instance, the British film *Southern Love* was given a one-night-only screening at the Royal Albert Hall to a reported audience of 9,000 and at an estimated cost of £1,000. The film was projected onto a screen sixty feet wide fitted up against the organ, and accompanied by a sixty-piece symphony orchestra and three singers of the British National Opera Company. There was also a musical prologue with forty Gypsy performers who gave what was described in advance as "a 'local' entertainment of their own on a special stage… The hall will be transformed into something resembling a Spanish bull-ring flooded with colour-symphonies of light."[23] Somewhat less lavishly mounted prologues and atmosphere were also typical of an exploitation run in a West End theatre. From the renters' point of view the idea of the pre-release, often in a "legitimate theatre" such as the New Scala in Charlotte Street, or the Capitol in New Oxford Street, was that this would add prestige to the film, and put up its eventual price.[24]

The inclusion of this range of live performances alongside the feature film was only the latest turn in a long history of the appearance of moving pictures in mixed programmes, of course. From 1895 through to the 1930s, 1940s, and beyond, moving pictures were routinely screened alongside live musical, dramatic, and variety performances. Given the patchiness of our knowledge of film's early sonic practices both internationally and within individual countries, it is difficult to make generalizations. However, what we know of practices in the United States and Britain indicates that the nature of mixed entertainment programmes changed with broader industry developments over those years (illustrated songs in the nickelodeon and penny theatre era versus cinema organ interludes in the 1920s and through the early years of sound film), and varied according to location (country, region within a given country, rural area, urban area, wealthy neighbourhood, working-class neighbourhood, etc.), as well as type of venue (film as a variety item on a music hall bill versus the apex of a picture palace's mixed programme), availability of resources (solo piano or mechanical instrument as against full orchestra), and even the ambition of the exhibitor. Nevertheless, unlike most of these other live entertainments, the prologue, in its various incarnations, bore a direct relation to the feature film and had a particular purpose: namely, helping to immerse the audience into the specific world of the feature film. This type of cinema sought not only to offer mixed entertainment programmes but almost to fuse the dramatic core of the feature film with live theatre. It was very far from an attempt to end the stage (cf. Jacques Derrida's claim discussed by Derek Scott in this book).[25]

AMERICAN SOURCES FOR BRITISH PROLOGUES?

Notwithstanding Mangan's few published diagrams, prologues were fundamentally ephemeral theatrical forms, as were so many aspects of early film culture: they may never have existed in the form of a script, or written-out scenario or staging, let alone that the latter may have been kept for posterity; nor were they routinely remarked upon in the wider press. Trade reporting is therefore extremely important to historians. It is also potentially misleading.[26] For this chapter I have surveyed prologue reporting from 1919 through to the end of 1927 in three British trade papers (*Kinematograph Weekly*, *The Bioscope*, and *Cinema News and Property Gazette*) with the aim of reading both with the grain (for trade PR and aspiration, which dominate) and against the grain (for the often telling admissions).[27] During the early 1920s the volume and promotional nature of the coverage tends to leave a reader with the impression that the concept of the live prologue was imported from the United States and widely adopted across Britain throughout that period. Yet on 14 January 1926 one of its key apologists, *Kinematograph Weekly*'s Showmanship columnist H. F. Kessler-Howes—himself a producer of prologues—let slip that "Even now prologues are not very popular with British exhibitors, and only occasionally half-hearted attempts are made to stage one."[28] Kessler-Howes' comment appeared at a point when overt promotion of prologues had started to wane, and suggests that the dense reporting of the previous six or seven years was a distortion of reality.[29] Such a comment not only brings into question the relationship between trade press reporting and dominant practice; the context in which it was uttered also sheds light on how the British trade press made use of American reporting, and how promotion of immediate trade interests could seem to wipe from collective memory the earlier achievements of local exhibitors. Let us take these points in turn.

Although it provoked dedicated trade paper attention, the prologue and elaborate staging associated with *Broken Blossoms* in 1920 were not the first of either in Britain.[30] In mid-August 1919 *With Allenby in Palestine* opened in London at the Royal Opera House and made use of an elaborate, atmospheric staging and live prologue specific to the film.[31] For what was initially billed as an "Illustrated travelogue on the British Campaigns", charismatic film lecturer Lowell Thomas recalls having hired the band of the Royal Welsh Guards to provide about twenty minutes of music before the prologue proper began—presumably to help establish the mood of colonial military adventure.[32] When the lights went out a live prologue was performed, after which Thomas started to lecture.[33] He borrowed an opera set from Sir Thomas Beecham, which had been used for the "Moonlight on the Nile" scene from Handel's *Joseph and his Brethren*, and by way of prologue had an "oriental dancer" perform a dance of the seven veils to "atmospheric Eastern music" that his wife had arranged, after which a musical setting for the Muslim call to prayer was sung offstage by an Irish tenor.[34] Once the show transferred to the Royal Albert Hall the overall presentation was expanded to include more atmospherically targetted music variously embracing British nationalist sentiment, militarism, and orientalist fantasy: organist Quentin Maclean provided overtures ("Triumphal March" from Verdi's *Aida*, Concert Overture in C minor by Alfred Hollins, and both "Chant Pastoral" and "Alleluia" by Dubois) and interlude music (Allegro Maestoso from Widor's Sixth Symphony, "Reverie du Soir," from Saint Saëns's *Suite Algérienne*, and Elgar's *Pomp and Circumstance*, no. 1 in D), and played Frank Bridge's *Allegro Marziale* after the National Anthem.[35] Notwithstanding the spectacular popular success of Lowell Thomas's show, the fact that it was a species of travelogue dependent on him as charismatic lecturer, as opposed to a fictional feature film able to be promoted to the industry at large, may help to explain the trade papers' alternative focus on *Broken Blossoms*, which, being another Griffith milestone, may have seemed of greater significance to industry interests. Lowell Thomas even claimed that the live-prologue idea originated from his London show.[36]

If British atmospheric theatrical presentation did not originate in Griffith, nor was Rothafel directly responsible for this advance in the way Dench's 1919 article in *Kinematograph Weekly* implies. Notwithstanding the publication pressures to which the journal was undoubtedly subject, its decision to print Dench's assertion in a British trade paper without comment is perhaps a little surprising. Indeed, during a short visit to London in February 1923 Rothafel addressed the London branch of the Cinematograph Exhibitors' Association (CEA) over a luncheon in his honour and noted that on his previous visit in 1914 the art of presentation had been better understood in England than in America.[37] Exemplary atmospheric presentation dated from even earlier than 1914 in some large London theatres. At the London Scala in late 1911 a Kinemacolor programme involving films depicting a bull arena in Madrid was afforded a theatrical stage setting of a Roman interior and "an original system of stage lighting."[38] Another early film event which came even closer to later concepts of special presentation and prologue was that for Alfred De Manby's film *Mephisto*, shot in Kinemacolor and screened at the Scala Theatre, London, in August and September 1912: "an entirely novel entertainment," according to *The Bioscope*, "which can best be described as a series of mystic and elaborate illusions portraying the temporary dominance of human nature by 'Mephisto,' and his ultimate overthrow by the angels of Virtue."[39] The fifty-minute presentation made use of full orchestra and choir, and its music employed "themes" from Gounod's *Faust*. A detailed advertisement describes it as opening with a staged scene showing Mephisto in his underground haunts, after which the action moved to the screen for the story of man's downfall in the face of gold, during which the "disembodied" Mephisto appeared on screen; then it was back to the stage for another cavern scene, followed by more "dovetailing" of stage scene and moving pictures. One staged scene involved a dancer, while the climax involved Mephisto singing "Mankind is mine; the world is mine":[40]

> Those accustomed to the usual methods of exhibiting animated pictures will be surprised to find how many departures from conventional ideas are contained in this subject, staged scene and moving picture story being dovetailed into one another in so surprisingly realistic a fashion that, as the pictures themselves will be presented in natural colors by Kinemacolor, it will be difficult at times to be sure where actuality begins and moving picture ends.[41]

The Royal Opera House presentation of Max Reinhardt's film of Karl Vollmoeller's mystery play *Das Mirakel* (*The Miracle*) on 21 December 1912 also used the stage to supplement film, and was closer to the atmospheric "live prologue plus feature film" pairing to be found in Britain in the 1920s. The film itself was based on Reinhardt's extravagant pantomime-cum-pageant production at Olympia, London, which reportedly involved more than 2,000 actors, a choir of 500, and an orchestra of 200 including an organ.[42] In order to augment the necessarily scaled-down screen version of the pantomime, the Royal Opera House auditorium was converted "into the exterior of a church, similar to the scheme carried out at Olympia," and an orchestra and chorus numbering 200 were used.[43]

> The stage front presents the exterior of an ancient cathedral at Pechtoldsdorf, with coloured-glass windows above and at the sides, and when the great doors are opened the audience sees the whole enactment of the play as though it were in the church itself.[44]

Engelbert Humperdinck's music for the stage production had been adapted to accompany the moving picture version, and was performed using not only a large orchestra but also "a large, unseen chorus [which] gives the accustomed effect to the chants of the nuns and priests, and the cries and murmurs of the crowds."[45] The resulting presentation was described by the *Daily Telegraph* as having been "as much operatic as cinematographic".[46] When American exhibitor Al Woods travelled to London to secure the US rights for the film, he saw the Royal Opera House production and appears to have used it as inspiration for his own staging. In New York, however, he had the chorus parade down the aisle dressed as nuns, rendering visible and theatrical a choir that in London had been invisible, and turning an effects device into a species of pageant prologue.[47]

Both London and New York presentations of *The Miracle* stemmed directly from a desire to recreate within a regular theatre a transfer to screen of what had been a theatrical event, a pageant, at the enormous London Olympia, and which had been dramatically reduced in scale by being filmed. Like *Mephisto* before it, it was a theatrical screen transfer that was bursting at the seams; in London comparisons were made between the screen and London Olympia versions, which those responsible for the film presentation probably anticipated.[48] With *Mephisto*, however, the screen–stage relationship seems to have served in part to articulate a distinction between very physical happenings (stage) and more ghostly or magical happenings (screen). Either the use of staging and live performance were effects for a film screening, or the moving pictures were effects for a stage play—exploiting their ability to create illusions. In practice it was both or neither, and anticipated most twentieth-century mixed-media art works involving film. The stage decorations for the bull-arena films, like the "exotic" stage decorations, prologue, and musical framing of *With Allenby in Palestine*, could also be understood in terms of old traditions of enhancing films, especially travel and topical films, using special sound effects.[49] Indeed, as discussions of presentation and prologues developed in the trade papers some British exhibitors were curious as to the difference between the "up-to-date cinema terminology" of "presentation" and "atmosphere" on the one hand, and the old concept of "effects" on the other: a *Bioscope* columnist admitted in September 1920 that the only difference was in degree.[50]

CRITIQUE AND DIFFICULT CONDITIONS

Notwithstanding the misleading impression projected by the trade papers concerning the prologue's origins and the sense that this was all somehow very new, there is also the faltering take-up in the early twenties admitted by H. F. Kessler-Howes. Having put together major prologues for trade shows, Kessler-Howes was himself a practitioner of "special presentation", and his comment in early 1926 that prologues had never been terribly popular almost threatened to undermine his own industry prestige. But it could equally be read as a canny signal from a key player in the exhibition sector, someone who sensed that the tide was turning against the prologue and felt that he could and should reposition himself at the forefront of new industry trends. It appeared in his regular Showmanship column alongside his report of a criticism of prologues published in the *New York Telegram* by Major Bowes of the Capitol, Broadway, New York, who had complained that live prologues which anticipate the story of the feature film defeat the work of filmmakers who write and direct pictures.[51] Kessler-Howes immediately lays claim to the same view, also observing that "trade moves in America usually have some sort of an effect on the Trade in England, and if the prologue is finished in America, it might easily finish in England." Kessler-Howes's column may therefore be read as an attempt simultaneously to anticipate the likely future direction of the trade in Britain, and to flatter fellow British exhibitors by implying that their limited embrace of the prologue means that they sensed this problem all along. He may also have felt that his future in the exhibition industry was safe enough to risk such a confession given the return of mixed variety within British picture theatres around 1925, which he had been reporting for months (of which, more below).[52]

Bowes's critique was either shared or taken to heart by Francis A. Mangan, who later that year was reported by *Kinematograph Weekly* not to believe in prologues in the sense of "the reproduction of the big scene from the film, played by living characters before the picture starts".[53] However, related concerns about their dramatic position within the film programme had already long been expressed, if one reads the trade papers closely. One committed exponent of staged atmosphere before the feature film drew the line at including the spoken word in 1923, on the grounds that it detracted from, rather than added value to, the film. Preceding films with

> acted prologues, song scenas, dramatic sketches, excerpts from the action of the picture, operettas…have allowed comparison between screen and stage to creep in, usually to the detriment of the screen. The spoken word cannot immediately precede a sub-title without the value of the latter suffering considerably in consequence.[54]

Others expressed faith in the power of film itself: "Is not the film capable of diffusing its own atmosphere without the aid of draperies and whatnots hired from the theatrical furnishers?"[55] *Kinematograph Weekly* columnist E. Fletcher-Clayton felt that prologues were already in decline in August 1923, arguing that they were either presented excessively in cinemas with good stage facilities, or in a derisory way in smaller theatres. They had given up on their usefulness.[56] He pulled no punches: many prologues involving a monologue or a song were simply tedious; tableaux pantomimed in grossly exaggerated proportions with equally strange words, were all "deliberate eccentricity"; in some cinemas prologues had even started to elide with old-style ballyhoo—namely some sort of stunt on the street, which culminated in the stunt people marching into the cinema and up to the front. Some prologues—especially the cheap local productions, often drawing on local talent and usually promoted in the trade papers in positive terms as helping to localize the show—were simply poor, even laughable. "The cry is: Cut it out and get on with the show!"[57] West End theatres were not immune from such criticisms: one particularly lame prologue staged at Marble Arch was described by a columnist as "a miracle of futile endeavour".[58]

Another critical element was the cost. Quite early in the prologue's heyday, some exhibitors—especially small exhibitors—questioned the return on investment it represented and used costs to explain why "the British exhibitor has been slow to come under the influence of the special 'prologue.'"[59] Norwich publicity manager Hastings Pye was one, questioning whether prologues themselves drew audiences in, and arguing that if they did they certainly did not do so to the extent that they justified the amount of money spent on them.[60] Modestly appointed cinemas could only charge a certain entry fee anyway. The entertainment tax, introduced during the war, also served to discourage the increase of overheads. The mounting of atmospheric prologues risked racking up costs, which would in turn require increased ticket prices. Since the tax operated on a sliding scale, raising ticket prices carried with it the threat of having to pay a higher tax rate.[61] Columnists acknowledged the cost issue when reporting lavish prologues by offering suggestions for downscaling (see Figure 11.2). But some, like Hastings Pye, made the case for creating "advance prologues", that is, presentations that were like prologues but which had mutated into a species of advertisement.[62] Pye described a cheap way to produce an advance "tableau" prologue for Buster Keaton's *The Navigator*, which was due to feature in his own cinema the following week. His design involved a simple, but creatively lit and minimally animated tableau-style poster, the visual details of which were gradually revealed while the orchestra played "A Life on the Ocean Wave", starting pianissimo and working up in a crescendo. The presentation culminated in the illumination of "Next week" on the trousers of the sailors (see Figure 11.3). Small-town cinemas reported having found such presentations a particularly useful way of maximizing limited advertising and performance budgets. Some advance prologues were elaborate, however, and some were even used in conjunction with moving-image film trailers.[63] In February 1925, for instance, the exhibitor at the Brixton Palladium put on a "prologue" to *The Thief of Bagdad* consisting of "an attractively staged and artistically dressed song-scena…consisting of an Eastern scene in which…[t]wo appropriate songs were rendered…[. T]he theme of the play was subsequently indicated by a series of conjuring tricks by 'Morimura,' a well-known Oriental illusionist."[64] The performance ran in the week prior to *The Thief of Bagdad*, immediately after the trailer of the film (not before!), and according

FIGURE 11.3 Culminating tableau of Hastings Pye's budget "advance prologue" for Buster Keaton's
The Navigator. Kinematograph Weekly, 13 August 1925: 69.

to *Kinematograph Weekly*, was "in itself a big success", and "resulted in countless inquiries concerning the screening of Fairbanks' big picture". This mutation of the live prologue into an entertainment item which creates anticipation for a film at a week's remove is an interesting aspect of prologue discourse; it stretches the theatrical conception of a "prologue," but does so by giving a specific commercial purpose to its function of preparing the audience for what follows—though now a whole week later.[65]

Other local conditions, not only broader historical considerations, but also the interconnected matters of restrictive venue-licensing laws and less variety-oriented programme construction in the early 1920s may have helped to slow down the prologue's progress in Britain. Some felt that the First World War was partly to blame. When Rothafel noted in 1923 that Britain had earlier been ahead of the United States in terms of presentation, a *Cinema* columnist blamed the war, though with surprising reasoning. He claimed that during the war and for the two years following the Armistice there was not only "a superabundance of money", but also a demand for amusement that far exceeded supply. As a result, exhibitors did not have to try very hard to entice people into their theatres, and "the composition of a picture programme degenerated into an almost mechanical calculation of so many feet of film in so many minutes."[66] Even to the untrained eye this seems an unlikely account of wartime exhibition circumstances, and according to Michael Hammond quite the opposite was true: a building boom in 1913–14 had resulted in a high ratio of seats per person in most large and medium-sized cities and towns, which led to fierce local competition during the war.[67] If the war did have an impact on the development of the prologue in Britain, it is more likely to have been as a result of its impact on the construction of new purpose-built super cinemas with stage facilities able to cater for theatrical productions of suitable scope, and possibly also the shortage of relevant personnel. F. E. Adams, managing director of Provincial Cinematograph Theatres, Ltd. (PCT), the largest British circuit in 1920,[68] answered one call in 1922 to look towards American exhibition practices by venting his frustrations in *Kinematograph Weekly*, where he claimed that "95 per cent" of cinemas in the country in early 1922 were pre-war theatres, with limited seating capacity and no stages or other facilities for running the types of entertainments that were becoming typical of the mixed programmes in the United States at the time.[69]

"RIDICULOUS LOCAL REGULATIONS"

During the twenties in the United States, the sort of programme found in picture palaces and imitated in smaller houses stabilized as a mixed one: usually an orchestral overture, followed by newsreel, then a short musical novelty, possibly a short scenic or serial, then a vocal solo, then a two-reel comedy, then a prologue preceding the feature film, followed by a concluding organ item.[70] The ideal type "combined an idea of artistic unity with the need for diversity in entertainment", as Vinzenz Hediger puts it.[71] It is harder to talk about an average cinema programme in Britain at this time, not only because of the exhibition sector's highly stratified nature (which was also true of the United States) but also because of its variable approaches to licensing. A strong trend—"a fetish", according to *Kinematograph Weekly*—in the early twenties was for exhibitors to construct programmes involving two feature-length films.[72] Samuel Rothafel argued strongly against this exhibition policy on grounds of audience boredom and of its halving of effective "seating capacity"; moreover, his concept of atmospheric programming worked best with a prologue prior to a feature film, which itself was the apex of a mixed entertainment format.[73] With two features it was inherently difficult to tailor special atmosphere. Special to which feature? At the same time, other columnists reported that some exhibitors were still, in early 1925, using the continuous-exhibition model, which would likewise not lend itself to "special presentation" or to the idea of a carefully conceived, timed, and executed "atmospheric prologue".[74] Continuous programming also survived well into the late twenties, and possibly later still.[75] Trade papers began arguing vigorously against the two-feature policy, and in favour of a more mixed cinematic programme, in 1925, at which point there was a distinct turn to mixed variety programming (again).[76] Concessions to licensing restrictions as regards the appearance of variety turns in cinemas were made in 1927, even if some restrictions remained.[77] Nevertheless, in the early twenties, when the trade was pushing the prologue, the broadly mixed programme with one feature film at the heart—which lent itself so well to the total thematization of the programme and the rise of the atmospheric prologue in the United States—was apparently less widespread in Britain.

Britain's idiosyncratic licensing laws were linked to the question of programming, inasmuch as they helped to determine what was even possible, though their impact was far less prominently reported in the trade papers than were examples of the sort of dramatic and musical prologue presentations a showman might ideally aim towards. Numerous stories reveal the extent to which imaginatively conceived prologues came into direct conflict with local licensing laws, however. As Jon Burrows has demonstrated in connection with the penny theatre period in London, theatre licensing laws had an enormous impact upon the live and especially musical entertainments that ran alongside film exhibition in Britain.[78] This remained true in certain localities in the early twenties.

For instance, notwithstanding the wide praise it attracted, the Alhambra's prologue and epilogue for *Broken Blossoms* could not simply be copied, or even scaled down, elsewhere. By the time the film arrived in Leeds, local authorities ("ridiculous local regulations", according to *Cinema*[79]) had already precluded the use of human characters, "as in the noted prologue and epilogue as at the Alhambra". Instead the New Gallery Kinema staged what *Kinematograph Weekly* described as "a short scenic", which involved the creation of an elaborate Chinese-themed stage set, the accommodation of the orchestra behind a latticework screen "artistically covered with Chinese blossom", and the use of singing birds, said to have added "considerably to the effectiveness of the atmosphere".[80] Girl ushers and pay-box clerks were all dressed in Chinese costumes, though the stage scene itself apparently ran with neither actors nor singers. Another way to create prologues that adhered to restrictive licenses was proposed by Louis Blattner, a Manchester-based producer of prologues interviewed for *The Bioscope* in November 1922. Blattner suggested that it was "possible to have a prologue filmed with concealed vocalists singing in absolute synchronism in cases where an acting license is unobtainable."[81] Although restrictions relating to live performance before or after screenings of films applied in certain venues, music and even singing were often possible *during* a film, because it was deemed integral to the film.

As late as November 1925, Birmingham's Public Entertainments Committee was still seeking to clarify the status of prologues in the eyes of the licensing laws there. Permission had been sought to employ up to a maximum of four vocalists "to sing to pictures without special sanction from the Justices".[82] In the end, the Joint Committee decided (apparently attempting to mediate between CEA and "legitimate" theatre and music hall interests) that although four vocalists together could *not* sing just before a film, one singer could do so. More than one singer might appear on stage in costume, but only subject to stringent conditions:

> Vocalists may appear in costume suitable to the character on condition that they do not "dress" at houses not provided with proper dressing accommodation, it being understood that managers' offices and similar rooms do not constitute such accommodation.
>
> A vocalist will be allowed to sing actually before the film comes on to the screen, instead of only during the exhibition of the film, so long as the song is incidental to the film.
>
> With regard to the association's request that the annual license should include that more than one vocalist can sing at the same time, a formal application would be made by the association at the annual theatre sessions, when others interested could have the opportunity of placing their views before the Justices.[83]

The 1922 broadside that Adams of PCT made, following an earlier call to look to American Exhibition practices, also lamented these locally managed licensing arrangements:

> He suggested that we should follow in the footsteps of America and immediately add to our already overburdened programs [*sic*] the prologues, ballets, fantasies and light vaudeville which have been tacked on to the picture shows there.
>
> It sounds very nice, but … [he] is quite ignorant of the regulations and conditions under which we labour in this country. It may interest him to hear that if I attempted to engage a solo singer for any of my theatres (with eleven minor exceptions), *the police* would immediately come down and close my doors! In three towns only have I power to put on the simplest ballet! In many instances the local regulations are simply idiotic; for instance, in a large proportion of my theatres I may not use a brass instrument without losing my licence. Mr. Wanger will probably gasp when I tell him that quite recently I took a costly P.C.T. Symphony Orchestra to a town which was not doing too well, and was immediately informed by the police the Symphony Orchestra must be withdrawn or I must close the theatre.[84]

Even if the live atmospheric prologue did not take root in Britain as quickly and thoroughly before 1926 as the trade papers suggest, and even if similar approaches to presentation had long existed in Britain, or at least London, in less integrated ways, Kessler-Howes's January 1926 speculations about its possible imminent death were clearly much exaggerated. Two months after his comments the Plaza Theatre, London, opened and Kessler-Howes himself would soon promote its presentation manager Francis Mangan as a model exponent and even feature his stage designs on his Showmanship page. The prologue's survival into the very late 1920s is witnessed not only by continued, if reduced, coverage in the trade papers, but also in suggestions to bear them in mind when designing new super cinemas.[85] Some of the early descriptions of "electrical reproducers" (essentially, electrical gramophone players) even consider the need to provide prologues. One discussed in the supplement to the *Kinematograph Weekly* in early 1929 notes that "at the Tivoli recently the film 'Trail of '98' was preceded by a prologue expressing the theme of the picture, the record having previously been made by a well-known elocutionist."[86] It remains for further research to trace the trajectory of the prologue in Britain through the late twenties and into the thirties. But in the early phases of their trade paper promotion, it is ironic not only that before the war Britain had been ahead of the United States in terms of thematized exhibition, but also that America's "apostle of 'presentation'", Rothafel (hailed as such by *Cinema News and Property Gazette* in 1923[87]), was an all but isolated voice pointing this out, albeit that he spun a quite different story in the United States, as James Buhler shows in chapter 8 of this volume. Cine-variety's reemergence towards the end of 1924 meant that from that point trade paper column space previously devoted to prologues was increasingly assigned to more broadly based discussions of "variety" into which the prologue was absorbed. Premature though they were, Kessler-Howes's musings on the prologue's mortality nevertheless prove revealing in other ways—alerting us to the slowness of a cultural embrace only occasionally glimpsed otherwise, and revealing much about how transatlantic industry voices intertwined on questions of exhibition. And yet, though the live prologue may have initially struggled in Britain, it was an important part of the rich and complex landscape of film exhibition in the 1910s and 1920s, and another place where music and sound served a critical role in film exhibition.

NOTES

1. West End first runs were sometimes called "exploitation runs" (see *The Bioscope*, 28 Aug. 1924, 23) or "presentation runs" (*Bioscope*, 26 Feb. 1925, 29). I would like to thank Andrew Higson, Jim Buhler, Christine Gledhill, and Annette Davison for their helpful comments on this chapter.

2. "'Presenting' a Masterpiece", *Bioscope*, 10 June 1920, 26.

3. "Editorial Chat. A Notable Film 'Premiere'", *Cinema News and Property Gazette* (hereafter, *Cinema*), 18 Mar. 1920, 31.

4. Reported in Christine Gledhill, *Reframing British Cinema, 1918–1928: Between Restraint and Passion* (London: BFI, 2003), 12. Gledhill draws attention to live prologues as an example of the wider theatricalization of British Cinema in the twenties.

5. "'Presenting' a Masterpiece", 26–26a. It was described as "the same as" New York in "'Broken Blossoms'. 'Atmosphere' for films", *The Times*, 16 Mar. 1920, 14. For more on the presentation of *Broken Blossoms*, see Russell Merritt, "In and Around *Broken Blossoms*", *Griffithiana* 48/49 (Oct. 1993): 12–19.

6. Ernest A. Dench, "How Stage Settings Enhance Film Projection", *Kinematograph and Lantern Weekly*, 24 April 1919, 77. Dench was billed as author of *Making the Movies* (New York: Macmillan, 1915).

7. Dench notes that although at the Strand Theatre, New York, atmospheric stage settings were generally permanent, or at least seasonal (reflecting the seasons of the year), "some exhibitors prefer to change their sets for every production": Ibid. Samuel Rothafel anglicized the spelling of his name (dropping the "p") around June 1920, using his appointment as director of presentation at the Capitol Theatre, New York, to launch the new spelling. See Ben M. Hall, *The Best Remaining Seats: The Story of the Golden Age of the Movie Palace* (New York: Clarkson N. Potter, 1961), 66. Because the current chapter relates mainly to Rothafel's activities after 1920, I use the anglicized spelling unless citing an article he authored using the previous spelling or quoting others. See also Ross Melnick, *American Showman: Samuel "Roxy" Rothafel and the Birth of the Entertainment Industry* (New York: Columbia University Press, 2012), which, however, appeared after the present volume went into production.

8. S. L. Rothapfel, "Your House in Order", *Kinematograph Weekly* (hereafter, *KW*), 26 Aug. 1920, xi (cont. xiii); "Real Service", *KW*, 30 Sept. 1920, xi; "Stage and Lobby", *KW Supplement*, 21 Oct. 1920, xv; "Program Building", *KW Supplement*, 2 Dec. 1920, xiii. *Kinematograph Weekly's* invocation of the famous New York showman contrasts with the American trade papers' initial dependence upon developments in exhibition in Britain and continental Europe. As James Buhler shows in this book, reporting shifted to the exhibition practices of home-grown Rothafel in US trade paper *Moving Picture World* in late 1913.

9. See for instance, Robb Lawson, "The Science of Exploitation (No. III): The Art of Presentation", *Bioscope*, 14 July 1921, 10b–10c. On architecture, see Ben M. Hall, *The Best Remaining Seats*; Marianne Triponi, "The New Ironwood Theatre in Context: Movie Palace as Symbol", *Journal of American Culture* 13/4 (1990): 1–7.

10. See Rothapfel, "Program Building."

11. Rick Altman describes prologues as first popularized by Roxy at the Regent, in *Silent Film Sound* (New York: Columbia University Press, 2004), 385. Rudmer Canjels also claims that the shows of Rothafel and Sid Grauman were where "the prologue concept was first used"; "Featuring on Stage: American Prologues from the 1920s", in *Limina/Le soglie del film. Film's Thresholds*, ed. Veronica Innocenti and Valentina Re (Udine: Forum, 2004), 309. On Griffith, see David Mayer, *Stagestruck Filmmaker: D. W. Griffith and the American Theatre* (Iowa: University of Iowa Press, 2009) and Charles Beardsley, *Hollywood's Master Showman: The Legendary Sid Grauman* (New York: Cornwall, 1983). For an overview of the prologue in North America, see Vinzenz Hediger, "'Putting the Spectators in a Receptive Mood'", in *Limina/Le soglie del film. Film's Thresholds*, ed. Innocenti and Re, 291–308.

12. *Footlight Parade*'s plot concerns a company producing assembly-line prologues for touring as a way of adapting to the advent of the talkies, in the way American sister-and-brother dance team of Fanchon and Mark Wolfe, known professionally as Fanchon and Marco, did in ever-dwindling size until 1937. See Robert S. Birchard, "A song-and-dance spectacular", *American Cinematographer* 86/11 (2005), 66.

13. Cf. Hediger, "'Putting the Spectators in a Receptive Mood'", 294–7.

14. British columnists routinely used the traditional term "scena" to describe scenes either from or involving operatic music.

15. On *The Sea Hawk*, see *Cinema*, 23 Oct. 1924: 36–37 and *KW*, 23 Oct. 1924: 88; on *Her Reputation*, see *Bioscope*, 22 May 1924, 32; on *Passion*, see *Daily Express*, 29 Nov. 1922, 6. Ernst Lubitsch's film *Madame Dubarry* was shown under the title *Passion* in Britain.

16. See *Cinema*, 22 Nov. 1923, 5. On the film itself, see Andrew Higson, *Waving the Flag: Constructing a National Cinema in Britain* (Oxford: Clarendon, 1995), 26–97.

17. See *Daily Express*, 21 June 1921, 7.

18. A brief feature about Francis Harris appears in *KW Supplement*, 15 Oct. 1925, vi.

19. *KW*, 6 Aug. 1925, 44.

20. *Cinema*, 6, 13, 20 May 1926, 59.

21. For photos of lavish stage settings at the Plaza, see *KW*, 23 Dec. 1926, 30; *KW*, 30 Dec. 1926, 25; *Cinema*, 6, 13, and 20 May 1926, 59 (these three issues were published as one). Articles by Mangan, which published the sorts of diagrams to which we rarely have access, include *KW*, 27 Jan. 1927, 69; 3 Feb. 1927, 64; 24 Feb. 1927, 81 (reproduced as Figure 2).

22. *KW*, 15 Dec. 1927, 62. The Tiller Girls also regularly appeared at the Plaza: *KW*, 12 May 1927, 61.

23. *Daily Express*, 12 Jan. 1924, 3. Other such cases included *The Blackguard* (*Bioscope*, 2 April 1925, 7) and *Captain Blood*. As Rachael Low points out, these special evening trade shows were eventually replaced by the "premiere"; Low, *The History of the British Film, 1918–1929* (London: Allen and Unwin, 1950), 50.

24. In time both practices started to irritate sections of the trade, which feared that extravagant trade shows might have been masking poor films, and at any rate effectively inflated the cost of the film to the trade (*Cinema*, 27 Nov. 1924, 1 (cont. 29)), and that West End "exploitation runs" primarily made the film more valuable to the renter: because they tended to run at a loss, the renter had had more profits to recoup from the provincial exhibitor. "West End Presentation", *Bioscope*, 28 Aug. 1924, 23.

25. I am unable here to explore prologues conceptually, but an essay with the provisional title "'From the World of Actuality into the Kingdom of Shadow Dreams'?: The Live Cinema Prologue and the Myth of Immersion" is in preparation.

26. On the need to approach trade papers with care, see also James Buhler and Jon Burrows, chapters 8 and 6 respectively in this volume.

27. Eileen Bowser notes that one needs to read "the small type" of film trade papers in *The Transformation of Cinema, 1907–1915* (Berkeley: University of California Press, 1994), 121.

28. H. F. Kessler-Howes, "Showmanship", *KW*, 14 Jan. 1926, 73.

29. Close reading reveals that at least one person was writing about prologues in the past tense in November 1925. One short column reads "In the days of the prologues, Mr. Renouf staged some very effective examples ...", *KW Supplement*, 12 Nov. 1925, ii.

30. *The Cinema News and Property Gazette*, for instance, described *Broken Blossoms*'s special presentation as "the first time such an effort has been made in this country", "Editorial Chat. A Notable Film 'Premiere'", *Cinema*, 18 Mar. 1920, 31.

31. It opened at the ROH on 14 August 1919. When Thomas Beecham needed to start his opera season, overwhelming public success demanded Thomas's show continue, and it transferred to the Royal Albert Hall on 27 October 1919. In early December it moved on to the Philharmonic Hall, and later that month to the Queen's Hall.

32. A programme relating to the Royal Opera House run, dated 14 August 1919, is held at the Victoria and Albert Theatre and Performance Archives.

33. Thomas, quoted in Kevin Brownlow, *The War, the West and the Wilderness* (London: Secker and Warburg, 1979), 447.

34. From interview with Thomas for WPEN radio in 1965: audio file 1790.03 Marist Special Collections. This is available as Audio Clip #2: http://www.cliohistory.org/thomas-lawrence/show/groundbreaking-production/ [accessed 3 August 2012]. The dancer, the use of a special stage set and big orchestra were apparently Thomas's own ideas, not those of Percy Burton, the British impresario who brought him to London from New York: see cliohistory website, above. Thomas recalls his wife arranging the music, in a personal interview published in 1979 in Brownlow, *The War, the West and the Wilderness,* 447. See also Richard Aldington, *Lawrence of Arabia: A Biographical Inquiry* (London: Collins, 1969), 284ff.

35. "A programme from this period" is quoted on Jeremy Wilson's blog available at: http://blog.castlehillpress.com/chpblog/2010/04/03/lowell-thomas-in-london-1919-20/ [accessed 3 August 2012]. A part-reconstruction of the film lecture was put together by Luke McKernan and Neil Brand at the British Silent Festival, Phoenix Square, Leicester, April 2010.

36. Brownlow, *The War, the West and the Wilderness,* 447.

37. "Rothafel's Home Truths!", *Cinema,* 15 Feb. 1923, 4.

38. According to advance reports in *Daily Express,* 21 Oct. 1911, 9.

39. *Bioscope,* 29 Aug. 1912, 614.

40. This may be a creative appropriation of Méphistophélès's line "Ici, je suis à ton service, Mais là-bas, tu seras au mien!" from Gounod's *Faust.*

41. *Kinematograph and Lantern Weekly Supplement,* 29 Aug. 1912, c.50. See also *KLW,* 5 Sept. 1912, 1383: "Special scenery has been painted".

42. J. L. Styan, *Max Reinhardt* (Cambridge: Cambridge University Press, 1982), 100.

43. As reported in advance by *New York Times,* 9 Dec. 1912, 5. Advertisements in Britain claimed the 200 musicians; *New York Times,* an orchestra "100-strong" plus choir.

44. *Daily Telegraph,* 23 Dec. 1912, 6. *Daily News and Leader* (23 Dec. 1912, 3) reports clearly that the pictures appear through the door.

45. *Evening Standard,* 23 Dec. 1912, 13. See also *Observer,* 22 Dec. 1912, 10.

46. *Daily Telegraph,* 23 Dec. 1912, 6.

47. See *New York Times,* 29 Dec. 1912, 27; and 18 Feb. 1913, 13.

48. See for instance *Observer,* 22 Dec. 1912, 10; and *Daily News and Leader,* 23 Dec. 1912, 3.

49. See, for instance, Stephen Bottomore, "The Story of Percy Peashaker: Debates about Sound Effects in Early Cinema", in *The Sounds of Early Cinema,* ed. Richard Abel and Rick Altman (Bloomington: Indiana University Press, 2001), 137; and Rick Altman, *Silent Film Sound,* 139–55.

50. Pitticus, "Effects or Presentation?" *Bioscope,* 2 Sept. 1920, 28.

51. H. F. Kessler-Howes, *KW,* 14 Jan. 1926, 73. For more on Bowes's intervention, see Hediger, "'Putting the Spectators in a Receptive Mood'", 299–300.

52. From November and December 1924 variety starts to be reported intensively, though it had already started earlier in the year.

53. "The Plaza Presentations", *KW*, 23 Sept. 1926, 78.

54. "Chas. Penley, Presentation Expert, Foreshadows Alterations in Theatres", *Bioscope*, 3 May 1923, 106–7.

55. Hubert Waring, "That Blessed Word 'Presentation'", *Bioscope*, 24 July 1924, 32. Interestingly, this article was printed only a couple of weeks before Sid Grauman was in London, and three weeks before *The Bioscope* ran a one-and-a-half-page feature based on an interview with Grauman. "Great American Showman Tells How", *Bioscope*, 14 Aug. 1924, 34–5.

56. E. Fletcher-Clayton, "Film Prologues—I", *KW Supplement*, 2 Aug. 1923, vi.

57. Ibid.

58. I. P. Gore, "Vaudeville in the Kinema", *KW*, 30 Oct. 1924, 102. Complaints also came from regular audience members, as seen in a letter to the *Daily Express* complaining about the use of various operatic excerpts as part of the prologue to the German film *Passion*: *Daily Express*, 29 Nov. 1922, 6.

59. *Bioscope*, 18 May 1922, 35.

60. Hastings Pye, "The Prologue as a Paying Proposition", *KW*, 13 Aug. 1925, 69.

61. By 1920, following a "small remission of tax on the cheapest seats", the sliding scale of the tax was configured thus: nothing levied under 2*d.*, a penny on a 2½ –4*d.* ticket, 2*d.* on a 4*d.*–7*d.* ticket, and up to 2*s.* on seats of 10*s.* 6*d.*–15*s.* This was altered a little in June 1924, but only by shifting the threshold points (nothing up to 6*d.*; and reduced on tickets up to 1*s.* 3*d.*). Low, *History of the British Film, 1918–1929*, 48–9.

62. "[T]he habit of devising advance prologues to arouse advance curiosity is growing", *Bioscope*, 19 Feb. 1925, 76. See also *KW Supplement*, 12 Nov. 1925, iii.

63. More elaborate advance prologues are discussed in *KW*, 3 Sept. 1925, 84; and *KW*, 7 May 1925, 64.

64. *KW*, 5 Feb. 1925, 79.

65. Although the same mutation also took place in the United States, the entertainment tax may have acted as a particular brake on British exhibitor spending. On "advance prologues" in the United States, see Vinzenz Hediger, *Verführung zum film: Der Amerikanische Kinotrailer seit 1912* (Marburg: Schüren, 2001), 105–8. For more on attempts to reduce costs by trying to make parts of shows, including prologues, portable, see Hediger, "'Putting the Spectators in a Receptive Mood'", 293–5.

66. "Rothafel's Home Truths!", 4.

67. Hammond, "Letters to America: A Case Study in the Exhibition and Reception of American Films in Britain, 1914–1918", in *Young and Innocent? The Cinema in Britain, 1896–1930*, ed. Andrew Higson (Exeter: University of Exeter Press, 2002), 129.

68. See Low, *History of the British Film, 1918–1929*, 41–2. PCT grew from thirty-three cinemas in 1920 to seventy-five in 1926, more than three times more than its nearest rival, Scottish Cinema & Variety Theatres. The average size of most circuits in 1926 was only five theatres, and the average size of larger circuits was fifteen.

69. F. E. Adams, "Adams replies to Weigall", *KW*, 12 Jan. 1922, 40 (cont. 42). This sentiment is echoed in *Bioscope*, 18 May 1922, 35.

70. Altman, *Silent Film Sound*, 380.

71. Hediger, "'Putting the Spectators in a Receptive Mood'", 293.

72. *Bioscope*, 23 June 1921, 16, contains a letter complaining about programmes involving two features plus comedies—programmes lasting two and a half to three hours. The "fetish" quote is from "The Bases of Interest: Using the Effect of Variety to Affect the Attendance", *KW*, 26 April

1923, 119–20. H. F. Kessler-Howes described the average programme as two feature films, with "little opportunity of crushing even a topical in", and explained the phenomenon with reference to a recent lack of availability of shorts: *KW*, 31 Dec. 1925, 71.

73. S. L. Rothapfel, "Program Building".

74. In January 1925 Kessler-Howes argued that with long "super" films of seven to twelve reels the continuous programme was no longer tenable: *KW*, 29 Jan. 1925, 71. Yet, an alternative perspective is given by "A Layman" who, in September 1925, reported that the average picture programme consisted of at least four different films (one feature and three others), which for him was an argument for prologues over "atmospherics" *per se*. Atmospherics could only be sympathetic with one of those four films; thus, "rightly conceived and executed", a prologue "which does not interfere with the other films in the programme" has the advantage over "atmospherics" on the stage. "Prologue or Atmosphere—Which?" *KW*, 17 Sept. 1925, 100.

75. See James Sedgworth, "The Continuous Programme", *KW*, 14 July 1927, 55.

76. The two feature programme would nevertheless eventually became the sound film standard.

77. Christine Gledhill (*Reframing British Cinema*, 12) notes that by February 1927 the Variety Artistes' Federation (VAF) had secured local-authority licensing for variety acts throughout the country, and went on to a successful recruitment drive. Despite the VAF's perception of a resolution, licensing issues continued to arise in the trade papers. For instance, on "renewal day" for licences in Preston borough in mid-1927 it was decided that only two variety turns would be possible: *KW*, 14 July 1927, 45.

78. Jon Burrows, "Penny Pleasures [I]: Film Exhibition in London during the Nickelodeon Era, 1906–1914", *Film History* 16/1 (2004): 60–91. See also this volume, chapter 6.

79. *Cinema*, 20 May 1920, 15.

80. *KW*, 20 May 1920, 124.

81. *Bioscope*, 30 Nov. 1922, 33.

82. "Vocalists at the Kinemas: Birmingham's Battle for Prologue Facilities", *KW Supplement*, 5 Nov. 1925, liii.

83. *KW*, 12 Nov. 1925, 73.

84. "Adams replies to Weigall", 42.

85. For instance, cinema builders and lighting designers were advised to take prologues and kine-variety into consideration: *Kinematograph Year Book 1928* (London: Kinematograph Publications, 1928), 217.

86. *KW Supplement*, 31 Jan. 1929, 23.

87. "Rothafel's Home Truths!"

12

Animating the Audience: Singalong Films in Britain in the 1920s

Malcolm Cook

THE MID-1920S SAW the brief but vigorous popularity of singalong films in Britain. This alternate sonic practice utilized an animated "bouncing ball" or similar device to indicate the lyrics of a song with the intent of promoting a communal singalong in the audience. As will be demonstrated in the first section of this chapter, communal singing was not in itself an innovation and there are a number of precedents that provide an important context for these films. Nevertheless, the sudden initiation of ten or more regular series of films in this genre by a variety of producers is indicative of a geographically and historically specific moment. The appearance of these films coincided with the community singing movement, a broader cultural trend formalized in the foundation of the Community Singers Association by Gibson Young in 1925 and given considerable press attention by the *Daily Express* in 1926–7. Both the singalong films and the community singing movement can be seen as engaging with the new technologies of sound reproduction: gramophone, telephone, and especially radio. These technologies would play a central role in the arrival of synchronized sound in cinemas and the singalong films may be considered a reflection of the debates about what the emerging sound cinema would sound and look like.

The first singalong films to be released in Britain were Reciprocity's *Milestone Melodies* from January 1926, with Mercury's *Famous Melody* series also released in that month.[1] While these films reached cinemas first, Pathé had been promoting the American-produced *Song Car-tune* series since August 1925 for release in March 1926.[2] They were clearly successful as Pathé instigated a British-produced series called *Pathésongs* in 1926 and by their own account achieved the "huge success of cinema singing".[3] This prompted them to release a third series later in the same year, titled *Super-Songs*.[4] Alongside these, British cinemas were flooded with new releases in 1926 and 1927. These included British-produced series such as Ideal's *Singsong* series,[5] Pioneer's *Famous Song Scenes*,[6] Pioneer/Luscombe's *Community Song* series,[7] Parkinson's *Syncopated Melodies*,[8] as well as Film Box Office's (FBO) American-produced *Song Parodies*.[9] The secondary status of short films at this time meant the trade press did not list or review every release in each series, though it is clear they were all intended to have a regular and frequent release schedule. Ideal's *Singsong* series was "to be released fortnightly" with at least twelve films being released.[10] Pioneer/Luscombe's *Community Song* series was planned for twenty-six episodes.[11] Parkinson's *Syncopated Melodies* included at least twelve releases.[12] Given that these films would also have been eminently repeatable it can be assumed they were a mainstay of the cinema programme in 1926 and 1927. From 1928, however, references to the films became scarce in trade papers. To an extent this may reflect that the films had simply become an unremarkable part of the cinema programme, but it also coincides with two important changes to be examined later in this chapter: first, the emergence of synchronized sound cinema in this period, and second, the slow decline in popularity of the community singing movement.[13]

As the titles of these series suggest, the films were fully intended to provoke a communal vocal reaction. One review writes of the *Pathésongs* series: "the popular song…and clever sketches and good timing ensure that any audience will be both interested and quickly moved to song".[14] Advertising for the *Singsong* series also emphasizes the interactive nature of these films as their primary purpose as "they comprise familiar British songs and melodies that people love to sing together" and that they contain "songs they all sing—heartily".[15] The cartoons accompanying the Ideal advertisements feature large groups, many holding song sheets in front of them, with their mouths wide open in song, again emphasizing the communal and interactive nature of the experience (Fig. 12.1).[16] While these films indicate particular interest in communal singing at this time in Britain, it was not an original idea. The following section examines three precedents which offer important background to the films in question.

SINGALONGS: PRECURSORS AND CONTEXT

Communal singing was strongly associated with music hall, though given the latter's long history, from its origins in the 1830s through to gentrified forms of variety in the early twentieth century, it would be a simplification to suggest that it was always

FIGURE 12.1 Advertisement for Ideal's "Singsong" Series. *Kinematograph Weekly*, 24 June 1926.

characterized by an active, vocal audience. Dagmar Kift's research has indicated the historical and geographic specificity of audience behaviours in music halls. She compares London with the provinces, and identifies significant shifts in managers' and proprietors' attitudes to audience expressions in different periods.[17] In the period of the singalong films' production such historical specificity was not always acknowledged. A 1927 editorial in the *Musical Times* makes a case for community singing having a long history, contrary to the *Daily Express*'s claims of its recent innovation. It describes a recent scene at the Alhambra music hall in which the audience was provoked into a lively "communal performance...so that it was difficult to quieten them when the interval was over". It goes on to imply this was a consistent music hall scene over three generations, the only difference being the song titles: "their grandfathers sang 'Beer, glorious beer'".[18] As will be discussed later, the singalong films' debt to music hall lay less in any specific period or place than in this idealized, ahistoric sense.

Vocal audience response in music halls was also a component of other acts, including lightning cartooning. I have argued elsewhere that this act involves a particular form of active spectatorship as well as being an important precedent for animated cartoons, including those that would feature in many of the singalong films of the 1920s.[19] Established as an important act from 1880, the lightning cartoon would present an artist rapidly producing a drawing, most commonly of public figures in the political or entertainment realm. This would encourage a type of guessing game, a narrative of perception, in which the audience actively sought to discern what was being drawn and responded to it. This active spectatorship extended to a vocal response to the political caricatures that emerged.[20] From 1896 music halls were an important venue for the earliest moving-image presentations in Britain and films of lightning cartoonists were part of these shows; it may be presumed the vocal response was also a component of these early animated cartoons.[21] The association of animated cartoons with vocal participation continued up to the end of the First World War. As Nicholas Hiley has shown, cinema audiences continued to be vocal into the 1910s, although "from 1909 onwards the working class cinema audience was subjected to a concerted effort at controlling its behaviour," including dampening vocal responses.[22] Nevertheless, audiences continued to be vocal throughout this period especially in animated cartoons, but in a manner controlled by the exhibitor and his musical director. In 1917 Anson Dyer's film *The Kaiser's Record* featured a series of famous music hall songs, including "We don't want to fight, but by Jingo if we do" and "All dressed up and nowhere to go", that would be very familiar to the audience and would likely result in a singalong.[23] This result was to be encouraged, according to *The Bioscope* reviewer who stated that cinemas "with a musical director who can play up to the artist are sure of a hearty welcome".[24] Music hall, cartooning, and vocal spectatorship had a tripartite relationship that carried on into cinemas and would play an important role in the singalong films under discussion.

Illustrated songs form a second key precursor to singalong films. In the United States, illustrated songs were a central part of the presentation both in vaudeville (the American equivalent to Britain's music hall) and the nickelodeon, an important exhibition venue in the United States between 1906 and 1910. Illustrated songs comprised between sixteen and twenty mass-produced magic lantern slides with illustrative photographic scenes, the final slide showing the lyrics of the song.[25] The majority of the song was performed by professional singers, either employed by the theatre or supplied by the music publisher to promote the song, with the singer often receiving star billing on advertising. The audience would join in with a singalong only on the last slide where the lyrics were present. Richard Abel suggests that the illustrated song is defined by this mix of local popular culture expressed through live performance combined with mass-produced cultural commodities.[26]

Here is a centrally controlled mass entertainment which contains clearly demarcated roles and behaviours for the audience, as well as a form of popular culture which allows space for self-expression and local variation, a description which might easily describe the singalong films of the 1920s.

The illustrated song is often considered a purely American phenomenon, as indicated by the title of Abel's landmark discussion, in which he suggests illustrated songs were unknown in France and Germany; elsewhere he has suggested that "attempts to export illustrated songs to countries such as Great Britain and Sweden, around 1909–1910, proved unsuccessful".[27] Yet an examination of the catalogue of the Yorkshire-based Bamforth company reveals that very similar magic lantern slides were being produced in Britain from the mid-1890s, reaching a peak in 1910.[28] Bamforth's 1890s slides were predominantly religious, featuring established songs and did not yet feature a final chorus slide with lyrics, although some sets did present the words to hymns on each slide. The early 1900s saw the slides begin to feature printed lyrics to encourage audience participation, and they used more recent popular and secular songs. By 1909 the songs featured were exclusively recent hits, and consistently featured a final chorus slide for audience participation; this slide also featured the publisher of the song, its address, and even the price of the sheet music. By 1914 and the outbreak of war, Bamforth had stopped producing their song slides, to concentrate on the picture postcard industry as well as film production, including animated cartoons created by in-house postcard artist Douglas Tempest.

The final important precursor to the singalong films is the *Koko Song Car-tune* series of films produced from 1924 by the Fleischer brothers, Dave and Max Fleischer. The Fleischers were best known at this time for their animated cartoon series *Out of the Inkwell*, featuring Koko the Clown, whose name was used in the title of the *Song Car-tunes* to promote the series.[29] The *Koko Song Car-tunes* presented popular songs' lyrics on screen with a bouncing ball, which encouraged the audience to participate in the performance. The idea of using animated cartoon techniques to present popular songs in this manner is credited to Charles K. Harris, a famous songwriter since the 1890s.[30] This origin story is revealing for two reasons. Firstly, as Daniel Goldmark argues, it indicates the importance of the Fleischer singalong films' connection with songwriters and with the promotion of recent popular music. Goldmark's analysis of the specially orchestrated score for one of the series, *Has Anybody Here Seen Kelly?* (1926), finds that the film emphasized performance in the interests of promoting the song, and that "whether the audience sings or not is inconsequential".[31] Harris's involvement also makes a definite link between the illustrated song slides of the prior decades and the singalong films of the Fleischers. Harris's songs had been adapted for a number of song slides, including at least fourteen manufactured by Bamforth, from "And a Little Child Shall Lead Them" (1900) to "Don't Give Me Diamonds,

All I Want is You" (1912). His suggestion was thus made in full knowledge of the practices of song slide manufacturers in the previous decade, including their explicit promotion of new popular songs in association with music publishers.

SINGALONG FILMS AND COMMUNITY SINGING

Important as these predecessors are to singalong films, the most revealing influence on the sudden popularity of singalong films in Britain in the mid-1920s is the parallel rise and decline of the community singing movement. This movement was inaugurated by Gibson Young's founding of the Community Singers Association (CSA) in April 1925.[32] The organization was well supported by the musical community with an "executive committee" of established figures including Sir Richard Terry (director of music at Westminster Cathedral),[33] Percy Pitt (music director at the BBC),[34] Sir Hugh Allen (director of the Royal College of Music),[35] and W. G. Whittaker (founder of the Newcastle-upon-Tyne Bach Choir and future first principal of the Scottish National Academy of Music).[36] The organization held a number of events over the next year, including concerts at the Royal Albert Hall, but it was the adoption of the movement by the *Daily Express* in October 1926 that brought the activity to the attention of the newspaper's large readership and the wider public.[37] Following a series of high-profile events, including further concerts at the Royal Albert Hall, the movement reached its peak with community singing at the 1927 Football Association (FA) Cup Final with the king in attendance.[38] While events continued over the next few years, the profile of the movement and the CSA soon declined, and by 1930 a commentator could write of them in the past tense: "community singing, to be sure, as we recently knew it, had a short and varied life in this country."[39]

The community singing movement and the singalong films that are the primary focus of this chapter clearly share a common goal, "the choral singing of the man in the street", although their relationship is more substantial than just a shared aim.[40] As already suggested, community singing and singalong films shared a common history derived from music hall, and the dates of their main activity, between 1926 and 1928, are congruous, but there are further similarities. There was a common language used in describing both the films and community singing. Most obvious is the naming of Pioneer/Luscombe's *Community Song* series, but Ideal's *Singsong* series is also named after a phrase commonly used in discussion of community singing.[41] While community singing took place in many venues, including public parks and as part of football matches, cinemas also provided a venue for the activity.[42] Lastly, some screenings of the singalong films were indivisible from the community singing movement, as with a number of events held at the Prince of Wales Picture Playhouse in Lewisham, for example, which Pathé heralded as "cinema singing", but which were treated by *The Times* as "community singing".[43] Despite these close links, community singing and the singalong films were distinct. A comparison of the two helps bring out their shared qualities as well as the unique characteristics of the singalong films in a number of areas, including song repertoire, the balance between the musical and the visual, the cultural specificity of communal singing, and the relationship with sound-reproduction technologies.

SONG REPERTOIRE

As Dave Russell has documented, the community singing movement had an extremely restricted repertoire, in number and range. The song books may have featured over one hundred songs, but in practice only twenty to thirty songs received regular performances.[44] These were drawn from three categories. First, items described as "national song": older songs, sometimes of indistinct origin, which were nevertheless felt to reflect the national consciousness in some way. Second, songs strongly associated with the First World War, the only music hall songs to be used in the repertoire. Third, hymns, especially "Abide with Me", which formed an important part of many community singing events.

Characterizing the repertoire of the singalong films released in 1926–7 is more difficult. The association with community singing is apparent in some selections, such as First World War song "There's a Long Long Trail a-Winding" and "D'ye Ken John Peel", which had regularly featured as a national song in community singing events.[45] Both the *Syncopated Melodies* and the *Community Song* series featured a rendition of "The More We Are Together," otherwise known as the Froth Blowers' Anthem because it was the official song of the Ancient Order of Froth Blowers, which was established in 1924.[46] It was hugely popular at the time and was featured in numerous community singing events, as well as the films mentioned.[47]

The singalong films were not restricted to the categories of songs used in community singing. Unlike community singing, all music hall songs were an important point of reference, not just those associated with the war. Ideal's *Singsong* series drew on music hall hits, and often those that date from the earliest days of film and before. Ideal chose to emphasize the songs' origins by listing the names of the music hall performers associated with them alongside the song names in their advertising.[48] Vesta Tilley's "The Midnight Son", used in a September 1926 edition, had been debuted by Tilley, one of the most popular music hall stars, in 1897.[49] Tilley had also helped popularize another Ideal *Singsong*—"Burlington Bertie"—a song she first sang in 1900.[50] Another Ideal *Singsong* featured Harry Lauder's "Stop Y'r Ticklin Jock", a song Lauder had been performing since at least 1904 and which was strongly associated with his Scottish persona.[51] Lauder had been performing in music halls since

1895 and was knighted in 1919 in recognition of his work during the First World War.[52] By 1926 he would be considered a national treasure and one of the most recognizable music hall and variety performers.

The continued influence of illustrated song slides is apparent in the selection of some singalong films. "Sally in our Alley" had been released as an illustrated song slide set by Bamforth in 1902 and featured in one of Ideal's *Singsongs* in 1926.[53] FBO's *Song Parodies* lampooned "Annie Laurie" which had been released twice by Bamforth, in 1901 and 1912.[54] Mercury's *Famous Melody Series* featured "Alice, Where Art Thou?", an 1861 song which had been popular enough to warrant Bamforth's releasing it on three different slide sets, in 1898, 1905, and 1912.[55] By using songs connected with either song slides or music hall, the singalong films were drawing on long-established material already strongly associated with communal singing. These songs would probably evoke a nostalgic sense of these prior forms of entertainment, which had also promoted a vocal audience, but in the different setting of the cinema.

The singalong films did not just feature popular songs of the past. They also showcased recent hits, following the practice of song slide manufacturers by coordinating with music publishers to explicitly promote sheet music. Jeff Smith has shown how this practice was adopted by film producers in the 1910s in America.[56] It was also a feature of British film making prior to the singalong films' appearance. The creation of songs about the main characters of films was especially associated with animated cartoons. While *Felix the Cat* was an American import to Britain, his huge popularity led to several British songs being written in his name, including "Felix Kept on Walking" (1923).[57] Written by Ed. E. Bryant and Hubert W. David, the song was a popular hit, encouraging them to follow it in 1924 with "Here He Is Again! (Being More Adventures of Felix)".[58] Harry Tilsley also wrote a "Felix" song, "Fido Followed Felix", published in Britain in 1924.[59] The British producers of the *Jerry the Troublesome Tyke* series also adopted cross-media promotion: their feline star was associated with a popular song that was then promoted by being played on the *Radio Radiance* radio show conducted by James Lester.[60]

The association of recent popular songs with films, including animated cartoons, was a well-established practice by the time the singalong films adopted this approach. Pioneer/Luscombe's *Community Song* series included "Perhaps You'll Think of Me", from 1926, "Am I Wasting My Time on You?", again from 1926,[61] and "Shepherd of the Hills", from 1927.[62] Parkinson's *Syncopated Melodies* went further in the attempt to promote recent music. As well as including recent popular tunes, such as Irving Berlin's "Because I Love You" (1926), the films were also associated with famous dance bands of the time such as "Jack Hylton's, the London Radio Dance Band, the Savoy Havana... and John Lester's Cowboy Syncopators" with gramophone records of the bands available as an alternative to sheet music.[63]

The repertoire of the singalong films as a whole was heterogeneous, with no discernible pattern beyond the requirement that they could be communally sung by an audience. In some cases even individual series show no distinct pattern; for instance, Ideal's *Singsong* series initially used very old folk songs or those associated with song slides, but shifted its approach after nine films to focus on music hall songs.[64] Pathé similarly covered all bases, with its films featuring "All the most popular Old Time Songs and Melodies also An Extensive Selection of Modern Favourites".[65] This heterogeneity may simply be considered part of an insatiable appetite for novelty. It may also be considered a symptom of the emergence of sound cinema and an uncertainty about the exact form this would take, as I discuss below.

THE MUSICAL AND THE VISUAL

Community singing was intended as a primarily musical movement, as Gibson Young's manifesto makes clear, the crowd being led "to a better and a higher appreciation of the best in music".[66] There was some debate over the extent to which the communal singing of songs simple enough to be grasped by hundreds of singers simultaneously could raise the musical standards of the general public, but the CSA's backing by the leading figures of the musical world indicates this was a genuine aim of the movement.[67] There is no indication that the singalong films held such aspirations. These were commercial films produced to entertain and amuse, as is indicated by Ideal advertising that the orchestrations supplied with its *Singsong* series contained "quaint and novel orchestral effects" rather than aspired to musical excellence.[68]

Given the musical focus of community singing, there was very little attention paid to its visual component, beyond the spectacle of a huge crowd taking part in an activity in unison, the aspect highlighted by the *Illustrated London News*.[69] There was one further important visual aspect to the movement that indicates an affinity with the singalong films: the conductor. *The Times*'s account of the community singing at the 1927 FA Cup Final vividly reports the gymnastics of T. P. Ratcliff who conducted many community singing events. It describes "the strange spectacle of a white figure, plump but athletic, vigorously waving his arms about, on a movable, black-painted platform" and emphasizes "the whiteness of the figure and the blackness of the platform", an arrangement that was common for community singing events.[70] This description closely matches the experience of watching Pioneer/Luscombe's *Community Song* series, the only example of the British singalong series known to have survived, three films being preserved in the BFI National Archive. These films feature an animated version of the mythological figure Orpheus who acts as conductor, leaping around the screen and waving his arms to guide the audience. The similarity is not only a resemblance between the monochrome colour scheme and animated antics of a conductor, but also the importance of this figure in guiding and controlling audience involvement.[71] A similar form of animated indicator for the lyrics appeared in all these films, whether a conductor in the *Community Song* series, the common bouncing ball, or in the case of the Ideal *Singsong* series, the production company's trademark moving from word to word.[72] Each of these indicators provided a visual focal point to guide the audience's involvement. Both community singing and singalong films featured an animated figure concerned with directing, or animating, the audience.

The visual element of the singalong films was central to their appeal. Ideal's advertising highlighted the "drawings by Norman Cobb", and the use of cartoon images in the advertising indicates the equal status given to the visual. As discussed above, cartooning had a long association with active vocal spectatorship from the lightning cartoon. This was clearly still a factor in the 1920s, with Ideal advertising that their *Singsong* films contain "the pictures the people yell at".[73] The association with lightning cartooning also carried into the films themselves, with the bouncing ball replaced by an animated conductor's hand holding a baton which points to each word in turn in the *Community Song* series, for example. While ostensibly musical in reference, the image evokes the iconography of the lightning cartoon, the artist's hand holding a pen or pencil. Animation was important to some singalong films because it encouraged and was associated with active vocal participation. Yet as with the song repertoire, singalong films cannot be easily characterized as a whole by this tendency. Ideal's *Singsongs* and Pioneer/Luscombe's *Community Song* series were fully animated, but Reciprocity's *Milestone Melodies* and Mercury's *Famous Melody* series used photographic footage which would be associated with a very different mode of spectatorship. With so few of these films surviving, other series cannot be clearly identified as using one technique or the other. As will be argued below, this reflects not simply a diverse differentiated marketplace, but a tension over the emergence of synchronized sound and what sound films should look and sound like.

"BRITISH THROUGH AND THROUGH"

Both the community singing movement and the singalong films derived part of their appeal from their evocations of a particularly British, or English, cultural tradition. The use of "national" songs and the notion of "Merrie England" characterized community singing as specifically British, despite founder Gibson Young's Australian roots and the origins of the movement in Australia and the United States.[74] The community singing movement was not, at its establishment, concerned with political ideology. In his statement of intent for the CSA, Young wrote "music is beyond sect, political party, or clique of bohemia".[75] Yet following the General Strike in 1926 it was increasingly involved with political ideology and associated with both sides of the political spectrum. In a February 1927 article for the *Illustrated London News*, G. K. Chesterton defended the movement from the claim "that Community Singing was identified with Communist Singing".[76] Whether in reaction to this claim, or through long-held political belief, a number of those involved in the community singing movement lent their services to right-wing events. Conductor T. P. Ratcliff contributed to Conservative party political events, including one at the Royal Albert Hall in which the singing and the Prime Minister's speech were relayed to Hyde Park for an "overflow meeting" estimated at thirty thousand people.[77] Gibson Young lent his services to the "Anti-Socialist and Anti-Communist Union" conducting community singing as part of a political rally in Hyde Park in May 1927.[78] The political affiliations of community singing became a major part of this event which was scheduled in direct opposition to and on the same day as the long-standing Labour and Socialist May Day march in Hyde Park, which according to *The Times* had a strong Communist contingent in 1927.[79] This event would have been highly charged, coming in the aftermath of the General Strike and coinciding with the House of Commons debate on the Trade Unions Bill, which would place greater restrictions on strikes and make changes to union membership. Both political groups were thus engaged in the use of community singing to lay claim to a particular vision of Britain's future, the Socialists and Communists singing the "Marseillaise" and "The Red Flag", the Anti-Socialist Union singing "John Peel" and "John Brown's Body".[80]

This highly charged political atmosphere is entirely absent from any discussion of the singalong films in trade press, beyond their advertising claim to being "British through and through" and "All British".[81] As commercial products the films were primarily concerned with reaching as wide an audience as possible, an aim that was incompatible with expressing overt political viewpoints. Nevertheless, this social context should not be dismissed as irrelevant to the discussion of these films. As has been demonstrated, the singalong films were intimately connected with community singing, which was in turn becoming entwined with the political debates of the day. While the films do not express overt political viewpoints, they do engage with underlying principles: individuality versus communal activity, control versus freedom to act, local specificity versus national or international standardization. These issues, as with the other areas already identified in previous sections, would play an important role in the way singalong films negotiated the introduction of sound reproduction and the emergence of sound cinema.

SINGALONG FILMS AND THE NEGOTIATION OF TALKING PICTURES

As has been indicated throughout this chapter, singalong films in Britain arose at a time of major change in the film industry: the coming of sound. Clearly it is beyond the scope of this chapter to address the myriad aspects of this complex technological, economic, aesthetic, and social shift, either as it specifically affected British production and exhibition, or in international terms. Nevertheless, there are several key points which pertain directly to the arguments laid out here regarding the relationship of singalong films with sound-reproduction technology, and which are derived from Donald Crafton's comprehensive study of the topic.[82] Crafton's field of study goes beyond the film industry to identify the complex structural relationships from which sound cinema emerged. The technology of sound cinema was not invented for the purpose of creating moving pictures. It owed little to previous attempts to synchronize sound with film in the first thirty years of moving images; rather it utilized and was an exploitation of many different technologies and parallel areas of research from areas such as telephony, radio, and phonography.[83] Further to this, Crafton demonstrates that although by 1931 sound was fully incorporated aesthetically into the narrative feature film and that "the film style of the previous fifteen years changed little", in the period prior to this the notion of what sound film might look and sound like was open to question and experimentation. A number of different approaches were tried, from the technological replacement of the cinema orchestra with canned music to a "virtual Broadway", in which musical and other performances supplemented narrative film making, as well as to the eventual dominant mode of the talkies of Crafton's title.[84] This final section will address these two aspects of the emergence of sound cinema in relation to the singalong film in Britain.

The community singing movement has been understood by many commentators, both at the time and in histories of the movement, as being opposed to modern or mass culture, and specifically the reproduction of sound in the new technologies of radio and the gramophone. *The Times* published an editorial comment which praised the movement in these terms:

> it is, therefore, an extremely good thing in an age which encourages Everyman, by machinery and propaganda, to turn listener, that Everyman should insist on taking some part, if only a humble one, in *doing* something musical.[85]

Here community singing, and by inference singalong films, stand in opposition to a passivity associated with technology (especially that of sound reproduction). Appealing as this binarism is, it is apparent that community singing and singalong films have a more complex and ambivalent relationship with the technologies of sound and their personal or social implications. Sound reproduction was important to community singing in a number of ways. From the outset many of the community singing events were broadcast on radio by the BBC.[86] While not explicitly acknowledged in most discussions, amplification was an important component of community singing.[87] Finally, a number of recordings of community singing events were released as gramophone records.[88]

The singalong films held a similarly ambivalent relationship with sound reproduction. Ideal's *Singsong* series most clearly aspired to the live immediacy of community singing, emphasizing in its advertising the "free orchestral score specially written by Horace Shepherd" that accompanied its films.[89] Of course the synchronization between the musicians and the on screen film would be difficult to achieve and a number of reviews highlight the importance of an "efficient musical director" who would need to take "reasonable care...in conducting".[90] The singsong films were thus revealing of one of the technical limitations of film presentation with live music and may have helped to make the case for synchronized, reproduced sound. Of course mechanically reproduced sound was equally subject to the synchronization problem. The *Pathé Super Songs* were accompanied by gramophone records, which a review optimistically suggested would be synchronized "with ordinary care from a good operator".[91] In this case the gramophone record was simply providing a direct replacement for live cinema musicians, what Crafton calls the "virtual orchestra".[92] The 1927 *Syncopated Melodies* took this approach further, using gramophone records of famous dance bands of the time, which were promoted in advertising for the series. In using star performers, these films moved towards another of Crafton's categories, "virtual Broadway".[93] Here the reproduction technology was used to bring the greatest stars from the largest cities to any cinema equipped to screen the films. Clearly there was an appeal in the democratization of this process, making the finest musical acts available to everyone. Yet it would also degrade two of the key appeals of the singalong film. First, it would remove the immediacy of the live event, especially given the difficulties of synchronizing a gramophone record with a film. Second, it would shift the focus away from the audience back to the performers, returning the audience to passive spectatorship.

A number of different approaches were adopted by singalong film series to deal with these issues. *Famous Song Scenes* did not use reproduced sound but were distributed not only with "specially arranged complete scores" but also "competent vocalists" to perform the songs.[94] Pioneer's *Cameo Operas* were also intended to be presented by professional singers, with a trade show featuring the British National Opera Company "which suggests a line of treatment for exhibitors who book the series".[95] The performance-led approach of these series would clearly return the immediacy of live performance, but at the expense of audience participation as well as synchronization problems, an issue highlighted by trade paper reviewers.[96] Stephen Bottomore explores an earlier attempt to deal with the synchronization difficulties that resulted from performance-led films in chapter 9 of this volume, on Selsior dance films; in these a conductor was filmed within the frame of the image.

Immediacy could be returned to these films in other ways as well, such as the association with the latest in sound technology, the radio. Starting in April 1926, the orchestra at the Prince of Wales Picture Playhouse made regular appearances involving vocal performances on the BBC 2LO station.[97] On 27 August 1926 its broadcast included community singing, using one of the *Pathésongs* films, an event which, according to Pathé's advertising, produced considerable press and public interest.[98] On release the Pathé *Super Songs* were heralded as being accompanied not only by gramophone records, but also radio broadcasts: "an irresistible and compelling tie up", according to press reviews.[99] While it is not clear how many of the broadcasts from this cinema featured community singing (which continued until 1931)[100], a repeat event in November 1926 suggests they were a regular part for the peak period of interest in community singing and singalong films.[101] Radio broadcasts would communicate the community singing experience to a much wider, geographically dispersed audience while retaining a sense of live performance, and they would also promote the singalong films.

The sense of transcending geographical distance was also a key factor in the singalong films' association with the other important technology of sound reproduction, the telephone. In 1927 the *Community Song* series featured the hit "Shepherd of the Hills", written by the Americans Edgar Leslie and Horatio Nicholls. This song was unremarkable musically, but attracted considerable attention due to its having been transmitted to London via newly available transatlantic telephony. The first successful engineering test across the Atlantic had occurred only in March 1926.[102] Less than a year later, on 10 February 1927, the writers of the song were able to communicate their new song by telephone to bandleader Jack Hylton "only a few days before the show" of the singalong film, which was quickly reviewed in the 3 March edition of *Kinematograph Weekly*.[103] The story of its rapid dissemination was central to the song's popularity, with the British sheet music given the tagline "the 3,000 miles a second New York–London Hit!"[104]

The use of radio and telephone technology associated the singalong films with the latest advances in sound reproduction, but it also changed the nature of the singalong film. Community singing and some earlier singalong films, such as Ideal's *Singsongs*, had emphasized national specificity and allowed space for local musical variations. In contrast, the use of internationally written songs, whose music and lyrics tended towards a transatlantic non-specificity, meant the singalong films became another area of cinema presentations dominated by American mass entertainment. Furthermore, radio broadcasts, which needed to appeal to a broader audience, could therefore not acknowledge the specificity of their local cinema audience, such as the diversity of London's many audiences.

CONCLUSION

Despite the shared goal of invoking communal singing and the clearly delineated dates of peak activity, it is the heterogeneity of the singalong films which characterizes them. Some films recalled, through their repertoire, prior forms of communal singing, such as music hall and illustrated song slides. Yet others preferred recent popular songs and promoted them in association with music publishers. Some films used animation, calling on an established association of cartooning with active vocal participation. Yet several series used photographic images to illustrate the songs, visuals which could have very different associations for the audience. Some films emphasized their British credentials and placed national specificity at their centre, yet they failed to clearly define the meaning of this and did not engage with the political use of community singing to define "Britishness". Other films used American songs and had no geographical specificity. The connection of the singalong films with the parallel community singing movement is of central importance, suggesting a shared concern with live, communal experience and active participation. Yet many of the films experimented with the new sound-reproduction technologies of radio, phonography, and telephony as well as reintroducing the use of professional performers. It is these latter associations which underpin the heterogeneity of the singalong films. The singalong films probe what the combination of cinema and these technologies—which were central to the emergence of sound cinema—would look and sound like. Would it create, or simulate, a sense of live immediacy as found in performance, or provide an easily reproducible mass entertainment? Would it enhance the "realistic" qualities of the photographic image or provide a space for alternative practices with aural equivalents to animation? Would it provide a space for local and national specificity or would it allow further dominance of standardized American mass entertainment? Would it create a space for an active, vocal audience or silence them into passivity? The singalong films did not provide any final answers to these questions and examples of all of these tendencies can be found among their ranks. The final statement is made by the singalong films' disappearance at the same time synchronized sound was being institutionalized into the cinema, with audiences increasingly listening rather than singing.

NOTES

1. *Kinematograph Weekly* (hereafter, *KW*), 5 Nov. 1925, 43.
2. *KW*, 27 Aug. 1925, lxix.
3. *KW*, 2 Sept. 1926, 15.
4. *KW*, 18 Nov. 1926, 74.
5. *KW*, 1 July 1926, 2.

6. *KW*, 21 Oct. 1926, 63.

7. *KW*, 3 Mar. 1927, 54.

8. *KW*, 10 Mar. 1927, 59.

9. *KW*, 7 Oct. 1926, 63; *Film Daily*, 5 Dec. 1926, 13.

10. *KW*, 19 Aug. 1926, 8.

11. *KW*, 3 Mar. 1927, 54.

12. *KW*, 10 Mar. 1927, 59.

13. *Times*, 25 April 1927, 6.

14. *KW*, 20 May 1926, 68.

15. *KW*, 24 June 1926, 2; *KW*, 16 Sept. 1926, 26.

16. Full-page advertisements featuring these cartoons appear in *KW* on 24 June 1926, 2; 1 July 1926, 2; 15 July 1926, 2; 19 Aug. 1926, 8; 16 Sept. 1926, 26.

17. Dagmar Kift, *The Victorian Music Hall: Culture, Class and Conflict* (Cambridge: Cambridge University Press, 1996), 70.

18. *Musical Times*, 1 Mar. 1927, 239.

19. Malcolm Cook, "The Lightning Cartoon: Animation from Music Hall to Cinema", *Early Popular Visual Culture* (Forthcoming).

20. *Era*, 12 Nov. 1881, 4

21. *Era*, 28 Mar. 1896, 18.

22. Nicholas Hiley, "The British Cinema Auditorium", in *Film and the First World War*, ed. Karel Dibbets and Bert Hogenkamp (Amsterdam: Amsterdam University Press, 1995), 165.

23. *Bioscope*, 12 July 1917, 198.

24. *Bioscope*, 12 July 1917, 180.

25. Rick Altman, *Silent Film Sound* (New York: Columbia University Press, 2004), 183.

26. Richard Abel, "That Most American of Attractions, the Illustrated Song", in *The Sounds of Early Cinema*, ed. Richard Abel and Rick Altman (Bloomington: Indiana University Press, 2001), 143–55.

27. Ibid., 145; Richard Abel, "Illustrated Songs", in *Encyclopedia of Early Cinema*, ed. Richard Abel (London: Routledge, 2005), 310.

28. *A Detailed Catalogue of Photographic Lantern Slides, Life Models &C.*, (Holmfirth: Bamforth, 1910). The Bamforth catalogue is represented along with reproductions of many of the slide sets on the DVD-Rom, "The Illustrated Bamforth Slide Catalogue", ed. Richard Crangle and Robert MacDonald (London: Magic Lantern Society, 2009). Rachael Low describes Bamforth as "fairly important dealers in lantern slides". An article in the *Optical Magic Lantern Journal* from 1902 describes the Bamforth storage room with "hundreds of thousands" of slides packed ready for delivery, in addition to "many thousands" being prepared for delivery and another room with "four tiers of shelves 52 feet long, 8 feet high, with capacity for another 1,500,000 slides." Rachael Low and Roger Manvell, *The History of the British Film, 1896–1906* (London: Allen and Unwin, 1948), 15; *Optical Magic Lantern Journal*, Oct. 1902, 7.

29. Donald Crafton, *Before Mickey: The Animated Film, 1898–1928* (Cambridge, MA: MIT Press, 1982), 175.

30. Daniel Goldmark, "Before *Willie*: Reconsidering Music and the Animated Cartoon of the 1920s", in *Beyond the Soundtrack: Representing Music in Cinema*, ed. Daniel Goldmark, Lawrence Kramer, and Richard Leppert (Berkeley: University of California Press, 2007), 233.

31. Ibid., 239.

32. Gibson Young, "Recreative Singing: Community Singing in Industry", *The Sackbut*, May 1925, 300.

33. John Harper, "Terry, Sir Richard Runciman (1864–1938)", in *Oxford Dictionary of National Biography* (Oxford: Oxford University Press, 2004); online edn, http://www.oxforddnb.com/view/article/36463 [accessed 3 Aug 2012].

34. Stephen Follows, "Pitt, Percival George (1869–1932)", ibid.; online edn, http://www.oxforddnb.com/view/article/60854 [accessed 3 Aug 2012].

35. W. K. Stanton, "Allen, Sir Hugh Percy (1869–1946)", ibid.; online edn, http://www.oxforddnb.com/view/article/30386 [accessed 3 Aug 2012].

36. Michael Brown, "Whittaker, William Gillies (1876–1944)", ibid.; online edn, http://www.oxforddnb.com/view/article/60852 [accessed 3 Aug 2012].

37. *Daily Express*, 4 Oct. 1926, 1.

38. Dave Russell, "Abiding Memories: The Community Singing Movement and English Social Life in the 1920s", *Popular Music* 27/1 (2008): 117–33

39. *Musical Mirror*, Nov. 1930, 329.

40. Young, "Recreative Singing", 301. *Daily Express*, 4 Oct. 1926, 1.

41. *Times*, 6 July 1926, 14.

42. *Times*, 27 Oct. 1927, 8.

43. *KW*, 2 Sept. 1926, 15. *Times*, 27 Aug. 1926, 8; 12 Nov. 1926, 21.

44. Russell, "Abiding Memories", 122.

45. *KW*, 20 May 1926, 68; 1 July 1926, 2; Russell, "Abiding Memories", 122.

46. *KW*, 10 Mar. 1927, 59; 3 Mar. 1927, 54; *Times*, 23 May 1931, 10.

47. *Times*, 27 Jan. 1927, 12; 2 Dec. 1927, 12.

48. *KW*, 16 Sept. 1926, 26.

49. *KW*, 23 Sept. 1926, 70; *Era*, 6 Nov. 1897, 19.

50. *KW*, 16 Sept. 1926, 26; *Era*, 22 Sept. 1900, 19.

51. *KW*, 16 Sept. 1926: 26; *Judy: The London Serio-Comic Journal*, 16 Nov. 1904, 1172.

52. *Era*, 17 Aug. 1895: 16; Dave Russell, "Lauder, Sir Henry [Harry] (1870–1950)", in *Oxford Dictionary of National Biography*; online edn, http://www.oxforddnb.com/view/article/34419 [accessed 3 Aug 2012].

53. *Bamforth's Artistic Life Model Lantern Slides: Supplementary List* (Holmfirth: Bamforth, 1912). *KLW*, 1 July 1926, 2.

54. *Bamforth's Artistic Life Model Lantern Slides: Supplementary List*. *KLW*, 7 Oct. 1926, 68.

55. *Bamforth's Artistic Life Model Lantern Slides: Supplementary List*. *KLW*, 5 Nov. 1925, 43.

56. Jeff Smith, "Banking on Film Music: Structural Interactions of the Film and Record Industries", in *Movie Music: The Film Reader*, ed. Kay Dickinson (London: Routledge, 2003), 66–68. See also, Jeff Smith, *The Sounds of Commerce; Marketing Popular Film Music* (New York: Columbia University Press, 1998).

57. Ed. E. Bryant and Hubert W. David, "Felix Kept on Walking" (London: Worton David, 1923).

58. Ed. E. Bryant and Hubert W. David, "Here He Is Again! (Being More Adventures of Felix)" (London: Worton David, 1924).

59. Harry Tilsley, "Fido Followed Felix" (London: Cecil Lennox, 1924).

60. *Bioscope*, 3 Sept. 1925, 38.

61. *Musical Times*, 1 Jan. 1927, 41.

62. Edgar Leslie and Horatio Nicholls, "Shepherd of the Hills" (London: Lawrence Wright Music, 1927).

63. *KW*, 10 Mar. 1927, 59.

64. *KW*, 1 July 1926, 2; *KLW*, 19 Aug. 1926, 8.

65. *KW*, 15 April 1926, 10a.

66. Young, "Recreative Singing", 301.

67. *Musical Times*, 1 April 1927, 336–42.

68. *KW*, 24 June 1926, 2.

69. *Illustrated London News*, 30 April 1927, 782.

70. *Times*, 25 April 1927, 6; Russell, "Abiding Memories", 118.

71. For more on the possibilities afforded by an on screen conductor, see Stephen Bottomore's discussion of the Selsior dancing films in chapter 9 of this volume. For these a conductor was filmed in the corner of the frame to enable a live orchestra in the theatre to provide music for the on screen dancers who synchronized with their movements.

72. *KW*, 23 Sept. 1926, 70.

73. *KW*, 1 July 1926, 2.

74. Russell, "Abiding Memories", 126.

75. Young, "Recreative Singing", 300.

76. G. K. Chesterton, "Our Notebook", *Illustrated London News*, 19 Feb. 1927, 290.

77. *Times*, 10 May 1927, 9.

78. *Times*, 29 April 1927, 11.

79. *Times*, 2 May 1927, 14.

80. *Times*, 2 May 1927, 14.

81. *KW*, 1 July 1926, 2; *KW*, 15 July 1926, 2.

82. Donald Crafton, *The Talkies: American Cinema's Transition to Sound, 1926–1931* (Berkeley: University of California Press, 1999).

83. Ibid., 9.

84. Ibid., 11–18.

85. *Times*, 13 Aug. 1927, 8.

86. *Times*, 1 May 1925, 24.

87. *Times* 22 June 1925, 12; 5 Aug. 1927, 13; 29 April 1929, 6.

88. *British Musician*, Jan. 1929, 28.

89. *KW*, 1 July 1926, 2.

90. *KW*, 18 Nov. 1926, 74; 7 Oct. 1926, 68.

91. *KW*,18 Nov. 1926, 74.

92. Crafton, *The Talkies*, 70–75.

93. Ibid., 63–70.

94. *KW*, 21 Oct. 1926, 63.

95. *KW*, 30 June 1927, 68.

96. Ibid.

97. *Times*, 16 April 1926, 7; 25 June 1926, 8.

98. *KW*, 2 Sept. 1926, 15; *Times*, 27 Aug. 1926, 8.

99. *KW*, 18 Nov. 1926, 74.

100. *Times*, 30 June 1931, 19.

101. *Times*, 12 Nov. 1926, 21.

102. *Times*, 8 Mar. 1926, 16.

103. *Times*, 29 Feb. 1928, 5; *KW*, 3 Mar. 1927, 54.

104. Leslie and Nicholls, "Shepherd of the Hills".

PART FOUR

Musicians, Companies and Institutions

13

Workers' Rights and Performing Rights: Cinema Music and
Musicians Prior to Synchronized Sound

Annette Davison

> Silent films functioned as if they had been
> designed to create jobs for musicians.
>
> CYRIL EHRLICH, *The Music Profession in Britain*[1]

IN 1911 ONLY 460 musicians in England and Wales identified themselves as
employed by "picture theatres", just ten percent of those engaged as "Musicians
employed in theatres, music halls and picture theatres".[2] As Jon Burrows explains in
chapter 6 in this volume, by the end of 1912 half of the licensed cinemas in London
employed an orchestra of some kind (typically five to seven players at this time),
rather than a lone pianist; a situation that evidence suggests was true across Britain
generally. Cinema was cheap, by comparison with music hall and theatre. There
were no stars, no stage performers, and no backstage crew beyond the projectionist.[3] An orchestra, however, was a major expense that the best cinemas could not do
without. Opportunities for cinema musicians grew exponentially as the size and
seating capacity of cinemas were increased over the next decades, though the provision of lone pianists continued in smaller venues, and during quieter periods of the
programme in larger halls. At the Cinema House, which opened in the centre of
Glasgow in December 1911 with a seating capacity of approximately 600, the cost

of the musicians was twice that of the manager's salary. A trio performed from 7 to
10.30p.m. each night, with two pianists engaged for longer hours. Within months,
however, additional musicians were sought for the afternoon programme, and for
the presentation of particular films in the evening.[4] Despite these rising costs, the
original band received six nights' holiday plus a bonus after six months, with a further bonus paid at the anniversary of the cinema's opening.

The rebuilding of the Cinema House in the mid-1920s more than doubled the seating capacity to 1,314.[5] The lone pianist was replaced by a "quintette", and the larger
orchestra for afternoon and evening programmes was also augmented.[6] By September
1926, the total weekly cost of the musicians was almost a quarter of the cinema's total
running costs, at £97 5s. per week.[7] Here the orchestra's augmentation was probably
due to fears about competition: a new "super"—the Green's Playhouse—was nearing
completion along the street.[8] It opened the following year with a seating capacity of
more than 4,300, with an orchestra of thirty on a platform, raised to the height of the
stage by hydraulics for the musical interlude.[9] While super cinemas were concentrated
in urban centres, musicians were required by film exhibition venues of all classes, size,
and location. By 1924 "quite half of the musicians employed in the entertainment
business [were] employed in cinemas".[10] By 1928 cinemas accounted for "between 75
and 80 per cent of 'paid musical employment'",[11] or, "at least 16,000 full-time jobs".[12]

Employers had limited options as to how to cut the cost of musicians, who were
among the first groups in the entertainment industry to form a trade union; the
Amalgamated Musicians' Union (AMU) was formed in 1893 in Manchester. Total
union membership in Britain stood at one and a half million then, but with the
expansion of unionization to semi-skilled and unskilled workforces, by 1920 membership had reached more than eight million. With the power afforded to the trade
unions by the election of union executives as Members of Parliament, legislation
was developed which supported the unions and increased their strength.[13] National
Joint Industrial Councils were established from 1919, as a result of the Whitley
Report, and local Conciliation Boards, with representation from both employers
and workers, were created to settle disputes concerning wages and conditions, and
avoid strikes.[14] The Performing Right Society (PRS), established in 1914, benefitted both the composers and publishers of music heard in cinemas, and was funded
by the licences that venues were required to pay for the right to perform copyright
music administered by the PRS: another music-related cost borne by cinemas. On
the surface it would seem that the odds were stacked in favour of the musicians. The
reality was that other factors, such as the war, the entertainments tax, and a period
of extreme economic volatility, together generated a rather more complex situation
for this sector of the labour market. In this chapter I explore the situation of cinema
musicians and composers in the two decades that followed the Cinematograph Act

of 1909, through their relations with musicians' unions, the employers, and the PRS. Examples are drawn primarily from evidence relating to the situation in Scotland.

MUSICIANS, UNIONS AND THE CINEMA

In the same year that Joseph Williams, a twenty-one-year-old clarinettist at the Comedy Theatre, Manchester, established the AMU, Fred Orcherton, a flautist in the Queen's Hall Orchestra, started the London Orchestral Association (LOA), later the National Orchestral Association.[15] As its name suggests, the LOA retained its focus on London, initially at least, despite competition from the AMU. The AMU was established as a trade union, accepting everyone, including "second jobbers", female musicians, and amateurs; anyone who drew an income from performing music. By contrast, the LOA was established as a society for the very best "professionals", and expressed disgust at the notion of music as a "trade".[16] It admitted neither women nor part-time musicians. Within a year, AMU membership, at 2,400, was more than double that of the LOA.[17] By September 1919, AMU membership was up to 16,000.[18] By the point of the AMU–LOA merger in 1921, the AMU was significantly larger than its London-based counterpart, which had only 2,700 members.

Cinema musicians are first mentioned specifically as a group by the AMU in 1912, when the Glasgow branch published its prices for picture shows: a Leader at £2 per week, 1st instruments £1 15s., and 2nd Instruments £1 10s. When engaged alone, a pianist was to receive £2 2s. per week. Playing hours were not to exceed twenty-five per week.[19] The minimum would provide an annual salary of between £78 and £109 per year, the upper end of the scale equating to the average salary received by a female teacher in 1913 (£104 6s.), though not a male teacher (£154).[20] At these rates the musical director (MD) or lone pianist was better paid than many lower-level clerks, with a salary that almost matches that received by Civil Service clerical officers (£116).[21] Salaries at the lower end of the scale were still better than those paid to unskilled workers, calculated at an average of £56 5s. per annum.[22] While musicians had additional expenses—learning to play an instrument, learning to read music, buying and maintaining instruments—the investment also brought rewards, in the form of opportunities to supplement regular income, such as fees for instrumental lessons, overtime payments for hours worked in continuous houses above those agreed for the union minimum wage, and playing at trade shows. Such opportunities were dependent on the skill of the musician, and the location in which they worked, and make calculating an average salary for cinema musicians in the period difficult, though union minimums and negotiations with the employers offer a useful starting point.

There were great hopes for the improvement of wages and conditions for cinema musicians when the LOA and AMU finally merged in 1921, forming the Musicians'

Union (MU).[23] An editorial in the *Musicians' Journal* expressed relief that at long last the employers, in the form of the Cinematograph Exhibitors' Association (CEA), would no longer be able to play off the AMU and the LOA against one another for its own benefit.[24] But the timing could not have been worse; the MU achieved dominance over the sector in the midst of a period of severe economic volatility.[25]

The CEA had been established in 1912 and had become the largest of the employers' associations. Membership grew rapidly from less than ten members originally, to 965 by April 1914 (controlling 1,468 theatres), with 2,882 members by 1928.[26] Formed as a company with liability limited by guarantee, in July 1916 the secretary, W. Gavazzi King, took the unusual step of proposing that the CEA become a trade union "for the full protection of its members, and the accomplishment of its ultimate ends",[27] which it did in 1917. Key among these "ultimate ends" was the abolition of the entertainments tax, introduced in the budget of April 1916 and applied to all cinema tickets.[28] The tax was one of several difficulties facing the exhibitors at that point, which included censorship, block booking, and the high costs of rentals. It seems clear that the transformation from a trade association into a union was due to the CEA's perceived lack of control over such problems. Against this backdrop, claims for wage increases from the musicians appear more of a minor irritation than a major issue for the employers.

The merger of the AMU and LOA in 1921 followed the formation of a joint committee in 1915.[29] In 1916 the AMU began to press for minimum pay for cinema musicians.[30] Musicians generally received a fixed rate wage, thus when the cost of living began to rise—first steadily, then rapidly during the First World War—the value of their wages fell dramatically in real terms.[31] Negotiations began falteringly, but slowly agreements with regional branches of the CEA were reported. In March 1918, for example, the Glasgow and West of Scotland branch of the CEA agreed to the AMU's demand for a twenty-five percent increase in wages for cinema musicians: a rise of 7s. 6d. per week, giving a total of £2 12s. 6d. for twenty-two hours work in a first-class house in Glasgow, and £2 7s. 6d., second class.[32] The increased 1918 minimum is put into sharp relief when considered in terms of the findings of the Working Classes Cost of Living Committee, which projected the weekly expenditure of a standard family on food in the summer of 1918 as 47s. 3d. (or £2 7s. 3d.); a figure that did not include fuel, rent, clothing, or violin strings.[33] Although further increases were obtained, musicians' wages did not keep pace with the price of goods and services. The cost of living virtually doubled between 1914 and 1918, peaking at around two and half times 1913 levels in 1920, after which it began to fall, relatively sharply to 1923, then slowly over the next ten years.[34] In 1922 the chairman of the Musicians' Union, J. S. Ratcliffe, calculated that musicians had lost more than £300 each in real terms since 1914.[35] In addition, significant differences in cinema musicians' pay persisted, both locally and regionally, with

the campaign for a national minimum frustrated in part by the relative decentraliza-
tion of both the CEA and AMU/MU administration.

The introduction of the CEA–AMU conciliation boards in the late 1910s led
to agreements in pay and conditions that covered larger areas, even the whole of
Scotland on one occasion, but they did not harmonize pay.[36] In January 1920, for
example, the union minimum for six nights' work as a cinema musician varied from
£2 15s. for musicians in "little country places", up to £3 10s. in first-class houses in
Glasgow. In Scotland, Glasgow's cinema musicians reaped the highest rewards, both
in terms of pay rates and opportunities for overtime in continuous houses.[37] They
continued to be paid less than theatre musicians, however, and such differences
were frequently, if unsuccessfully, cited by the union as the basis of applications for
increases. But, as the economic situation worsened in the early 1920s, the MU began
to look weak. The union continued to apply for significant increases, but these were
now met by equivalent applications for reductions from the CEA. The duration of
agreements got shorter. Conciliation board negotiations were protracted or began
to fail.[38] The tide had turned in favour of the employers.

While a study of cinema musicians as a labour market can tell us something of the
situation of these musicians within society more generally and of the strength of the
union in relation to the employers, it raises further questions concerning the music
heard in cinemas. Key among these concerns is the quality of musical performance,
about which we know very little beyond the fact that it varied enormously. Using
union musicians probably offered exhibitors a guarantee of sorts about a basic level
of skill and professionalism.[39] The musical selections submitted to trade journals by
musical directors provide an indication of performers' skill levels, where they are
reported as being well executed, at least. It seems likely though that skill levels were
affected most by the supply and demand of musicians. The onset of war in 1914
brought about a changed situation in terms of the constituency of cinema musicians.
As Cyril Ehrlich highlights: "Native musicians at every level found it easier to get
jobs: leading players because there was less competition from foreigners; part-timers
because the trenches emptied the pits."[40] With the introduction of conscription in
1916, demand outstripped supply and quality suffered. As a "Lady Instrumentalist,
AMU" explained: "Continuous picture shows…combined with the scarcity of
properly trained musicians" had allowed "a perfect deluge of incompetent amateur
musicians of both sexes who, with no further qualifications than a few hurried lessons on some sort of instrument, have the impertinence to undertake important
engagements, accepting disgraceful lowering terms, and impossibly long hours of
work."[41] During the war it seems that exhibitors could find musicians willing to play
for very low rates of pay, though probably not the best players. The return of musicians from the war, alongside an increase in graduates from music colleges, led to

an oversupply of musicians from the late 1910s into the 1920s, probably resulting in improved standards of performance.[42]

High standards of musical performance did not guarantee a sympathetic and effective accompaniment for films, however, as J. Morton Hutcheson emphasized in his *Bioscope* column. Complaints about orchestras "playing at" rather than "playing to" the pictures raise questions about when practices changed and where, with probable differences in practices at the local and/or regional level, which may or may not have been in step with those favoured and encouraged by columnists, as both Jon Burrows and Andrew Higson explore in chapters 6 and 7 of this volume.[43]Where, in the United States, the impresario Samuel "Roxy" Rothafel was considered something of a visionary figure, particularly in terms of the "premium" he placed on music in the theatres he managed (as Jim Buhler mentions in chapter 8 of this volume), the apparent lack of such a figure in Britain may have deferred aesthetic standardization in British cinemas.[44] The appointment of musical advisors to the growing number of circuits was possibly more influential in generating standardization in musical practices across multiple cinemas. Although producer- and distributor-led musical suggestions, cue sheets, and occasionally even original scores increase through the period, we have as yet been unable to assess their impact in aesthetic terms. Although also contingent on other factors, such as the increased duration of films, conditions outlined in union agreements between the musicians and the employers (hours worked, timing and duration of breaks, etc.) might also have affected the standardization of both the cinema programme and the place of music in it. Despite the strength of the CEA and exhibitors in the 1920s relative to the workers, musical decisions continued to be made by the musicians and musical directors and advisors, with interference from the employers restricted to financial matters: the money spent on musicians' wages, and thus the size of the orchestra, and/or music bought or hired. The establishment of a collection agency for performing rights in Britain brought different economic considerations into play.

THE PERFORMING RIGHT SOCIETY

Changes to British copyright law were required following the modifications to the Berne Convention for the Protection of Literary and Artistic Works (1886) made in Berlin in 1908. The music publisher William Boosey was appointed to the committee created to explore the necessary changes and, though initially highly critical of the changes that would need to be made to UK legislation, the publisher's view soon changed entirely, as he stated in his autobiography, published some years later:

> I foresee the day when composers will depend almost entirely for their income
> upon the fees obtained for them by the Performing Right Society, more

particularly as the broadcasting authorities have had to recognise that they are powerless to reproduce music for public performance except by treaty with those who hold the copyright.[45]

Music publishing in Britain was somewhat unstable at the time, however. The industry had been severely bruised by piracy in the previous decades, and the audience for serious music appeared to be waning. Though popular music continued to flourish, audience interest in the influx of American offerings was growing.[46]Boosey's prescience notwithstanding, in general the publishers looked backwards rather than forwards, seeing sheet music as their key means of income generation, thus focussing on concerns about piracy. Indeed this was probably the main reason why Britain was so resistant to the notion of controlling performing rights for music: both music publishers and composers believed that remuneration for music should come from sales of sheet music. The situation in France was different: here performing rights were considered vital. The French collection agency, the Société des Auteurs, Compositeurs et Éditeurs de Musique (SACEM), established in 1851, had collected payments in Britain for the performance of the music it controlled via a representative in London since the 1880s. By contrast, the performing rights of British composers were not protected in Britain, or not on a regular or formalized basis.[47]

In February 1912 H. S. J. Booth, the director of the popular and light music publisher Ascherberg, Hopwood and Crew, addressed other music publishers on the potential benefits of a performing right "association", drawing upon the situation in France.[48] He highlighted that a great deal of SACEM's income came from "picture houses" and concerts, and noted that the current boom in cinema building "provided an unprecedented opportunity: 'the figures are dazzling'".[49] After significant procrastination on the part of other publishers, by late 1913 the situation had begun to change, as authors and composers began to look elsewhere for support for the performing right. SACEM's representative based in London, Pierre Sarpy, drew up a series of draft rules that were discussed by the Publishers' Association.[50] In December 1913 representatives from ten publishers signed an agreement to establish an association, and the society was registered on 6 March 1914. Its committee would comprise eight authors or composers and eight publishers, with a chair drawn from the latter.

The society faced a number of problems, however. Primarily, persuading people to pay for a right that they had previously enjoyed free of charge. For this recourse was made to the courts, where the society was supported by a series of judges' rulings. Several attempts were made to overturn the need to pay for the performing right, including the formation of the British Music Union in 1918,[51] and later, the

International Council of Music Users. Protracted campaigns by both groups were ultimately overcome, following the defeat of the private members' bills they sponsored in Parliament.[52] A second key problem was that not all publishers joined the society, which left a reasonable proportion of repertoire outside the society's purview. Arguments for and against the society were played out in correspondence in the national press. One publisher expressed fear that claiming a fee for the performing right would involve an "'un-English' and 'inquisitorial' undertaking",[53] which would thus restrict sales of sheet music. Directors at Novello were sympathetic and had been involved in discussions, but would not join unless fees were collected only from those "using music for the purpose of making money".[54] Light music composer Montague Ewing stated that composers were "in a cleft stick": they needed to join the society to benefit from much-needed income, but doing so would risk alienating the publishers that had not joined.[55]

Other difficulties included formulating a basic mechanism by which the society could carry out its *raison d'etre*: the collection and analysis of the information it needed to distribute its revenues fairly. Decisions concerning the relative *value* of works were even more problematic: in the early years of the society numerous composers and publishers argued over the distinction drawn between the benefits for "serious musicians" versus those who wrote popular music, with the latter seen to benefit more from the performing right in the main, though the balance of power in the society was in the favour of "serious music". Over time this was to develop into a dispute that concerned the classification of works and how income was distributed among its members.

THE PRS AND MUSIC IN CINEMAS

The Cinema House in Glasgow, mentioned above, was one of many first-class, city-centre venues that paid an annual fee to SACEM in order to perform the music controlled by the French society prior to the establishment of the PRS.[56] Sarpy began the process of transition to the PRS by systematically offering British titles to existing SACEM licensees for an increased fee. An initial group of important music users thus became PRS licensees almost immediately. Sarpy then began to make collective agreements at discounted prices through trade associations, allowing the society to reach an even larger number of potential licensees quickly. The CEA was among the first.[57] In return for the preferential rate enjoyed by CEA members, each venue was required to send a weekly return to the society detailing the music played.

In 1915 the cinema tariff was charged according to the number of musicians: two guineas per annum for one musician or mechanical instrument, with each additional player (or mechanical instrument) charged at a further guinea. By charging per musician rather than per venue it is clear that the conception of performing rights in Britain at this time was similar to that of sheet music sales, with the right to perform charged as though it were a set of parts for a music score, that is, by a levy on musicians. SACEM, by contrast, was founded following a court case brought by a composer concerning the unauthorized use of his music at a café-concert: a levy on venues for the use of music as promotion. Under the PRS cinema licence up to three variety turns were allowed; more than that, or if films comprised less than half of the total entertainment, and a music hall licence was required.[58] The 1918 tariff was organized on the same basis though at an increased cost, with CEA members offered licences at discounted rates.[59]

The PRS had made a new enemy, though. The tariff increases, the mode of tariff calculation, and the difficulty involved in finding out which music the PRS controlled (there was no catalogue), together formed a catalyst for Joseph Williams, still general secretary of the AMU. Early in 1918 he asked the union's general office to suggest to AMU members that they use "as little PRS music as possible".[60] By the end of the year this had escalated to a boycott of music controlled by the PRS that began on 1 January 1919. Williams intended to bring down the society it seems. He demanded that copyright law be reformed, with the cost of the performing right subsumed under the cost of the sheet music, which suggests that Williams too still understood performing rights to be a levy on musicians, rather than a means of distributing income to publishers and composers for the use of music as venue promotion.[61] Then in the same year a number of important popular publishers resigned from the society, taking with them the composers they represented; I return to this below.[62] This was grist to the mill for Williams who deduced that some eighty percent of available music now lay outside of the control of the society.[63] Cinema managers were urged not to buy PRS licences and musical directors were told not to fill in the society's forms on which they listed the music played.[64] Williams's campaign against the society was not wholly successful though because managers were not willing to risk court action by refusing to take out PRS licences.[65]

Where successful, cases brought against infringers were reported widely and were vital in establishing both the legality and strength of the society.[66] To identify infringers, the society sent locally based inspectors to investigate venues in which music was performed but which did not hold a licence. Inspectors noted the details of each piece of music played, so that it could be ascertained whether the PRS held copyright over the music. Inspectors were told to sit near to the musicians and note whether the music was performed from sheet music or from memory; a distinction that made no difference in terms of infringement, but could be considered to affect the strength of the evidence collected by the inspector.[67] In addition, supporting Larway's fears that the system would be inquisitorial, inspectors should ideally "interview the performer or leader of the band, and obtain admission of the performance of the works heard, in case the performance is subsequently denied."[68]

A small number of these reports survive as evidence for the court cases brought by the society against infringers. In 1918, a cinema in Epsom was accused of playing two PRS-controlled numbers without a licence. "The defendant claimed that his pianist had been told to extemporize and avoid copyright sheet music. He added the opinion that the PRS was merely 'engaged in the practice of fomenting and encouraging litigation in connection with Copyright.'"[69] These claims and accusations were summarily dismissed. The judge found in favour of the society, explaining that it performed "a very useful function", and that its objects were "in every respect legitimate".[70] In a classic declaration of the society's right to function that is familiar even today, Judge Atkin continued: "'One has very little sympathy when a thief complains of the organization of the police force' but many people otherwise 'honourable in every transaction of life...have very loose notions as to the honesty of dealing with other persons' property in such matters as copyright.'"[71]

The main reasons for the popular publishers' desertion of the society were most likely the harm caused by Williams's assault and their belief that membership of the society would limit returns from sheet music sales. Ehrlich suggests that competition from new publishers also contributed, since none of them joined the society. By contrast to the music halls, the withdrawal of the popular publishers may not have affected the licensed cinemas greatly. The AMU boycott would have had a rather more serious impact, though, since much of the standard repertoire in cinemas was focussed in the categories of light music and popular classics, and key publishers of those categories remained in the PRS.[72] The boycott was met by an injunction, but not until considerable damage had been sustained. A settlement of sorts followed in February 1920 that involved the appointment of Williams to the society in a "consultative capacity".[73] Williams used his position to encourage a change to the way tariffs were calculated.

The tariff for general PRS licences for cinemas (i.e., for non-CEA-affiliated venues) was changed to that used for music halls, that is, "a percentage of the monetary value of the seating capacity of cinemas", though PRS licences for CEA members continued to be calculated on the basis of the number of musicians.[74] Both modes were considered "unsatisfactory", however: orchestras were frequently augmented or reduced during the course of a year, and returns from applicants were "not wholly reliable". It was simply not practical to check such information in any systematic way.[75] After considerable negotiation, the two systems were finally harmonized in 1924, with the tariff for both CEA and non-CEA PRS licences for cinemas organized in line with the CEA's own grading system for cinemas, with grades decided by the "total money holding capacity of a hall for one performance".[76]

PRS licences for cinemas were henceforth charged at the same rate that a venue would be charged for CEA membership, but with CEA members receiving a discount of a third on a PRS licence. A hall graded AA by the CEA would pay £14 to the PRS for an annual licence, an A-graded hall, £7, a B-graded hall, £3 10s., and a C-graded hall £1 8s.[77]

This changed mode of tariff calculation clearly benefitted the PRS, given that the seating capacity of cinemas increased throughout the period. Certainly both the smallest and the largest venues with CEA membership stood to benefit. Under the new system, the smaller B- or C-graded halls paid a licence fee that would previously have limited them to two musicians with a PRS–CEA cinema licence, while the A and AA halls paid fees that would have granted them five or twelve musicians respectively, under the previous system. Orchestras could also now be augmented (or reduced) without any impact on the venue's licensing agreement. It is unclear whether the change made any difference to the life of musicians working in cinemas, though it may have led to increased job opportunities in cinemas: larger orchestras and more of them. The cost of an annual licence was negligible in comparison with the weekly cost of musicians' salaries, however. The change in tariff calculation might thus be better regarded as a symbolic victory for Williams and the union, rather than one that had an unequivocal impact on cinema musicians.

H. S. J. Booth's pre-society assessment that cinemas presented huge potential in performing rights was proven correct. As early as the society's second year of operation, CEA licences had raised £1889, almost half of the society's total income of £4067.[78] Indeed, it was the success of the cinemas that enabled the PRS to endure the difficulties of 1918–1920. The income generated from cinema licences was greater than that from music halls by a factor of five as the latter fell into decline.[79] Ehrlich notes that by the mid-1920s "Members of the Cinematograph Exhibitors' Association, which covered most but not all cinemas, took out some 2,500 licences, approximately half of the total for every kind of user issued by the Society."[80] Cinemas thus bolstered the society during its early years, though the approach to classification was of greater benefit to those whose works were performed in the concert hall. Easily the most complicated of the society's roles, the means by which income was distributed would never satisfy all of its members.

THE PRS AND DISTRIBUTION: MUSIC FOR CINEMAS

The classical publishers tended to dominate in questions of classification, a situation that was to continue at least until the international success of pop in the 1960s. The society's original plan for the distribution of income was based on the weekly return from each venue listing the music performed. The first system classified works on a sliding scale according to type and duration, so that "Selections, medleys, potpour-ris" of a minimum duration of eight minutes, were assigned 10 points, while a symphony was allocated 50 points. Works shorter than eight minutes were all allocated 5 points.[81] In this way an attempt was made to recognize the likely frequency of performance (larger-scale works were performed less often), and the amount of time spent producing them (larger-scale works generally took longer to compose). The analysis of weekly returns was fraught with difficulty, however. First the title of the work had to be correctly identified, then the rights in the work had to be identified and correctly allocated, with the latter frequently involving "a bewildering variety of fractional entitlements".[82] When the society came to make its first distribution of income in 1917—£5,201 to 297 members—it was soon recognized that the means of recording the music performed was inadequate.[83]

Albert W. Ketèlbey, a composer of cinema and light music, was first elected to membership of the society in 1918, but he believed the society's system of distribution failed to reflect the popularity of his work. Following complaints from a number of quarters, adjustments were made to the classification system. Under the new scheme, composers, arrangers, and authors were classified into ten categories, with a further grading submitted by publishers as to the "popularity of sales" of their works. Publishers too were then also graded. Such decisions inevitably led to discord. Further adjustments were made in 1924, but these too failed to satisfy Ketèlbey and his publisher, Bosworth and Co. Ehrlich states that Ketèlbey's *In a Persian Market*, whether in full or in part, was "probably more frequently played, at home and abroad, than any other work in the history of English music, with the possible exception of the national anthem."[84] It was apparently reported in 1924 that "one or other of Ketèlbey's compositions could be heard 'three or four times a day in most cinemas and restaurants'."[85] Bosworth and Co. organized "an independent check of performances in a number of cinemas,... submitted the results as evidence of underpayment, and demanded that such figures be used in calculating future distributions."[86] The committee refused to accept the figures presented. The complaints continued and in 1926, following a revised classification system submitted by cinema composer George Clutsam, cinema music was given its own classification, which was used as the basis for the April 1926 distribution (see Table 13.1).

Comparing this classification with the general class grouping, the work's duration is the defining issue, with the exception of dances (1 point) and "Medleys and pot-pourris" (2 points regardless of length). "Distinctive" light music is allotted 2 points for up to five minutes' duration, 4 points for between five and eight minutes (class C). The longest, and most serious works receive the highest point allocations. Works of between eight and twelve minutes receive 10 points, with larger works allotted

TABLE 13.1 Classification of works within cinema music category.[87]

Class F: Cinema Music	Points per film performance
Selections of musical numbers used as thematic melos	1
Numbers of 2 to 4 minutes used in entirety	2
Numbers of 4 to 5 minutes	3
Numbers over 5 and not exceeding 8 minutes (as in class "C")	4
Music specially composed for an entire film	4 points for each 5 minutes
Music played in Cinema Houses, apart from association with the projection of a film, to revert to its place in the general class grouping.	

points on a sliding scale, 20 points for twelve to twenty minutes, rising to 90 points for an hour's music. An hour's special score for the cinema (48 points) is thus worth only a little over half the points given for a work of an hour's duration *not* composed for the cinema (90 points).

For the year ending January 1929 the composers and publishers of music heard most often in the cinema received a boost: revenue from dance halls and cinemas would henceforth be separated from other society revenue. The system was considered much improved; in 1930 Ketèlbey received £1,630 from the society, a significant improvement on the £12 15s. he received in 1918, and £151 19s. 1d. in 1923.[88] However, a comparison of the income received by two light and two serious composers through the century provided by Cyril Ehrlich in his history of the PRS highlights that while income is higher for popular or light composers in the short term, in the longer term successful serious composers can reap far higher rewards.[89]

CONCLUSION

Ehrlich puts the total number of musicians in Britain who lost their jobs following the virtual extinction of silent film by 1932 as between 12,000 and 15,000.[90] The 1931 census indicates that thirty-eight percent of all male musicians, and thirty-two percent of all female musicians were out of work, proportions that were "more than double the average, and from nine to twenty times worse than in the professions".[91] Virtually all of these were undoubtedly cinema musicians. As victims of technological change rather than cyclical change, cinema musicians could not expect their jobs to return in the future.[92] A relatively small number would continue to work in the film industry, and only those who lived in, or moved to London, where performing for the recording of film scores in the early sound era offered "the most highly paid form of [orchestral] work".[93]

Although the world of the cinema musician had truly boomed and bust by the early 1930s, just five years earlier cinemas had been "largely responsible for the fact that more live music was being performed by professional musicians than at any other time in the country's history".[94] Cinemas had led to unprecedented employment for musicians in the 1920s and provided the PRS with a steady income through the decline of the music halls, prior to the increased fees that were negotiated with broadcasters.

The return of the popular publishers was an enormous boost to the society in 1926 with the enlarged repertoire that it signalled. This probably benefitted cinemas and their musicians as a result of the influx of new repertoire that was covered by the PRS licence, such as the Sam Fox Moving Picture Music collections, available via Keith Prowse.[95] On the other hand, the return of the popular publishers to the PRS may not have made much difference to the music played in cinemas. Since many of these companies waived their right to performing fees in the first half of the 1920s, cinema musicians may well have continued to play the music of the popular publishers, and possibly also the music of ASCAP composers distributed in Britain by the popular publishers, until the return of these publishers to the society.[96] Their return was due in part to declining sheet music sales, but just as important, the beginnings of performing rights for broadcasting, and soon after, the synchronized sound film. These modes of distribution enabled composers and publishers to reach a larger audience more quickly, and thus more effectively maximize the shorter-term profits associated with popular music. Record companies also benefitted from licensing opportunities offered by new technologies: Phonographic Performance Ltd. (PPL) was established in 1934 as the result of a legal ruling against a restaurant in Bristol where customers were entertained by a recording without permission from the copyright owners. PPL collects fees for licences to broadcast or play recordings in public settings, with income distributed to record companies.

By contrast to the fate of cinema's musicians, PRS income did not diminish with the demise of cinema orchestras in Britain: the society continued to receive revenue from the licensing of music performed in cinemas, though now from synchronized music primarily; and, just as the cinema orchestras were being disbanded, so changes to licensing tariffs for the emerging broadcasting industry increased PRS revenue dramatically. The replacement of one source of performance (cinema orchestras) by another (radio) meant that the composers of the much-loved light music and popular classics performed so frequently in cinemas over previous years also continued to receive a substantial income from performing rights.[97] Composers, publishers, and record companies were thus able to adapt income-generating mechanisms to the new technologies of radio and sound cinema in ways that performing musicians could not, beyond lucrative work for a minority. While music publishers, record companies, and collection agencies focussed on how they might best benefit from these new technologies and their modes of distribution, the MU spent crucial months, even years, opposing recording, broadcasting, and sound cinema, understanding them as a threat to performing musicians' livelihoods, to the probable detriment of musicians' livelihoods. This transitional moment in cinema history, from live to recorded music in the form of the synchronized soundtrack, resulted in the decline of the musician, but also the rise of the publisher. Thus, more broadly, it also describes the transition from a nineteenth-century to a twentieth-century form of entertainment.

NOTES

1. Cyril Ehrlich, *The Music Profession in Britain Since the Eighteenth Century: A Social History* (Oxford: Clarendon Press, 1985), 194. I would like to thank Simon Frith, Trevor Griffiths, and Julie Brown for their insightful comments on earlier drafts of this chapter, and also Ray Luker of the PRS Archive, and Karl Magee of the University of Stirling.

2. Census for England and Wales, 1911, Vol. X, part 1, p. xxiv.

3. Ehrlich, *Music Profession in Britain*, 194.

4. As happened with the performances for *Siegfried* in November 1912, for example.Scottish Screen Archive (SSA) 5/22/3, Glasgow Picture House Ltd. Minute Book 1, 1 Nov. 1912.

5. Bruce Peter, *100 Years of Glasgow's Amazing Cinemas* (Edinburgh: Polygon, 1996), 22. Peter states that the refurbishment of the Cinema House took place in 1920, though Minute Book 3 indicates long periods of closure in 1924 and 1925 to refit and extend the cinema. SSA 5/22/4, Glasgow Picture House Ltd. Minute Book 3, 31 March 1924; 9 Jan.1925; 24 Dec. 1925. The cinema's name was subsequently changed to the Regent.

6. SSA 5/22/4, Glasgow Picture House Ltd. Minute Book 3, letter from Manager [n.d.]. Meeting on 20 Sept. 1926 refers to the manager's requests.

7. SSA 5/22/4, Glasgow Picture House Ltd. Minute Book 3, 20 Sept. 1926; and AGM, 22 Nov. 1926.

8. Rachael Low, *The History of the British Film, 1918–1929* (London: Allen and Unwin, 1971), 42.

9. [n.a.] "Glasgow", *Musicians' Journal*, Oct. 1927: 11.

10. B. Newton Brook, "Organiser's Notes [London]", *Musicians' Journal*, Oct. 1924, 15.

11. Ehrlich, *Music Profession in Britain*, 199.

12. Ibid.

13. The overturning of the notorious court ruling of the "Taff Vale Railway Co. versus the Amalgamated Society of Railway Servants", in which the union was made liable for the employers' costs incurred by the strike was key, for example. See Henry Pelling, *A History of British Trade Unionism* (Harmondsworth: Penguin, 1976), 123–7.

14. The Whitley Report was published by the Ministry of Reconstruction. The National Archives, Committee on Relations between Employers and Employed, *Final Report* (1918), Cmnd 9153.

15. Later, this association was also known as the National (sometimes, London) Orchestral Union of Professional Musicians.

16. Ehrlich, *Music Profession in Britain*, 152.

17. Ibid., 148

18. *Musicians' Report and Supplement*, Sept. 1919, 1

19. *Musicians' Report and Supplement*, June 1912, 1. Additional payments were to be made for matinees ("not to exceed two hours") and any performers who were required for more than twenty-five hours a week were to receive overtime payments of 1s. 6d. per hour.

20. Guy Routh, *Occupation and Pay in Great Britain 1906–79*, 2nd edn (London: Macmillan, 1980), 70.

21. Ibid., 90.

22. Ibid., 113.

23. The formation of the Industrial Council for the entertainment industry appears to have been the catalyst for the merger, as the employees refused to agree to two societies representing musicians within the council. C. Jesson, MP, "London Organiser's Notes", *Musicians' Report and Journal*, July 1919, 4.

24. *Musicians' Journal*, Aug. 1921, 1. The dissolution of a smaller union, the National Federation of Professional Musicians (NFPM), in 1914 had resulted in a similar outcome. According to J. S. Ratcliffe, then the AMU's Scottish organizer, competition between the two organizations in Glasgow meant that musicians had not gained the best rates. With the dissolution of the NFPM, the single remaining union, the AMU, was in a stronger position to negotiate for higher wages. J. S. Ratcliffe, "Organiser's Notes", *Musicians' Report and Journal*, Mar. 1914, 19.

25. To see just how unusual this period of economic volatility was, see Figure 1, "Composite Price Index: annual percentage change: 1751–2003", in Jim O'Donoghue, Louise Goulding, and Grahame Allen, "Consumer Price Inflation since 1750", *Economic Trends* 604 (Mar. 2004), Office for National Statistics, 40.

26. *Bioscope*, 9 April 1914, 179, cited in Rachael Low, *The History of British Film, 1906–1914* (London: Allen and Unwin, 1949), 81, 82; *Bioscope*, 8 Mar. 1928, 52, cited in Low, *History of the British Film, 1918–1929*, 45.

27. *Bioscope*, 20 July 1916, 253.

28. Initially the levy was set at ½d. on seats up to 2d., with a sliding scale rising in relation to ticket prices. The April 1917 budget proposed increases, raising the levy to 1d. on seats up to 3d., and 2d. on seats priced above 3d. but less than 6d., 3d.on seats prices at 6d.up to 1s., and so on. The CEA asked that the tax be reduced such that the 1d.levy be applied to all seats up to 6d. The government refused, "because 80 per cent of the revenue from this duty came from the 6d. tickets and below". A compromise was agreed, however, with the tax on tickets up to 4d. tickets reduced to 1d. *The Entertainer*, 5 May 1917, 9; 7 July 1917, 14.

29. By this point the two remaining smaller unions (NFPM and London Society of Musicians) had ceased to function, and the LOA had decided to reorganize itself along the lines of a trade union, albeit an unregistered one. J. S. Ratcliffe, "Looking Forward", *Musicians' Report and Journal*, July 1915, 2. The September 1915 issue explains the agreement to form a joint committee of representatives of the two organizations.

30. See, for example, J. Morton Hutcheson, "The Musician in the Cinema. The AMU Active", *Bioscope*, 6 July 1916, 44; 3 Aug. 1916, 424.

31. Ehrlich, *Music Profession in Britain*, 179.

32. *Bioscope*, 14 Mar. 1918, 87; 21 Mar. 1918, 3. A meeting of the AMU and the CEA in Newcastle resulted in the formation of a conciliation board to deal with the wages and conditions of cinema musicians in the North the same month. *Bioscope*, 28 Mar. 1918, 10. See also Rachael Low, *The History of British Film, 1914–1918* (London: Allen and Unwin, 1950), 121.

33. Cited in Arthur Lyon Bowley, *Prices and Wages in the United Kingdom, 1914–20* (Oxford: Clarendon Press, 1921), 58.

34. See, for example, John Burnett, *A History of the Cost of Living* (Harmondsworth: Penguin, 1969), 306–9; Routh, *Occupation and Pay in Great Britain*, 134–7.

35. J. S. Ratcliffe, "Organiser's Notes, Scotland", *Musicians' Journal*, 3 Jan. 1922, 19. Ratcliffe based his calculation on the rates for first-class theatre and music hall musicians, which were generally higher than those for cinema musicians. The cost was thus likely to have been even greater to cinema musicians.

36. J. S. Ratcliffe, "Organiser's Notes", *Musicians' Report and Journal*, July 1919, 8

37. Following a rise of 15*s*. per week for musicians in cinemas of all classes in December 1920, the minimum in first-class houses in Glasgow stood at £4 5*s*., with the lowest minimum, in rural areas, at £3 10*s*. This put the weekly earnings of a player performing for thirty-three hours in a continuous house in Glasgow at £6 7*s*. 2*d*., almost double the salary of a musician in a small rural cinema.

38. The composition of the boards was part of the problem, given that the employers' representation often reflected the diversity of venues (and thus priorities and values) covered by the CEA.

39. With more stringent entrance requirements, the LOA was perhaps in a position to guarantee a higher level of musical skill than the AMU, prior to the merger in 1921.

40. Ehrlich, *Music Profession in Britain*, 186.

41. *Musicians' Report and Journal*, Aug. 1916, 1–2, also cited in Ehrlich, *Music Profession in Britain*, 189.

42. Ehrlich, *Music Profession in Britain*, 190.

43. The information provided by J. Morton Hutcheson, music columnist for *The Bioscope*, following his tour of cinemas in Edinburgh and Glasgow in the late summer of 1916, presents a fascinating snapshot of the range of accompaniment practices in play in cities. "Music in the Cinema", *Bioscope*, 31 Aug. 1916, 816–17; 7 Sept. 1916, 945–7; 14 Sept. 1916, 1041, 1043; 21 Sept. 1916, 1123.

44. See Brown and Buhler, chapters 11 and 8 respectively in this volume, for more discussion of "Roxy" and his influence.

45. William Boosey, *Fifty Years of Music* (London: Ernest Benn, 1931), 176.

46. Ehrlich, *Harmonious Alliance: A History of the Performing Right Society* (Oxford: Oxford University Press, 1989), 13–14

47. There were exceptions in the case of individual works, however. For example, Ehrlich notes that Oliver Hawkes had an agreement with Balfour Gardiner for his popular "Shepherd Fennel's Dance"; Ehrlich, *Harmonious Alliance*, 6.

48. Ibid., 15.

49. Ibid.

50. Ibid.

51. An organization originally representing dance schools, but later expanded to include restauranteurs, hoteliers, and some town councils; Ehrlich, *Harmonious Alliance*, 31.

52. Ibid., 31–4, 54–62.

53. J. H. Larway, *Daily Telegraph*, 13 July 1914, cited in Ehrlich, *Harmonious Alliance*, 18.

54. Novello, *Daily Telegraph*, 16 July 1914, cited in Ehrlich, *Harmonious Alliance*, 20.

55. Ewing, cited in Ehrlich, *Harmonious Alliance*, 19.

56. SSA 5/22/3, Glasgow Picture House Ltd., Minute Book No. 1, Committee Meeting Minutes 9 July 1913. For the music performed at the Cinema House, the company paid two guineas to SACEM for its annual licence.

57. The initial cost for a licence was reported as 10s. 6d. in "Musical Copyright: How the PRS came into being", in *Scottish Cinema*, 12 July 1920, 8. Presumably this was the additional cost SACEM licensees in the CEA paid for a PRS licence initially. See also the "Memorandum of Agreement" between the CEA and PRS, dated 1 August 1915; PRS Archive, British Music House, Berners Street, London.

58. PRS Archive, "Tariff for Licences for Provincial and London Surburban Theatres and Music Halls, and for Cinemas, 1918".

59. Twenty-five per cent up to three guineas, and a further fifteen per cent costs beyond this.

60. PRS Archive, Basement Box 1207, Copies and Correspondence with and relating to the AMU leading to litigation, File No. 1 (1914–1919): Letter from Williams to AMU General Office (Manchester), 27 Jan. 1918.

61. Ehrlich, *Harmonious Alliance*, 29. Williams's history with the society pre-dated this debacle. In the years before the PRS he had worked as a "sub-agent" for Sarpy and SACEM. Following Sarpy's sudden death early in 1915, the PRS took advantage of an offer of assistance from Williams, to provide "information concerning the grading of Theatres, the number of Musicians in the Orchestras of Music Halls and Cinemas, and to get reports of infringements of our Copyright at Establishment in the Provinces." The agreement was terminated in 1917, but had been problematic from the start, presenting Williams with a conflict of interest; given that tariffs were based on the number of instrumentalists, information from Williams might have resulted in the loss of musicians' jobs if venues wanted to reduce a tariff or maintain a lower one. PRS Archives, Basement Box 1207, Folder of letters to J. B. Williams (30 Nov. 1915–6 Oct. 1920): Letter from Frank Hill, General Manager and Secretary, PRS, to J. B. Williams, dated 19 June 1916.

62. These publishers were Feldman, Star, and Lawrence Wright, followed by Goldsmith and Laurilland.

63. Ehrlich, *Harmonious Alliance*, 29. Williams highlighted that the war had meant the removal of all Austrian and German music as alien, and that there had been little from France in the same period. He provided a list of the publishers who had not joined the society, adding the recently withdrawn popular publishers.

64. Ibid., 29–30.

65. Ibid., 30.

66. See, for example, a letter from the PRS Controller, John Woodhouse, to Messrs. Croft-Gray and Gibb, Edinburgh Agents suggested by their solicitors, dated 22 December 1920, concerning action taken against the Palace Picture House, Leith: "I would, however, like to add that I was in hopes the settlement may take such a form that we should be able to make use of it in our propaganda, and terms be such that we might cite them in our records of successful cases in the pamphlets we issue. An important feature of these settlements is to be able to say that an Interdict (Injunction) was granted." PRS Archive, PRS vs. Leith Public Hall Co. Ltd.

67. PRS Archive, PRS, "Instructions to Inspectors", Dec. 1928, Point 3.

68. Ibid., Point 12.

69. Cited by Ehrlich, *Harmonious Alliance*, 27–8.

70. Ibid., 28

71. Ibid.

72. Ibid., 36.

73. PRS Archive, Box 1, Minute Book 2, Minutes of Executive Committee Meeting on 19 Dec. 1918, and Committee Meetings on 3 Jan. 1919; 16 Jan. 1919; 5 Feb. 1919; 12 Mar. 1919; 10 April 1919; 15 April 1919, and a General Committee Meeting on 4 Feb. 1920, and an Emergency Meeting of the General Committee, 18 Feb. 1920. See also Ehrlich, *Harmonious Alliance*, 27.

74. PRS Archive, Box 1, Minute Book 3, Committee Meeting, 22 Sept. 1921. See also Box 1, Minute Book 2, Committee Meeting 14 Feb. 1919; Tariff Subcommittee, 21 July 1920.

75. PRS Archive, Box 1, Minute Book 3, Committee Meeting, 22 Sept. 1921.

76. PRS Archive, W. Gavazzi King, "Licences to Perform Copyright Music: How to obtain a CEA Licence from the Performing Right Society, Ltd.", 5 April 1924. "The money-holding capacity is calculated upon the maximum evening prices (excluding Saturdays), after deduction of Entertainments Tax."

77. C-graded halls had a total money-holding capacity for one performance of up to £12 10s.; for a B-graded hall this capacity exceeded £12 10s., but it did not exceed £25; for an A-graded hall, a single performance had the potential to generate more than £25 but not more than £166; an AA-graded hall had a total money-holding capacity for one performance of more than £166.

78. PRS Archive, Box 1, Minute book 1, Committee Meeting Minutes, 23 Nov. 1915.

79. Ehrlich, *Harmonious Alliance*, 36.

80. Ibid.

81. PRS Archive, Box 1. Minute book 1.Committee Meeting Minutes, 16 April 1915.

82. Ehrlich, *Harmonious Alliance*, 40.

83. PRS Archive, Box 1, Minute book 1, Committee Meeting Minutes, 23 Feb. 1917: Distribution of Fees.

84. Ehrlich, *Harmonious Alliance*, 37.

85. Ibid., 38.

86. Ibid., 39.

87. PRS Archive, Distribution Committee, Minute Book 1, Committee Meeting Minutes, 2 Nov. 1926.

88. Ehrlich, *Harmonious Alliance*, 164. I am grateful to Ray Luker for providing details of Ketèlbey's income from performing rights in 1918 and 1923. According to Ketèlbey's biographer, John Sant, an article in the *Performing Right Gazette* in October 1929 stated that, on the basis of his income, Ketèlbey should be recognized as "Britain's greatest living composer". Cited in John Sant, *Albert W. Ketèlbey, 1875–1959: From the Sanctuary of His Heart* (Sutton Coldfield: Manifold, 2000), 52. It should be noted, however, that I have not been able to locate this reference in the *Performing Right Gazette*.

89. For example, although Ketèlbey's earnings of £1,630 for 1930 dwarfed those of Gustav Holst in the same year, by 1955 the situation had reversed, with Holst's earnings almost double those Ketèlbey. And the gulf continued to widen. By 1985, Holst's estate was earning six times that of Ketèlbey's. See Appendix I: Income Tables, Table 4: "Performing Right Earnings of Four Composers (£)", in Ehrlich, *Harmonious Alliance*, 164.

90. Ehrlich, *Music Profession in Britain*, 210.

91. Ibid.

92. Ibid.

93. Thomas Russell, managing director of the London Philharmonic Orchestra in the 1940s, "The Orchestral Player." In *A Career in Music*, ed. Robert Elkin (London: William Earl and Company, 1950), 142.

94. Ehrlich, *Harmonious Alliance*, 35

95. Ibid., 43.

96. In an advert in *The Era*, 4 May 1921, for example, three popular publishers state clearly, "We are not members of the Performing Right Society Ltd." A list of the American popular publishers they represented was printed alongside, with the notice that their music could "still be played without fee or licence". Also cited in Ehrlich, *Harmonious Alliance*, 28.

97. See Appendix I: Income Tables, Table 4: "Performing Right Earnings of Four Composers (£)", in Ehrlich, *Harmonious Alliance*, 164. In addition, those composers whose music was used in synchronized sound films continued to enjoy performance rights from films.

14

Sound at the Film Society

John Riley

THIS CHAPTER INVESTIGATES the Film Society's accompaniment of silent films from 1925 onwards, arguing that while its approach was necessarily the product of a certain pragmatism, it was also often innovative. A complete collection of programme notes for the society survives, and has been published.[1] There is also an incomplete collection of associated documentation, comprising letters, invoices, and architectural plans.[2] Sufficient material survives to show that the society used a variety of approaches to film accompaniment, from screening films in complete silence to affording them full orchestral accompaniments, even within the same programme. The aural environment of some Film Society performances was often as diverse as some of its film programmes.

Founded by a group of intellectuals and cinephiles in London in 1925 and operational until April 1939, the Film Society aimed to show "pictures of a high class character", films which it argued were "in some degree interesting and which represent[ed] work which has been done, or is being done experimentally in various parts of the world".[3] Part of its mission was "to explain", which meant that some of its events were informational and even somewhat didactic. Its mission is explicit in the manifesto: "It is in the nature of such films that they are (it is said) commercially unsuitable for this country; and that is why they become the especial province of the Film Society."[4] The society hoped that under the influence of these high-class pictures British films would improve, though the first annual report observed a lack of enthusiasm from commercial filmmakers. The moving spirit was the Hon. Ivor Montagu, aristocrat-communist, vole-expert, table-tennis pioneer, filmmaker, critic and, later, spy, who conceived of the group with actor Hugh Miller, though neither was among its founders.[5] Montagu did join the council, but resigned soon afterwards to spare the society embarrassment when he became vice-chairman of what he described as the "avowedly political" Workers' Film Federation.[6] Three of the other main figures were Adrian Brunel, Thorold Dickinson, and Iris Barry.[7]

The society's annual programme of eight monthly Sunday afternoon "performances" was popular with London's artists and bohemian intelligentsia, though its annual reports suggest that the same enthusiasm did not spread to the musical community. However, if the society was concerned about the absence of those with a special interest in film music, the annual reports do not make this explicit. Even in 1970, when some of the surviving council members were considering reprinting the programmes, one option for reducing costs was to omit the front page, the argument being that it "almost never contained any information except the number of the performance, the date, time, theatre *and conductor.*"[8] Nevertheless, the Film Society did approach live sound and music with a seriousness that was unusual for British institutions of the period, albeit that some of its decisions seem in retrospect somewhat unconventional.

The society's 108 performances spanned the mid-twenties up to 1939, when every film-producing country in the world had moved to sound. Nevertheless, it continued to show silent films far longer than commercial cinemas. Indeed, the society kept a collection of silent films until the very end of its existence, though by then it rarely showed them and the vault charges were the subject of an ongoing correspondence.

A combination of reasons probably accounts for this ongoing interest in silent film. Its members had a natural liking for them, to start with. Even as sound film began to dominate, some cinephiles continued to hold that silent cinema was superior, as a sample of their arguments outlined below shows. It was also part of the society's agenda to show and maintain interest in older films. The first three performances included four "Film Society Resurrections" of pre-First World War titles. It subsequently dropped the series title (along with other "Film Society Series"), but continued to show such films. The society also routinely showed experimental films, whose aesthetics or budgets sometimes precluded synchronized sound. It showed unsynchronized films by Marcel Duchamp, Man Ray, Walter Ruttmann, and others, and as the makers sometimes made no particular recommendations about the accompaniments, some were shown in silence. Some of the films came from Japan and the USSR, countries which, for different reasons, were among the slowest to move from silent to sound cinema. In the USSR,

Stalin's insistence on developing Soviet sound-recording equipment rather than using Western technology, combined with a poorly developed network of sound cinemas meant that silent films were still being made in the mid-1930s. In Japan, the popularity of film narrators (*benshi*) meant that sound films penetrated the market more slowly than elsewhere, again coming to dominate only in the mid-1930s.

The society employed a variety of approaches to accompanying silent films and had a somewhat ambivalent attitude both to synchronized tracks and to live accompaniment. Often it was positive, such as in 1927 when the society said:

> a film seen without a musical accompaniment scrupulously adjusted by rehearsal is in a form as imperfect and rudimentary as is the printed book of a play when compared with its living reality on the stage. Accordingly it is desirable, and essential for the perfect realisation of the aims of the Society, that the performances should be given in a cinema of modern design (rather than in a theatre...or a clubroom without organ or orchestra).[9]

Ivor Montagu also stressed the importance of high-quality musical accompaniment. In his memoirs he recalled:

> We must have the best West End cinema for the purpose, the best orchestra and the best music. Remember—these were in the days of silent films [*sic*] and a special score well played was an intrinsic part of the impression that could make or kill a film.... [O]ur real motive, unavowed even perhaps to ourselves, was that we liked pictures, and that without the subscriptions of the like-minded enthusiasts who joined the society, we should ourselves never have been able to afford to see them with a big audience and the right music—both essentials for proper appreciation."[10]

Only certain types of music were acceptable at the Film Society, however. Adrian Brunel ran "hate parties" where, following the evening's screening, participants would "turn on everything in cinema that we most hated: renters or Wurlitzer organs or mottled title backgrounds".[11] Likewise, only certain types of audience behaviour were acceptable. Most important from the point of view of sound was the fact that the audience was encouraged to be quiet. Even the programme leaflets introducing the films were printed on paper that did not rustle, and the council was sometimes moved to include reminders of the injunction to silence. Although the usefulness of the leaflets varied, just as their comments on the music differed in length, accuracy, and degree of insight, they were consistent in their unobtrusiveness.

MUSICAL PERSONNEL

The society started with a gesture towards "high quality" in the musical domain by drawing on some impressive musical credentials. Its first performance was conducted by Eugene Goossens, Snr, then aged fifty-eight and about to take over the British National Opera Company, while the musical director was Frederick Laurence. However, Goossens's involvement was probably a ploy to create an opening splash. By the second performance he had been replaced by his friend Myer De Wolfe, whose company provided stock music, which De Wolfe selected, arranged, and conducted. He in turn left the podium after the first season (though he continued to provide other services) and thereafter the conductors were Gaumont's Ernest Grimshaw, Fred Kitchen, and Harry Fryer, though there were also occasional guests. John Reynders, music director on several Hitchcock films, oversaw the society's presentation of the Japanese film *Ashes* (1929); Dennis Arundell (musical all-rounder and actor) compiled and conducted a score for Pudovkin's *The Story of a Simple Case* (1933); Ernest Irving (occasional composer and dedicatee of Vaughan Williams's *Sinfonia Antartica*), conducted Meisel's music for Eisenstein's *October* (1927), while composers Hans Zeller and Edmund Meisel conducted their own scores to, respectively, Lotte Reiniger's films and *The Battleship Potemkin* (1926).

For presentations of silent films in the sound years Jack Ellitt frequently received a credit for arranging "non-synchronous music," presumably selecting records and operating the gramophone on which they were played. The first person to be credited with this role (30 October 1932) was Dallas Bower, who had recorded the famous "knife" scene in Hitchcock's *Blackmail* (1929) and went on to become a producer, notably of Olivier's *Henry V* (1944). Ellitt also wrote a score for Len Lye's *Tusalava* (shown at the society on 1 December 1929), though the rest of that programme was conducted by Grimshaw. Even though the society had co-funded the film, the money did not run to a synchronized print and the committee then asked Ellitt to arrange his two-piano score for a single player, which in the end proved unperformable.[12]

The budget for music was always tight at the Film Society, but some music directors seemed to feel this more than others. Before its launch, the society costed musical accompaniment and received a quote from an unidentified company in 24 Berners Street.[13] Including music hire, conductor, and one rehearsal the company said it would charge:

10 players £35.10.0, plus £8.17.6 (rehearsal) = £44.7.6
12 players £38.0.0, plus £9.12.6 (rehearsal) = £47.12.6
14 players £39.10.0, plus £10.7.6 (rehearsal) = £49.17.6

It would negotiate to reduce the Sunday performance double rate. There is no record of the correspondence's continuation but the society clearly found a better deal.

The society seems initially to have set a music budget of around £50 per performance, a total of about £400 per season. De Wolfe, the society's first real musical director, provided a complete service but his invoices don't give a full breakdown.[14] Presumably, the fee covered "fitting" (i.e., choosing and synchronizing the music), hire charges from De Wolfe's library, musicians, rehearsals, and his conducting fee. It is clear that De Wolfe somehow provided more musicians than the anonymous quote. On one of the more detailed invoices (14 February 1926), £50 covered his own services, an orchestra of nineteen and a solo organist. To this he added the £4 hire of a reed organ, which may have come from De Wolfe's own stock; the company later became the monopoly importer of Wurlitzer organs.[15]

De Wolfe seems in turn to have been dropped by the society, and from the second season the music was provided by Gaumont's own orchestra, usually conducted by Ernest Grimshaw. Financially this suited the society no better, and after the performance on 28 November 1926 (Walter Ruttmann's "Kriemhild's Dream of Hawks" sequence from Fritz Lang's *Die Nibelungen*, Part 1, and Lang's *Dr Mabuse, the Gambler*), Sidney Bernstein (who had recently taken over responsibility for his family's Granada chain of cinemas) wrote querying a £60 invoice, saying that the music had never cost more than £52. Gaumont's A. W. Jarratt replied offering to reduce it to £55, but suggesting that it had become used to De Wolfe paying for fewer players and that this was the real cost.

EXHIBITION VENUES

In his memoirs, Ivor Montagu recalled that the Film Society occasionally used a "full-sized orchestra".[16] In practice, the music and sound that the society was able to use for its screenings was not only a function of budget, but also a function of the venue in which it held its gatherings; the society was semi-itinerant and negotiated venues for each season. As Table 14.1 shows, over the course of the society's existence, it had eleven separate spells in five different theatres.

Most of the performances (sixty) were in the New Gallery on Regent Street (which closed in 1953), with the second largest number (forty-two) in the Tivoli on the Strand (demolished in 1957). Each venue offered different facilities for music and musicians, but as cinemas moved from using live musical accompaniment to synchronized sound, the size of their orchestra pits, and with it the number of musicians they could accommodate, became less important than

TABLE 14.1 Venues used for Film Society performances

Performances	Dates	Venue
1–32	25 October 1925 to 5 May 1929	New Gallery Kinema
33–46	10 November 1929 to 8 March 1931	Tivoli, Strand
47A and B	12 April 1931	Phoenix Theatre
48–50	3 May 1931 to 6 December 1931	Tivoli, Strand
51–52	10 January 1932 to 31 January 1932	Astoria Theatre
53–57	28 February 1932 to 30 October 1932	Tivoli, Strand
58	20 November 1932	New Victoria Theatre
59–63	11 December 1932 to 2 April 1933	Tivoli, Strand
64	21 May 1933	Astoria Theatre
65–80	5 November 1933 to 12 May 1935	Tivoli, Strand
81–108	27 October 1935 to 23 April 1939	New Gallery Kinema

their preparedness for amplification. At their most spacious the pits were around fifty feet across and up to seventeen feet from front to back, but as they were sometimes ornately shaped not all of the area was usable.[17] They could therefore accommodate only a modest number of musicians, especially when some of the space was taken up by the organ console.[18] When Montagu refers in his memoirs to a "full-sized orchestra", he is referring to what would have been at most around twenty players.

Of the Film Society's five venues, only the Tivoli and the New Gallery were used in both the silent and the sound eras, which makes them the most interesting to consider in terms of their orchestra pits, the modifications necessary for sonorization and the society's programming, though the performances at the other venues bring their own points of interest as the society experimented with a range of approaches to accompaniment.

When the society arrived at the Tivoli in November 1929, the pit was 44 feet wide and 16 feet 10 inches from front to back, though the unusual shape meant that the usable space was smaller. The pit also accommodated an organ, whose console would have taken up around 5 feet square of that space. In November 1928 Provincial Cinematograph Theatres (PCT) made various changes to the theatre among which was its replacement of the Jardine organ with a Wurlitzer.[19] The Tivoli was also the first London cinema to show sound films using the DeForest Phonofilm system and in late 1931 it applied for permission to build a stage 5 feet 6 inches above the floor of the pit, stipulating a hardwood floor. This latter request was presumably made in order to improve sound projection, not only for the non-synchronized films, but because as with numerous venues it divided its time between operating as a cinema and a theatre. Nevertheless, around 1934 the society contributed a significant sum towards the installation of a "non-synchronous attachment" in the Tivoli, presumably to allow it to continue the practice of accompanying films with gramophone records, even though the venue had long been wired for synchronized sound.[20] Such a decision is a clear indication of the society's occasionally exacting approach to sound.

There is less specific information about the pit at the New Gallery, a venue chosen at least in part because Montagu had negotiated a very cheap deal from Lord Ashfield. In the late teens the New Gallery had boasted of having the largest cinema orchestra in London.[21] However, the installation of a Wurlitzer organ— only the third in the United Kingdom and the first in the West End—may have reduced the space for musicians, as at the Tivoli.[22] As organs were used to give orchestras a break, the society may also have seen the instrument as a cheaper alternative for full programmes; if so it perhaps indicates that its approach had become more pragmatic since Brunel's "hate parties." In 1927 the cinema was sonorized using the Western Electric System (Fox-Case Movietone), but the Film Society did not avail itself of the facility and it was only with its move to the Tivoli (10 November 1929) that it showed its first synchronized film, *The Barn Dance* (1929).

ATTITUDES TOWARDS SYNCHRONIZED SOUND FILM

The transition to synchronized sound, which began a few years after the Film Society's birth, brought an intensification of long-running debates on the role of sound in the cinema. But the society itself had already approached silent film accompaniment in a number of experimental ways.

Many in the "art film" community, when they weren't outright hostile to sound, were at least ambivalent about it. Proponents of "pure"—that is, abstract— cinema insisted that silent cinema reigned supreme, and some went so far as to claim that silence was the ideal aural environment. This attitude sometimes even extended to discussions of sound films. The variety of approaches can be seen in responses to the 1932 sound film *Silt*, which the society showed on 31 January 1932. The Film Society programme described its technique, stressing its audio-visual counterpoint:

It begins by associating the theme sounds of lake, dredger and river with the corresponding images, then by means of sound, picture and picture-sound montage endeavours to convey the deposit of sand by the slowed-up river, and with the addition of a shore sound recapitulates the whole process in sound and in picture.

However an anonymous article in *Close Up* treats it almost as a silent film:

> *Silt*, a one reel film made by Mr. Dan Birt to illustrate some of his theories of sound, was shown recently at the London Film Society. Dredgers, sand, sunlight on still water, the movement of buckets and arms, have acquired an audible, rather than a visual, sense even in the photography so that were the film to be shown silent, it would still be heard more than seen.[23]

Even those who felt that sound *might* prove positive, debated how it should work. The 1928 "Statement on Sound" by Eisenstein, Alexandrov, and Pudovkin was, for many, a template.[24] Its Soviet authors argued that the worst thing that could possibly happen would be for sound simply to reflect the images realistically, destroying cinema's poetry and reducing it to the banality of realism, a mere recording tool. Rather sound should dynamically counterpoint the images. In this sense, silent cinema, unshackled by specific languages, accorded with the internationalist agenda of the Left (which similarly promoted Esperanto). The Film Society rejected accusations that it was a left-wing organization; nevertheless, many of its supporters were prominent left-wingers and were, separately, members of more overtly political organizations. Some, such as Kenneth Macpherson and Robert Herring, came around to the idea of sound after initially adopting an anti-talkie stance. The most dramatic of these conversions was Basil Wright who, in the course of a single article in the form of a "dialogue" with Vivian Braun, moved from being completely against sound to being an enthusiastic proponent of "orchestrated abstract sound".[25]

Epiphanies such as Wright's fit well within the Film Society's "commercially unsuitable" agenda, and its concentration on non-naturalistic sound. Others were similarly concerned. George Pearson met Pudovkin at the society on 3 February 1929 and later recalled that "for both of us the moment was tinged with sadness, for though the great Russian films had touched the heights of the silent medium, the ominous arrival of Speech [capitalized] was in our thoughts. Yet I was convinced the Motion Picture had but one danger to avoid from Speech, dominance instead of service."[26]

By 1928–9, whatever the aesthetic approach, people were "beginning to think only in terms of sound film," as Rachael Low puts it.[27] So much so that one cinema preferred "paying forfeit rather than interrupt the succession of talking films by [the] exhibition of *Bolibar* or any other of the silent pictures for which it had contracted." In the case of *Bolibar*, the Film Society duly stepped in to save the day, and showed the film under the title *The Marquis of Bolibar* (5 May 1929). The following month, in June 1929, *Blackmail* opened and in September the society's fourth annual report stated that members had been asking about sound and talking films. In response the society pointed out that its programme selection would be limited by the cinema's sound system, but that in any case "no sound films produced in America or England [*sic*] has yet failed to secure wide public exhibition", which was a precondition for their eligibility for the society.[28] When a Mr Shapland wrote to enquire about sound films, Montagu's draft reply explained that it could use only Western Electric films and asked Miss Harvey to "send him the bunk above, but word it better!"[29]

Nevertheless, it began showing sound films the following season, starting with Disney's *The Barn Dance*—a film it is admittedly hard to imagine struggling to secure a wide release. The programme for the performance described the film as:

a model instance of synchronisation.... In his limited field, *Mickey Mouse* has achieved that perfect blend between visual and aural impulses towards which other sound-film technicians are yet striving, and of which Mr. Meisel's scores for *Potemkin* and *Berlin* were the first hints. (10 November 1929)

In accord with its "mission to explain," on 19 October 1930 the society showed five sound films, each employing a different recording system, as noted in the programme. Likewise, at the penultimate performance (26 March 1939), in an initiative by Anthony Asquith, it showed corresponding scenes ("the betrayal and death of Frankie brought about by his friend Gypo") from the 1929 and 1935 versions of *The Informer*. Max Steiner had won the Oscar for his music to Ford's film but the programme does not find room to mention that, nor does it give any indication of what accompanied the silent version.

Other innovations, perhaps involving an element of playfulness, included attempts to show how the soundtrack worked and to relate the visual aspects of film, even its physicality, to its aural side. In *Sound Rushes* (19 October 1930), the projector's masking was altered to reveal the RCA Photophone soundtrack of E. A. Dupont's *Cape Forlorn* (1930) with the programme warning the audience that the sound and its accompanying image were not in synchronization, while *A Demonstration of Sound Projected Backwards* (14 December 1930) is self-explanatory. The titles for both were the Film Society's own. They also showed Oskar Fischinger's drawn-soundtrack experiments with an explanation of how what is seen relates to what is heard (21 May 1933).

SAMPLE PROGRAMMES

The notes included in the Film Society programme leaflets are useful sources for understanding how the society chose to realize its aims. In line with wider exhibition norms of the time, the music at its events extended beyond the films. There was music before the film and during the interval, though it is usually unclear whether this was supplied on disc or performed by musicians live. The National Anthem concluded each show and, given the society's perceived leftist political stance, sometimes attracted more press attention than was given to the film accompaniment.

The committee took one of four approaches to screening silent films: intentionally silent, accompanied by live musicians, accompanied by records, accompanied by a narrator. Each performance usually involved some permutation of these, underlining the transitional nature of this period and reflecting the eclecticism of the society's film programming. The approach was far from consistent and did not necessarily reflect the filmmakers' wishes, even when they were achievable. But while the diversity of the film programming was the result of positive decisions, the diversity of sound approaches was sometimes more the result of pragmatism.

PERFORMANCE NO. 1 (New Gallery Kinema, October 25, 1925)
2:30 *"Absolute Films": Opus 1, 2 and 3* (1923–25)
2:50 *Film Society Resurrection Series No 1: Why Bronco Billy Left Bear County* (1912)
3:00 *Typical Budget* (1925)
3:15 *Waxworks* (1924)
4:35 *Champion Charlie* (1916)

As mentioned above, this opening performance was conducted by Eugene Goossens, Snr, under the musical direction of Frederick Laurence. Leni's *Waxworks* was conventionally approached with a compilation from pre-existing pieces, though alongside classical composers such as Mussorgsky and Cui there were more contemporary names such as Saint-Saëns, Sibelius, and Richard Strauss, as well as the cinema composer Giuseppe Becce.[30] That approach may have extended to the other films on the programme, though scores are not known to have survived for all of them.

Montagu recalled that the event began with a sonic experiment beyond the film: "From the moment the curtains drew apart punctually (in itself a triumph), and in silence (in itself an experiment), to disclose Ruttmann's absolute *Opera 2, 3 and 4* [*sic*], the Society was made."[31] The programme describes these films as "studies in pattern, with a drum accompaniment," implying that the orchestra's percussionist was featured. This would be even more extraordinary were it a solo percussionist, as Varèse's pioneering percussion piece *Ionisation* was only premiered in 1933 and the percussion interlude in Shostakovich's opera *The Nose* dates from 1927. Whatever happened, this was a consciously dramatic presentation: rather than, as might be usual, having music fill the pre-film aural void and run directly into the film accompaniment, the film and music would emerge simultaneously from (relative) darkness and (relative) silence, marking a definite break between "pre-performance" and "performance."

PERFORMANCE 3 (December 20, 1925, New Gallery Kinema)

2:30 *Film Society Resurrection Series, No 4: Muggins VC* (1911)

2:38 *Film Society Bionomics Series No 1* (1922–4) (reedited from *Secrets of Nature*)

2:45 *Raskolnikov* (1923)

4:20 An interval of ten minutes during which Comte Etienne will introduce his film

4:30 *A quoi rêvent les jeunes films* (1924–5)

The third performance is a good example of the diversity of sonic approaches that one might have encountered at a Film Society performance. *Muggins VC* was a popular pre-war comedy character who bests his "superiors" in a series of films. Here the film was accompanied by piano, while the scientific film had an orchestra (presumably a selection by De Wolfe). For *Raskolnikov* the programme note tells us that the council decided "by majority vote, that music and interval are alike unsuitable for this picture." It also noted that the film had been cut, and outlined some of the changes made to produce its ninety-five-minute version. However, the decision to run the film in silence was clearly not to everyone's taste and Montagu later drily opined: "we tried a two-hour show [referring to *Raskolnikov*] with no music but a battery of coughs."[32] After that came another coup: *A quoi rêvent les jeunes films*, with a score by the famous French conductor Roger Désormière (though he was not present at the performance).

But the details in the programme leaflet and other documentation raise as many questions as they answer about the musical arrangement. De Wolfe invoiced £50, plus £1.1s. for a solo pianist, but the invoice does not break the expenses down further than that. However, with *Muggins VC* accounting for the solo pianist and *Raskolnikov* being shown in silence, only the scientific film and *A quoi rêvent les jeunes films* required an ensemble. The French film is less than half an hour long and employs only seven players. Given that £50 would pay for around nineteen players, one wonders whether the society felt that to be a valid expense for the seven-minute scientific film? Perhaps, rather than employ an additional twelve players for such a short film, De Wolfe chose to put the money towards hire fees from his own library and arrangements for the same forces that were needed for Désormière's score. Whatever happened and whatever discussions occurred, there is no record of a complaint.

PERFORMANCE 4 (January 17, 1926, New Gallery Kinema)

2:30 *The Valse Mephistophilis of Liszt* (1925)

2:45 *Film Society Bionomics Series No 2: Dytiscus* (1913–25)

2:55 *Entr'acte* (1923–4)

3:15 *Film Society Bionomics No 3: an X-Ray Film* (1913–25)

3:17 *The Marriage Circle* (1924) [with interval].

The mid to late 1920s saw various inventions to synchronize sound and film and the society investigated one of them on 17 January 1926 in a programme that reveals some of the practical and aesthetic difficulties it faced. Perhaps keen to maintain its avant-garde profile, the society started with an innovation. The programme claimed that *The Valse Mephistophilis of Liszt* would be accompanied by "Piano, under the direction of Mr. Delacommune." This was a simplification. As was further explained, Charles Delacommune's Synchronismes Cinématographiques (patented in 1922 and 1923) "attempted to make a moving pattern each motion of which shall correspond exactly to a note in the Liszt waltz.... Mr. Delacommune will supervise the working of his synchronising apparatus." In practice, this "apparatus" was something like a player-piano, using "scores" comprising sheets with holes punched in them.

How the Film Society had learned of Delacommune's apparatus is unclear but Montagu went to Paris to negotiate its use.[33] The Synchronismes Cinématographiques so fascinated Fernand Léger that on 18 January 1924 he paid the inventor 300 francs to work on *Ballet Mécanique*, presumably to synchronize the score which George Antheil was writing.[34] The society must have been impressed with the apparatus when they screened *The Valse Mephistophilis of Liszt* as they went on to book it to accompany *Ballet Mécanique* at a subsequent performance. The project proved problematic, however. After the society had made its programme announcement, it became clear that the music by Antheil would not be ready in time, and so they cancelled.[35] But there was a subsequent change of heart, and they showed the film anyway (14 March 1926) with a selection of jazz records suggested by Léger. This is only one example of how last-minute some of the arrangements for music could be.

The ten-minute *Dytiscus* was shown in silence before *Entr'acte*. The programme admitted that the society could not provide the fifty-piece orchestra needed for

Satie's score for *Entr'acte*, so Jeffry Reynolds and Lyell Barbour played Milhaud's four-hand piano reduction. The X-ray film again was silent. It is worth noting that the society showed seven "bionomics" films over the years: the first was accompanied by orchestra, while these two were silent; there is no information for the other four. Perhaps this silent presentation was an investigation into whether the emotionality of music (a topic that came up in discussions of film music at the time) was inappropriate for a scientific subject.

The feature on this occasion was Lubitsch's *The Marriage Circle*, but after previewing it the council found it much duller than they remembered and chose to increase the projector speed.[36] How this affected the images and the music is not reported, but the film was accompanied by "A jazz band" which included a banjo and two saxophones.[37] De Wolfe presumably usually drew on a relatively standard ensemble of regular musicians from the Gaumont chain, employing occasional extras as necessary.

PERFORMANCE 47 (April 12, 1931, Phoenix Theatre[38])

2:30/8:30 *The Skeleton Dance, A Silly Symphony* (1929)
2:40/8:40 *Rain* (1929)
2:55/8:55 *Three Primitives* (n.d.)
    a) *Belshazzar's* [*sic*] *Feast*
    b) *Daniel in the Lion's Den*
    c) *The Persecution of the Christians*
3:00/9:00 *The Danube, Part One* (1930)
3:20/9:20 *Two Propaganda Films* (1930)
    a) *Hannevl Traumt—Bolle Milch*
    b) *Food for Thought—Cow and Gate Milk Food*
3:35/9:35 Interval of Ten minutes
3:45/9:45 *The Blue Express* (1929)

This programme took a variety of approaches, all to some degree following the filmmakers' wishes or expectations. Disney's *The Skeleton Dance* already had a synchronized track, which the society used. For Joris Ivens's twelve-minute impressionistic film *Rain*, the society announced that there was no musical accompaniment. The *Three Primitives* were accompanied by piano, though the programme does not name the pianist. Next on the bill was the first part of a documentary, *The Danube*, which had "a non-synchronised record accompaniment," comprising two pieces from the society's own record collection: Poulenc's eight-movement *Aubade* and Ravel's *Introduction and Allegro*. Running at nineteen and eleven minutes respectively, these records matched the film's thirty minutes, though they may not have been played in order. During the interval the audience was entertained by a recording of Delius's *On Hearing the First Cuckoo in Spring*.

After two synchronized "propaganda" (i.e., advertising) films, the feature was Ilya Trauberg's *The Blue Express*.[39] As a tribute to the recently deceased composer Edmund Meisel, the society intended to show the film with his music, which was available on record; alas, the disc for reel 5 was apparently missing, so they used Honegger's *Pacific 231* as a substitute.[40] This led to Constant Lambert's hitherto puzzling comment on that piece's effectiveness: "Those who are bored by *Pacific 231* in the concert hall would have been surprised at the brilliant effect it made when used in conjunction with the Soviet film *The Blue Express*."[41] Sadly, since then, the other discs have also been lost.[42]

PERFORMANCE 64 (May 21, 1933, Astoria)
2:30 *The Closing of the Zuyderzee Dyke* (1932)
2:43 *It's Fun to Be Fooled...It's More Fun to Know* (1929–32)
2:55 *Early Experiments in Hand-Drawn Sound* (1931)
3:00 *The Cultivation of Living Tissue* (1927–33)
3:20 Interval
3:30 *The Story of a Simple Case* (1931)

The performance on 21 May 1933 was a mixed programme which started with a sound film, included a collection of silents, and continued with an abstract sound-film. The programme again notes the recording system used for the sound film—Tobis—but does not individually identify the silent films shown under the group title *It's Fun to Be Fooled...It's More Fun to Know*. Judging by the description, however, one of them may have been *The Fugitive Futurist*, 1924. Most of the programme leaflet is devoted to explaining the complex sound history of *The Story of a Simple Case*. Pudovkin made this as a silent, but the programe notes that anticipating the introduction of sound, "an attempt was made to modify the treatment to embody 'unnatural' sounds and 'cut' sound counterpoint in accordance with the manifesto of Eisenstein, Alexandrov and Pudovkin."

> To this fact, of course, a measure of its weakness is due. A cutting construction, the images of which have been planned to be significant in association with sounds not causally connected with them, must obviously become obscure in the absence of such sounds.

Despite this, the society thought it worth seeing but either chose or were supplied with a silent print. The programme notes that "The musical accompaniment of the film has kindly been composed by Mr. Dennis Arundell; certain very general suggestions were received from the director."

The programme gives no indication about the accompaniment to *The Cultivation of Living Tissue*, but a lecturer was clearly used. According to the annual report, which sums up the season's achievements, "Dr Canti delivered a spoken commentary to his film." The society later preferred the French term *conférencier*, but what that annual report described as an "innovation" was, of course, no such thing.[43] They used the technique several times, though when they had shown three German films under the group title *The Film of Twenty Years Ago*, the programme balefully noted that: "Properly, a conferencier should explain these pictures, but no volunteer for that office is available to the Society" (4 March 1928). Similarly, the programme for 6 April 1930 might imply that *Voyage au Congo* was narrated:

> To obtain the full artistic effect of the expedition, M. Gide's travel-notes must be read for the atmosphere and colour of the regions visited, and their effect on the sensitive personality of the accomplished traveller.

—but it is not clear whether the "must" remained an aspiration.[44] Later the society also used a lecturer as a matter of expediency to narrate a couple of films that they could not get subtitled, either because there was no time or no money.

Oddly, however, when the society showed Japanese silents they did not use an equivalent of the traditional *benshi*, who narrated, explained, and provided the voices. For *The Tragedy of Temple Hagi* (1923) (8 January 1928) the society thanked the Japanese embassy for help including the loan of "suitable music"—though no details are given as to whether this was authentic Japanese music or Westernized Japonaiserie. After outlining the tradition of the *benshi* the programme explains that the society has tried to reproduce "as nearly as possible his [*sic*] effect," but by using intertitles, with backgrounds copied from fourteenth-century Japanese paintings. Why the society would go to the trouble and expense of creating a set of intertitles with elaborate backgrounds for a film which was never intended to have them is something of a mystery. However, part of the society's business plan was to seek to interest commercial distributors in the films they showed. Perhaps this film was a candidate for wider distribution, but they felt that relying on the *benshi* would hinder its commerciality.

Several of the silent films that the society showed had some sort of music, whether dedicated scores or general indications, but the society was not consistent about

following the instructions. Sometimes this was due to technical difficulties. The programme note for Walter Ruttmann's *Berlin: The Symphony of a City*[45] explained that
the film was

> cut by Mr. Ruttmann in close collaboration with Mr. Meisel…The music and
> pictorial scenes are thus welded to form a single rhythm. At the performances
> in Germany they are exactly synchronised by a special apparatus which it has
> not been possible here to reproduce. (4 March 1928)

Nevertheless they did manage to play Meisel's score (albeit without the "apparatus"),
but in other cases the music was generally provided by Ernest Grimshaw, who was
by now taking on the lion's share of the work. The programme for 21 October 1928
revealed that "In response to many requests from members…it should be known that,
unless otherwise stated, the orchestral score is to be attributed to Mr. Grimshaw."

The Film Society could hardly ignore the increasing hegemony of sound cinema,
though they continued to show silent films. The performance of Eisenstein's *October*
(11 March 1934) marked a watershed. At over £200, the musical accompaniment for
this single performance cost as much as some entire seasons (which Sidney Bernstein
questioned), but it was a complex film to synchronize: they had a copy from the
Russian negative, so the music of Edmund Meisel, which "fit" to the shorter German
version, had to be expanded and adjusted.[46] Ernest Irving employed three men who
were "up all night on Friday and Saturday doing the copying." Irving seems to have
foregone a fee for this work but was paid an additional £50 for the extra rehearsal
that was necessary.[47]

Though it could be counted a critical success, it seems to have been an exhausting experience. After this the society drew in its musical horns and accompaniments were limited to organ, piano, or records, though doubtless within those
limitations they continued to try to find "appropriate" soundscapes for each
film, while performances featured fewer silent films—usually as supports to
sound features. This change was driven by circumstance (the ubiquity of sound
cinema) and economics: the society's financial success was waning and the new
policy cost just a couple of pounds per show. However, with fewer silents on
each programme, the overall soundscape of the events became dominated by the
sound films.

Perhaps the 1934 screening of *October* was planned as a last hurrah for the
Film Society's live orchestral accompaniments. Whatever the larger agenda, by
then the society's work with regard to silent film and music was largely complete.
Over the previous decade it had brought an attitude to musical accompaniment
as eclectic as its programming of the films themselves. Despite its occasionally

eccentric decisions and the fact that few musical figures initially supported the society it did provide inspiration and experience for a number of people who were developing careers in sound film, and its decade of experimentation not only brought a range of responses to silent film music, but pointed some ways forward for sound films.

NOTES

1. London Film Society, *The Film Society Programmes, 1925–1939* (New York: Arno Press, 1972). Arno Press's 1972 facsimile of the complete Film Society programmes was the subject of a long and acrimonious correspondence about copyright and authorship. Subsequent quotations from this facsimile will be indicated in the text purely by date. Foreign films were erratically listed under original and translated titles; this essay will use the society's chosen form. See Ivor Montagu, "An Old Man's Mumble: Reflections on a Semi-Centenary", *Sight and Sound* 44/4 (Autumn 1975): 224.

2. The key collections are held at the British Film Institute (BFI) Library: the Film Society Collection and the Ivor Montagu Collection. Architectural plans are held at the London Metropolitan Archive.

3. Film Society: Memorandum and Articles of Association: paragraph 3(A) (22 June 1925). BFI, Ivor Montagu Collection, item 1. For more on the general background to the society, see Jamie Sexton, "The Film Society and the Creation of an Alternative Film Culture in Britain in the 1920s", in *Young and Innocent? The Cinema in Britain, 1896–1930*, ed. Andrew Higson (Exeter: Exeter University Press, 2002), 291–305.

4. George Amberg, unpaginated introduction in *The Film Society Programmes*.

5. The founders were listed, some with their occupations, in the society's articles of association: Iris Barry (film critic of *The Spectator* and the *Daily Mail*), J. M. Harvey (concert agent), Walter Mycroft (director, producer, screenwriter, and, at the time, film critic of the *London Evening Standard*), Anthony B. D. Butts ("of no occupation"), Frank Dobson (sculptor), and Sidney (later Baron) Bernstein.

6. Ivor Montagu resignation letter, 29 November 1929. BFI, Ivor Montagu Collection, item 7.

7. Brunel worked with Gainsborough Studios, and its head, Michael Balcon, forced him to step down from the Film Society Council, fearing that the society's highbrow approach was at odds with the studio's more populist fare. Dickinson was usually credited for "technical presentation" along with various others. Iris Barry was an author who knew many of the major modernist figures: she worked with Ezra Pound, had an affair with Wyndham Lewis, and T. S. Eliot encouraged her to submit her stories to *The Criterion*. She then became an influential film critic working for *The Spectator* and the *Daily Mail*. In 1935 she became the curator of the film department of the Museum of Modern Art.

8. Emphasis added. Film Society: Memorandum on a proposed Film Society Commemoration Book (30 September 1970). BFI, Ivor Montagu Collection, item 7.

9. Quoted in David Robinson, *The Life and Career of the Film Society* (unpublished manuscript, BFI, Film Society Collection, c.1963), unnumbered page, four from the last.

10. Ivor Montagu, *The Youngest Son: Autobiographical Sketches* (London: Lawrence and Wishart, 1970), 272–3.

11. Ibid., 275.

12. Disillusioned, Ellit withdrew from the premiere, and though he was credited as composer, the pianist was not credited. His wife recalled a chaotic performance: "The music was all rhythms—not a scrap of melody and difficult to follow. The pianist did his best but there were places where he gave up and just ran his fingers up and down the keys." The score itself is lost. See Roger Horrocks, *Len Lye: A Biography* (Auckland: Auckland University Press, 2001), 69–71.

13. The quote refers to the Tivoli, though of course the first performances were at the New Gallery: it seems that even at this late stage—less than a month from the first performance—the venue had not been finalised. Anon. Letter to Film Society (30 Sept. 1925). BFI, Film Society Collection, item 13.

14. Invoices and other financial statements are held within the BFI's Film Society and Ivor Montagu Special Collections.

15. "Nitrate/Bit-Rate: 100 Years of De Wolfe Music"; http://www.dewolfe.co.uk/help/news/Nitrate_to_Bitrate2.pdf [accessed 3 August 2012].

16. Montagu, "An Old Man's Mumble", 220.

17. The London Metropolitan Archive holds plans and accompanying correspondence of some of the Film Society's venues. The most comprehensive interior plans are for the Tivoli (GLC/AR/BR/19 360), the New Victoria Theatre (LCC/AR/BR 194168), and the Astoria (GLC AR/BR/19/3083A).

18. Newer, specially designed cinemas were better appointed: the New Victoria had a band room and another devoted to the music library. New Victoria Theatre, Preliminary Plan (revised). London Metropolitan Archive LCC/AR/BR 19 4168

19. Eyles and Skone, *London's West End Cinemas* (Sutton: Keytone, 1991), 44. Other alterations included re-routing a pipe that fed the curtain drencher which had extended a long way into the pit, perhaps indicating the importance originally attaching to the musicians' facilities.

20. Film Society Profit and Loss Account, 1933–34. BFI, Film Society Collection, item 24c–f.

21. Eyles and Skone, *London's West End Cinemas*, 43.

22. Ibid.

23. Anon., *Close Up* 9/1 (Mar. 1932): 69.

24. Sergei Eisenstein, Grigori Alexandrov, and Vsevolod Pudovkin, "Statement on Sound", in *S. M. Eisenstein: Selected Works*, Vol. 1: *Writings, 1922–34*, ed. and trans. Richard Taylor (London: BFI, 1988), 113–14. The first English translation (by Ivor Montagu) appeared in *Close Up* 3/4 (1928): 10–13 under the title "The Sound Film: A Statement from USSR".

25. Basil Wright and B.Vivian Braun. "Manifesto: Dialogue on Sound—Its Proper Use in Film", *Film Art* 3 (Spring 1934): 28–29. Reproduced in *Traditions of Independence: British Cinema in the Thirties*, ed. Don Macpherson (London: BFI 1980), 178–9.

26. George Pearson, *Flashback: The Autobiography of a British Film-maker* (London: George Allen and Unwin, 1957), 155. Pearson's other reminiscences of the society cover just two pages (132–3) and imply that he played a small part.

27. Rachael Low, *The History of the British Film, 1918–1929* (London: Allen and Unwin, 1971), 184.

28. Film Society: Annual Reports. BFI, Ivor Montagu Collection, item 2.

29. Ivor Montagu, Draft letter (14 March 1929) to Mr. Shapland. BFI, Ivor Montagu Collection, item 7.

30. The score is now held in Cambridge University Library; details at http://ul-newton.lib. cam.ac.uk/vwebv/holdingsInfo?bibId=528855 [accessed 3 August 2012].

31. Montagu, "The Film Society, London", *Cinema Quarterly* 1/2 (Autumn 1932): 44. This innovation seems to have been dropped later. The programme to Performance 97 (14 Nov. 1937) says that the soundtracks of parts of the pot-pourri *Chants et danses de l'Armée Rouge* were used as a pre-film overture. Note that the programme lists as *"Absolute Films": Opus 1, 2,* and *3* what were in fact Ruttmann's *Opus 2, 3,* and *4*. Montagu recycled parts of this text in various accounts of the Film Society, for instance, Montagu, *The Youngest Son,* 32–3.

32. Montagu, "The Film Society, London", 44.

33. An undated pencil note has the inventor's address and phone number and reminders of various other errands. Undated (1925?) itinerary and notes. Ivor Montagu Collection, item 7.

34. Judi Freeman, "Bridging Purism and Surrealism: The Origins and Production of Fernand Léger's *Ballet Mécanique*", in *Dada and Surrealist Film,* ed. Rudolf E. Kuenzli (New York: Willis, Locker, and Owens, 1987), 34.

35. When Antheil finally delivered the score it was far longer than the film, and the ensemble, including sixteen player pianos, impractical. He later edited and re-orchestrated it so that it would be performed separately. In 2000 Paul D. Lehrman devised a synchronization to go with a recently discovered print of the film that is thought to be the original.

36. Oswell Blakeston, "British Solecisms", *Close Up* 1/2 (August 1927): 18. Reproduced in *Close Up, 1927–1933: Cinema and Modernism,* ed. James Donald, Anne Friedberg, and Laura Marcus (Princeton: Princeton University Press, 1998), 41–3.

37. The invoice lists those instruments separately.

38. A problem led to a last-minute relocation to the Phoenix Theatre in Charing Cross Road for the society's only show there. Also uniquely, the performance was repeated in the evening, hence the two start times for each film.

39. The film was presented under the English title.

40. Film Society record list (undated). BFI, Film Society Collection, item 24c–f. Ironically the society showed Tsekhanovsky's 1932 film interpretation of *Pacific 231* on 17 April 1932 and 12 March 1933.

41. Lambert, *Music Ho! A Study of Music in Decline* (London: Penguin, 1948), 176. Lambert's discussions of films and their music are clearly informed by Film Society performances. Some of those in *Music Ho!* are "*La Nouvelle Babylone*" (Kozintsev and Trauberg's *New Babylon*) and [*The Battleship*] "*Potemkin*" (p. 65), which he rates more highly than *The General Line* (p. 12), though he still says that Meisel's music is no match for the film (pp. 189–90). For more on Meisel, see Fiona Ford, chapter 15 in this volume.

42. A frustratingly undated and anonymous typed response to an enquiry speculates on the fates of discs and sheet music for films, some of which were shown at the Film Society: *Berlin: Die Sinfonie der Grosstadt* ("Berlin: Symphony of a City"), *Der heilige Berg* (*The Holy Mountain*), *Der blaue Expreß* (*The Blue Express*), and *Panzerkreuzer "Potemkin"* (*Battleship Potemkin*). In the last two cases, the problem was the failure of the German company Prometheus, which had, allegedly, recorded a reduced orchestra version of Meisel's score for *Potemkin* (Film Society lost records list).

43. See, for instance, Joe Kember, chapter 1 in his volume.

44. Jean Prévost's 1927 article in *Close Up* had made no mention of any musical accompaniment: Prévost, "André Gide and Marc Allégret's Voyage to the Congo", trans. K. Macpherson, *Close Up* 1 (July 1927): 38–41.

45. Again, the film was shown under the English title.

46. *The Film Society Programmes* (11 March 1934).

47. J. M. Harvey, Letter to Sidney Bernstein (13 March 1934). BFI Film Society Collection, item 13.

15

Edmund Meisel's "Visual Sound" in *The Crimson Circle* (1929): The Case of the Vanishing Part-Talkie

Fiona Ford

ON 1 MARCH 1929 British International Film Distributors (BIFD) held a trade show in London for *The Crimson Circle*.[1] This was a retitled version of a recent German silent film, *Der rote Kreis* (Efzet-Film GmbH, 1928; directed by Friedrich Zelnik), based on Edgar Wallace's thriller from 1922. The plot concerns a mysterious stranger who controls a murderous blackmail gang in London. The gang is pursued by Inspector Parr and a private detective, Derrick Yale (played by Stewart Rome). Parr's daughter, Thalia Drummond (played by Lya Mara), works undercover as a mysterious secretary-cum-petty-thief to help her father unmask Yale as the criminal mastermind. The film was subsequently re-released in August 1929 with dialogue, sound effects, and a score postsynchronized on discs using British Talking Pictures equipment. This re-release provides us with an interesting case study of a British film company negotiating the transition to synchronized sound.[2] The score and sound effects were devised by Edmund Meisel, the Austrian composer notorious for his propulsive accompaniment to *Das Jahr 1905 (Panzerkreuzer "Potemkin") (Battleship Potemkin)* in April 1926.[3] Neither the print nor the discs from *The Crimson Circle* are known to survive, but glimpses of the composer's intentions and style can be gleaned from contemporaneous press reports and articles. The surviving documentary evidence, when set within the context of Meisel's extant film scores, illuminates many aspects of the lost soundtrack to *The Crimson Circle*.

Meisel was based in Berlin for most of his career, but spent over a year in London working on sound-film experiments. Like many other film composers,

Meisel had a background in music for the stage. He continued to compose incidental music alongside his film work, chiefly for the epic stage productions of the left-wing director Erwin Piscator. Virtually nothing survives of Meisel's incidental music, making it almost impossible to establish firm connections between this arena and his film scores. Nevertheless, copious evidence in his extant film scores suggests that he composed with the immediacy typical of a theatre composer. In relation to his earlier silent film score for *Der heilige Berg* (*The Holy Mountain*),[4] Meisel proclaimed how "a filmic image stimulates me in such a way that the moment I see it I experience a distinctive accompanying sound shape for the relevant scene."[5] Similarly, a press release for *The Crimson Circle* encapsulated Meisel's compositional approach, stating that the music for *The Crimson Circle* had been "spontaneously composed to suit the action of the story".[6] Due to tight deadlines and other commitments, Meisel was certainly often compelled to produce his film scores within ridiculously short timescales. He allegedly composed his *Potemkin* score within twelve days and nights,[7] and that for *Der blaue Expreß* (*The Blue Express*) in five.[8] Meisel also helped to carry over many traditional practices from incidental music into film accompaniment. These practices include the use of music apposite to the action, accompanying dialogue to intensify its dramatic effect, using motifs, sound effects, and musical rhetoric (or "mickey mousing") to enhance the narrative. These elements are already present in his silent scores to varying degrees, but with *The Crimson Circle* Meisel developed them in a new way.[9]

MEISEL'S SOUND EXPERIMENTS

While Meisel had the luxury of almost three months' preparation for *The Crimson Circle*, much of this time was probably taken up by experiments in the recording studio.[10] Meisel had been experimenting with recorded sound for various stage and screen projects since at least the autumn of 1927. For Piscator's stage production of *Die Abenteuer des braven Soldaten Schwejk* ("The Adventures of the Good Soldier Svejk"), first performed in Berlin in January 1928, his incidental music and sound effects were recorded and played back on gramophone discs.[11] He had intended to include some recorded sound effects during live performances of his orchestral score to *Zehn Tage, die die Welt erschütterten* (*October*) in April 1928, but this may have been unrealized.[12] However, he did create a set of six general purpose sound effects discs for use in cinema presentations, released by Deutsche Grammophon in the summer of 1928.[13] These recreated typical soundscapes for trains, stations, city streets, machinery, and so on. Meisel's sound effects were generated through varying combinations of orchestral, jazz, and percussion instruments, apparatus familiar to backstage sound effects men in the theatre (metal sheets, dried peas in a tincan, etc.), and, latterly, an electrically powered "sound effects desk" invented by the composer and allegedly first used for his incidental music to *Schwejk*.[14] His fascination with the recreation of everyday noises had reached its apogee during his collaboration with Walther Ruttmann on *Berlin. Die Sinfonie der Großstadt* ("Berlin: Symphony of a City"; Fox-Europa-Film, 1927), an abstract celebration of the German capital. The director and composer joined forces again on *Deutscher Rundfunk* ("German Radio", also known as *Tönende Welle*), a sound short commissioned for the fifth German Radio Exhibition in Berlin, which opened on 31 August 1928. The film, now lost, was a mélange of location footage and sound recordings made on a tour of the regions surrounding the nine biggest radio stations in Germany, capturing radio broadcasts, speech, music, and sounds emanating from city streets, leisure parks, and major industrial sites. For the soundtrack, Meisel blended field recordings with sections of his own original music and sound effects, for example replacing an unusable field recording of the Rhine Falls.[15]

MEISEL IN LONDON

At the end of October 1928 Meisel informed Sergei Eisenstein that he and his wife Els were "setting off for London early tomorrow, for the recording of a new large-scale sound film with a newly established English sound film company. It is still uncertain how long the recording might last."[16] The success of *Deutscher Rundfunk* may have been the catalyst for Meisel's trip to England, but he appears to have been enticed abroad on false pretences: the promised work failed to materialize and he spent several months without any substantial occupation. Despite his reputation in Germany, Meisel was generally unknown in London, except among the membership of the Film Society, who had witnessed Ruttmann's *Berlin* at the New Gallery Kinema on 4 March 1928, with Meisel's cacophonous accompaniment conducted by Ernest Grimshaw.[17] Once in London Meisel soon became involved with the Film Society and collaborated with Grimshaw over the musical accompaniment for *The End of St Petersburg*,[18] screened on 3 February 1929 with the director in attendance.[19] During the same period the composer made some fruitless attempts to generate income through various self-scripted scenarios, including a proposed sound feature entitled *A Symphony of London* (similar to his *Berlin* collaboration with Ruttmann).[20] He was on the verge of returning to Berlin when he received a contract from British Talking Pictures in April 1929 to postsynchronize four films.[21] A later press release described his contract in more detail: "At the invitation of B.I.F.D., Mr. Edmund Meisel, the eminent [Austrian]

composer and conductor, is writing original musical compositions, synchronisation and sound effects to the company's films. The first production...is 'The
Crimson Circle.'"[22]

British Talking Pictures was part of a film business portfolio owned by Isidore W.
Schlesinger, an American magnate with a virtual monopoly over the distribution
and exhibition of films in South Africa. Schlesinger began to invest in the British
film industry in 1926, joining the board of British International Pictures to guarantee him a supply of the best British films to screen in Africa.[23] Within two years he
had taken over the British rights to Lee de Forest's Phonofilm process (a sound-on-
film system), acquired studio premises at Wembley, and formed three interrelated
companies to handle equipment sales and studio hire, sound film production, and
film rentals. These were, respectively: British Talking Pictures, British Sound Film
Productions, and British International Film Distributors.[24] By the time Meisel
arrived in London, British Talking Pictures had a soundproof studio at Wembley
capable of producing short sound films, with additional facilities for postsynchro-
nizing silent pictures; larger studio premises for producing feature-length films were
completed in September 1929.[25]

British sound studios were at least a year behind their American counterparts in
terms of investment and output, so early British sound features from 1929 tend to
have more in common with the American product from 1928 than the American
sound films exhibited in London during 1929. Many of the early sound features
released by American studios in 1928 had actually been silent films "retrofitted with
music, sound effects, and perhaps a little post-dubbed dialogue".[26] The part-talking
version of *The Crimson Circle* was advertised as having precisely these features:
"Dialogue! Synchronized! Sound Effects!"[27] Such part-talking films were a valid
commercial response at a time when British studios were still acquiring experience
in recording technology and generally lacked sound studios capable of making
feature-length sound films. These hybrid films are fascinating for film music historians, because they often have a much more extensive and varied musical accompaniment than many later sound films from the 1930s, when music was often confined
to a brief overture, a closing fanfare and moments of music making within the film's
action.

Sinclair Hill, formerly a director at Stoll Picture Productions, was hired to direct
the talking sequences for *The Crimson Circle*. Hill had been directing short sound
films for British Sound Film Productions since the beginning of 1929, including the
comic sketch *Mr Smith Wakes Up*.[28] Generally, the reviews praised the recording
quality and direction of Hill's dialogue sequences in *The Crimson Circle*. Presumably
these were all postdubbed, since it would have been too expensive and impractical

to shoot extra scenes. The only evidence regarding the positioning of the dialogue scenes comes from the *Bioscope* review:

> The dialogue is introduced in the early scenes when the Scotland Yard detective and the bogus detective [Yale] discuss plans for tracking down the mysterious gang, during the frantic rush of people at the run on the bank, and again in the finale when the real culprit is dramatically exposed. The recording of the various voices is extremely good, those of Stewart Rome and Lya Mara being particularly so. A novel feature is a supposed broadcast from 2LO, and the announcement of a further mysterious murder.[29]

This suggests that Hill went to some lengths to integrate the new dialogue within the drama, rather than merely bolting on a reel of dialogue at the end as an additional flourish, as was often the case.[30] Hitchcock took a similarly artistic approach in *Blackmail* (British International Pictures, 1929), inserting around thirteen minutes of dialogue throughout his film. The English actor Stewart Rome was definitely involved in the new sound version of *The Crimson Circle*,[31] but there was speculation in the press regarding the voice of his Latvian co-star: "Considering the difficulties of synchronising certain of the scenes, Mr. Sinclair Hill has acquitted himself admirably.... That we have been unable to discover whether Lya Mara had a speaking double or not is a great tribute to the director." [32]

In the autumn of 1929 Ivor Montagu prepared a cost estimate for Meisel's proposed (but unrealized) postsychronization of *The General Line* (*Staroye i novoye,* Sovkino, 1929, directed by Sergei Eisenstein). To reduce costs, Meisel suggested a remuneration of £500 for composition, conducting, and rights for *The General Line,* "half of his normal fee from B.I.F.D. for the same work". [33] This suggests that Meisel's contract for BIFD was a lucrative one and that he received the princely sum of £1000 for his work on *The Crimson Circle.* Having secured his finances, Meisel installed a projector in his London flat,[34] recreating the working conditions he had enjoyed in Berlin for *Potemkin.*[35] Now he was able to compose at a piano while watching the film print, closely aligning his score to salient points of the drama. Twenty-six musicians were hired for the synchronization and rehearsals began in the middle of June. These rehearsals were interrupted on the fourth day by a strike over remuneration rates, instigated by the Musicians' Union, and only recommenced a few days later once new terms had been agreed and the musicians had been replaced.[36] A later press release stressed that all musicians hired for the recording were British,[37] since sufficient British personnel and studio facilities had to be employed to guarantee that the sound version of *The Crimson*

Circle qualified as "British made" under the terms of the Cinematograph Films Act, 1927, despite the film's German origins, the international cast, and foreign composer.

We can deduce from the lengthy rehearsal time (more than four days) that Meisel's score required many detailed points of synchrony during the live recording. It is perhaps surprising that the sound was recorded onto discs, given that British Talking Pictures chiefly employed a sound-on-film process (Lee de Forest's Phonofilm). The decision may have been taken to promote their new disc attachment, advertised around the time *The Crimson Circle* was being recorded,[38] or to take into account the existing number of cinemas with sound-on-disc equipment. Alternatively, Meisel may have insisted on using disc technology, due to his previous recording experience in Berlin.

MEISEL'S "OPERATIC" SCORE

Press releases published prior to the trade shows for *The Crimson Circle* promote the operatic nature of Meisel's score as the film's unique selling point and how it closely reflected the action:

> [This is] the first "talkie" film to have music composed for it on definitely operatic lines.... Mr. Edmund Meisel... makes some of the instruments "talk" in exact accompaniment to certain of the words the characters utter. In addition to giving every character his or her motive, and modifying these themes to suit each part of the action, the music is composed to suggest in turn colour, light, words, effects and impressions.[39]

> [Meisel] has given not only each character a motif, but each theme of the film—the circle, the letter, the Buddha, &c,—a motif as well; so that there will be a harmony of texture in the sound, as there is a harmony of texture in the images.... The trade mark of B.I.F.D. has even a motif to itself.[40]

> The music...will express dialogue, colour, emotion, mystery and dancing. Through Meisel's musical interpretation, people will be seen and "heard" running. A man calling "Thalia" will be heard in music. When a prison door opens, a cell becomes lighter and lighter. The change is expressed by sound.[41]

Audiences at the trade presentations were handed publicity material explaining how every character and salient detail had a distinctive motif in Meisel's score, each rendered by means of appropriate instrumentation, and that sometimes these motifs would be contrapuntally intertwined in accordance with the dramatic conditions.[42]

This recourse to themes and motifs reflects Meisel's established compositional approach, particularly in *Der heilige Berg*, discussed below. It also concurs with what would become the dominant purpose of thematic accompaniment in film music during the synchronized-sound era: namely a narrative device whereby the traits of a particular character are instantly recognizable through a "clear music-to-character correspondence".[43]

While Meisel created a network of themes for *Der heilige Berg*, his handling of these themes can best be described as apposite but unsophisticated: his themes are hardly ever transformed or combined.[44] *The Crimson Circle* appears to have had more examples of themes in combination, but trade show reviews imply that Meisel's thematic approach was still crude and at times overdone:

> The film opened with a scene of detective Yale in his study [...].
>
> The "Yale" motif is heard, strange, expectant; rather like a gramophone running at the wrong speed. Inspector Parr is announced. "Parr" motif, then "Parr" and "Yale" motifs interwoven in conversational undertones, but still in the strange timbre of a gramophone turning too fast.[45]

> When a gold Chinese Buddha is being sold to a pawnbroker the ear is filled with music which suggests the stately march of mandarins in some musical comedy while the mind is wholly indifferent to the object which is being bartered; the meaning of the scene to us is that in it an apparently innocent typist is shown to be a thief.[46]

In the second citation, above, Meisel's spontaneous response appears to be no different from the archetypal pianist accompanying a silent film: he saw a Chinese Buddha and immediately produced some stereotypical Chinese music, just as he would for the Chinese labourers in *Der blaue Expreß*.[47]

ACCOMPANIED DIALOGUE

Where Meisel's score takes on a quite experimental character is in his handling of dialogue and sound effects. There are many examples in Meisel's silent film scores where he accompanied the "dialogue" present in the intertitles or mouthed onscreen in a manner that suggested the verbal content. The score to *Der heilige Berg* has extended sequences where the composer generated declamatory melodies with exact or near-exact rhythmic replication of the dialogue exchanges in the intertitles. The first encounter in the mountains between Diotima, a dancer played by Leni Riefenstahl, and the enigmatic mountain climber (Luis Trenker) is reproduced in Example 15.1.[48]

DIOTIMA: Have you come from above [the summit of the mountain]? It must be beautiful up there.

CLIMBER: Beautiful, tough, and dangerous!

DIOTIMA: And what does one look for up there?

CLIMBER: Oneself!

DIOTIMA: And nothing else?

CLIMBER: And what are you looking for then at the top…in nature?

DIOTIMA: Beauty!

CLIMBER: And nothing else?

Example 15.1. Example of accompanied dialogue from *Der heilige Berg* with translation.

This example demonstrates how the intertitle words appear directly above the appropriate bars, that every syllable has a corresponding note in the melody and that each dialogue line is delimited by a caesura, giving the orchestra some leeway for synchronization in live performance. Meisel's stereotypical contrasts in orchestration and tessitura also help to delineate the gender and personality of his characters: solo oboe in a high range for Diotima and interjections from solo brass and clarinet in a lower range for the mountain climber. Meisel was still advocating the same approach to accompanying silent film dialogue in an interview published in *Cinema News*, given primarily to promote his *Symphony of London* scenario:

> Instruments should, on occasion, "speak" the subtitles—that is to say, they should accompany the sentence, with proper intonation for a question, or an exclamation, and the dramatic effect of certain subtitles can be much enhanced by this means.[49]

Moreover, Meisel returned to this technique for his final score, *Der blaue Expreß*, particularly for the scene near the beginning of the film, where the Chinese railway fireman is overjoyed to be reunited with two of his family members.

The notion of Meisel making instrumental melodies shadow the contours of actual dialogue in a sound film seems at best bold and experimental or at worst foolhardy, especially at a time when it was all too easy to drown the voice with any simultaneously recorded background sounds. In an article later published in *Melos*, Meisel described how he had experimented with four different ways in which to accompany the dialogue in *The Crimson Circle*, varying orchestration and microphone positioning to overcome this danger:

> In daily co-operation with the sound technicians I tried out all possible combinations.
>
> For example: repeatedly recording the same piece in various orchestrations, moreover modifying the positions of the instruments around the microphone—dialogue recordings accompanied throughout with music, or only the gaps in conversations filled with music, or individual words emphasized with music.... The performance of individual instruments as an accompaniment to the appropriate personalities in the dialogue...[50]

Examples representing each type of accompaniment can be found in the press reports. *Cinema News* praised the climax of *The Crimson Circle* for the effective manner "in which music and voices are dramatically blended",[51] a concrete example where dialogue had a continuous accompaniment; Meisel would create similar blends for crowd scenes in his postsynchronization of *Potemkin* in 1930.[52] A *Close Up* review cited an example where Meisel filled in the gap after a shout:

> Yale leaves Parr and an assistant, and enters the next room. We hear him fall heavily. Parr rushes to the locked door and shouts "Yale!!" Swifter than an echo a "composed" shout follows...[53]

This example is directly comparable to a moment in Max Steiner's score to *The Informer* (RKO, 1935; directed by John Ford), where a solo violin echoes the vocal pitch intonation after the main character's girlfriend calls out his name, "Gypo!"[54] A press release for *The Crimson Circle* in *Bioscope* stated that "A man calling 'Thalia' will be heard in music".[55] Emphasizing an individual word—particularly a name—was not a new idea for Meisel: his *Der heilige Berg* score has several musical representations of one character calling out the name of another. The names, made visually explicit via intertitles and the overt mouthing of words, are synchronized in the score with an appropriate imitation of the vocal contour and syllabic pattern, as for example when Diotima calls the name of her young friend Vigo after he wins a ski race. Similar musical surrogates for the human voice can be found in the Movietone score for *Sunrise: A Song of Two Humans* (Fox Film Corporation, 1927; directed by F. W. Murnau; score credited to Samuel Rothafel, conducted by Ernö Rapée)[56], where mournful horn calls represent the farmer desperately calling for his missing wife, and in Albert Cazabon's score for *The Flag Lieutenant* (Astra-National, 1926; directed by Maurice Elvey), where a trumpet embodies Lascelle's shout.[57] It is possible that the "Thalia" shout in *The Crimson Circle* immediately shadowed the recorded voice, as in the "Yale!!" example, rather than being heard simultaneously. Finally, Meisel's *Melos* article mentioned a scene from *The Crimson Circle* where he chose instrumentation appropriate to character and situation in a similar manner to the example from *Der heilige Berg* in Figure 15.1, above:

> An old misanthropist irately approaches his young secretary...to angry, clipped figurations from a *forte*, muted, solo trombone. The tentative reply of the intimidated young girl...*piano legato* solo oboe. The ranting fury of the old man...screeching muted gabbling of the trombone, turning *diminuendo* into the clattering of the typewriter, to where the young girl with tiny *pizzicato* footsteps has taken refuge.[58]

SOUND EFFECTS

As demonstrated above, Meisel had a tendency to create isomorphic and iconic representations of the emotions present in the human voice during dialogue scenes. He had a similar approach to the handling of sound effects. This is apparent from his description of the scene between the old misanthropist and his young secretary, which continues:

> Cumbersomely the old man gets up, in order to go after her...a deep sound accompanies each of his movements: sitting...first sound. Gazing at the girl,

his arm lying on the table…second sound. Standing up…third sound. Beating the table with his fist…fourth sound,—the sounds continually intensifying![59]

The fear engendered in the young girl as the old man rises menacingly from the table may have been accompanied by Meisel's trademark ascending sequence, where a simple rhythmic idea is repeated at successive chromatic steps as the action intensifies. He famously used this simple technique at the climax of *Potemkin* when the mutinous ship encounters the approaching squadron and anxiously waits to see if it will be attacked. An ascending sequence may also have been appropriated for the scene "when a prison door opens, a cell becomes lighter and lighter. The change is expressed by sound."[60] Throughout his career, Meisel had shown a preference for sound effects to be "composed" and integrated within the measured metre of his score. The synchronization of these effects was therefore under the control of the conductor's baton, rather than being freely added by a lone percussionist or sound effects operator closely watching the screen action. Again, this is evident from his interview in *The Cinema*:

> In the interpretation of scenes into music [Meisel] introduces a number of distinctive ideas. One is, the elimination of "effects" as such, in deference to music that suggests the sound to be indicated. Telephone bells, for instance, should not be "rung" in the ordinary way, but should be worked in as an integral part of the music.[61]

Hay Chowl was surprised and disappointed that Meisel, whom he described as "the mid-European pioneer of counterpoint sound and sight", had resorted to such synchronized mimetic sound effects, seemingly eschewing the recent "Statement of Sound" issued by Meisel's Russian friends (Eisenstein, Alexandrov, and Pudovkin):

> When someone is seen typing and tapping noises are heard, whether it is the typewriter itself or "composed" tappings that are heard; substantially, it is *hearing* what is *seen*. And that, I understand, is taboo in the best counterpoint circles.[62]

Composed synchronized sound, when it mirrors the on screen choreography or gives shape to an emotion—now described as "mickey mousing"—appears to be directly at odds with the statement in the famous Russian sound manifesto, namely that: "*The first experiments with sound must be directed towards its pronounced non-coincidence with the visual images. This method of attack only will produce the requisite sensation, which will lead in course of time to the creation of a new orchestral counterpoint of sight-images and sound-images.*"[63] To confound matters, Eisenstein became a huge fan of Mickey Mouse and Disney. The director hurried to see Disney cartoons "on the very first day of his arrival on British soil" and was fascinated by the way in which Disney meticulously choreographed the movements of his cartoon characters to music, graphically following the contour of a melody.[64] Christopher Morris has suggested in his analysis of Meisel's *Der heilige Berg* score that Meisel's approach is too "easily dismissed as a naïve prototype of film scoring technique", one which

> often comes uncomfortably close to an orchestral version of a poor cinema pianist, who reacts to each shot with the first musical idea that pops into his/her head. But it complicates the synchronized vs. contrapuntal binary that would soon preoccupy film music theory, resituating aspects of so-called synchronized scoring (associated above all with Hollywood practice) as gestures toward music-film counterpoint.[65]

Like Disney's first composers, chiefly Wilfred Jackson and Carl Stalling, Meisel created a close choreography of movements and sound effects in his scores, drawing on age-old musical rhetorical figures for expressive effect. This approach—developed in his scores for silent film—proved to be a practical solution to the technological limitations of the recording studio, enabling several elements of the soundtrack to be recorded within the one take. William Hunter, who experienced several of Meisel's scores at Film Society screenings between 1928 and 1934, described how Meisel's music ultimately functioned as "visual sound":

> I have heard the scores of *Potemkin*, *Berlin*, and Trauberg's *Blue Express*. To consider them as "music" is completely to misunderstand their purpose.... Meisel's "music" is rather "visual sound"—and extremely difficult to define....
> When [Meisel's scores] are onomatopoeic... they are not an imitation of the sound so much as a symbolism of it, and reinforce, in a manner which a musical accompaniment... or the actual noises could not do, the emotional and intellectual context in which they are found.[66]

Similar sentiments were expressed in a review of *The Crimson Circle* in *Close Up*:

> We should remember how Mara [Thalia Drummond] comes into a room and sits down to read a letter, all to the tune of a highly rhythmetised tango. That was worth a lot when you consider Mara—which Meisel helps you to do—in this light. He Meisels her into your subconscious. Nothing else could. Remember too the typewriter's cute tappetytap, and specially a harpsichordish *con brio* tinkling round the somberer noises of a business interview.[67]

PRESENTATION AND RECEPTION

Meisel invited members of the Film Society to attend the London trade show at the New Gallery Kinema, Regent Street, on 27 August[68] and there were further trade presentations in Manchester, Leeds, Birmingham, Glasgow, and Cardiff between 30 August and 11 September 1929.[69] There were several complaints regarding the over-amplification of the sound at these presentations,[70] a problem common in many cinemas newly equipped for sound reproduction. However, much of the over-amplification during *The Crimson Circle* was intentional, if perhaps overdone in practice, since "cue-sheets giving the right volume for each scene" were used at the trade shows.[71] This meant that, in addition to synchronizing each sound disc with its matching film reel, an operator had to adjust the volume during the screening at prescribed points to create a greater dynamic range in reproduction than was possible during the recording. Hence "a saxophone had a sound close-up, and one man's voice was amplified until it expressed a whole crowd."[72] The latter example is reminiscent of Pudovkin's famous statement regarding the expressive possibilities of sound film, where one might "combine the fury of a man with the roar of a lion".[73]

A few days after the London trade show, Meisel wrote enthusiastically about the future of sound film to Eisenstein:

> I have just shown enormously great possibilities here through an experiment, with great success. Dialogue with instruments, composed car chases, close-ups of instruments, etc. The artistic creation of any noise is possible ...
>
> Already in the case of my film the press here are writing that my way is the correct one and worthy of imitation.[74]

In reality, *The Crimson Circle* was not the unmitigated success implied by Meisel's comments. Because of the emphasis in the press releases on the "operatic" nature of his score, many critics had been inadvertently primed to expect that Meisel's music would be considered too highbrow for commercial cinema. Consequently the *Kinematograph Weekly* reviewer found it "a little too advanced in technique to appeal to the masses. The discordant noises, instead of creating atmosphere, only succeed in taking one's mind off the picture."[75] By contrast, *The Cinema*'s reviewer was pleasantly surprised:

> We state frankly that [Meisel's score] is not as bizarre from the popular point of view as we had thought conceivable, but is actually a score which even the most unintelligent film patron can appreciate. It is certainly something different, although in his desire to interpret the actions of the players Herr Meisel

occasionally attracts relatively too much attention to his music. It is, nevertheless, consistently interesting.[76]

Those critics who were more familiar with Meisel's other scores—typically the Film Society cognoscenti—questioned why Meisel's talents had been wasted on an Edgar Wallace plot in the first place.[77]

It is not known how many bookings for *The Crimson Circle* were generated as a result of the trade shows and I have yet to find any listings for it, even in London. Presumably Schlesinger's chain of cinemas—United Picture Theatres—was obliged to screen it. The film had a short run in the Little Picture House, New York, but was criticized for having a "poorly synchronized score…sounding very much like romantic Oriental music trying to go modern".[78] Meisel was not involved in the next major release from BIFD, a full-talking feature entitled *Dark Red Roses*, again directed by Sinclair Hill. *Dark Red Roses* had a successful trade show just days before a serious fire at the Wembley studios in the early hours of Sunday, 20 October 1929.[79] Miraculously, their newest sound studio for recording feature-length films emerged relatively unscathed, as did their main film vault. Press reports stated that *Dark Red Roses* had been saved, but made no mention of *The Crimson Circle*: it had already been forgotten.[80] Despite their initial promise, Schlesinger's enterprises were ultimately unable to compete with the American sound-film companies and within a few years were brought to financial ruin through some costly multinational and multilingual productions. The Wembley studios ended up being leased out to independent producers, becoming a busy production centre for Fox-British quota films in the 1930s.[81] Meisel did not fulfil the remainder of his contract with British Talking Pictures and returned to Berlin in January 1930, his reputation tarnished by his lack of a significant success in London.

Kurt London, one of Meisel's contemporaries, stated that "[Meisel's] first attempts in sound-films, after which death overtook him, showed that he died with the silent film, in a kind of common destiny: apparently it was only with difficulty and reluctance that he managed to submit to the laws of the sound-film."[82] His influential opinion remained largely unchallenged for almost half a century, until Werner Sudendorf described Meisel as "one of the few film musicians and one of the few film making artists in Germany generally who favoured sound film from the beginning."[83] This examination of the soundtrack to *The Crimson Circle* fully corroborates Sudendorf's stance. The score to *The Crimson Circle* baffled some British critics in its day, primarily because it was much more intrusive than was usual for silent or early sound film accompaniment. In many ways it appears to have been a pioneering attempt at an integrated soundtrack. Many of its "visual sound" techniques would soon become the conventions of "classical" Hollywood scoring practice for sound features in the 1930s and 1940s, as exemplified in the scores of Max Steiner and Erich Korngold. Far from being reluctant to accept the new laws of sound film, Meisel demonstrated an eagerness to experiment with microphone and recording technology, fully embracing sound film and all its possibilities.

NOTES

1. Trade show advertisement for "The Crimson Circle", *Bioscope*, 27 Feb. 1929, 6–7.

2. I would like to thank Tony Fletcher for generously sharing his research on the sound version of *The Crimson Circle*.

3. German release of the silent film *Bronenosets Potyomkin* (Goskino, 1926; directed by Sergei Eisenstein).

4. Ufa, 1926; directed by Arnold Fanck.

5. Edmund Meisel, "Wie schreibt man Filmmusik?", *Ufa-Magazin* (Berlin) 2/14, 1–7 April 1927. Reproduced in *Der Stummfilmmusiker Edmund Meisel*, ed. Werner Sudendorf, Schriftenreihe des Deutschen Filmmuseum Frankfurt (Frankfurt am Main: Deutsches Filmmuseum, 1984), 58. Unless indicated, all translations from the German are by the author.

6. "Meisel's Method", *Bioscope*, 21 Aug. 1929, 41.

7. Edmund Meisel, "Wie schreibt man Filmmusik?"

8. German release of the silent film *Goluboi ekspress* (Sovkino, 1929; directed by Ilya Trauberg). See Dr. K. L., "Im Mozartsaal: Der blaue Expreß. Meisels Originalmusik", *Der Film*, 25 Oct. 1930, Beilage: "Kritiken der Woche".

9. This proclivity to tailor his music closely to the action is most pronounced in films with more archetypal narratives.

10. "First 'Film-Opera': New Methods for 'The Crimson Circle'. Meisel's Music for Edgar Wallace Thriller", *The Cinema News and Property Gazette* (hereafter, *Cinema*), 13 Aug. 1929, 2.

11. C. D. Innes, *Erwin Piscator's Political Theatre: The Development of Modern German Drama* (Cambridge: Cambridge University Press, 1972), 82.

12. German release of the silent film *Oktyabr'* (Sovkino, 1928; directed by Sergei Eisenstein). See Meisel to Sergei Eisenstein, Berlin, 29 January 1928. Reproduced in Sudendorf, *Der Stummfilmmusiker*, 79–80.

13. Listed in *Polydor Records Chief Catalogue 1929. Green Label: Electrical Recordings. Series "Polyfar": All Electrical Records issued up to and including July 1929* (Berlin: J. Schmidt, 1929), 129.

14. Meisel may have incorporated his invention, or an earlier prototype, in his score to Walther Ruttmann's *Berlin*, which had its Berlin premiere in September 1927. See Oswald Blakiston [Oswell Blakeston], "Composer as Director's Associate: Writer of 'Berlin's' Music on Sound Films", *Film Weekly*, 11 Feb. 1929, 15.

15. Recollection of the sound engineer Karl Brodmerkel, "Zur Vorgeschichte der deutschen Tonfilmindustrie", *Bild und Ton* (Berlin, DDR) 6/8 (1953): 244; cited in Jeanpaul Goergen, *Walter Ruttmann: Eine Dokumentation* (Berlin: Freunde der Deutschen Kinemathek, 1989), 32, and 50, n. 12.

16. Meisel to Sergei Eisenstein, Berlin, 31 October 1928. Reproduced in Sudendorf, *Der Stummfilmmusiker*, 85.

17. London Film Society, *The Film Society Programmes 1925–1939* (New York: Arno Press, 1972), 85–8.

18. *Konets Sankt-Peterburga* (Mezhrapbom Rus, 1927; directed by Vsevolod Pudovkin).

19. *Film Society Programmes*, 112–15.

20. See "*Symphony of London*: Famous German Composer's Unique Scenario", *Cinema*, 21 Feb. 1929, 8; "Film and Sound—The New Production Technique: Famous Composer on Writing for the Microphone", *Cinema*, 6 Mar. 1929, Technical Section: vii.

21. Meisel to Sergei Eisenstein, London, 18 April 1929. Reproduced in *Eisenstein und Deutschland: Texte, Dokumente, Briefe*, ed. Oksana Bulgakowa (Berlin: Henschel, 1998), 85–6.

22. "Meisel Composes Sound Film", *Bioscope*, 24 July 1929, 36.

23. Thelma Gutsche, *The History and Social Significance of Motion Pictures in South Africa, 1895–1940* (Cape Town: Howard Timmins, 1972), 179.

24. Rachael Low, *The History of the British Film, 1929–1939: Film Making in 1930s Britain* (London: Allen and Unwin, 1985; reprint, London: Routledge, 1997), 182–3.

25. "British Talking Pictures", *Bioscope British Film Number* Special Issue, 31 Dec. 1928: 105–6; Leslie Eveleigh, FRPS, "England's New Sound Studio: B.T.P.'s Big Achievement at Wembley", *Bioscope*, 4 Sept. 1929, Modern Cinema Technique: ix.

26. Donald Crafton, *The Talkies: American Cinema's Transition to Sound, 1926–1931* (Berkeley: University of California Press, 1999), 168.

27. Trade show advertisement for "The Crimson Circle", *Cinema*, 26 Aug. 1929, 3.

28. "BTP demo at Super Cinema, Charing Cross Rd. [21 February 1929]", *Bioscope*, 20 Feb. 1929, 15, also 30 and 38; "British 'Talkie' Success", *Bioscope*, 6 Mar. 1929, 50.

29. "The Crimson Circle", *Bioscope*, 28 Aug. 1929, 19–20.

30. Crafton, *The Talkies*, 13.

31. "Sinclair Hill putting Stewart Rome through his paces", British Film News, *Cinema*, 12 June 1929, 14.

32. L. H. Clark, "The Crimson Circle", *Cinema*, 28 Aug. 1929, 7.

33. Item 118: "Estimate for Cost of Synchronising 'The General Line'", Ivor Montagu Collection, BFI Special Collections, London.

34. Onlooker, Up & Down the Street, *Cinema*, 11 June 1929, 2.

35. Blakiston, "Composer as Director's Associate".

36. See "Wembley 'Talkie' Strike: Musicians Called Off Production. 'The Crimson Circle' Held Up", *Cinema*, 20 June 1929, 5; "Strike at Sound Film Studio: Musicians Called Out", *Times*, 20 June 1929, 8; "Film Musicians' Strike: Four Days' Pay in Dispute", *Times*, 21 June 1929, 19; "Talking Film Musicians' Strike", *Times*, 24 June 1929, 20; "Wembley Musicians' Strike: New Men already at Work", *Bioscope*, 26 June 1929, 18.

37. "Meisel Composes Sound Film".

38. "B.T.P. Disc System: New Attachment Evolved", *Bioscope*, 26 June 1929, 19.

39. "First 'Film-Opera'".

40. Robert Herring, "A Year's Talkies", The Week on the Screen, *Manchester Guardian*, 17 Aug. 1929, 9.

41. "Meisel's Method".

42. This material has not survived but is discussed in "The Crimson Circle: British Internationalizing Edgar Wallace. Musical Effects by Edmund Meisel", *Close Up* 5/4 (1929): 340–41; Hay Chowl, "A Tragedy", *Close Up* 5/4 (1929): 296.

43. Rick Altman, *Silent Film Sound* (New York: Columbia University Press, 2004), 375.

44. There is a comprehensive thematic analysis of the film score in Ulrich Rügner, *Filmmusik in Deutschland zwischen 1924 und 1934*, Studien zur Filmgeschichte, [Vol.] 3 (Hildesheim: Georg Olms Verlag, 1988), 164–190.

45. Chowl, "A Tragedy", 296–7.

46. "New Gallery Cinema: 'The Crimson Circle'", *Times*, 28 Aug. 1929, 10.

47. An aural record of Meisel's score survives on a sound-on-film print in the Cinémathèque Française, Paris, under the title *Le train mongol*, edited by Abel Gance in 1931.

48. The music survives as a piano-conductor score, with annotated suggestions for orchestration and cues to on screen action. The score is held by the Deutsches Filminstitut, Frankfurt am Main; the example has been taken from page 28.

49. "Film and Sound—The New Production Technique".

50. Edmund Meisel, "Erfahrungen bei der musikalischen Arbeit am Tonfilm", *Melos* (Berlin) 9/7 (July 1930): 313.

51. Clark, "The Crimson Circle".

52. The discovery of the sound discs for this version and their contents are discussed in Thomas Tode, "Ein Film kann einen anderen verdecken: Zu den verschiedenen Fassungen des *Panzerkreuzer Potemkin* und Meisels wieder gefundener Musikvertonung. Ein Forschungsbericht", *Medien & Zeit* 18/1 (2003): 23–40.

53. Chowl, "A Tragedy", 297. Chowl's disparaging remarks have been omitted.

54. This example is discussed in David Neumeyer, "Melodrama as a Compositional Resource in Early Hollywood Sound Cinema", *Current Musicology* 57 (1995): 82.

55. "Meisel's Method".

56. See Janet Bergstrom, "Murnau, Movietone and Mussolini", *Film History* 17/2–3, The Year 1927 (2005): 196.

57. Neil Brand, "Distant Trumpets: The Score to *The Flag Lieutenant* and Music of the British Silent Cinema", in *Young and Innocent? The Cinema in Britain 1896–1930*, ed. Andrew Higson (Exeter: University of Exeter Press, 2002), 219.

58. Meisel, "Erfahrungen bei der musikalischen Arbeit am Tonfilm", 313.

59. Ibid.

60. "Meisel's Method".

61. "Film and Sound—The New Production Technique".

62. Chowl, "A Tragedy", 296 and 297.

63. S. M. Eisenstein, W. I. Pudovkin, and G. V. Alexandroff, "The Sound Film: A Statement from USSR", *Close Up* 3/4 (1928): 12; translation by Ivor Montagu.

64. Jay Leyda, ed., *Eisenstein on Disney* (London: Methuen, 1988), 1 and 10; Eisenstein arrived in London on 30 October 1929.

65. Christopher Morris, "From Revolution to Mystic Mountains: Edmund Meisel and the Politics of Modernism", in *Composing for the Screen in Germany and the USSR: Cultural Politics and Propaganda*, ed. Robynn J. Stilwell and Phil Powrie (Bloomington: Indiana University Press, 2008), 82.

66. William Hunter, *Scrutiny of Cinema* (London: Wishart, 1932), 52–3, including some of footnote text marked with an asterisk in the original.

67. "The Crimson Circle. British Internationalizing Edgar Wallace".

68. Miss J. M. Harvey to members of the Film Society, 21 August 1929, London. See Item 15, Film Society Performances, Programme 33 Season 5 (1929–30) "Battleship Potemkin", Film Society Collection, BFI Special Collections, London.

69. *Cinema*, 28 Aug. 1929, 17; 4 Sept. 1929, 15.

70. For example, see the following reviews: "The Crimson Circle", *Bioscope*, 28 Aug. 1929, 19–20; Robert Herring, "Fashioning Talkies", The Week on the Screen, *Manchester Guardian*, 31 Aug. 1929, 11.

71. Herring, "Fashioning Talkies".

72. Ibid.

73. Pudovkin made his comments during a lecture given to members of the Film Society on 3 February 1929, reported in "Amazing Vista for Sound: Pudovkin the Prophet", *Cinema*, 6 Feb. 1929, 1 and 19.

74. Meisel to Sergei Eisenstein, London, 31 August 1929. Reproduced in Bulgakowa, ed., *Eisenstein und Deutschland*, 86–9.

75. "The Crimson Circle", *Kinematograph Weekly*, 29 Aug. 1929, 31.

76. Clark, "The Crimson Circle".

77. Herring, "Fashioning Talkies"; "The Crimson Circle. British Internationalizing Edgar Wallace", 341.

78. "Thriller Lacks Suspense: 'The Crimson Circle'—A Mystery Picture of the Old School", *New York Times*, 28 Dec. 1929, 15.

79. "Fire at Wembley Studios: Extensive Damage to Buildings", *Times*, 21 Oct. 1929, 16.

80. Ibid.; also "Wembley Studios Gutted: £100,000 Fire Damage—No Hold-Up in Deliveries", *Bioscope*, 23 Oct. 1929, 27.

81. Patricia Warren, *British Film Studios: An Illustrated History* (London: Batsford, 1995), 183.

82. Kurt London, *Film Music: A Summary of the Characteristic Features of its History, Aesthetics, Technique; and Possible Developments*, trans. Eric S. Bensinger (London: Faber & Faber, 1936), 94.

83. Sudendorf, *Der Stummfilmmusiker*, 29. This was the only monograph on the composer prior to Fiona Ford, "The Film Music of Edmund Meisel (1894–1930)", PhD. diss. University of Nottingham, 2011.

Abel, Richard. "'Pathé Goes to Town': French Films Create a Market for the Nickelodeon". *Cinema Journal* 35/1 (1995): 3–26.

———. "That Most American of Attractions, the Illustrated Song". In *The Sounds of Early Cinema*, ed. Richard Abel and Rick Altman, 143–55.

———. "Illustrated Songs". In *Encyclopedia of Early Cinema*, ed. Richard Abel, 310–12.

———, ed. *Encyclopedia of Early Cinema*. London: Routledge, 2005.

Abel, Richard, and Rick Altman, eds. *The Sounds of Early Cinema*. Bloomington: Indiana University Press, 2001.

Allen, Michael. "In the Mix: How Mechanical and Electrical Reproducers Mediated the Transition to Sound in Britain". In *Film Music: Critical Approaches*, ed. K. J. Donnelly, 62–87. Edinburgh: Edinburgh University Press, 2001.

Aldcroft, Derek H. *The British Economy between the Wars*. Oxford: Philip Allan, 1983.

Aldington, Richard. *Lawrence of Arabia: A Biographical Inquiry*. London: Collins, 1955.

Allen, Robert C. "Manhattan Myopia; or Oh! Iowa!" *Cinema Journal* 35/3 (1996): 75–103.

Altick, Richard D. *The Shows of London: A Panoramic History of Exhibitions, 1600–1862*. Cambridge, MA: Belknap Press, 1978.

Altman, Rick. "The Silence of the Silents". *Musical Quarterly* 80/4 (1996): 648–718.

———. "The Living Nickelodeon". In *The Sounds of Early Cinema*, ed. Richard Abel and Rick Altman, 232–40.

———. *Silent Film Sound*. New York: Columbia University Press, 2004.

Anderson, Gillian. *Music for Silent Films, 1894–1929: A Guide*. Washington: Library of Congress, 1988.

Anderson, Tim. "Reforming 'Jackass Music': The Problematic Aesthetics of Early American Film Music Accompaniment". *Cinema Journal* 37/1 (1997): 3–22.

Armes, Roy. *A Critical History of the British Cinema*. London: Secker and Warburg, 1978.

Aronson, Michael G. "The Wrong Kind of Nickel Madness: Pricing Problems for Pittsburgh Nickelodeons". *Cinema Journal* 42/1 (2002): 71–96.

Bailleu, Bill, and John Goodchild. *The British Film Business*. Chichester: John Wiley, 2002.

Bakker, Gerben. "The Decline and Fall of the European Film Industry: Sunk Costs, Market Size, and Market Structure, 1890–1927. *Economic History Review* 58/2 (May 2005): 311–52.

———. "The Economic History of the International Film Industry". *EH.net Encyclopedia,* edited by Robert Whaples. February 10, 2008. Online. Available: http://eh.net/encyclopedia/article/bakker.film. January 18, 2012.

Balázs, Béla. *Theory of Film*. Trans. Edith Bone. London: Dobson, 1952. Originally published as *Filmkultúra*. Budapest: Szikra kiadás, 1948.

Ball, Robert Hamilton. *Shakespeare on Silent Film: A Strange Eventful History*. London: Allen and Unwin, 1968.

Bamforth's Artistic Life Model Lantern Slides: Supplementary List. Holmfirth: Bamforth, 1912.

Barnes, John. *The Beginnings of the Cinema in England 1894–1901*. Vol. 1: *1894–1896*. Exeter: University of Exeter Press, 1998.

———. *The Beginnings of the Cinema in England, 1894–1901*. Vol. 3: *1898: The Rise of the Photoplay*. Exeter: University of Exeter Press, 1996. 1983.

———. *The Beginnings of Cinema in England 1894–1901*. Vol. 4: *1899*. Exeter: University of Exeter Press, 1996.

Barr, Charles, ed. *All Our Yesterdays: 90 Years of British Cinema*. London: BFI, 1986.

The Battle of the Somme. DVD. The War Office. 1916; London: Imperial War Museum, 2008. SN6540.

Baugh, Christopher. "Philippe de Loutherbourg: Technology-Driven Entertainment and Spectacle in the Late Eighteenth Century". *Huntington Library Quarterly* 70/2 (June 2007): 251–68.

Beardsley, Charles. *Hollywood's Master Showman: The Legendary Sid Grauman*. New York: Cornwall, 1983.

Bennett, Colin N. *The Handbook of Kinematography*, 2nd edn. London: Kinematograph Weekly, 1913. Reproduced in *A History of Early Film*, Vol. 2, ed. Stephen Herbert, 59–440.

Billman, Larry. *Film Choreographers and Dance Directors: An Illustrated Biographical Encyclopedia*. Jefferson, NC: McFarland, 1997.

Bilitereyst, Daniel, Richard Maltby and Philippe Meers, eds. *Cinema, Audiences and Modernity: New Perspectives on European Cinema History*. London: Routledge, 2012.

Birchard, Robert S. "A song-and-dance spectacular". *American Cinematographer* 86/11 (2005): 66–73.

Blacker, Harry. *Just Like It Was: Memoirs of the Mittel East*. London: Vallentine, Mitchell, 1974.

Blackman, Robert D. *Voice, Speech and Gesture*. Edinburgh: John Grant, 1908.

Blakeston, Oswell. "British Solecisms". *Close Up* 1/2 (August 1927): 17–23. Reproduced in *Close Up, 1927–1933: Cinema and Modernism*, ed. James Donald, Anne Friedberg, and Laura Marcus, 41–3.

Bolter, Jay David, and Richard Grusin. *Remediation: Understanding New Media*. Boston: MIT Press, 2000.

Boosey, William. *Fifty Years of Music*. London: Ernest Benn, 1931.

Booth, Michael R. *Victorian Spectacular Theatre, 1850–1910*. London: Routledge & Kegan Paul, 1981.

Bottomore, Stephen. "An International Survey of Sound Effects in Early Cinema". *Film History* 11/4 (1999): 485–98.

———. "The Story of Percy Peashaker: Debates about Sound Effects in Early Cinema". In *The Sounds of Early Cinema*, ed. Richard Abel and Rick Altman, 129–42.

———. "Rediscovering Early Non-Fiction Film", *Film History* 13/2 (2001): 160–73.

Bowley, Arthur Lyon. *Prices and Wages in the United Kingdom, 1914–20*. Oxford: Clarendon Press, 1921.

Bowers, Q. David. *Nickelodeon Theatres and their Music*. New York: Vestal Press, 1986.

Bowser, Eileen. *The Transformation of Cinema, 1907–1915*. Berkeley: University of California Press, 1994.

Brand, Neil. "Distant Trumpets: The Score to *The Flag Lieutenant* and Music of the British Silent Cinema". In *Young and Innocent? The Cinema in Britain, 1896–1930*, ed. Andrew Higson, 208–24.

Brewster, Ben. "Periodization of Early Cinema". In *American Cinema's Transitional Era: Audiences, Institutions, Practices*, ed. Charlie Keil and Shelley Stamp, 66–75. Berkeley: University of California Press, 2004.

Brooker, Jeremy. "The Temple of Minerva: Magic and the Magic Lantern at the Royal Polytechnic Institution, 1837–1900". PhD. diss, Birkbeck College, University of London, 2012.

Brown, Julie. "Audio-Visual Palimpsests: Resynchronizing Silent Films with 'Special' Music". In *The Oxford Handbook of Film Music Studies*, ed. David Neumeyer New York: Oxford University Press, forthcoming.

Browning, H. E., and A. A. Sorrell. "Cinemas and Cinema-Going in Great Britain". *Journal of the Royal Statistical Society*, Series A (General), 117/2 (1954): 137–70.

Brownlow, Kevin. *The War, the West and the Wilderness*. London: Secker & Warburg, 1979.

———. "Silent Films—What Was the Right Speed?" In *Early Cinema: Space, Frame, Narrative*, ed. Thomas Elsaesser with Adam Barker, 282–90.

Buchanan, Judith. *Shakespeare on Silent Film: An Excellent Dumb Discourse*. Cambridge: Cambridge University Press, 2009.

———. "Shakespeare and the Magic Lantern". *Shakespeare Survey* 62 (2009): 191–210.

Bulgakowa, Oksana, ed. *Eisenstein und Deutschland: Texte, Dokumente, Briefe*. Berlin: Henschel, 1998.

Burch, Noël. *Life to Those Shadows*. Trans. and ed. Ben Brewster. Berkeley: University of California Press, 1990.

Burnett, John. *A History of the Cost of Living*. Harmondsworth: Penguin, 1969.

Burrows, Jon. "Penny Pleasures [I]: Film Exhibition in London during the Nickelodeon Era, 1906–1914". *Film History* 16/1 (2004): 60–91.

———. "Penny Pleasures II: Indecency, Anarchy and Junk Film in London's 'Nickelodeons', 1906–1914", *Film History* 16/2 (2004): 172–97.

———. "*West is Best!*; or, What We Can Learn from Bournemouth". *Early Popular Visual Culture* 8/4 (2010): 351–62.

Burrows, Jon, and Richard Brown, "Financing the Edwardian Cinema Boom, 1909–1914". *Historical Journal of Film, Radio and Television* 30/1 (March 2010): 1–20.

Burton, Alan, and Laraine Porter, eds. *The Showman, the Spectacle and the Two-Minute Silence: Performing British Cinema before 1930*. Trowbridge: Flicks Books, 2001.

Canjels, Rudmer. "Featuring on Stage: American Prologues from the 1920s". In *Limina/Le soglie del film. Film's Thresholds*, ed. Veronica Innocenti and Valentina Re, 309–20.

Carlson, Marvin. *Theatre Semiotics: Signs of Life*. Bloomington: Indiana University Press, 1990.

Chanan, Michael. *The Dream that Kicks: The Prehistory and Early Years of Cinema in Britain.* London: Routledge and Kegan Paul, 1980.

Charney, Leo, and Vanessa R. Schwartz, eds. *Cinema and the Invention of Modern Life.* Berkeley: University of California Press, 1995, 1–12.

Châteauvert, Jean, and André Gaudreault. "The Noises of Spectators, or the Spectator as Additive to the Spectacle". In *The Sounds of Early Cinema*, ed. Richard Abel and Rick Altman, 183–91.

Christie, Ian. "*The Magic Sword*: Genealogy of an English Trick Film". *Film History* 16/2 (April 2004): 163–71.

———. "The Anglo-Boer War in North London: A Micro-Study". In *Picture Perfect: Landscape, Place and Travel in British Cinema before 1930*, ed. Laraine Porter and Bryony Dixon, 82–91. Exeter: University of Exeter Press, 2007.

Comstock, Andrew, and James Allan Mair. *The Model Elocutionist: A Manual of Instruction in Vocal Gymnastics and Gesture.* London: William Collins, 1874.

Condon, Denis. *Early Irish Cinema, 1895–1921.* Dublin: Irish Academic Press, 2008.

Cook, Malcolm. "The Lightning Cartoon: Animation from Music Hall to Cinema". *Early Popular Visual Culture.* Forthcoming.

Cook, Patricia. "Albany Ward and the Development of Cinema Exhibition in England". *Film History* 20/3 (2008): 294–307.

Crafton, Donald. *Before Mickey: The Animated Film, 1898–1928.* Cambridge, MA: MIT Press, 1982.

———. *The Talkies: American Cinema's Transition to Sound, 1926–1931.* Berkeley: University of California Press, 1999.

Crangle, Richard. "'Next Slide Please': The Lantern Lecture in Britain, 1890–1910". In *The Sounds of Early Cinema*, ed. Richard Abel and Rick Altman, 39–47.

Crangle, Richard, Robert MacDonald, eds. *The Illustrated Bamforth Slide Catalogue.* London: Magic Lantern Society, 2009. DVD-Rom.

Crary, Jonathan. *Suspensions of Perception: Attention, Spectacle, and Modern Culture.* Cambridge, MA: MIT Press, 1999.

Dahlquist, Marina. "Global versus Local: The Case of Pathé". *Film History* 17/1 (2005): 29–38.

Derrida, Jacques. *Writing and Difference.* Trans. A. Bass. Chicago: University of Chicago Press, 1978.

A Detailed Catalogue of Photographic Lantern Slides, Life Models &C. Holmfirth: Bamforth, 1910.

Dewey, Peter. *War and Progress. Britain, 1914–1945.* Harlow: Longman, 1997.

Donald, James, Anne Friedberg, and Laura Marcus, eds. *Close Up, 1927–1933: Cinema and Modernism.* Princeton: Princeton University Press, 1998.

Eco, Umberto. *Travels in Hyperreality: Essays.* Trans. William Weaver. London: Pan, 1987.

Ehrlich, Cyril. *The Piano: A History.* London: Dent, 1976.

———. *The Music Profession in Britain Since the Eighteenth Century: A Social History.* Oxford: Clarendon Press, 1985.

———. *Harmonious Alliance: A History of the Performing Right Society.* Oxford: Oxford University Press, 1989.

Eisenstein, Sergei, Grigori Alexandrov, and Vsevolod Pudovkin. Trans. Ivor Montagu. "The Sound Film: A Statement from USSR". *Close Up* 3/4 (1928): 10–13.

Elkin, Robert, ed. *A Career in Music.* London: William Earl, 1950.

Elsaesser, Thomas, with Adam Barker, ed. *Early Cinema: Space, Frame, Narrative.* London: BFI, 1990.

Eyles, Allen, and Keith Skone. *London's West End Cinemas*. Sutton: Keytone, 1991.

Fischer-Lichte, Erika. *The Semiotics of Theater*. Trans. Jeremy Gaines and Doris L. Jones. Bloomington: Indiana University Press, 1992. Originally published as *Semiotik des Theaters*. Tübingen: Gunter Narr Verlag, 1983.

Fletcher, Tony. "Sunday and Holy Days". In *Networks of Entertainment: Early Film Distribution, 1895–1915*, ed. Frank Kessler and Nanna Verhoeff, 235–45.

———. "Sound before *Blackmail* (1929)". In *The Showman, the Spectacle and the Two-Minute Silence: Performing British Cinema before 1930*, ed. Alan Burton and Laraine Porter, 6–11.

Ford, Fiona. "The Film Music of Edmund Meisel (1894–1930)". PhD. diss., University of Nottingham, 2011.

Freeman, Judi. "Bridging Purism and Surrealism: The Origins and Production of Fernand Léger's *Ballet Mécanique*". In *Dada and Surrealist Film*, ed. Rudolf E. Kuenzli, 28–45.

Garry, Rupert. *Elocution, Voice and Gesture*. London: Bemrose, 1888.

Gates, B. H. "Cinema in Aberdeen". In *Educational Film Bulletin* 33 (Sept. 1946): 16–20.

Gaudreault, André, and Germain Lacasse. "Editorial: Le bonimenteur de vues animées". *Iris* 22 (Autumn 1996): 3–9.

———. "Le bonimenteur de vues animées (1895–1930)", GRAFICS website: http://cri.histart. umontreal.ca/grafics/fr/bonimenteur.asp [accessed 4 Aug. 2012].

Gaudreault, André, with Jean-Pierre Sirois-Trahan. "Le retour du [bonimenteur] refoulé ... (où serait-ce le bonisseur-conférencier, le commentateur, le conférencier, le présentateur ou le 'speacher'?)" *Iris* 22 (Autumn 1996): 17–32.

Geduld, Harry M., ed. *Film Makers on Film Making*. Harmondsworth: Penguin, 1967.

George, W. Tyacke. *Playing to Pictures: A Guide for Pianists and Conductors of Motion Picture Theatres*. London: Kinematograph Weekly, 1912.

Gifford, Denis. *Books and Plays in Films, 1896–1915: Literary, Theatrical and Artistic Sources of the First Twenty Years of Motion Pictures*. London: Mansell, 1991.

———, ed. *The British Film Catalogue. Vol. 1: Fiction Film, 1895–1994*. London: Fitzroy Dearborn, 2000.

Gledhill, Christine. *Reframing British Cinema, 1918–1928: Between Restraint and Passion*. London: BFI, 2003.

Goergen, Jeanpaul. *Walter Ruttmann: Eine Dokumentation*. Berlin: Freunde der Deutschen Kinemathek, 1989.

Goldmark, Daniel. "Before *Willie*: Reconsidering Music and the Animated Cartoon of the 1920s". In *Beyond the Soundtrack: Representing Music in Cinema*, ed. Daniel Goldmark, Lawrence Kramer, and Richard Leppert, 225–45.

Goldmark, Daniel, Lawrence Kramer, and Richard Leppert, eds. *Beyond the Soundtrack: Representing Music in Cinema*. Berkeley: University of California Press, 2007.

Greasley, David, and Les Oxley, "Discontinuities in Competitiveness: The Impact of the First World War on British Industry". *Economic History Review*, 2nd series, 49/1 (1996): 82–100.

Green, Benny, ed. *The Last Empires: A Music Hall Companion*. London: Pavilion Books, 1986.

Grimoin-Sanson, Raoul. *Le Film de Ma Vie*. Paris: Henry Parville, 1926.

Gunning, Tom. "The Scene of Speaking: Two Decades of Discovering the Film Lecturer". *Iris* 27 (Spring 1999): 67–79.

———. "Dance films". In *Encyclopedia of Early Cinema*, ed. Richard Abel, 163–4.

Gutsche, Thelma. *The History and Social Significance of Motion Pictures in South Africa, 1895–1940*. Cape Town: Howard Timmins, 1972.

Guy, Stephen. "Calling All Stars: Musical Films in a Musical Decade". In *The Unknown 1930s: An Alternative History of the British Cinema, 1929–39*, ed. Jeffrey Richards, 99–119.

Haggith, Toby. "Reconstructing the Musical Arrangement for *The Battle of the Somme* (1916)". *Film History* 14/1 (2002): 11–24.

Hall, Ben M. *The Best Remaining Seats: The Story of the Golden Age of the Movie Palace*. New York: Clarkson N. Potter, 1961.

Hammond, Michael. "Letters to America: A Case Study in the Exhibition and Reception of American Films in Britain, 1914–1918". In *Young and Innocent? The Cinema in Britain, 1896–1930*, ed. Andrew Higson, 128–43.

Hanson, Stuart. *From Silent Screen to Multi-Screen: A History of Cinema Exhibition in Britain since 1896*. Manchester: Manchester University Press, 2007.

Hardcastle, Ephraim. *Wine and Walnuts*. London: Longman, Hurst, Rees, Orme, 1824.

Harper, Sue. "A Lower Middle-Class Taste-Community in the 1930s: Admissions Figures at the Regent Cinema, Portsmouth, UK". *Historical Journal of Film, Radio and Television* 24/4 (2004): 565–87.

Hartley, Charles. *How to Speak Well in Public and Private*. London: Groombridge, 1884.

Hediger, Vinzenz. *Verführung zum film: Der Amerikanische Kinotrailer seit 1912*. Marburg: Schüren, 2001.

———. "'Putting the Spectators in a Receptive Mood'". In *Limina/Le soglie del film. Film's Thresholds*, ed. Veronica Innocenti and Valentina Re, 291–308.

Hepworth, Cecil. "Those Were the Days". In *Penguin Film Review* 6 (1948). Reprinted in *Film Makers on Film Making*, ed. Harry M. Geduld, 40–45.

———. *Came the Dawn: Memories of a Film Pioneer*. London: Phoenix House, 1951.

Herbert, Stephen, ed. *A History of Early Film*, Vol. 2. London: Routledge, 2000.

Herbert, Stephen, Colin Harding, and Simon Popple, eds. *Victorian Film Catalogues: A Facsimile Collection*. London: Projection Box, 1996.

Hewitt, Martin. "Beyond Scientific Spectacle: Image and Word in Nineteenth-Century Popular Lecturing". In *Popular Exhibitions, Science and Showmanship, 1840–1914*, ed. Joe Kember, John Plunkett, and Jill A. Sullivan, 79–96.

Higson, Andrew. *Waving the Flag: Constructing a National Cinema in Britain*. Oxford: Clarendon Press, 1995.

———. "Polyglot Films for an International Market: E.A. Dupont, the British Film Industry, and the Idea of a European Cinema, 1926–1930". In *"Film Europe" and "Film America"*, ed. Higson and Maltby, 274–301.

———. "A Visit to the Cinema in 1912: 'The Sense of Touch'". In *Reading the Cinematograph*, ed. Andrew Shail, 240–56.

———, ed. *Young and Innocent? The Cinema in Britain, 1896–1930*. Exeter: University of Exeter Press, 2002.

Higson, Andrew, and Richard Maltby, eds. *"Film Europe" and "Film America": Cinema, Commerce and Cultural Exchange, 1920–1939*. Exeter: University of Exeter Press, 1999.

Hiley, Nicholas. "The British Cinema Auditorium". In *Film and the First World War*, ed. Karel Dibbets and Bert Hogenkamp, 160–70. Amsterdam: Amsterdam University Press, 1995.

———. "'At the Picture Palace': The British Cinema Audience, 1895–1920". In *Celebrating 1895: The Centenary of Cinema*, ed. John Fullerton, 96–103. London: John Libbey, 1998.

———. "'Nothing More Than a "Craze"': Cinema Building in Britain from 1909 to 1914". In *Young and Innocent? The Cinema in Britain, 1896–1930*, ed. Andrew Higson, 111–27. Exeter: University of Exeter Press, 2002.

Horrocks, Roger. *Len Lye: A Biography*. Auckland: Auckland University Press, 2001.

Hubbert, Julie, ed. *Celluloid Symphonies: Texts and Contexts in Film Music History*. Berkeley: University of California Press, 2011.

Hunter, William. *Scrutiny of Cinema*. London: Wishart, 1932.

Ingarden, Roman. *The Literary Work of Art*. Trans. George G. Grabowicz. 3rd edn. Evanston: Northwestern University Press, 1973. Originally published as *Das literarische Kunstwerk*. Halle (Saale): Niemeyer, 1931.

Innes, C. D. *Erwin Piscator's Political Theatre: The Development of Modern German Drama*. Cambridge: Cambridge University Press, 1972.

Innocenti, Veronica, and Valentina Re, eds. *Limina/Le soglie del film. Film's Thresholds*. Udine: Forum, 2004.

Kember, Joe. *Marketing Modernity: Victorian Popular Shows and Early Cinema*. Exeter: University of Exeter Press, 2009.

———. "'Go thou and do likewise': Advice to Lantern and Film Lecturers in the Trade Press, 1897–1909". *Early Popular Visual Culture* 8/4 (2010): 419–30.

Kember, Joe, John Plunkett, and Jill Sullivan, eds. *Popular Exhibitions, Science and Showmanship, 1840–1914*. London: Pickering and Chatto, 2012.

Kessler, Frank, and Nanna Verhoeff, eds. *Networks of Entertainment: Early Film Distribution, 1895–1915*. Eastleigh: John Libbey, 2007.

Kift, Dagmar. *The Victorian Music Hall: Culture, Class and Conflict*. Trans. Roy Kift. Cambridge: Cambridge University Press, 1996.

King, Elspeth. "Popular Culture in Glasgow". In *The Working Class in Glasgow, 1750–1914*, ed. R. A. Cage, 142–87. Beckenham: Croom Helm, 1987.

King, Norman. "The Sound of Silents". *Screen* 25/3 (1984): 2–15.

Klenotic, Jeffrey. "'The Sensational Acme of Realism': 'Talker' Pictures as Early Cinema Sound Practice". In *The Sounds of Early Cinema*, ed. Richard Abel and Rick Altman, 156–66.

Knight, Arthur. "The Movies Learn to Talk: Ernst Lubitsch, René Clair, and Rouben Mamoulian". In *Film Sound: Theory and Practice*, ed. Elisabeth Weis and John Belton, 213–20.

Koszarski, Richard. "Laughter, Music and Tragedy at the New York Pathé Studio". *Film History* 14/1 (2002): 32–9.

Kuenzli, Rudolf E., ed. *Dada and Surrealist Film*. New York: Willis, Locker, and Owens, 1987.

Lacasse, Germain. *Le Bonimenteur de Vues Animées. Le Cinéma Muet entre Tradition et Modernité*. Paris: Méridiens Klincksieck, 2000.

———. "The Lecturer and the Attraction". In *The Cinema of Attractions Reloaded*, ed. Wanda Strauven, 181–91.

Lambert, Constant. *Music Ho! A Study of Music in Decline*. London: Penguin, 1948.

Lang, Edith, and George West. *Musical Accompaniment of Moving Pictures: A Practical Manual for Pianists and Organists and an Exposition of the Principles Underlying the Musical Interpretation of Moving Pictures*. Boston: The Boston Music Company/London: Winthrop Rogers, 1920.

Lecointe, Thierry. "La sonorisation des séances Lumière en 1896 et 1897". *1895. Mille huit cent quatre-vingt-quinze* 52 (2007): http://1895.revues.org/1022 [accessed 3 August 2012].

Leyda, Jay. *Kino: A History of the Russian and Soviet Film*. London: George Allen and Unwin, 1960.

———, ed. *Eisenstein on Disney*. Trans. Alan Upchurch with an introduction by Naum Kleiman. London: Methuen, 1988.

Ligensa, Annemone, and Klaus Kreimeier, eds. *Film 1900: Technology, Perception, Culture*. New Barnet: John Libbey, 2009.

Lindsay, John. *Corporation of Glasgow. Review of Municipal Government in Glasgow*. Glasgow: William Hodge, 1909.

Lindsay, Vachel. *The Art of the Moving Picture*. New York: Macmillan, 1915.

London Film Society. *The Film Society Programmes 1925–1939*. New York: Arno Press, 1972.

London, Kurt. *Film Music: A Summary of the Characteristic Features of its History, Aesthetics, Technique; and Possible Developments*. Trans. Eric S. Bensinger. London: Faber & Faber, 1936.

Loobey, Patrick. *Cinemas and Theatres of Wandsworth and Battersea*. Stroud: Tempus, 2004.

Low, Rachael. *The History of the British Film, 1906–1914*. London: Allen and Unwin, 1949.

———. *The History of the British Film, 1914–1918*. London: Allen and Unwin, 1950.

———. *The History of the British Film, 1918–1929*. London: Allen and Unwin, 1971.

———. *The History of the British Film, 1929–1939: Film Making in 1930s Britain*. London: Allen and Unwin, 1985.

Low, Rachael, and Roger Manvell. *The History of the British Film, 1896–1906*. London: Allen and Unwin, 1948.

MacInnes, Colin. *Sweet Saturday Night*. London: MacGibbon and Kee, 1967.

Macpherson, Don, ed. *Traditions of Independence: British Cinema in the Thirties*. London: BFI, 1980.

Maloney, Paul. *Scotland and the Music Hall, 1850–1914*. Manchester: Manchester University Press, 2003.

Mannoni, Laurent. "Phonoscènes". In *Encyclopaedia of Early Cinema*, ed. Richard Abel, 518.

Manvell, Roger, and John Huntley. *The Technique of Film Music*. London: Focal Press, 1957.

Marks, Martin Miller. *Music and the Silent Film: Contexts and Case Studies, 1895–1924*. New York: Oxford University Press, 1997.

Matuszewski, Bolesław. *La Photographie Animée: Ce Qu'elle Est; Ce Qu'elle Doit Être*. Paris: Noizette, 1898.

May, Lary. *Screening Out the Past: The Birth of Mass Culture and the Motion Picture Industry*. New York: Oxford University Press, 1980.

Mayer, David. *Stagestruck Filmmaker: D. W. Griffith and the American Theatre*. Iowa: University of Iowa Press, 2009.

Mayhew, Henry. *London Labour and the London Poor (1851)*, ed. Victor Neuburg. London: Penguin Books, 1985.

McCalman, Iain. "The Virtual Infernal: Philippe de Loutherbourg, William Beckford and the Spectacle of the Sublime". *Romanticism on the Net* 46 (May 2007): http://www.erudit.org/revue/ron/2007/v/n46/016129ar.html [accessed 3 August 2012].

McKernan, Luke. "'Something More than a Mere Picture Show': Charles Urban and the Early Non-Fiction Film in Great Britain and America, 1897–1925". PhD. diss., Birkbeck, University of London, 2004.

———. "'Only the Screen Was Silent …': Memories of Children's Cinema-Going in London before the First World War". *Film Studies* 10 (2007): 1–20.

Medhurst, Andy. "Music Hall and British Cinema". In *All Our Yesterdays*, ed. Charles Barr, 168–88.

Meisel, Edmund. "Wie schreibt man Filmmusik?". *Ufa-Magazin* (Berlin) 2/14 (1927). Reprinted in *Der Stummfilmmusiker Edmund Meisel*, ed. Werner Sudendorf (Frankfurt am Main: Deutsches Filmmuseum, 1984), 57–60.

———. "Erfahrungen bei der musikalischen Arbeit am Tonfilm". *Melos* 9/7 (July 1930): 312–3.

Meisel, Martin. *Realizations. Narrative, Pictorial, and Theatrical Arts in Nineteenth-Century England*. Princeton: Princeton University Press, 1983.

Melnick, Ross. *American Showman: Samuel "Roxy" Rothafel and the Birth of the Entertainment Industry, 1908–1935*. New York: Columbia University Press, 2012.

Mera, Miguel and Ben Winters. "Film and Television Music Sources in the UK and Ireland". *Brio* 46/2 (Autumn/Winter 2009): 37–65.

Merritt, Russell. "In and Around *Broken Blossoms*". *Griffithiana* 48/49 (October 1993): 12–9.

Metz, Christian. "The Imaginary Signifier". Trans. Ben Brewster. *Screen* 16/2 (1975): 14–76.

Miskell, Peter. *A Social History of the Cinema in Wales, 1918–1951: Pulpits, Coalpits, and Fleapits*. Cardiff: University of Wales Press, 2006.

Montagu, Ivor. "The Film Society, London". *Cinema Quarterly* 1/2 (Autumn 1932): 42–6.

———. *The Youngest Son: Autobiographical Sketches*. London: Lawrence and Wishart, 1970.

———. "An Old Man's Mumble: Reflections on a Semi-Centenary". *Sight and Sound* 44/4 (Autumn 1975): 220–4, 247.

Morris, Christopher. "From Revolution to Mystic Mountains: Edmund Meisel and the Politics of Modernism". In *Composing for the Screen in Germany and the USSR: Cultural Politics and Propaganda*, ed. Robynn J. Stilwell and Phil Powrie, 75–92. Bloomington: Indiana University Press, 2008.

Morris, Robert J. "Urbanisation and Scotland". In *People and Society in Scotland. Vol. 2: 1830–1914*, ed. W. Hamish Fraser and Robert J. Morris, 73–102. Edinburgh: John Donald, 1990.

———. "Clubs, Societies and Associations". In *The Cambridge Social History of Britain, 1750–1950. Vol. 3: Social Agencies and Institutions*, ed. F. Michael L. Thompson, 395–443. Cambridge: Cambridge University Press, 1990.

———. "Leisure, Entertainment and the Associational Culture of British Towns, 1800–1900". Unpublished paper, 1996.

Musser, Charles. "The Nickelodeon Era Begins: Establishing the Framework for Hollywood's Mode of Representation". In *Early Cinema: Space, Frame, Narrative*, ed. Thomas Elsaesser with Adam Barker, 256–73.

———. "A Cinema of Contemplation, a Cinema of Discernment: Spectatorship, Intertextuality and Attractions in the 1890s". In *The Cinema of Attractions Reloaded*, ed. Wanda Strauven, 159–79.

———. "The Eden Musee in 1898: Exhibitor as Co-Creator". *Film and History* 11/4 (1981): 73–83.

Narath, Albert. "Oskar Messter and his Work". In *A Technological History of Motion Pictures and Television*, ed. Raymond Fielding, 109–17. Berkeley: University of California Press, 1967.

Nasaw, David. *Going Out: The Rise and Fall of Public Amusements*. Cambridge, MA: Harvard University Press, 1999.

Neumeyer, David. "Melodrama as a Compositional Resource in Early Hollywood Sound Cinema". *Current Musicology* 57 (1995): 61–94.

O'Brien, Charles. *Cinema's Conversion to Sound: Technology and Film Style in France and the U.S.* Bloomington: Indiana University Press, 2005.

O'Donoghue, Jim, Louise Goulding, and Grahame Allen. "Consumer Price Inflation since 1750". *Economic Trends* 604 (March 2004): 38–46. Office for National Statistics.

Pearsall, Ronald. *Edwardian Popular Music*. Newton Abbot: David and Charles, 1975.

Pearson, George. *Flashback: The Autobiography of a British Film-maker*. London: Allen and Unwin, 1957.

Pearson, Roberta. "Transitional Cinema". In *The Oxford History of World Cinema*, ed. Geoffrey Nowell-Smith, 23–42. Oxford: Oxford University Press, 1996.

Pelling, Henry. *A History of British Trade Unionism*. Harmondsworth: Penguin, 1976.

Peter, Bruce. *100 Years of Glasgow's Amazing Cinemas*. Edinburgh: Polygon, 1996.

Pitches, Jonathan. *Vsevolod Meyerhold*. London: Routledge, 2003.

Powell, Hudson John. *Poole's Myriorama!: A Story of Travelling Panorama Showmen*. Bradford-on-Avon: ELSP, 2002.

Prévost, Jean. "André Gide and Marc Allégret's Voyage to the Congo". Trans. K. Macpherson, *Close Up* 1 (July 1927): 38–41.

Prevots, Naima. *Dancing in the Sun: Hollywood Choreographers, 1915–1937*. Ann Arbor: UMI, 1987.

Pulch, Harald. "Messters Experiment der Dirigentenfilme", *KINtop* 3 (1994): 53–64.

Puttkammer, Claudia, and Sacha Szabo. *Gruß aus dem Luna-Park. Eine Archäologie des Vergnügens. Freizeit- und Vergnügungsparks Anfang des zwanzigsten Jahrhunderts*. Berlin: Wissenschaftlicher Verlag Berlin, 2007.

Raymond, George L. *The Orator's Manual: A Practical and Philosophical Treatise on Vocal Culture, Emphasis, and Gesture*, 3rd edn. New York and London: Putnam's, 1910; first publ. 1879.

Reynolds, Herbert. "Aural Gratification with Kalem Films: A Case History of Music, Lectures and Sound Effects, 1907–1917". *Film History* 12/4 (2000): 417–42.

Richards, Jeffrey, ed. *The Unknown 1930s: An Alternative History of the British Cinema, 1929–39*. London: Tauris, 1998.

Richards, Lily May. *Biography of William Haggar*. Unpublished manuscript, National Fairground Archive, Sheffield.

Robinson, David. *The Life and Career of the Film Society*. Unpublished manuscript, BFI Film Society Special Collection, c.1963.

Routh, Guy. *Occupation and Pay in Great Britain, 1906–79*, 2nd edn. London: Macmillan, 1980.

Rügner, Ulrich. *Filmmusik in Deutschland zwischen 1924 und 1934*. Studien zur Filmgeschichte, Vol. 3. Hildesheim: Georg Olms Verlag, 1988.

Russell, Dave. "Abiding Memories: The Community Singing Movement and English Social Life in the 1920s". *Popular Music* 27/1 (2008): 117–33.

Russell, Thomas. "The Orchestral Player". In *A Career in Music*, ed. Robert Elkin, 139–58. London and Bournemouth: William Earl, 1950.

Salt, Barry. "Film Style and Technology in the Thirties: Sound". In *Film Sound: Theory and Practice*, ed. Elisabeth Weis and John Belton, 37–43.

Sanders, Lise Shapiro. "'Indecent Incentives to Vice': Regulating Films and Audience Behaviour from the 1890s to the 1910s". In *Young and Innocent? The Cinema in Britain, 1896–1930*, ed. Andrew Higson, 97–110

Sant, John. *Albert W. Ketèlbey, 1875–1959: From the Sanctuary of His Heart*. Sutton Coldfield: Manifold, 2000.

Scheide, Frank. "The Influence of the English Music-Hall on Early Screen Acting". In *Moving Performance: British Stage and Screen, 1890s–1920s*, ed. Linda Fitzsimmons and Sarah Street, 69–79. Trowbridge: Flicks Books, 2000.

Schneider, Ulrich. *Die Londoner Music Hall und ihre Songs, 1850–1920*. Tübingen: Niemeyer, 1984.

Scotland, John. *The Talkies*. London: Crosby Lockwood and Son, 1930.

Scott, Derek B. *The Singing Bourgeois: Songs of the Victorian Drawing Room and Parlour*. Milton Keynes: Open University Press, 1989.

———. *Sounds of the Metropolis: The 19th-Century Popular Music Revolution in London, New York, Paris, and Vienna*. New York: Oxford University Press, 2008.

Sexton, Jamie. "The Film Society and the Creation of an Alternative Film Culture in Britain in the 1920s". In *Young and Innocent? The Cinema in Britain, 1896–1930*, ed. Andrew Higson, 291–305.

Shail, Andrew. "'A Distinct Advance in Society': Early Cinema's 'Proletarian Public Sphere' and Isolated Spectatorship in the UK, 1911–18". *Journal of British Cinema and Television* 3/2 (2006): 209–28.

———, ed. *Reading the Cinematograph: The Cinema in British Short Fiction, 1896–1912*. Exeter: Exeter University Press, 2010.

Singer, Ben. "Feature Films, Variety Programs, and the Crisis of the Small Exhibitor". In *American Cinema's Transitional Era: Audiences, Institutions, Practices*, ed. Charlie Keil and Shelley Stamp, 76–100. Berkeley: University of California Press, 2004.

———. "The Ambimodernity of Early Cinema: Problems and Paradoxes in the Film-and-Modernity Discourse". In *Film 1900: Technology, Perception, Culture*, ed. Annemone Ligensa and Klaus Kreimeier, 37–52.

Sims, George Robert. *The Lifeboat, and Other Poems*. London: J. P. Fuller, 1883.

Smith, Albert E., with Phil A. Koury. *Two Reels and a Crank: From Nickelodeon to Picture Palace*. Garden City: Doubleday, 1952.

Smith, Jeff. *The Sounds of Commerce: Marketing Popular Film Music*. New York: Columbia University Press, 1998.

Sopocy, Martin. "A Narrated Cinema: The Pioneer Story Films of James A. Williamson". *Cinema Journal* 18/1 (1978): 1–28.

Sparshott, F. E. "Basic Film Aesthetics". *Journal of Aesthetic Education* 5/2, "Film II, the Teaching of Film" (Special Issue) (1971): 11–34.

Stanislavski, Constantin. *An Actor Prepares* [1936]. Trans. Elizabeth R. Hapgood [1948]. New York: Routledge, 1989.

Strauven, Wanda, ed. *The Cinema of Attractions Reloaded.* Amsterdam: Amsterdam University Press, 2006.

Styan, J. L. *Max Reinhardt.* Cambridge: Cambridge University Press, 1982.

Sudendorf, Werner, ed. *Der Stummfilmmusiker Edmund Meisel.* Schriftenreihe des Deutschen Filmmuseum Frankfurt. Frankfurt am Main: Deutsches Filmmuseum, 1984.

Talbot, Frederick A. *Moving Pictures: How They Are Made and Worked.* London: William Heinemann, 1912.

Thomson, Michael. *Silver Screen in the Silver City: A History of Cinemas in Aberdeen, 1896–1987.* Aberdeen: Aberdeen University Press, 1988.

Titchener, Edward Bradford. *A Primer of Psychology.* New York: MacMillan, 1898.

Tode, Thomas. "Ein Film kann einen anderen verdecken: Zu den verschiedenen Fassungen des *Panzerkreuzer Potemkin* und Meisels wieder gefundener Musikvertonung. Ein Forschungsbericht". *Medien & Zeit* 18/1 (2003): 23–40.

Toulmin, Vanessa. "'Local films for local people': Travelling Showmen and the Commissioning of Local Films in Great Britain, 1900–1902". *Film History* 13/2 (2001): 118–37.

———. "Cuckoo in the Nest: Edwardian Itinerant Exhibition Practices and the Transition to Cinema in the United Kingdom from 1901 to 1906". *Moving Image* 10/1 (2010): 52–79.

Toulmin, Vanessa, and Martin Loiperdinger. "Is It You? Recognition, Representation and Response in Relation to the Local Film". *Film History* 17/1 (2005): 7–18.

Triponi, Marianne. "The New Ironwood Theatre in Context: Movie Palace as Symbol". *Journal of American Culture* 13/4 (1990): 1–7.

Ulff-Møller, Jens. "Hollywood's 'Foreign War': The Effect of National Commercial Policy on the Emergence of the American Film Hegemony in France, 1920–1929". In *"Film Europe" and "Film America": Cinema, Commerce and Cultural Exchange, 1920–1939,* ed. Andrew Higson and Richard Maltby, 181–206.

Verdone, Mario. *Gli Intellettuali e Il Cinema.* Roma: Bulzoni, 1982.

Vibart, Henry M. *The Life of General Sir Harry N. D. Prendergast.* London: Eveleigh Nash, 1914.

Visschedijk, Ruud. "Introduction" to Max Nabarro, "This is My Life". *Iris* 22 (Autumn 1996): 183–200.

Warren, Low. *The Film Game.* London: T. Werner Laurie, 1937.

Warren, Patricia. *British Film Studios: An Illustrated History.* London: Batsford, 1995.

Wedel, Michael. "Messter's 'Silent' Heirs: Sync Systems of the German Music Film, 1914–1929". *Film History* 11/4, "Global Experiments in Early Synchronous Sounds" (special issue) (1999): 464–76.

Weis, Elisabeth, and John Belton, eds. *Film Sound: Theory and Practice.* New York: Columbia University Press, 1985.

Williams, David R. *Cinema in Leicester, 1896–1931.* Loughborough: Heart of Albion Press, 1993.

———. "The 'Cinematograph Act' of 1909: An Introduction to the Impetus behind the Legislation and Some Early Effects". *Film History* 9/4 (1997): 341–50.

Wilson, Larry C. "Phyllis Dare", *Silent Film Monthly* 5/7 (Sept. 1997): 1–4.

Winans, James Albert. *Public Speaking: Principles and Practice.* Ithaca, NY: Sewell, 1915.

Wolf, Steffen. "Geschichte der Shakespeare-Verfilmungen (1899–1964)". In *Shakespeare im Film,* ed. Max Lippmann, 15–33. Wiesbaden: Deutsches Institut für Filmkunde, 1964.

Wright, Basil, and B. Vivian Braun. "Manifesto I: Dialogue on Sound—Its Proper Use in Film". *Film Art* 3 (Spring 1934): 28–9. Reproduced in *Traditions of Independence: British Cinema in the Thirties*, ed. Don Macpherson, 178–9.

Young, Gibson. "Recreative Singing: Community Singing in Industry". *The Sackbut* (May 1925), 300–301.

INDEX